STILL THE BEST HOPE

STILL THE BEST HOPE

Why the World Needs
American Values to Triumph

DENNIS PRAGER

BROADSIDE BOOKS
An Imprint of HarperCollinsPublishers
www.broadsidebooks.net

HarperCollins books may be purchased for educational, business, or sales promotional use. For information, please e-mail the Special Markets Department at SPsales@harpercollins.com.

Broadside Books™ and the Broadside logo are trademarks of HarperCollins Publishers.

A hardcover edition of this book was published in 2012 by Broadside Books, an imprint of HarperCollins Publishers.

FIRST BROADSIDE BOOKS PAPERBACK EDITION PUBLISHED 2013.

The Library of Congress has cataloged the hardcover edition as follows:

Prager, Dennis [date]
    Still the best hope : why the world needs American values to triumph /
Dennis Prager.
        p.   cm.
    ISBN 978-0-06-198512-6 (hardback)
    1. Social values—United States.   2. Right and left (Political science)   3. Islamic fundamentalism.   I. Title.
    HN90.M6.P73 2012
    303.48'273—dc23
                                                                2011049595

ISBN 978-0-06-198513-3 (pbk.)

17 18 19 20   OV/RRD   10 9 8 7 6 5 4

To my sons, David and Aaron

CONTENTS

Contents

Part II: Islam and Islamism

Part III: America and Its Unique Values

Preface to the Paperback Edition

Wʜᴇɴ I ᴡʀᴏᴛᴇ *Still the Best Hope*, I wrote it in the hope that it would long remain relevant. The good news is that I did not have to change anything for this paperback edition. The bad news is precisely the same.

Both Islamism and Leftism, the two doctrines most antagonistic to what I call the American Trinity—"Liberty" (small government), "In God We Trust" (ethical monotheism and Judeo-Christian values), and "E Pluribus Unum" (national rather than ethnic or racial identity)—continue to gain adherents and power.

Regarding Islamism, I hope that one day the great majority of Muslims will reject the idea that a society, even one in which Muslims are the majority, should be governed by Sharia. The day that the Islamic world recognizes this will probably not arrive in this generation. But one day it will, because the Islamist model will be unsustainable. Islamist societies will implode.

I am less hopeful about Leftism's demise. For over a century it has been the most dynamic religion in the world. Almost everything it has strongly influenced, it has, over time, either harmed or destroyed: education, religion, the arts, and economics are prominent examples. But its allure is evidently too powerful for most people to resist. It appeals to almost every aspect, good and bad, of human nature: altruism, the emotions, narcissism, envy, love of power, desire for community, and the lure of self-esteem, to name only some. What it does not have is wisdom or objective standards that make moral demands on the individual. And neither of those is highly valued at this time.

The American Founders believed that only a society whose citizens hold themselves accountable to a moral God and who practice moral religion can be both good and free. Neither the Leftist godless model nor the Islamist theocratic model can do that.

The American system of values has uplifted more downtrodden people than any other system, while ultimately producing what has become the least racist, most altruistic, most prosperous, and most opportunity-giving society in world history. But, again, it does not appeal to the nearly universal desire to be taken care of. Rather, it demands that every individual who is capable of doing so must take care of himself—and then his family, community, and even the oppressed of other countries.

In that way, among others, American values are not—and America until the present has not been—in accord with human nature. To demand that people take care of themselves is less "natural" than the Leftist promise to be taken care of. As of this writing, more Americans than ever have come to depend on the state for unearned money. And free money may be more addictive, and more difficult to wean oneself from, than narcotics. It certainly seems that way in Europe, where Leftism has supplanted Christianity as the continent's dominant faith.

I will end on a personal note.

We mortals have a very finite time to live. Life is, in the words of the Jewish liturgy, "as a passing shadow." All of us must therefore ask ourselves what we shall do with our limited time on earth.

Thanks to my wife, Sue, my domestic life is one of peace and tranquility. Thanks to God or luck, I have excellent health. Thanks to my friends, I have love and support. Thanks to my sons, I have hope in the future. Thanks to my listeners and my employers, I have a microphone through which I can talk to millions of people.

Consequently, I am free to do what I want. And I what I want is to devote my life to making the case for the values that I believe to be the only ones that can increase human goodness, liberty, and prosperity. They are liberty, which necessitates small government—that great, but unnatural and uniquely American idea; ethical monotheism; Judeo-Christian values as preached and practiced throughout American history; reason-based rather than emotion-based social policies; and personal responsibility.

I am engaged in this effort through this book—the culmination of a lifetime of thought on goodness, on America, on God, and much else; through my daily radio show, heard in America on radio and everywhere on the Internet; and through the Internet-based Prager University, where the finest minds in the world present intellectually and visually exciting five-minute courses on everything from sexuality to economics to God's existence in an attempt to undo the moral and intellectual decline that I describe at length and with scores of examples in this book. Prager University is accessed at www.prageru.org.

When Abraham Lincoln said that America was "the last best hope of earth," he was right. And it remains true today, But only if Americans understand why. That is the reason for this book.

Dennis Prager
La Cañada Flintridge, California
April 2013

STILL THE BEST HOPE

Why This Book

I HAVE WRITTEN THIS BOOK because I am convinced that there is a way to end most evil.* And ending evil is the most important task humans can ever undertake.

The only proven way to achieve this on any large scale is the American value system. These values are proclaimed on every American coin: "Liberty," "In God We Trust," "E Pluribus Unum." Each one is explained at length, and each one is adaptable to just about any society in the world.

I have written this book with a number of audiences in mind:

It is written first for Americans who already affirm American values. To those who would argue that this is an unnecessary exercise in "preaching to the choir," I would say that, unfortunately, this is not the case. Most of the choir have forgotten the melody. Few Americans can articulate what is distinctive about American values, or even what they are.

---

* By evil I mean the deliberate infliction of death, cruelty, oppression, and other injustices on fellow human beings. It is a sign of the times in which we live—and one of the reasons for this book—that I feel compelled to define "evil." It is necessary to define a term that should not need to be defined because a generation of Westerners has been taught that good and evil are subjective terms—that one man's evil is another man's good. In this morally confused modern world, evil needs to be defined.

There is, in fact, a thirst among Americans for rediscovering and reaffirming American values. I know this from my daily radio show, and I know this from a personal experience. A few years ago, at a public forum at the University of Denver, I was asked by the moderator, former Colorado senator Bill Armstrong, what I thought the greatest problem confronting America was. I answered that it was that the last two generations of Americans have not communicated what it means to be American to their children. Someone in the audience videotaped my response and put it on YouTube, where millions of people have seen it. A lot of Americans realize we have forgotten what we stand for.

The second audience consists of those—Americans and all others—who either do not believe that the American value system is as described, or that it is the best ever devised, or that there is even such a thing as a specifically American value system. I welcome these readers. I have in many ways designed this book for them.

The third audience is non-Americans. As this book goes to press, it is finally becoming obvious that the European attempt to create a welfare state alternative to the American model has failed. Begun after World War II, the secular welfare state offered Europeans and sympathetic non-Europeans an alternative to American religiosity and to what the welfare state's supporters depict as cutthroat, heartless American free market capitalism. But some fifty to sixty years later, it is clear that this state is economically—and, as I show in the book, morally—unsustainable. Of the two democratic models—the European and the American—only the American one works and can endure. And the beauty of it as far as non-Americans are concerned is that it does not demand that any group give up its national or religious culture (except insofar as the culture holds values in conflict with the American value system). On the contrary, Americanism, as this value system is called, *wants* all peoples to retain their national culture and allegiances.

A word about the way arguments are formulated here: I make a generalization and then support it with one or more examples. To those readers who object to generalizations, I respond: First, there is no wisdom without generalizations. Generalizations are what enable us to make sense of the world. If one cannot generalize, one cannot see patterns, and therefore one cannot make sense of reality. "Seat belts save lives" is a generalization. Now, everyone knows that sometimes seat belts actually cause the death of a driver or passenger. Does that invalidate the generalization? Of course not. The existence of exceptions does not invalidate a generalization. Moreover, if we could not make this particular generalization, many people would die needlessly. Therefore, the objection to a person making a generalization cannot be "You're generalizing," as if doing so is inherently wrong. The only valid objection to a generalization is "Your generalization is untrue." For that reason I always offer examples to illustrate the generalization.

One major goal of this book is to present as thorough a dissection of Leftism as has been written. There are many brilliant works on aspects of the Left—and I have greatly benefitted from many of them. But what we need most—and if I did not believe this was needed, I would not have devoted so much time to writing this book—is an overall explanation of the inherent moral and intellectual defects of Leftism, along with an explanation of why so many people believe in it despite its terrible track record. *Still the Best Hope* is the product of a lifetime's thought and study. I began formal study of the Left while in graduate school at the Russian Institute of Columbia University's School of International Affairs and have never stopped.

As I repeatedly make clear, I almost never judge the motives or the character of people with Left-wing views. I do not for many reasons, but chief among them is that I know personally many people—in my extended family and among friends and acquaintances—who hold those views, and whom I adore. The family is a great institution for many obvious reasons. Here is a less obvious one: It teaches us how to love people with whom we may have major disagreements. It's easy to love friends—we choose them. It's not always as easy to love family members with whom one strongly differs on some of the most important issues of life.

One of the worst features of the Left is its assumption that those on the Right are bad people. It is not a view I reciprocate. Indeed, my understanding that so many people with Left-wing views mean well is what enables me to analyze the Left as thoroughly as I do. After all, if everyone you differ with is bad, there is nothing to analyze. You just label them bad and move on.

While on the subject of Leftism, two other issues need to be addressed.

One is the use of the words "liberal" and "Left"—they are used more or less interchangeably. The reason is implicitly explained, but I need to address it explicitly. There was a difference between liberals and the Left for many decades. In the United States, the distinction ended after the Vietnam War. The John F. Kennedy–type liberal—anti-Communist, in favor of using American power to spread liberty, and for lower taxes to stimulate economic growth—essentially died with his assassination on November 22, 1963.

When the *New York Times* began identifying the *Nation*, among the most Left-wing journals published in America, as "liberal," that exemplified the Left-wing takeover of the term "liberal." Many people who hold Left-wing views still prefer to call themselves "liberal," but their views are indeed Left-wing. They simply prefer the term "liberal" because they do not wish to see themselves, or have others see them as, Leftists. If the *New York Times* editorial page is liberal, what is Left? I cannot come up with one major difference between the *Nation* and the *New York Times* editorial page.

This in turn leads to the other issue that needs to be clarified. I am sure that many readers, upon encountering a Left-wing position, will say to themselves, or perhaps yell to anyone within hearing distance, "I'm a liberal [or 'on the Left'] but I don't hold that view— what's this guy talking about?"

My response is that in this book I have no interest in identifying Leftist individuals. I am interested in identifying Leftist positions. The fact that any given liberal or Leftist does not hold a certain view does not mean the view is not Leftist. For example, opposition to the death penalty for murder is a Left-wing position despite the fact that some people who call themselves liberal or Left are in favor of the death penalty. It is my belief, in any event, that many Americans who call themselves liberal actually hold many conservative positions. But thanks to the brilliantly successful, nearly century-long campaign to demonize the Right and identify "liberal" with compassion, decency, fairness, and "social justice," these people would never allow themselves to identify as conservative, let alone to vote Republican.

As for Muslims, I hold out the hope that without dropping belief in the Koran or in Muhammad as Allah's messenger, Islam can be reformed and become a major world force for liberty, justice, and goodness. There are hundreds of millions of good and decent people in the Muslim world who can use their Muslim identity as a force for good. Why Islam has too rarely been such a force is the focus of the chapters on Islam and Islamism. It would bring me great joy if this book were translated into Arabic and the languages of other major Muslim populations—as I note in some detail, there are already believing Muslims, especially in America, who are working on combining the American value system with their Muslim theological beliefs.

Finally, I return to my opening—my hatred of evil as the ultimate reason for this book.

To put it in a nutshell, evil has been the norm. America has been the aberration.

The list of horrors people have endured at the hands of fellow human beings dates back to the beginning of recorded history. It is likely that about a billion human beings have been killed—not to mention enslaved, beaten, and tortured—by other human beings.

That, plus all the world's natural suffering, is why the great Russian writer Fyodor Dostoyevsky felt he could sum up human existence with this line from *The Brothers Karamazov*: "There is suffering and suffering; degrading, humiliating suffering. . . ."

That is why the Buddhist worldview is predicated on the assumption of life as suffering, and why Christianity is founded on the belief that God became human and suffered a torturous death at the hands of human beings.

Even if Dostoyevsky exaggerated somewhat—after all, most of us do not only suffer in life—the problem of unjust human suffering is the central problem of human existence. And most of that suffering has been, and is even more so in modern times, man-made suffering.

Because of all the man-made suffering in history, most societies have sought a solution to this terrible problem. This quest is the genesis of higher religion and of modern political movements: How do we make a better world?

The Buddhist would respond that it is best to simply leave this pain-filled world by following the Buddha and ultimately abandoning our ego-based existence. The Muslim would respond that living a Muslim life, that is, one based on the Koran as understood by Islam since the time of Muhammad—along with universal conversion to Islam—is the answer. The Christian would respond that faith in Jesus Christ and following biblical precepts is the answer for the individual and for all humanity. The traditional Jew would respond that Judaism and its laws are the way for the Jew and that following the basic moral precepts ("The Seven Laws of the Children of Noah") is the way for all mankind. The secular humanist, that is, a follower of the Enlightenment, would argue that reason and science provide the answer. Modern-day men and women on the Left ("progressives," "social democrats," "liberals") equally fervently believe that their values and their models (for example, the Scandinavian countries and Western Europe generally) are the best ones to solve the problem of evil and make a good society.

This book argues that the best—really the only—answer to making a better world is the American value system. Or, to put it another way, if you are disturbed by the amount of unjust suffering most human beings have endured and vast numbers continue to endure, nothing approaches the American value system as humanity's best hope. It was true when President Abraham Lincoln declared in his message to Congress in 1862 that America is "the last best hope of earth." And it is true today.

Humanity at the Crossroads: The Future Will Be Leftist, Islamist, or American

THERE ARE THREE IDEOLOGIES competing for the allegiance of mankind. This competition shapes much of the present world, and the outcome will shape humanity's future.

They are Islamist, Leftist, and American.

"Islamist" does not refer to the 1.3 billion people around the world who identify as Muslims. I am referring to those within the Muslim world who wish to see as much of the world as possible governed by Sharia, Islamic law. The word *Islam* means "submission" (to Allah), and that submission is manifested by adherence to Islamic law in a state that is governed by Sharia and whose leaders are Muslim clerics (though, strictly speaking, there are no clergy in Islam).

"Left" refers to the values associated with the Western welfare state, secularism, and the vast array of attitudes and positions identified as Left from Karl Marx to contemporary socialist democrat parties and today's Democratic Party in the United States. Identifying Leftist values and explaining why people adopt them is far more difficult than identifying and explaining American values or Islam and its values. That is one reason more space is devoted in this book to the Left than to Islam or Americanism.

American values, or Americanism, refers to what I call the "American Trinity": "Liberty," "In God We Trust," and "E Pluribus Unum" ("Out of Many, One"), the three values that appear on all American coins.

"Liberty" represents personal freedom, which according to Americanism is dependent upon small government, a free economy, and a God-based (which until now has meant a Judeo-Christian) society.

"In God We Trust" represents a society that regards its liberty, its human rights, and its moral values as ultimately emanating from God. It was axiomatic to those who founded America—including the so-called deists Thomas Jefferson and Benjamin Franklin—that America would fail if it ever became godless.

"E Pluribus Unum" originally meant out of thirteen colonies one nation, but came to represent the American value of a society based on neither ethnicity nor race. In effect, as many of the American Founders themselves said, America is producing something new, people defined by an (American) identity that transcends blood, ethnicity, nationality, class, and race (though the latter took much longer to transcend). Obviously, Americans did not always live up to this or any of its noblest values. This proves that Americans are flawed, not that American values are not better than other value systems. If one judges values by their fruit, Americans, along with their values, will come out ahead. As we shall see, Americans have done more good for more people than any other society in history.

There Are Good People in Each Group

IT IS VITAL TO RECOGNIZE that there are good people who adhere to all three ideologies. There are good people who advocate Leftist values, there are good people who practice fundamentalist Islam, and there are good people who adhere to American values. There are also bad individuals within each group.

This is critical to note because my advocacy of Americanism as opposed to Islam or Leftism is not an attack on all people who adhere to Leftism or Islam. Nor is it a claim that all those who espouse American values are good people.

Nevertheless the existence of both good and bad people within each group says little about the ideologies of each group. There were surely many good people who believed in Zeus. But it would be very difficult to argue plausibly that belief in Zeus caused their goodness, or that Zeus-belief is the best ideology for creating a good society.

The question, therefore, is not whether there are good Leftists and good believing Muslims as well as good Americans; it is which of the three ideologies is more likely to produce better people and a better society.

The Three Ideologies Are Incompatible

THE THREE IDEOLOGIES are not compatible. This does not mean that a Leftist or a practicing Muslim cannot be a good American citizen, let alone a good person. Though it sounds paradoxical, there are many good and loyal American citizens who hold values that are not American. That one's values may be in conflict with American values does not make the holder of those values a bad or unpatriotic American. There are many Americans who have held Leftist values who have risked or given their lives fighting for America. That is why it would take a deliberate mischaracterization of this book to claim that I read American Muslims (the great majority of whom, in any case, are not Islamists) or American Leftists out of the American nation, or that I claim that they are un-American, or disloyal to America, or do not love America. I neither imply nor believe any of those things.

Nevertheless, the fact is that the three ideologies are incompatible. *Any one of them succeeds at the expense of the other two.* All Islamists know this, and many Leftists know this, but most of those holding American values do not. This book explains why they are incompatible, but I will cite some examples here. The American value of "Liberty" is at odds with a Sharia-based society and with the Leftist commitment to material equality; "E Pluribus Unum" is at odds with the Leftist commitment to multiculturalism; and "In God We Trust" conflicts with both the Leftist commitment to secularism and the Islamic ideal of a Sharia-based state (since the God in "In God We Trust" does not want a theocracy).

Of the Three, Only Americans Do Not Proselytize

TWO OF THE THREE IDEOLOGIES proselytize; one does not. Faithful Muslims and Leftists vigorously proselytize; adherents to American values once did but rarely do today. The major reason for this is that while most Leftists and Muslims know what they believe in, most Americans have forgotten or never learned what is distinctive about American values. And you cannot advocate what you cannot articulate.

One Is Being Promoted Violently

IT IS A FUNDAMENTAL tenet of Islam that all of mankind should be Muslim.

This, in and of itself, is not necessarily troubling. After all, most Christians would like the whole world to be Christian; most Leftists want the whole world to adhere to Leftist values; and I, among others, would like the whole world to adopt American values (which, it should be noted, allow, even encourage, people to keep their religious, ethnic, and cultural identities).

What is troubling in the Muslim case is that more than a few Muslims are prepared to spread Islam violently. Polls repeatedly indicate that at least 10 percent of Muslims support Islamic terror.

That equals about 130 million people. And that number does not include those Muslims who, though not necessarily prepared to support terror, would nevertheless support the use of force to spread Islam. Historically, most countries that became Muslim did so via the sword.

Concerning contemporary Muslim violence, about one million black Sudanese Muslims and non-Muslims have been killed by Sudan's Arab Islamist regime in large measure because of their race and/or because they have resisted the violent imposition of Islam. The latter is the primary reason for Muslim-Christian violence in Nigeria as well: Christians there have resisted the violent imposition of Islam. And this is a major reason for Islamic terror—to enable Islamist groups to gain control of a terrorized society, such as Afghanistan, or to weaken countries, particularly the United States and Israel, that stand in the way of the spread of Islam.

Nor is the individual Islamist terrorist the primary problem. Islamist regimes are. The goal of Iran has been clearly enunciated by its Islamist leader, Mahmoud Ahmadinejad: "Is it possible for us to witness a world without America and Zionism?" Ahmadinejad asked at "The World Without Zionism" Tehran conference in 2005. "You had best know that this slogan and this goal are attainable, and surely can be achieved," adding that Iran has a "war preparation plan [for] the destruction of Anglo-Saxon civilization."[1]

That Muslims who push Islam through violence are in the minority of Muslims is true. That they may even be opposed (though almost always silently) by the majority of Muslims may also be true. But neither presumption negates the fact that Islam is, in some significant instances, being spread through violence.

Leftism as a Religion

MOST PEOPLE DO NOT REGARD Leftism as analogous to Christianity or Islam. They do not see it as the secular religion or as the all-embracing ideology that it is. Yet Leftism is not only a secular form of religion; in our time it is much more vigorous in its proselytizing than Christianity. In the Western world, there are many more organizations promoting Leftism than Christianity. Western readers of this book are more likely to have been asked to sign a petition for a Leftist cause than for a Christian one, and more likely to have been asked to join a Leftist cause than to embrace Jesus Christ. And, of course, students throughout the Western world are taught Leftist, not Christian, beliefs and values in their high schools and universities.

Most adherents to Leftist values fervently seek to spread Leftism. This is not some conspiracy, secret or otherwise; nor is it an indictment. Indeed, few Leftists would deny it. Wherever the Left exists, it seeks power for its adherents and for its ideas.

And it has been wildly successful. Its values and worldview have so taken over the non-Muslim world (not only the Western world) that the Leftist worldview is considered by many to be the one normal way to view the world.

This last point is vital. For the majority of people in the West, the Left's view of life is not considered only the Left's view, but in fact the only legitimate view of life. That is why it is so difficult for most people, including many who consider themselves Leftists, to acknowledge that Western news media and Western educational institutions are overwhelmingly Leftist. They just seem, well . . . normal.

Yet Leftism dominates just about every university in the non-Muslim world and just about every news source in the world—with the important exceptions of American conservative talk radio, the *Wall Street Journal* editorial page (not news pages), conservative websites, one cable news network in America, and a handful of newspapers and magazines in the English-speaking world. Few of these Leftist universities or media call themselves liberal, let alone Leftist.

There are essentially no differences in outlook among the world's leading newspapers and electronic news media. If you read *Le Monde*, France's most prestigious newspaper, you have essentially read the *New York Times* in French, and vice versa. In terms of values, the editors of the *New York Times* have everything in common with the editors of *Le Monde* and little in common with at least half their fellow Americans. The editors of the *Los Angeles Times* would feel more comfortable at a meeting in Paris, where they had to converse with the editors of France's leading newspapers using translators, than at a meeting of the Rotary or Kiwanis clubs of Los Angeles.

Most of all, Leftism is a religion because those who believe in its tenets often do so as fervently as religious Jews, Muslims, and Christians believe in their tenets. The Left believes in the welfare state with the same passion that a Muslim believes he should fast during Ramadan. A Leftist believes in the moral virtue of expanded government as deeply as a religious Christian believes in the moral virtue of stopping abortion. Western European Leftists and their American (and Canadian and Latin American) supporters are as passionate about secularism, economic equality, and the welfare state as believing Muslims are about Muhammad, the Koran, and Islam. And they want Leftist values to dominate the world as much as orthodox Muslims want Islam to.

That is religion.

America Is the Major Impediment to Leftist Success

BECAUSE THE LEFT'S WORLDVIEW is so different from the American worldview and because only America seems to stand in the way of the Left's conquering of the non-Muslim mind, the worldwide Left is anti-American. America represents the last great holdout against Leftism in the non-Muslim world. In this sense, America represents the same thing to the Leftist as it does to the Islamist: the greatest barrier to its success. Islam and the Left are ideological enemies, but as long as America is strong and neither Muslim nor Leftist, both fundamentalist Islam and the Left are allied in one way— anti-Americanism.

That is why the Left around the world runs interference on behalf of Islamists. Criticism of Islam or Muslims, no matter how nuanced or free of malice, is attacked by the Left as "Islamophobic." Sometimes the Left is so vigorous in its defense of Muslims that it acts more "Catholic than the pope." This is what happened during the "Ground Zero mosque" controversy in 2010. The majority of Americans supported objections expressed by many relatives of those murdered on 9/11 to the building of a hundred-million-dollar mosque and Islamic center two blocks from the World Trade Center, where thousands of Americans had been murdered by Muslims in the name Islam. It was the Left, much more than Muslims, that excoriated the opponents: Around the world some leading Muslim authorities actually sided with the American objectors.

The Left understands on a visceral, if not always fully conscious, level that a strong and self-confident America is a threat to its ascendancy. Though a vigorous Islam is no friend of the Left, the Left (correctly) feels much more threatened at this time by Americanism than by Islamism.

Since 1980, the largest demonstrations in Western Europe—always involving people on the Left and/or led by groups on the Left—have often been against America, and, not coincidentally, have taken place when the American president was a conservative (Ronald Reagan and George W. Bush). It is difficult to cite a single Leftist demonstration against any of the worst evils since World War II. Why? Because all those evils were committed by Leftist and Islamist regimes or groups, not by America.

Nor have Leftist peace activists demonstrated in any great numbers against war. It is America (or Israel) at war, not just any war, that disturbs the Left. That is why there have been few demonstrations, and none of any size, against the mass murder of Sudan's blacks; the genocides in Rwanda, Cambodia, or Congo; China's crushing of Tibet; or Saddam Hussein's wars against Iran, Kuwait, and Iraq's own Kurds. Though there are always admirable individual exceptions, the Left has not been nearly as vocal about these large scale atrocities as it is about America's wars. One additional reason is that, in general, atrocities committed by non-whites rarely interest the

Left—and therefore "world opinion," which is essentially the same thing as Leftist opinion.

Leftist university professors in Western Europe and the United States have also been agitated about one other country's wars—Israel's. Hence the numerous attempts by Leftist professors at Western universities to boycott Israeli professors and universities. But, of course, Chinese professors and universities are not only exempt from boycotts; they are enthusiastically sought after despite the lack of elementary freedoms in China, the Chinese government's incarceration of dissidents in psychiatric wards, the decimation of much of Tibetan culture, and the increasing Chinese occupation of that ancient country.

Impediments to the Spreading of American Ideals

UNLIKE LEFTISM AND ISLAM, there are serious impediments to spreading American values.

First, while the other two ideologies—Islam and socialism/secularism—dominate many countries, the third ideology only dominates one: America. There is no other country that claims to be Judeo-Christian and has such strong support for free markets and small government.[2] Therefore, while both militant Muslims and Leftists have a great number of supporters around the world, the American value system has few. That is why America goes it alone—with the partial exceptions of Israel, Britain, Canada, and Australia (especially when those countries have conservative governments).

Second, neither Judeo-Christian nor individual liberty nor free market values are secure in America. Many Americans, including most members of America's intellectual class, are as hostile to Judeo-Christian and other conservative values as European socialists are.

Third, almost no one is teaching the next generation of Americans what constitutes the American value system, let alone what is superior, or even simply unique, about it. American children are overwhelmingly educated by people who believe in European, not American, values.

In sum, since no other culture or society is offering an ideology that can be embraced by all the world's countries, the competition is among the Leftist, the Islamist, and the American.

The American way can only prevail if Americans believe in it. That is why, as important as the military battles against militant Islam and militant Leftism (Communism) have been, the most important battle is the ideological one within America. But with America's universities, labor unions, mainstream news media, entertainment media, and one of its two major parties ideologically aligned with European socialist values, and with big businesses frequently aligning themselves with the cultural Left, the battle within America itself for America's unique values is far from won.* And given that only America offers a viable alternative to both militant Islam and secularism-socialism, if American values do not prevail in America, humanity has a dark future.

The purpose of this book, therefore, is to explain American, Leftist, and Islamic values. If the explanations are convincing, the reader will understand why the world's hope lies with the American value system.

Is There a Fourth—the Chinese—Alternative?

IN 2010, the *New York Times* foreign affairs columnist Thomas Friedman wrote:

> [S]peaking of phrases I've never heard here before, another goes like this: "Is the 'Beijing Consensus' replacing the 'Washington Consensus'?" Washington Consensus is a term coined after the cold war for the free-market, pro-trade

---

* The idea that big business is conservative is a Leftist belief. But it is not so. Big business overwhelmingly aligns itself with whatever ideology is more powerful.

and globalization policies promoted by America. As Katrin Bennhold reported in the *International Herald Tribune* this week, developing countries everywhere are looking "for a recipe for faster growth and greater stability than that offered by the now tattered 'Washington Consensus' of open markets, floating currencies and free elections." And as they do, "there is growing talk about a 'Beijing Consensus.'"

The Beijing Consensus, says Bennhold, is a "Confucian-Communist-Capitalist" hybrid under the umbrella of a one-party state, with a lot of government guidance, strictly controlled capital markets and an authoritarian decision-making process that is capable of making tough choices and long-term investments, without having to heed daily public polls." [3]

Friedman and Bennhold are not alone among experts who contend that the Chinese model may prove appealing to various societies.

In the recent past, experts have predicted that any number of alternative political-economic models would surpass America. Many said that Japan's government-business model—"Japan, Inc."—was the future. Japan has been in recession for decades. The entire Left-wing world has pointed to the Western European welfare state as the only viable model of a humane and economically successful system. As this book goes to press, it is clear that the welfare state is economically (and for reasons explained in the section on Leftism, morally) unsustainable. And now, some see the Chinese model as overtaking the American way of life.

I do not. Either China will become a freer society or it, too, will fail. And along with liberty, it will still have to affirm values beyond material success in order to succeed as America has. Thus, I have not included the Chinese authoritarian-capitalism model as a fourth possibility for mankind because, among other factors, there is no ideology involved. Its appeal is largely restricted to would-be dictators. The Chinese model is based on the ability of a small group of people (the Chinese Communist Party in this case) to control a society. Confucianism, with its emphasis on stability and hierarchy, may play some role in the ability of many Chinese to give up most personal freedoms for economic gain and a largely conflict-free society. But the Chinese government does not offer Confucianism to its own people, let alone to others.

Having said this, if America were to weaken considerably—economically and militarily—dictatorships would most likely proliferate, and some of them would undoubtedly find the Chinese Communist model appealing.

But that, of course, only makes the case for America and its values all the more compelling.

Part I

LEFTISM

I

What Is Leftism?

A Secular Religion

LEFTISM IS BOTH A WAY of understanding the world and a value system. It is, in fact, a form of religion, albeit a secular one. Many of its adherents believe in it with the same passion as religious Jews, Christians, and Muslims believe in their respective religions. They direct their lives by it, and more than a few have been willing to die—and many have killed—for various Leftist ideologies. In much of the world outside the Muslim world, Leftism is the dominant ideology. It influences the values and actions of nearly as many people as does Christianity or any other religion. It even influences many believing Christians and Jews. For these reasons *Left*, *Leftist*, and *Leftism* are capitalized in this book.

One example of the religious nature of Leftism was the term adopted by Hillary Clinton when she was First Lady of the United States—"the politics of meaning." The term was highly meaningful to the Left, but meaningless to conservatives. The reason is that conservatives do not look to government and politics for meaning. They look to their own lives—their families, their work, their friends, their hobbies, and most of all, their God-based religions. But with the collapse of God-based religion on much of the Left, Leftist religion has filled the meaning void. For the Left since Marx, utopia is to be created here and now, on earth. Politics becomes the vehicle to achieving this and therefore politics provides much more meaning to Leftists than to those on the Right. For the Left, politics is the way to transform the world; for conservatives, politics is primarily the way to stop the Left from doing so. The former is much more fulfilling than the latter.

THIS IS NOT APPARENT—
EVEN TO MANY WHO HOLD LEFTIST BELIEFS

Unlike those who hold Christian beliefs and call themselves Christian, or those who hold Muslim beliefs and call themselves Muslim, many people who hold Leftist values do not call themselves "Leftist," and do not even think of themselves as such.

This is also true of organizations. While virtually every Christian or Muslim or Jewish organization identifies itself in that way, virtually no Left-wing organization includes the word *Leftist* in its name. In America, a list of leading Leftist organizations would include groups as diverse as the American Library Association, the American Civil Liberties Union (ACLU), People for the American Way, the National Organization for Women, and the National Council of Churches. Not one of their names even hints at a Leftist orientation and if asked, many of their members would deny that these organizations are Leftist.

The great majority of the world's labor unions are Leftist institutions.

The great majority of liberal arts colleges and universities in the Western world are Leftist. The social science departments of Western universities are essentially Left-wing seminaries. Just as the purpose of Christian seminaries is to produce committed Christians, the primary purpose of most Western universities is, consciously or not, to produce committed secular Leftists. The major difference between them is that Christian seminaries declare their purpose, and Western universities do not.

The great majority of the world's news media are on the Left.

And, just as significant, there are so many Leftists in other institutions that those institutions become de facto Leftist even when they are ostensibly committed to other ideals. An example would be Western religious institutions that come to be dominated by Leftists. The Anglican Church in Britain and many mainstream Protestant churches in the United States have Leftist values that are indistinguishable from those of other Left-wing institutions. However, because no one calls the Presbyterian Church (U.S.A.) the "Leftist Presbyterian Church U.S.A.," it is not immediately identified as a Left-wing institution.* Likewise, there is no mainstream Leftist position that the leadership and many rabbis of the Reform movement of Judaism do not hold, but the institution is called Reform Judaism, not Leftist Judaism, and most Left-wing rabbis in Reform Judaism would be insulted if they were described as having Leftism-rather Judaism-based values.†

If asked how they would identify themselves socially or politically (and usually only if asked), Leftists will call themselves "progressive," "open-minded," "liberal," "feminist," "environmentalist," "enlightened," or any combination of these, but relatively few will label themselves "Leftist." Many people with primarily

---

* To be precise, it is the leadership of the PC (U.S.A.) that is Leftist. And insofar as the leadership determines the church's positions on American and world issues, such as divestment from companies doing business with Israel, one can say that the PC (U.S.A.) is Leftist, even though many of its lay members and some clergy are not on the Left.

† Two examples will illustrate the Left-wing politics of Reform Judaism. At its biennial convention in 2005, the Union for Reform Judaism, the umbrella group for all Reform Jews, passed a resolution calling for statehood for Washington, D.C. Fair-minded people will ask what this has to do with Reform Judaism. A second example took place in 2007, when the then head of the Union for Reform Judaism, Rabbi Eric Yoffie, gave a speech to the annual convention of the Islamic Society of North America (ISNA). Yoffie said, "Why should anyone criticize the voluntary act of a woman who chooses to wear a headscarf or a veil? Surely the choice these women make deserves our respect, not to mention the full protection of the law." The rabbi's commitment to multiculturalism led him to defend the Muslim practice of covering women's faces with a veil, one of the behaviors most dehumanizing to women practiced in the world today.

Left-wing views think of themselves as "centrists." And that is understandable. Because almost none of these institutions, from the universities to the world's mainstream news media, calls itself Leftist and because the views of the university and of the news media are the only views to which the average person with Left-wing views is ever seriously exposed, it makes perfect sense that many people on the Left would consider themselves—and Left-wing views—to be centrist.

No Official Creed or Scripture

Another obstacle to identifying Leftism is that, unlike traditional religions, Leftism has no official creed or scriptures. If you want to know what Judaism is, you can read the Torah, the rest of the Hebrew Bible, the Talmud, and rabbinic literature. If you ask a Christian what Christianity is, a Protestant will refer you to the Old and New Testaments and a Catholic will refer you to the Bible and to Church teachings. Muslims likewise will refer to their holy works beginning with the Koran and the Hadith.

But even though there are hundreds of thousands of Left-wing books and an innumerable number of essays and articles written from a Leftist perspective, there are no official Leftist scriptures. At one time, perhaps, one would have pointed to the works of Marx and Engels, but no longer.

Unlike the beliefs of traditional religions, Leftism's beliefs must often be inferred. One knows that a Christian is one who affirms belief in the Christian Trinity. But it is not nearly as easy to label people Leftist as it is to label them Christian. The dogmas to which virtually all Christians assent are listed or easily identified by asking virtually any Christian clergyman. But the dogmas of Leftism are not listed and there is no official Leftist clergy.

Nevertheless it would be absurd to deny that there is such a thing as Leftism.

What the Left Believes

TWO IRRECONCILABLE VISIONS

Most Americans want to believe that liberal America and conservative America can be united. That was a major allure of the 2008 presidential campaign of Barack Obama. But the unhappy fact is that there are two Americas, and they are not a rich one and a poor one; economic status plays little role in this division. Rather, there is a conservative America and a liberal America.

The reason people in America believe (more so than in Europe, which is used to deep ideological divisions) in the possibility of unity between Left and Right is that they think the two have essentially the same vision for America—that Right and Left share the same ends—and therefore really differ only in their ways to achieve that vision. That is not the case. Right and Left differ in their visions of America, not just in having different roads.

- The Left wants America to look as much like Western European countries as possible. The Left wants Europe's quasi pacifism, cradle-to-grave social democracy, socioeconomic egalitarianism, and secularism in America. The Right shares none of those goals. It regards pacifism as an accessory to evil; the cradle-to-grave welfare state as economically and morally untenable; socioeconomic egalitarianism as subversive of liberty; and secularism as undermining both ultimate meaning and objective morality.

- The Left wants America not only to have a secular government, but to be a secular society as well. The Left argues that if people want to be religious, they should do so at home and in their houses of prayer, but not to inject their religious values into society.* The Right wants

---

* The Left, however, deems it acceptable and even desirable for religious people to inject liberal values into society. When the United States Conference of Catholic Bishops comes out against abortion

America to continue to be what it has always been—a God-centered (Judeo-Christian) society with a secular government that is not indifferent to God and religion.

- The Left wants Americans to identify as citizens of the world; it fears nationalism, especially of the American variety. This distrust of nationalism has been true for the European Left since World War I, and for the American Left since World War II. The Right, on the other hand, first identifies as citizens of America, and celebrates American (and other countries') nationalism.

- The Left therefore regards the notion of American exceptionalism as an expression of chauvinism and conceit. It often views European and world opinion as better than America as arbiters of what is good. The Right, on the other hand, has a low opinion of the United Nations and of world opinion as moral compasses. It sees both as having a much poorer record in identifying and confronting evil than America has.

- The Left is ambivalent about, and often hostile to, overt displays of American patriotism. That is why, for example, one is far more likely to find American flags displayed in conservative neighborhoods on national holidays than in liberal neighborhoods such as Santa Monica, California; Manhattan; and San Francisco.

- The Left subscribes more to the French Revolution, whose guiding principles were "Liberty, Equality, Fraternity." The Right subscribes to the American Revolution's formula, "Life, Liberty, and the Pursuit of Happiness." The French/European notion of equality (which goes far beyond the American belief that all people are created equal) is not mentioned. The Right

---

or same-sex marriage, the Left accuses it of violating the separation of church and state. But when the same bishops come out against capital punishment or for nationalized health care, the Left considers them valuable allies.

rejects the French Revolution and does not hold Western Europe as a model. The Left does.

- The Left envisions an egalitarian society; the Right
does not. The Left values equality of economic status
above other societal values—most important, above
liberty. This is what propels the Left to advocate laws
that would compel employers to pay women the same
wages they pay men not only for the same job but for
"comparable" jobs. This Left-wing emphasis on egalitarianism is what led the United Nations World Health
Organization to rank health care in the United States
and in Cuba as essentially tied—because the United Nations values equality, and in America, while the poor get
far superior health care to almost anyone in Cuba, there
is nevertheless less equality in health care than in Cuba,
where almost no one (except Communist Party leaders)
has decent health care.

- The Left wants a world—and therefore an America—
devoid of nuclear weapons. The Right wants America
to have the most advanced nuclear (and other) weapons
in the world. The Right trusts American might more
than it does universal disarmament as a vehicle to world
peace.

- The Left wants, as Barack Obama repeatedly stated
when running for president, to "fundamentally transform" America. Conservatives want America improved,
not fundamentally transformed.

- For these and other reasons, calls for a unity among
Americans that transcends Left and Right are either
naive or disingenuous. America will be united only
when the great majority affirm either Left-wing or conservative values.

1. MATERIALIST EXPLANATIONS FOR
HUMAN BEHAVIOR

Whether or not an individual who espouses Left-wing ideas considers himself a Marxist—and few have since the fall of the Soviet Union—Left-wing ideas are predicated on Marx's materialist understanding of life. In popular jargon, "materialism" means an excessive love of material things. But philosophically, "materialism" means that only matter is real; there is no reality beyond the material world.

This in turn means:

No Reality Other Than the Material

Nothing non-material is real. Love, for example, is ultimately chemistry, since the mind is nothing more than the physiological activities of the brain. So, too, free will does not exist—all our decisions are determined by our genes and our environment. And, therefore, God and religious beliefs are nonsense—frequently dangerous nonsense.

Religion Is Opposed Because It Prevents Revolution

From Marx on, the Left has fought against religion because it is non-materialist and because Leftists have understood that so long as people were religious, they would not engage in what the Left considers the necessary revolution to better their material lives. Religion teaches people how to accommodate to their material condition—precisely by relegating the material world to a lower rung than other spheres of life, such as the spiritual, the moral, and the intellectual.

Economics Explains Most Human Behavior

The Left does not view actions that Judeo-Christian society has labeled "good" and "evil" as the products of people's moral values and self-control but as the products of material equality or inequality. Thus the Left ascribes most violent crime to poverty, not to the violent criminal's defective character or defective value system.

2. MATERIAL INEQUALITY IS THE GREAT EVIL

The Left's great fight is with material inequality, not with evil as normally understood. Thus, *the Left has always been less interested in fighting tyranny than in fighting inequality.* That is why Leftist dictators—from Lenin to Mao to Pol Pot to Ho Chi Minh to Fidel Castro and Hugo Chavez—have had so much support from Leftists around the world. Many of these dictators were mass murderers, but to much of the world's Left it was more important that they opposed material inequality (and America).

This explains the Left's relative disinterest in creating wealth. The enormous and unsustainable debts facing the individual American states and the United States as a country from 2009 on have disturbed the American Right far more than the American Left. The same has been true for nearly all the European countries saddled with unsustainable debt. The reason is that the Left is not nearly as interested in creating wealth as it is in erasing inequality.

3. THE STATE IS THE VEHICLE TO UTOPIA

End all these social and economic inequalities and you will have created a beautiful world, essentially a utopia. The further Left one goes, the greater the belief in creating a this-world paradise. Unfortunately, however, attempts at creating utopia in this world lead to dystopia in this world. The conservative view is that the best is the enemy of the better and attempts to create a utopia usually destroy much of what is good in a society. That is why conservatives marvel at how good America is while Leftists seek to "transform" it.

Beginning with the chancellor of the German empire, Otto von Bismarck (1815–98), known as the father of "state socialism," the view steadily arose among Western progressives that the state should take care of its citizens. This was not the American view, which had always been that the state should be as small as possible and that the individual, the family, the community, and religious and other charitable institutions should take care of people.

There is an additional reason for the Leftist love of the state—it gives the Left power to achieve its goals. The Leftist combination of belief in its good intentions and its certitude that Leftist intellectuals are smarter inexorably leads to its commitment to enlarging the state.

Therefore the State Must Continually Tax and Spend

The Left argues that almost all social problems can be solved by the state taxing its citizens as much as possible in order to spend increasing amounts of money on social programs set up to solve those problems.

A prominent example is education. The Left is certain that a major reason for socioeconomic inequality in America is the inferior schools that poorer children—especially blacks and Latinos—attend. Therefore, America must continually spend more money on education.

But there are two empirical problems with this.

One is that increased spending has done nothing to improve American public school education, and has often harmed it. The United States spends enormous sums on education. According to the U.S. Department of Education's National Center for Education Statistics (2010), the United States spent $10,041 per pupil in its public elementary and secondary schools in 2006–2007. Compare this to 1960–61, when America spent $2,769 per pupil (in constant 2007–2008 dollars)—before the Great Society, the War on Poverty, and the establishment of the Department of Education. Nevertheless, American elementary school and high school graduates know less about everything important, and read and write more poorly, than they did when one-fifth the amount of money was spent on education.

An example of the irrelevance of massive increases in spending on education took place beginning in 1985, when a federal district judge took partial control over the Kansas City, Missouri, school district. The schools in that district were largely racially segregated, black students were performing poorly, and school buildings were often dilapidated. The judge ordered the state and district to spend nearly $2 billion over the next twelve years to build new schools, racially integrate classes, and raise student test scores up to national averages.

Over the next twelve years, the state and city spent these billions of dollars on fifteen new schools, with some of the best facilities and programs in America: an Olympic-size swimming pool, a state-of-the-art computer lab, television and animation studios, a model United Nations, student field trips to Mexico and Senegal (West Africa), higher teacher salaries, and a student-to-teacher ratio of just 13:1.

Fifteen years later, in 2000, Reuters reported that "Kansas City's public school district has become the first in the nation to lose its accredited status by failing all Missouri's performance standards, and could be abolished unless it improves." [1]

The $2 billion were wasted. Test scores remained as low as they were before, and the black-white gap in academic achievement remained the same. But the failure of the Kansas City experiment in massive funding of public education—like the trillions of dollars wasted on other Left-wing government programs—had no impact on the Left.

The Left not only overstates the importance of spending on education in explaining socioeconomic inequality; it also overstates the role of education itself.

Princeton University professor of psychology Daniel Kahneman, winner of the 2002 Nobel Prize in Economics and considered by many in his field to be the greatest psychologist of his time, describes the effect of education on income. *New York Times* columnist David Brooks summarized Kahneman's findings: "If everyone had the same education, the inequality of income would be reduced by less than 10 percent. When you focus on education you neglect the myriad of other factors that determine income. The differences of income among people who have the same education are huge." [2]

Why are there differences in income? Overwhelmingly because of the values and the hard work of those who make more money. As the *Washington Post* reported: "People who make less than $20,000 a year . . . told Kahneman and his colleagues that they spend more than a third of their time in passive leisure—watching television, for example. Those making more than $100,000 spent less than one-fifth of their time in this way—putting their legs up and relaxing. Rich people spent much more time commuting and engaging in activities that were required as opposed to optional."[3]

No one denies that there are many hardworking lower-middle-class Americans. Indeed, when these people pass values such as hard work, self-discipline, and marriage on to their children, those children will earn more—often considerably more—money than their parents.

But when conservatives argue that an individual's values and hard work are far more determinative of income than money spent on schools or the race of the individual, the Left's response is that this is "blaming the victim." No matter what evidence is brought, the Left wants more money spent on education. At a Democratic presidential debate in 2007, the candidates were asked to comment on issues pertaining to education. This was Connecticut senator Chris Dodd's response: "I've been asked the question over the years, 'What's the single most important issue?' I always say education because it is the answer to every other problem we confront as a people here."

It would be difficult to find any individual or institution on the Left that would differ with Senator Dodd. Yet they are all wrong. "The answer to every other problem we confront" is dependent upon the individual's values, character, moral education, wisdom, and common sense. It is not education per se, unless its purposes are character development, moral instruction, passing on the wisdom of the ages, and developing common sense. And since the Left took over education, these have not been taught.

Consequences of Ever-Expanding Government

The consequences of big government, of the welfare state, are as numerous as they are destructive.

- The most obvious consequence is that no society can afford the welfare state. At the time of this writing, the debt crisis in which Europe and America found themselves was the direct result of governments spending vast sums of money they did not have. As Jim Cramer, a Democrat, an Obama admirer, and host of CNBC's *Mad Money*, said of President Obama's meteoric increase in government spending within weeks of taking office: "This is the greatest wealth destruction I've seen by a president."[4]

Take the example of what had been the most economically dynamic and prosperous of American states: California.

For almost a generation California's Democratic legislature has been more or less able to do whatever it wants. In 2010, the *Wall Street Journal* described the results: "The Golden State—which a decade ago was the booming technology capital of the world—has been done in by two decades of chronic overspending, over-regulating and a hyperprogressive tax code . . ."[5]

One might argue that's this is a politically biased assessment. So here are some facts, not assessments:

- ★ California's state expenditures grew from $104 billion in 2003 to $145 billion in 2008.
- ★ In 2009, California's credit rating was the lowest in the nation.
- ★ As of 2011, California had the second-to-worst unemployment rate in the nation.
- ★ As of 2011, California had the second-highest home foreclosure rate.
- ★ California's taxpaying middle class has begun leaving the state because of the high taxes, because of the ever-increasing number of regulations on small businesses (which make up 83 percent of the state's businesses), and because

so many businesses have been fleeing to more business-friendly states.

* From 2000 on, California's job growth rate—which in the late 1970s was many times higher than the national average—lagged behind the national average by almost 20 percent.
* Beginning in 2001, California lost 25 percent of its industrial workforce. A typical example: In 2010, Intel, the world's largest maker of computer chips, announced that it would invest $7 billion to expand its facilities in Arizona, Oregon, and New Mexico—but not in California, the state in which Intel is headquartered.

- The bigger the government, the less the citizens do for one another.

If the state will take care of me and my neighbors, why should I? This is why Western Europeans, people who have lived in welfare states far longer than Americans have, give considerably less to charity and volunteer considerably less time to others than do Americans of the same socioeconomic status.

The greatest description of American civilization was written in the early nineteenth century by the Frenchman Alexis de Tocqueville. One of the differences distinguishing Americans from Europeans that he most marveled at was how much Americans—through myriad associations—took care of one another. Until President Franklin Roosevelt began the seemingly inexorable movement of America toward the European welfare state—vastly expanded later by other Democratic presidents—Americans took responsibility for one another and for themselves far more than they do today. Churches, Rotary clubs, free-loan societies, and other voluntary associations were ubiquitous. As the state

grew, however, all these associations declined. In Western Europe, they have virtually disappeared.

- The welfare state, though well intended, over time ends
up functioning like a Ponzi scheme.

    It is predicated on collecting money from today's
    workers in order to pay for those who paid in before
    them. But today's workers do not have enough money
    to sustain the scheme, and there are too few of them in
    any event. As a result, virtually every welfare state in
    Europe, and many American states, like California, are
    economically unsustainable.

- Citizens of liberal welfare states become increasingly
narcissistic.

    The great preoccupations of vast numbers of Brits,
    Frenchmen, Germans, and other Western Europeans are
    how much vacation time they will have and how early
    they can retire and be supported by the state.

- The liberal welfare state makes people disdain work.

    Americans work longer hours than Western Euro-
    peans, and contrary to liberal thought since Karl Marx,
    work is ennobling.

- Nothing more guarantees the erosion of character than
getting something for nothing.

    In the liberal welfare state, one develops an entitle-
    ment mentality—another expression of narcissism. And
    the rhetoric of liberalism—labeling each new entitle-
    ment a "right"—reinforces this sense of entitlement.

- The bigger the government, the more the corruption.

    Big businesses are also often corrupt. But they
    are eventually caught or go out of business. The state
    cannot go out of business. And unlike corrupt gov-
    ernments, corrupt businesses cannot print money and
    thereby devalue a nation's currency. Also, unlike the
    state, companies do not have police and cannot arrest

you. There is just no comparison between the amount of damage corrupt businesses can do and the amount of damage a corrupt government can do.

- The welfare state corrupts family life.

    Even many Democrats have acknowledged the destructive consequences of the welfare state in helping to create the underclass. It has rendered vast numbers of males unnecessary to females, who have looked to the state to support them and their children rather than to husbands. In effect, these women took the state as their husband. This is equally evident in the United Kingdom and elsewhere in Europe.[6]

- The welfare state inhibits the maturation of many of its young citizens into responsible adults. As regards men specifically, all previous generations of American men were raised to aspire to work hard in order to marry and support a wife and children. Many are no longer raised with these ideals and goals. One of the reasons many single women lament the prevalence of boy-men—men who have not grown up—is that the liberal state has told men they don't have to support anybody. They are free to remain boys for as long as they want.

- As a result of the Left's sympathetic views of pacifism and because almost no welfare state can afford a strong military, Europeans came to rely on America to fight the world's evils and even to defend their countries.

- The Leftist worldview sees society's and the world's great battle as between rich and poor rather than between good and evil.

    Equality therefore trumps morality. This is what produces the morally confused liberal elites who venerated a Cuban tyranny with its egalitarian society over a free, decent, and prosperous America that has greater inequality.

In sum, the bigger the government, the smaller the citizen.

Finally, the Left always seeks as much power as it can attain. One might respond that this is equally true of the Right. But it is not—by definition. The Left believes in ever-expanding government, while the Right believes in small government. Obviously those who want smaller government seek less power than those who want a big government and a powerful state, which, of course, they would lead or at least materially benefit from.

4. HIGH TAX RATES

Most people regard taxation as a necessary nuisance. The Left, however, regards taxes as the means to achieving two of its greatest goals: Taxation shifts power from the individual to the state, and it is regarded as the best way to decrease economic inequality.

Neither goal is part of the American value system. Taxes are viewed quite differently by those who uphold those values. They oppose increased state power and believe that liberty demands that people be allowed to keep as much of their legally earned money as possible. Moreover, in terms of economics, the higher the tax rates, the less an economy grows. Or, to put it another way, those most interested in producing wealth favor low tax rates.

But the Left (unlike classical liberals) is far more interested in producing economic equality than in producing wealth.

As President John F. Kennedy, a pre–Vietnam War liberal, not a Leftist, said in 1962, "This administration pledged itself last summer to an across-the-board, top-to-bottom cut in personal and corporate income taxes to be enacted and become effective in 1963. . . . The accumulated evidence of the last five years [is] that our present tax system, developed as it was in good part during World War II to restrain growth, exerts too heavy a drag on growth in peace time; that it siphons out of the private economy too large a share of personal and business purchasing power; that it reduces the financial incentives for personal effort, investment and risk-taking."[7]

5. SECULARISM AND OPPOSITION TO RELIGION

Though there are religious individuals on the Left, a fundamental aspect of Leftism is secularism.

From its beginnings in the works of Karl Marx, Leftism has rejected God and opposed religion. It is, after all, rooted in a materialist worldview. Man has supplanted the biblical God. "God is man," said Marx. And "man is God," said Engels.*

There are Leftist religious individuals and movements—examples include Catholic Liberation Theology and Jewish and Protestant Left-wing denominations. But the dominant Left-wing attitude toward traditional Jewish and Christian denominations has always been hostility. Unfortunately, however, there is considerably more respect among religionists for Leftism than among Leftists for religion. The reason is simple: Leftism has influenced Judaism and Christianity considerably more than Judaism or Christianity has affected the Left.

Why has the Left been hostile to religion? Because religion teaches people how to be content no matter what their material condition, because it defers utopian dreams to an afterlife or an end of times, because it emphasizes moral self-improvement (rather than, for example, economic equality), because it affirms a judging God and moral absolutes, and because it inoculates its adherents against secularism.

The classic Marxist reason was Marx's own: Human beings—specifically the poor—are supposed to make revolutions in order to better their material condition; and religion, by lulling them into accepting their low economic state, prevents them from doing so. Religion "is the opium of the people. The abolition of religion as the illusory happiness of the people is required for their real happiness." [8]

As it happens, there is truth to the Marxist analysis. All religions have taught their adherents how to achieve some contentment in

---

* I frequently use "man" in this book as the term for humans. I do so not because men are more human than women, an idea so preposterous that I feel foolish noting it. I use "man" and "he" only because they are linguistically more elegant than any egalitarian alternative.

this life despite their material poverty. For those who value human happiness, this is regarded as a great achievement. Indeed, religion increases the happiness of the rich as much as it does the poor. If anything, life is often more meaningless for the rich atheist than for the poor atheist. The poor always have some meaning and purpose in their lives—obtaining food and shelter. The rich, however, no longer derive meaning from obtaining food and shelter, both of which they take for granted. Therefore, the rich, and everybody else, need religious meaning at least as much as the poor do. It was the middle- and upper-class youth in America and Europe in the 1960s and '70s, not the poor, who lamented their angst about life's meaninglessness and their own "alienation."

Leftism then comes to the rescue of the well-educated secular middle and upper classes. It serves as a secular religion, providing meaning, purpose, camaraderie, an all-encompassing explanation of life, a division of the world between enlightened and nonenlightened, and much else that traditional religions provide.

Another reason for Leftist antipathy to religion is that religion presents the greatest organized obstacle to more widespread acceptance of Leftism. The more religious people are, the less they are attracted to it. Traditional Christians and Jews are the groups least likely to adopt Leftism. In addition to not seeking utopia in this world, religious Jews and Christians take the last of the Ten Commandments seriously—it is wrong to covet what belongs to their neighbor (Leftism depends on people coveting what the wealthier have).

How then can we explain Jews and Christians who adopt Leftist values? They belong to one of two groups. The first consists of secular Jews and Christians who nevertheless retain some attachment to a Christian or Jewish identity; they are known as "cultural Christians" and "secular Jews." The other group consists of Jews and Christians who do not consider themselves secular, who may strongly identify with their religion, and even attend synagogue or church. However, in the vast majority of cases they do not subscribe to many of the traditional beliefs of their faiths—especially divine scripture.

In the West, the great dividing line between Left and Right is not belief in God, since many on the Left—at least in the United States—believe in God (though often it is not the personal, morally judging, transcendent God of the Bible). Instead, the dividing line is belief in divine scripture. Those who believe that God is the ultimate author of their scripture (the Old and New Testaments for Christians, the Torah for Jews) are rarely Leftist. On the other hand, those Christians and Jews who believe that the Bible is entirely man-made are far more likely to adopt Leftist values.

Yet another reason for the Left's hostility to religion, especially Judeo-Christian religions, is that the values are in conflict. Jews and Christians who believe in the Bible certainly believe in helping the poor. In fact, religious Americans donate more and volunteer more time to charitable institutions than do secular Americans.[9] But they also believe in other biblical values that run counter to Leftism. They believe in the man-woman definition of marriage, that abortions not performed for health reasons are sinful (this is as true for Orthodox Jews as for traditional Christians), in a God who transcends nature, in objective good and evil, in reward and punishment in an afterlife, and much more that is contrary to Leftism.

In Western Europe, Leftism has largely succeeded in replacing Christianity as the dominant value system. For well over a century Christianity has been under attack morally and intellectually. Morally, it is considered useless at best, and harmful at worst. Virtually every Westerner who has attended university has been taught to reference the "Crusades" and "Inquisition" when discussing Christianity—as if those two events summarize the role of Christianity in history. And intellectually, traditional Christianity is dismissed as one would dismiss alchemy. The more Christianity shapes a person's life, the more the Left considers the person a buffoon.

Since the 1960s, wherever possible the American Left has sought to remove Christianity, and religion generally, from the public square. Obvious examples include the almost universal substitution of "Happy Holidays" for "Merry Christmas," the removal of Christmas plays and Christmas trees from nearly all schools, the banning of any nondenominational voluntary prayer from public schools, and the ban on any mention of God at school graduations (even "God bless the graduating class" has been deemed illegal).

There are many more examples.

On July 14, 2003, Reuters reported from Phoenix, Arizona: "After more than three decades at the Grand Canyon, three bronze plaques inscribed with biblical passages have been removed by U.S. park officials. . . . Officials said they had no choice but to remove the plaques from three popular spots at the majestic canyon's busy South Rim after an inquiry was made by the state chapter of the American Civil Liberties Union. 'They are religious plaques on federal buildings and that's not allowed based on the law,' said Maureen Oltrogge, a Grand Canyon National Park spokeswoman."

To understand the determination of the Left's campaign to remove God and religion from American life, one need only imagine how visually insignificant three plaques are in the immensity of the Grand Canyon. Yet even those plaques offended the secular Left.*

In 2004, the Los Angeles County Board of Supervisors voted 3–2 to remove a cross, the smallest image on the Los Angeles County seal, from the seal. This followed an ACLU threat to sue the county if it did not remove the cross.

To understand how extreme the movement to remove any vestige of America's religious origins is, it is necessary to know what the seal of Los Angeles County depicted.

There were six small panels, three going up and three going down each side. On the left side were panels depicting engineering instruments, a Spanish galleon, and a tuna representing the fishing industry. On the right side, the top panel contained oil derricks; the middle panel depicted the Hollywood Bowl, along with two

---

* As it happens, thanks to my Arizona radio stations, their listeners, and Republican members of the Arizona Senate, we successfully organized a campaign to restore those plaques to the Grand Canyon. It was a group of nuns who had placed them there, and I had the privilege of meeting those nuns at a synagogue in Phoenix. Here was a Jew along with evangelical Christians leading a campaign on behalf of plaques containing scripture from the Hebrew Bible placed by Roman Catholic nuns. The Left may have accomplished more for Christian-Jewish cooperation than Jews and Christians did in the two thousand years of Christian history.

stars representing the movie industry, and a small cross depicting, in the official words of the county, "the influence of the church and the missions of California." The lowest right side panel showed a prize cow.

By far the largest image was Pomona, the Roman goddess of gardens and fruit trees, who was drawn from top to bottom in the center of the seal. The cross was so small that when I first viewed the seal, I didn't see it.

The cross represented the Christian founding of Los Angeles County. The very name of the county, Los Angeles—"the Angels,"—bears testimony to its Christian origins. The cross no more advocated Christianity than the goddess Pomona advocated Roman paganism or the cow promoted Hinduism. It was dishonest to argue that Los Angeles County was promoting Christianity. As for the argument put forth by the ACLU that the tiny cross made non-Christians feel "unwelcome," as a Jew, I found the comment both absurd and paranoid. No Jews I spoke to, including Orthodox and other rabbis, felt "unwelcome." By the same logic, vegetarians should have felt unwelcome in Los Angeles County given that two panels depicted animals as food.

What we had here were the ACLU and the three liberal county supervisors erasing the Christian history of Los Angeles County.

Such efforts at extinguishing the religious nature of American life are not confined to the liberal coasts. In 2010, ABC News reported, "One week before the most solemn day in the Christian year, the city of Davenport, Iowa, removed Good Friday from its municipal calendar. . . . Taking a recommendation by the Davenport Civil Rights Commission to change the holiday's name to something more ecumenical, City Administrator Craig Malin sent a memo to municipal employees announcing Good Friday would officially be known as 'Spring Holiday.'"[10]

Consequences of Secularism and Leftism

There are, of course, secular conservatives. But most conservatives who are personally secular recognize that God-based morality is one of the pillars of the American value system. The consequences of secularism—especially when combined with Leftism—have been highly destructive on both the personal and societal levels.

No God, Life Is Absurd

First and most obvious, if there is no God then life is objectively meaningless. The materialist view of life renders the human being nothing more than self-conscious matter, with ultimately no more meaning than—but the same fate as—all other matter. Perhaps the best-known scientist of the late twentieth and early twenty-first centuries, Stephen Hawking, an atheist, goes even further. He essentially denies that there is any reality.[11]

No God, No Wisdom

There are intelligent and foolish people on both the Right and the Left. And there are both secular and religious fools. But the secular Left produces virtually no wisdom and almost all the foolish ideas believed by intelligent people have been produced by the secular Left intelligentsia. As George Orwell famously said, "Some ideas are so stupid only an intellectual could believe them."

Conservative intellectuals are sometimes wrong, but the list of foolish and dangerous ideas on the Left dwarfs the list of such ideas among conservatives: Marxism; Communism; people are basically good; poverty causes crime; men and women are basically the same; women are as likely to seek and enjoy sex without the prospect of commitment as are men; more government money solves most social problems; America was as responsible for the Cold War as was the Soviet Union; a human fetus has no worth unless the mother says it does; all things being equal, it is not better for a child to have a mother and father; humans are just another animal (with a bigger brain)—the list is almost as long as the list of all Left-wing ideas.

The Left-wing celebration of youth contributes to its rejection of wisdom. There is a Peter Pan–like aspect to much of Leftism. The desire to remain young manifests itself in America and especially in Western Europe in many ways: reluctance to marry; not wanting children; the belief that there is little difference between youth and adults; the public use of curse words; dressing at sixty as one did when one was twenty; the lack of desire to become an adult ("Call me Ted, not mister"); and more.

A major part of the reason for the foolishness of Leftist ideas is the secular world from which they emanate. Its rejection of the basic book of wisdom of the Western world, the Bible, and its similar rejection of almost all pre–twentieth century wisdom literature (as exemplified by its preference for racial diversity rather than excellence in literature) along with its emphasis on the value of "change" have led people to rely on their hearts for insights into life. And the heart is the worst place to find wisdom.

The religious certainly come up with irrational ideas of their own. It appears that the human being has to hold some irrational views and beliefs for a full life. Some of the deepest aspects of human life belong to the nonrational—love and music being two prominent examples. But—and this is a big but—in the Judeo-Christian world, the irrational is overwhelmingly confined to theology and religious life. A non-Christian may well argue that the Trinity and the Virgin Birth are irrational beliefs. A non-Mormon will view as irrational the Mormon prophet Joseph Smith's claims to have found and deciphered divinely placed golden plates. And non-Jews and non-Orthodox Jews can certainly find irrationality in Jewish law.

But unlike the irrational beliefs of the Left, these theological irrationalities rarely have an irrational, let alone harmful, impact on society. Unlike a committed Leftist, religious Mormons, Christians, and Jews rarely unleash their irrational beliefs onto society. Since the Reformation, religion in the West has generally confined its irrational beliefs to religion. Leftism, on the other hand, is all about affecting social policy and therefore its irrational beliefs have profound real-life consequences.

No God, No Free Will, No Punishment

If matter is the only reality, God, who is by definition a non-material being, does not exist. But neither does human free will. It is an illusion, since all of our behaviors are the product of either genes or environment. In order to believe that human beings have any free will, one has to posit that something non-material exists in the human being, such as a mind, a conscience, and/or a soul. This secular Leftist denial of human free will is one of the reasons the Left recoils from labeling evil as evil, and (correctly) ascribes talk about good and evil to the religious.

Aside from reducing human beings to sophisticated robots, the denial of free will has real-world consequences. It explains the Left's antipathy to punishing criminals: On what grounds can society punish people for acts they did not freely choose to engage in? It therefore regards punishment (especially capital punishment) as no more than revenge (as if just revenge is inherently ignoble).

Clarence Darrow, the most celebrated criminal defense lawyer in American history, and one of the best-known critics of religion in his day—in the famous Scopes "Monkey Trial," he defended John Scopes, the teacher who taught evolution—was opposed to all punishment of criminals. Darrow understood that in order to protect society, some criminals had to be placed in prisons, but beyond that, Darrow did not believe in punishing anyone because, as an atheist, he concluded what any atheist must conclude: Human beings have no free will.

"All people are products of two things," he declared, "and two things only—their heredity and environment. And they act in exact accord with the heredity which they took from all the past, and for which they are in no wise responsible, and the environment. . . . We all act from the same way." [12]

Thus, in Norway, one of the most Left-wing democracies, the maximum sentence allowed—no matter how heinous the crime—is twenty-one years in prison. Anders Breivik, the Norwegian who murdered seventy-seven of his countrymen in 2011, will be released from prison by age fifty-three.

Another characteristic example was the well-known case in Germany of cardiologist Dr. Dieter Krombach, who in 1996 was convicted of drugging and then raping a sixteen-year-old girl in his medical office. His nonpunishment? A suspended two-year sentence.

In 1993, Gunter Parche, a German fan of German tennis star Steffi Graf, ran onto the tennis court and stabbed Graf's opponent,

Monica Seles, nineteen, the world's top-ranked women's tennis player, between her shoulder blades with a nine-inch-long knife. Parche never served a day in prison. Instead he was given two years of free psychological treatment. Meanwhile Monica Seles could not play tennis for two years, and never fully regained her previous championship form. In her revulsion with the German justice system, she refused to ever play tennis again in Germany: "The justice system, in my case, really messed up."[13]

As reported in the *New York Times*, "Judge Gertraut Goring said a harsher sentence was not justified in view of the assailant's full confession, lack of former arrests and 'abnormal personality structure. . . . Our law does not function on the principle an eye for an eye,' Goring said."[14]

In the United States, especially in more conservative states, these outcomes would be inconceivable. Breivik would have been sentenced to death, and the rapist doctor and the fan who stabbed Seles would have served time in prison. The United States, the most religious of Western industrialized democracies, believes in free will and therefore in punishment.

No God, No Good and Evil

With the breakdown of Judeo-Christian belief in Europe and the West, the notion of objective good and evil has been relativized. There is no real good and evil; there are only subjective opinions about such matters. As British historian Paul Johnson notes in his magisterial *Modern Times*, the secular West wrongly applied Einstein's theories of relativity to morality: Not only were time and motion relative, so were good and evil. The moral confusion that has resulted in the secular Left world has been devastating to hundreds of millions of people. Secular Left intellectuals in the West come up with ideas, and peasants in China, Ukraine, Cambodia, Africa, and elsewhere are killed in the tens of millions.

The failure of the secular Left intellectual world to recognize and confront evil was acknowledged by Sam Harris, a leading atheist intellectual activist. Harris received a BA in philosophy from Stanford University and a PhD in neuroscience from UCLA. In his

2004 book, *The End of Faith: Religion, Terror, and the Future of Reason*, Harris argued that religion is the cause of the world's evils, and reason is the solution.

I conducted a dialogue/debate with him on my radio show. What follows is a part of that dialogue (italics added): [15]

> Dennis Prager: If I took a thousand Evangelical ministers—the folks that you have a certain fear of—and a thousand professors in the liberal arts, I would bet that the moral acuity of the thousand Evangelical ministers would dwarf the moral acuity of a thousand liberal arts professors. For which reason Lawrence Summers, for example, the president of Harvard, announced two years ago that the seat of anti-Semitism in America had shifted to the university. The university had also been the seat of support for Stalin. The university in Germany was the place to get Nazi philosophers. That you have such faith in secular reason is to me unbelievable, given the record of the secular rationalists.
>
> Sam Harris: Well, first, let me agree with you that liberal, ivory-tower discourse right now is certainly in many sectors bereft of real moral acuity, and the kind of discourse you have about Israel in particular vis-à-vis the conflict with the Palestinians—all of that is deplorable. But your first question, really, it all turns on what you mean by morality.
>
> Prager: Good and evil.
>
> Why is it that religious folks whom you fear turn out to be more morally accurate today than the secular folks at the university?
>
> Harris: I think that when you're talking about something as fundamental as recoiling from cruelty you would find that healthy people are going to be more or less the same across the board. But *I agree with you that about any number of things right now, academia has really become unhitched from morality as you and I know it.*
>
> Prager: I admire the fact that you, who are in academia,

would say that. But don't you ask what the root cause might be? To me it is clear: secularism.

Harris: Well, actually, no, I think the root cause in academia, certainly liberal academia now, is what we call "political correctness." I think that the problem we have to face now is that people are flying planes into our buildings because they believe their book was written by God.

Prager: Yet ironically, it is really only very strongly religious Christians, by and large—and I'm not a Christian, I'm a Jew—who have been at the forefront of criticizing Islam today. And they are called, by your whole secular liberal world, racists and bigots for doing so.

Harris: Right. I agree with you totally. I think it's profoundly ironic that the most sensible statements about Islam to appear in our culture have come from our own religious dogmatists.

Prager: It's not ironic. That's where you and I differ. It is their faith that gives them [their values and] the strength to say it. I think the university is a moral failure because it is radically secular. You think it's a failure because they're just weak-willed and politically correct.

If I lived in Europe two hundred years ago, I would have been tempted by the argument that reason alone, without God, religion, and sacred texts, can lead us to goodness. But after the depredations of the French Revolution; the horrors of two secular doctrines, Nazism and Communism; the low moral state of American and European universities; and the moral cowardice and appeasement of evil in contemporary secular Europe, one has to be—ironically—a true believer to believe that reason alone will lead us to a more moral world. Of course, we need reason. But we also need God and moral religion.

No God, No Beauty

It cannot be proved, but a strong argument can be made that the decline of religion in the West is correlated with the decline of beauty and excellence in music and art. Most of the great Western art was created with the goal of elevating man. But since there is no longer anything to elevate man to—no God, no holiness—Western art has sunk to the point where the deliberately ugly and even the scatological are celebrated in major art galleries in the Western world.

6. PACIFISM AND ANTIPATHY TO THE MILITARY

Beginning with the end of World War I, reaching its apex during the Vietnam War, and continuing until today, the Left has generally been hostile to anything to do with war, and has developed a great respect for pacifism, when not actually embracing it.

The bumper sticker "War Is Not the Answer" expresses a nearly universal Left-wing view. The Left believes that just about every conflict can be settled through negotiation, that war solves nothing, and that American expenditures on defense are a function of American militarism, imperialism, and the insatiable appetite of a "military-industrial complex." American use of military force, therefore, usually represents something nefarious.

The basic moral proposition that there is moral violence and immoral violence offends most Leftists, who regard the term "moral violence" as an oxymoron. Violence is deemed immoral, period. Many Leftists even oppose children viewing cartoons—like Bugs Bunny—that depict violence, not to mention playing with toy guns, water guns, or toy soldiers.

There are departments and institutes of "peace studies" at many American universities. Each can be assumed to hold Left-wing—specifically antiwar and pacifist—views. On the other hand, there are few "war studies" departments or institutes outside of military academies, even though war is frequently the only way to rid the world of some evil—and actually achieve some peace. The Nazi death camps were not liberated by "peace activists," but by people taught how to kill; that is, by soldiers.

Europe began its flirtation with pacifism at the end of World

War I, a conflict that extinguished virtually an entire generation of Europe's best young men for no apparent reason. Everything associated with going to battle came into disrepute—nationalism, a strong military, honoring the military, fighting, and the labeling of anything as "evil." Europe has never recovered from these effects of World War I.

It took nearly half a century for European antiwar sentiments to plant themselves on American soil. Antiwar (as well as anti-American) fervor reached its zenith during the American war in Vietnam. The world and gradually the American news media depicted the South Vietnamese regime and the American support of it as the immoral side in the Vietnam War. They did so despite the fact that the North Vietnamese Communist Party and the Viet Cong were as tyrannical, as squelching of all individual freedom, and as engaged in mass killing and torture as other Communist parties and regimes.

The American fight against Vietnamese Communism was therefore as moral as was its fight against the North Korean and Chinese Communists in the Korean War. But by that time, the Left dominated the news media, and had influenced a generation of young people—for the first time in American history, vast numbers of young Americans attended college.

The liberal media successfully depicted the American military victory in Vietnam that led to the North Vietnamese signing the Paris Peace Accords as a defeat. Then the Left ensured defeat once the Democratic Party took control of Congress in 1974, and ceased supplying the South Vietnamese government with arms, overturning what America had agreed to do in the Peace Accords.[16]

Shortly after South Vietnam fell in 1975, the Khmer Rouge ("Red Cambodians") murdered about one in every four of their fellow Cambodians. The Left had organized massive antiwar demonstrations when America was in Vietnam, but the Communist genocide in Cambodia was greeted with virtual silence. The antiwar demonstrations and riots were not about the Vietnamese, let alone opposition to tyranny; they were about opposition to possibly being drafted, and opposition to America at war. Left-wing antipathy to anything connected with the American military was so great that when Vietnam War veterans returned home they were frequently greeted with derision. The general Left-wing—and therefore media—view of them was that of men who were often losers who didn't or couldn't avoid getting drafted, and "baby killers."

Then, after succeeding in having America abandon Vietnam, Cambodia, and Laos to Communism, the international and American Left sought to undermine America's Cold War fight against the Soviet Union.

Since World War II, the Left has opposed fighting almost any evil. Even when Iraq's dictator, Saddam Hussein, invaded Kuwait in 1990 and sought to destroy that country and incorporate it into Iraq, the Left again opposed military intervention. One could hardly imagine a more morally acceptable use of military force than liberating Kuwait. It was even supported by the United Nations. Yet two-thirds of House Democrats and forty-six of fifty-six Democratic senators voted against that war; and they paid no political price for that opposition. For example, in 1998 the state of New York voted overwhelmingly to send Representative Charles Schumer, an outspoken opponent of the Gulf War, to the United States Senate. For the Left, "war is not the answer" even when the war's purpose is to save a country (Kuwait) from its would-be destroyer (Iraq).

7. CHANGE AS A SUPREME VALUE

Few words excite the Left as does *change*. The very name that the Left gives itself, *progressive*, implies, and necessitates, change. Therefore, the greater the Left's influence, the more widespread and radical the changes will be.

Every thinking person understands that there are times when changes are needed. But for the Left change is a value in and of itself.

Take the art world, for example. The Left dominates the worlds of music, ballet, art, architecture, theater, film, and literature. Artists, producers, musicians, actors, museums, galleries, choreographers, performers, critics, and academics are nearly all on the Left. What excites them most is not greatness (which, in any event, many would deny exists in any meaningful way), but change. Since the mid-twentieth century, the art world has esteemed what is new, what "pushes the envelope," and breaks with tradition—especially if it also offends conservative and middle-class tastes. That is one reason Norman Rockwell, probably the most beloved American painter of the twentieth century, is held in low esteem by the art world. He did everything wrong: He celebrated America, his paintings were completely intelligible, and the middle class loved him.

On the other hand, museums of modern or contemporary art feature works such as rotting fruit, fecal matter, menstrual blood, humans relieving themselves, nearly blank canvases, and other meaningless works.

This veneration of change rather than of greatness has also permeated classical music for about a hundred years. The music world, especially its music critics and university music departments, has been dominated by people who believe that change is great and incomprehensibility is deep. Typical was a famous 1952 piece for which John Cage, arguably the most influential American avant-garde composer, was best known. Titled *4'33"*, the "work" consists entirely of a performer sitting at a piano for four minutes and thirty-three seconds without playing any notes. This is deep stuff on the cultural Left.

Further poisoning musical judgment is the Left-wing value of diversity. In 2011, Anthony Tommasini, music critic of the *New York Times*, published his list of the ten greatest composers who ever lived. Absent from the list was Haydn, who Tommasini acknowledged was the father of the symphony, father of the string quartet, and father of the piano sonata. Indeed, one of the avant-garde's most celebrated modern composers (and a justly celebrated conductor), Pierre Boulez, "thinks Haydn a greater composer than Mozart,"[17] and one of the greatest pianists who ever lived, Glenn Gould, thought Haydn's piano sonatas were superior to Mozart's. So, why did the *New York Times* music critic omit Haydn? Because, he wrote, "If such a list is to be at all diverse and comprehensive, how could 4 of the 10 slots go to composers—Haydn, Mozart, Beethoven and Schubert—who worked in Vienna during, say, the 75 years from 1750 to 1825?" Diversity, not greatness, helped determine the *New York Times* list of the greatest ten composers. That is why Bartok, Debussy, and Stravinsky made the list but Haydn (and Handel) didn't.[18]

The Left-wing love of change has likewise devastated university courses in literature. According to Leftist professors, students were reading far too many DWEM, Dead White European Males. Their works, the literature upon which Western civilization had been built, were dropped in favor of inferior authors who were living and who were not white and European. Again, greatness doesn't matter. Change and diversity do.

In politics, change is equally revered. It is not characteristic of the Left to ask whether a policy change—no matter how radical—will work or what its costs are. If the change feels right, or if the change serves to expand the state's power—usually the same thing (except regarding national defense and security, where the Left prefers contracting the state's powers)—the Left advocates that particular change.

Obvious examples are the entitlement and social policies of the welfare state. They are called progressive because they represent changes—more and more government and state intervention in citizens' lives. What ailed American education that America needed a department of education and massive new outlays of money for public education? Virtually all the liberal changes in education—such as bilingual education for the children of immigrants, "whole language" instead of phonics to teach reading, an end to memorization, "new math," no more teaching of grammar or diagramming sentences, and ending core curricula in colleges—have seriously harmed American education. But they were changes.

It disturbs Leftists that there are unchangeable facts about human nature. People need to work hard is one of these unchangeable facts. Since Marx, the Left has desired to change this law of life and to create a society in which people work few hours, retire decades before they die, travel a great deal (the European Union declared international travel a fundamental human right),[19] and all the while be taken care of.

Faith in change has been a major reason the Left always supports the overthrow of non-Left-wing dictators. That this change may lead to far more evil does not concern the Left. So the Left was thrilled by the Russian Revolution even though the overthrown Russian czar was a boy scout in comparison to those who overthrew him. Decades later, the Left welcomed an Islamist tyrant from the Middle Ages, the Ayatollah Ruhollah Khomeini, because he overthrew the pro-American (and therefore Right-wing) shah of Iran. Liberals the world over welcomed the overthrow of Egypt's dictator, Hosni Mubarak. The dean of foreign policy commentators, Thomas Friedman of the *New York Times*, filed ecstatic reports from Cairo's Tahrir Square about the "Arab Spring." The liberal combination of change especially revolutionary change, and youth was irresistible.*

Meanwhile, in the summer of 2011, "mobs of ordinary Egyptians joined with soldiers to drive pro-democracy protesters from their encampment in Tahrir Square" in Cairo.[20] And in the Egyptian elections later in 2011, Islamist parties received about 75 percent of the votes.

The 2008 Barack Obama campaign for the American presidency was based on two words, one of which was *change*. (The other word was *hope*, which reflected the Left's exaggeration of how bad things are in America.) It was used multiple times in nearly every campaign speech, and it was often the one word that appeared on the banners that supporters waved at Obama rallies. A frequently expressed sentiment, as widespread as it was meaningless, was "We are the change we have been waiting for." The content of the change

---

* This conservative found the combination quite resistible. On March 1, 2011, within weeks of Mubarak's overthrow, I wrote a column titled "Eight Reasons Not to Be Optimistic about Egypt." As much as I wanted a free and prosperous Egypt, I saw little reason to believe that what would follow Mubarak would be a moral improvement. See http://www.nationalreview.com/articles/260953/my-pessimism-egypt-dennis-prager#.

was never delineated. What mattered to Obama supporters was that there would be change.

Why does the Left venerate change?

One reason is that the Left has utopian dreams. No matter how good life is, for the Leftist it is pretty awful compared with what it could be if only there were enough . . . change. America provides the best example. No place has been as good for as many people from as many backgrounds as has America; no country has done nearly as much good for other countries. Yet large numbers of Americans have been seduced by the Leftist depiction of America as sexist, intolerant, xenophobic, homophobic, racist, bigoted, imperialist, lacking in compassion for its poor, and afflicted with other moral flaws. Clearly, then, major changes are called for.

Non-Leftists, on the other hand, look at all the good that America has achieved and fear major changes. Conservatives recognize that the normal human condition is awful, that America is an aberration, and that therefore changes, especially radical ones, are much more likely to make society worse, not better.

Another reason for the Left-wing adoration of change may be that, according to just about every poll on happiness, people on the Left are generally less happy than conservatives. One consequence of this is that they will therefore look to change to bring them the happiness that has eluded them.

People on the Left respond that the rich are the ones who fear change lest it adversely affect their fortunate status. But the rich are as likely to be politically Left as the non-rich. To cite two examples: In 2008, the *New York Times* reported, "exit polls showed that 52 percent of voters who make $250,000 a year or more voted for Barack Obama."[21] And in 2011, the seven wealthiest U.S. senators were all Democrats.

8. THE CELEBRATION OF YOUTH

If you love change, you will venerate youth—young people embody change and young people love change. That is one reason the Left seeks to equate young people with adults. In the Leftist heydays of the 1960s and '70s, this was particularly evident. The voting age in America was lowered to eighteen. Whereas generations of Americans had assumed that few people under the age of twenty-one had sufficient wisdom to vote, in the youth-celebrating Leftist '60s, it was determined that eighteen-year-olds—seniors in high school—should be allowed to vote.

Likewise many young people demanded (and "demanded" is the appropriate term, since they often called what they wanted "non-negotiable demands") that colleges give them a say in determining their academic curriculum. And the liberal faculties relented. As a college student at the time, I was amazed that professional educators twice, three times my age did not believe that they knew better than I did what my core curriculum should be. But obviously they did not: After all, why would an adult know better than a young person what he or she should study? The very notion implies that adults are wiser than young people. That violated the Left-wing baby boomer 1960s motto: "Never trust anyone over thirty."

The 2004 Democratic National Convention provided an excellent example of Left-wing veneration of youth. One of the convention's featured speakers was a twelve-year-old girl. This was not some celebration of young people loving America. Her talk was reminiscent of the adult words put into the mouths of children in Hollywood films: The face is the face of a child, but the words are the words of an adult. (This, too, is a post-'60s phenomenon; in previous decades children in films spoke like children actually do.)

As the media reported, the highlight of the twelve-year-old's speech, and what brought the house down, was when she ridiculed vice president Dick Cheney.

This is not something conservatives would do. Using a child to publicly mock the vice president of the United States—at a national political convention, no less—is not a conservative value. I was there and wrote at the time that a twelve-year-old has not earned the right to publicly mock a vice president of the United States: "This girl has accomplished nothing compared to Dick Cheney. She has no wisdom, no humility, and no knowledge beyond the Leftist platitudes spoon-fed by her parents and schools. She is a mere child, more foolish than most, in that she actually thinks she has earned the right to publicly ridicule the vice president of the United States." [22]

The reactions from Left-wing readers were among the most intense I have ever received. In my next column, I wrote that "[n]o column has elicited so much anger, use of expletives and foolish thinking." [23]

9. ANTI-AMERICANISM

Anti-Americanism has been central to Leftism. The reason is that America embodies the opposite values of the Left—and yet has been the most successful country in history. American success is a refutation of Leftism. America is God-based (the most religious, indeed the one religious, major industrialized democracy);[24] is committed to the free market, individual liberty, small government, and nationalism; and executes murderers.[25]

The World Doesn't Hate America, the Left Does

One of the most widely held beliefs in the contemporary world is that, with a few exceptions, the world hates America—especially when its president is a conservative Republican. One of the Democrats' major accusations against the George W. Bush administration was that it increased hatred of America to unprecedentedly high levels. In many polls, the United States was held to be among the two or three greatest obstacles to world peace.

But it is not true that the world hates America. It is the world's Left that hates America. However, because the Left dominates the world's news media and because nearly everyone, understandably, relies on the news media for their understanding of what happens in the world, many people, including Americans, believe that "the world" hates America. And, of course, the Left-dominated media help to create much of the hatred for America that does exist. If I relied exclusively on the *New York Times* or *Le Monde* or the *Guard-*

ian or CNN International or virtually any of the world's major television and radio news stations and newspapers for all I knew about America, I would probably hold it in contempt as well.

Western Europeans who are not on the Left tend to hold America in high esteem. The prime minister of Spain from 1996 to 2004, Jose Maria Aznar, is a conservative who esteems America. He was elected twice, and polls in Spain up to the week before the 2004 election all predicted a third term for Aznar's party (Aznar had promised not to run for a third term as prime minister). Only the Madrid train bombings, perpetrated by Muslim terrorists three days before the elections, but which the Aznar government blamed on Basque separatists, turned the election against Aznar and his conservative party. The socialists won, and the usual negative views of America returned—along with Spain withdrawing its troops from Iraq.

Hundreds of millions of people around the world would rather live in America than in any other country, including those of Western Europe and including their own. Why would people want to come to a country they loathe? And why don't people want to live in Sweden or France as much as they wish to live in America? They, too, are rich and democratic countries—and according to the media, much more loved.

One answer is that most people know there is no country in the world more accepting of strangers than is America. After three generations, people who have emigrated to Germany or France or Sweden do not feel—and are not regarded as—fully German, French, or Swedish. Yet anyone of any background from any country is regarded as fully American the moment he or she becomes one. The country that the Left routinely calls "xenophobic" and "racist" is, in fact, the least racist and xenophobic in the world.

Two questions remain: Why does the Left hate America, and does the American Left hate America?

The answer to the first question is, as already noted, that America and especially the most hated parts of America—the conservative and religious—are the greatest obstacles to Leftist dominance.

To cite a few major examples:

- American economic success refutes the socialist-like ideals of the Left.
- American use of force to vanquish evil refutes the Left's pacifist tendencies.
- The Left strongly opposes the death penalty, and America is the last major democracy that allows for capital punishment.
- America, especially when governed by conservatives, uses the language of good and evil, language dismissed by the Left as "Manichaean" and even worse, as "religious."
- Most Americans still believe in Judeo-Christian values and in religions based on them, while the Left is aggressively secular.
- Americans are nationalistic and highly suspicious of international institutions such as the United Nations and the World Court, two venerated institutions of the Left, which is opposed to all nationalisms (except Palestinian).

And what about the American Left? Is anti-Americanism a characteristic of the American Left as well as the international Left?

One answer is that the American Left has contempt for the America that believes in American exceptionalism, that is prepared to use force to fight what it deems as dangerous evil, that affirms traditional Judeo-Christian values and religions, that believes in the death penalty, that supports the male-female definition of marriage, and that rejects big government, wants lower taxes, and prefers free market to governmental solutions.

All this notwithstanding, it would be untrue to say that all or even most American Leftists hate America. Many on the Left feel great love for the United States. But there is often a problem with this love.

For one thing, true Leftists have antipathy to the American

value system. They prefer secularism to "In God We Trust," egalitarianism to Liberty, and multiculturalism to "E Pluribus Unum." They also prefer the big European-type welfare state, and they reject American exceptionalism.

Additionally, while not denying the love that many Americans on the Left feel toward America, this love is often an odd one. If one really does believe, as the American Left continuously claims, that America is sexist, intolerant, xenophobic, homophobic, Islamophobic, racist, and bigoted, how lovable can such a place be? If a married individual thought as negatively about his or her spouse as the American Left does about America, we would find that individual's proclamations of deep love for the spouse difficult to believe. And we would certainly understand if the spouse constantly berated for such major moral deficiencies did not feel loved.

Perhaps it is an image of America's possibilities, rather than America as it is, that the American Left most loves. This seems quite plausible given American Leftists' belief that their country was founded by racists and remains essentially racist, that it is an imperialist nation, that tens of millions of Americans go hungry, that it invades countries for corporate profits, and that it is largely xenophobic.

Whatever the answer, the fact is that the further Left one goes, the greater the level of anti-Americanism, whether in America or abroad.

Here are a few examples:

Howard Zinn

Howard Zinn, an icon of the American Left, was professor of political science at Boston University, and author of *A People's History of the United States*, praised by the *New York Times* as "required reading" for all American students. A radical's depiction of American history, it became the single most widely read history text in American schools.

I dialogued with Howard Zinn on my radio show in 2006. Here is part of that dialogue:

Dennis Prager: I think a good part of your view is summarized when you say, "If people knew history, they would scoff at that, they would laugh at that"—that the United States is a force for the betterment of humanity. I believe that we are the country that has done more good for humanity than any other in history. What would you say . . . we have done more bad than good, we're in the middle, or what?

Howard Zinn: Probably more bad than good.

Prager: There is evil in the way we treated the Indians, there is no question about it. But there's also no question that the great majority died of disease and not deliberately inflicted disease.

Zinn: That's true that the great majority of Indians died of disease in the seventeenth century when the Europeans first came here. But after the American Revolution, when the colonists expanded westward, at that point we began to annihilate the Indian tribes. We committed massacres all over the country. . . .

Prager: What percentage of the Indians do you believe we massacred, as opposed to diseases ravaged?

Zinn: Oh, well it might have been ten percent.

Prager: Ten percent is very different from the generalization of "we annihilated the Indians."

Zinn: Well, ten percent is a huge number of Indians. So it's pointless I think to argue about whether disease . . . or deliberate attacks killed more Indians.

Prager: Ten percent is very different from what the general statement of "annihilate" tends to indicate. That's all I am saying.

Zinn: Okay.

Prager: If Europeans never came to North America and [the continent] was left in the hands of the American indigenous Indians, do you think the world would be a better place?

Zinn: I'd have no way of knowing.

Prager: So you're agnostic on that.

Zinn: Absolutely. We have no way of knowing what would have happened.

Prager: Well, we do have a way of knowing. If the Indians had never been intervened with, they would have continued in the life and the values of the societies that the American Indians made.

Zinn: Well, I suppose we could presume that. And many of their societies were very peaceful and benign, and some of their societies were ferocious and warlike. But the point is that we very often sort of justify barging into other peoples' territories by the fact that we are sort of bringing civilization. But if in the course of bringing civilization we kill large numbers of people—which we did in that case and which we have done in other cases—then you're led to question whether what we did deserves to be praised or condemned.

Prager: You can do both. You can condemn the massacres and you can praise the civilization that we made here. . . . Are you prepared to say that war is ever the best moral choice?

Zinn: No.

Prager: Never. Not even against Hitler?

Zinn: Well, I'm not sure about World War II.

Prager: Wow. . . . Do you feel that, by and large, the Zarqawi-world and the Bush-world are moral equivalents? [Abu Musab al-Zarqawi was head of Al Qaeda in Iraq and responsible for terrorist attacks in Iraq that killed thousands.]

Zinn: I do. I would put Bush on trial along with Saddam Hussein. . . .

Howard Zinn made five characteristic Left-wing points here about America: America has done more bad than good; Americans "annihilated the Indians" (even though, when challenged, he ac-

knowledged that Americans killed about 10 percent of the native
American population); maybe the world would have been better
had there never been a United States; no war is moral; and President
George W. Bush and the Islamic terrorists were moral equivalents.

Once again: This man's history of the United States is the most
widely used in American schools.

Amiri Baraka: New Jersey's Official Poet

In 2002, Amiri Baraka, formerly LeRoi Jones, a self-described
"Marxist-Leninist," was named by Democratic New Jersey governor James E. McGreevey as that state's official poet. Baraka came
to public notice in that role when Jewish groups pointed out that in
his post–9/11 poem, "Somebody Blew Up America," the Left-wing
poet wrote:

> *Who knew the World Trade Center was gonna get bombed*
> *Who told 4,000 Israeli workers at the Twin Towers*
> *To stay home that day . . . ?*

However, the poem turned out to be far more than a few anti-
Semitic lines. It was a 1,169-word tirade against whites and America.
The following is typical:

> *Who live on Wall Street*
> *The first plantation*
> *Who cut your nuts off*
> *Who rape your ma*
> *Who lynched your pa. . . .*
> *Who stole Puerto Rico*
> *Who stole the Indies, the Philippines, Manhattan*
> *Australia & The Hebrides*
> *Who forced opium on the Chinese. . . .*

Aside from the anti-Americanism, there is another characteristic Left-wing feature present here: Why would a Democratic gov-

ernor appoint a man with such views as his state's poet? The answer
is, in order to help keep the black vote Democratic and because an
America-loving black poet would not be deemed an authentically
black poet. For the Left, rage against America means you are an
authentic black.

Michael Moore and American Self-Hatred

As I witnessed—and the press reported—the most popular figure
at the 2004 Democratic National Convention was not the presidential nominee, Senator John Kerry, but the Left-wing filmmaker
Michael Moore.

As reported by David Brooks in the *New York Times*, here is
what this popular American Leftist said about America during an
international speaking tour in 2004:

"Before a delighted Cambridge [England] crowd: 'You're stuck
with being connected to this country of mine, which is known for
bringing sadness and misery to places around the globe.'

"In Liverpool, he paused to contemplate the epicenters of evil in
the modern world: 'It's all part of the same ball of wax, right? The
oil companies, Israel, Halliburton.'"

As Brooks noted, Moore told the London *Daily Mirror* that
Americans "are possibly the dumbest people on the planet . . . in
thrall to conniving, thieving, smug pricks."

"In an interview with a Japanese newspaper," Brooks wrote,
"Moore helped citizens of that country understand why the United
States went to war in Iraq: 'The motivation for war is simple. The
U.S. government started the war with Iraq in order to make it easy
for U.S. corporations to do business in other countries. They intend
to use cheap labor in those countries, which will make Americans
rich.'"[26]

Michael Moore and his Left-wing supporters may love America,
but with lovers such as these, America doesn't need haters.

American Media and American Military

American media have provided a sort of Moore-like view of America. The American military, in particular, has been repeatedly depicted in the most negative ways, often dishonestly.

In 2004, for more than a month, the *New York Times* ran stories about sexual humiliation inflicted by nine American soldiers on Iraqi prisoners at Baghdad's Abu Ghraib prison.

In 2005, *Newsweek* magazine published a "scoop." Based on an unnamed source, *Newsweek* informed the world that American interrogators of suspected Islamic terrorists at the Guantánamo Bay prison had flushed pages of the Koran down a toilet. If this were true, the interrogators would be both morally wrong and stupid, given that the words of the Koran and the pages on which they are written are considered intrinsically holy to Muslims. As it happens, however, the *Newsweek* story was not true. But it served the Left-wing goals of defaming George W. Bush and the American military.

In 2007, the *New Republic* published a series of articles by a pseudonymous American soldier about alleged American troop atrocities in Iraq. After being challenged, the *New Republic* stood by the stories for months. Finally, in December 2007, the magazine announced that it could no longer "stand by these stories."

America the Violent

Here is another typical Left-wing attack on America, made by a Canadian feminist professor in the presence of a member of the Canadian government in Ottawa:

> A [British Columbia] feminist told a cheering audience here that the United States government is more threatening to the world than international terrorism.
>
> Sunera Thobani received several standing ovations from about 500 delegates attending the Women's Resistance Conference on Monday.
>
> Her comments caused a political uproar, with oppo-

sition MPs condemning Secretary of State Hedy Fry for sitting silently as Thobani spoke. MPs called on the government to fire Fry, charging that she should have immediately condemned Thobani's statements.

"Today in the world the United States is the most dangerous and the most powerful global force unleashing horrific levels of violence," said Thobani, a women's studies professor at the University of British Columbia and former head of the National Action Committee on the Status of Women.

"From Chile to El Salvador to Nicaragua to Iraq, the path of U.S. foreign policy is soaked in blood . . ." [27]

Note that the Left-wing member of the Canadian government sat quiet during the America-bashing, while conservative members of Canada's parliament condemned that silence.

Gore Vidal on America the Corrupt

To much of the world's Left, America is simply the world's worst country. To the Left-wing novelist, essayist, and playwright Gore Vidal, described by *Newsweek* as "the best all-around American man of letters since Edmund Wilson," it may be worse than the Roman Empire at its most corrupt: "How we dare even prate about democracy is beyond me. Our form of democracy is bribery, on the highest scale. It's far worse than anything that occurred in the Roman Empire, until the Praetorian Guard started to sell the principate. We're not a democracy, and we have absolutely nothing to give the world in the way of political ideas or political arrangements." [28]

George Soros on the United States as Nazi-like

Speaking at the World Economic Forum in Davos, Switzerland, in 2007, George Soros, the billionaire who bankrolls many Leftist projects, said about America: "We have to go through a certain de-Nazification process," just as Germany did after World War II. The comment was hailed by the popular Left-wing website the *Daily Kos*: "Leave it to Mr. Soros to tell the unvarnished truth at a staid international forum like Davos."

The Left rejects American values. And American values reject the Left.

Why the Left Believes
What It Believes

I ASK AND RESPOND TO this question based on an important assumption—that many people who hold Left-wing views are well-intentioned. If one assumed that all those on the Left were mean-spirited people, there would be no purpose in explaining why people hold Left-wing beliefs. One would simply note that these are bad people (which is how the Left regularly explains the Right). But the question is far more complicated because many on the Left—and the many more who hold Left-wing beliefs but do not consider themselves Leftists—deeply believe that all they want is to do good. So, then, one needs to explain why people who want to do good do so much harm: Why do people who want to do good have Left-wing beliefs?

Man Cannot Live Without Religion

VERY FEW INDIVIDUALS can live a life without the meaning provided by religion. The religion may be noble or ignoble, rational or irrational, God-based or secular. But some guidelines for life, some camaraderie with like-minded souls, something that gives one hope for the future—these needs seem to be built into the human being.

With the collapse of Christianity in Europe, Leftism, fascism, and Nazism arose in its place. While the latter two seem to have been vanquished in Europe, Leftism—with its offshoots and related ideologies such as socialism, feminism, environmentalism, and egalitarianism—is as strong as ever.

The fact that it fills the hole left by the decline of Christianity is one reason so many people believe in Leftism.

Utopian Dreams

UTOPIAN DREAMS PLAY an enormous role in the emotional and political worlds of the Left. That is why, for example, those on the Left seek to "fundamentally transform" America, as candidate Barack Obama repeatedly promised to do if elected and attempted to achieve once in office.

Two famous statements encapsulate the operative liberal worldview.

The first was attributed to Robert F. Kennedy by his brother Senator Edward M. Kennedy: "There are those that look at things the way they are, and ask, 'Why?' I dream of things that never were, and ask, 'Why not?'"

The other is one of the most popular songs of the last fifty years, John Lennon's "Imagine," in which we are asked to imagine that there is no heaven or hell and that everyone lives for today; that there are no countries, nothing to kill or die for, and no religion; that everyone is living in peace; that there are no possessions, therefore no greed or hunger.

Regarding the Kennedy quote, a conservative would respond something like this:

Conservatives look at America and ask, how did something so decent, so different from other societies, ever get created and last more than two hundred years? Of course, we always seek to improve America, but more than anything else, we seek to preserve it—by preserving its core values. Conservatives do not "dream of things that never were" nearly as much as liberals do. Rather, we usually dream the same dream as our American forefathers did—to maintain a society committed to the values of E Pluribus Unum, Liberty, and In God We Trust. As for utopian dreams, we believe they are more likely to result in nightmares.

An almost perfect example of this utopianism and the Left's willingness to destroy what is good in the hope of creating utopia was expressed by Michael Moore, the Left-wing documentary maker, in an interview on CNN.

Moore told CNN's Anderson Cooper that today's "capitalism is an evil system set up to benefit the few at the expense of the many."

To which Cooper responded: "So, what system do you want?"

Moore replied: "Well there's no system right now that exists. We're going to create that system."[1]

For Moore, as for most Left-wing believers, those who lived before them are morally and intellectually defective. Nobody has come up with a good system of governance—Michael Moore will develop one. What did Jefferson, Madison, and Franklin—not to mention Moses or Jesus—know?

As for John Lennon's song, a conservative would respond:

Lennon's utopia is our dystopia. A world without God to give people faith that all their suffering is not meaningless is a nightmare. A world without religion means a world without any systematic way of ennobling people. A world without countries is a world without the United States of America, and it is a world governed by the amoral United Nations, where mass murderers sit on "human rights" councils. A world without heaven or hell is a world without any ultimate justice, where torturers and their victims have identical fates. A world without possessions is a world in which some enormous state possesses everything, and the individual is reduced to the status of a well-fed serf.

Liberals frequently criticize conservatives for fearing change. What we fear is transforming that which is already good. The moral record of humanity does not fill us with optimism about "fundamentally transforming" something as rare as America. Evil is normal. America is not.

Wishful Thinking

REALITY IS OFTEN WHAT THE LEFT WOULD LIKE IT TO BE

There are mature and immature people all across the political spectrum. But Leftist *positions* are usually childlike—because Left-wing positions are nearly all based on identifying one's wishes with reality.

- The Left would like to believe that people are basically good. Therefore the Left declares people to be basically good.
- The Left would like to believe that all cultures are equal. Therefore all cultures are equal.
- The Left would like to believe that all countries, cultures, and individuals want the same things—a peaceful, tolerant, open, free society. Therefore, they believe it.
- The Left would like to believe that men and women are essentially alike. Therefore the Left believes that men and women are essentially alike.
- The Left would like to believe that racism—not the breakdown of marriage and family, the absence of religious norms, a degraded popular culture, and other issues that all concern values—is the primary impediment to black progress in America. Therefore the Left declares racism the greatest impediment to black progress.
- The Left would like to believe that people commit violent crime primarily because of external forces over

which they have little control—poverty, racism, etc.
Therefore the cause of violent crime is held to be poverty and racism.

- The Left would like to believe that in order for America
  to stop relying on imported oil, often from hostile nations, all America needs to do is switch over to windmills and solar panels. Therefore windmills and solar
  energy are declared the solutions and enormous sums
  of money are spent on these "green" technologies even
  though North America has enough oil and natural gas
  reserves to supply America's energy needs for the foreseeable future.

The Rejection of Sad Facts

ANOTHER REASON LEFTISTS BELIEVE what they believe is related to
the childlike nature of the wishful thinking described above. Of-
tentimes they reject facts because they are sad or uncomfortable.
Leftists are not alone in this regard. Most human beings want to
reject uncomfortable truths. This includes social conservatives, who
do this when, for example, they assert that pornography leads to
rape. They so detest pornography that they reject the fact that a
causal link between pornography and rape does not exist: Rape
has been a terrible part of the human condition throughout history,
even when there was no porn, and the vast majority of men who
view pornography do not rape.

But the rejection of facts because they are sad is a distinguishing
feature of Leftism. For example, the belief that people are basically
good is an erroneous Leftist belief that is held, in large part, because
it denies the sad fact that people are not basically good. I learned this
after I devoted one of my columns in the *Jewish Journal of Los Angeles*
to analyzing why most Jews believe that people are basically good despite the fact that this belief is neither rational nor Jewish and despite
the fact that Jews, of all people, know how cruel humans frequently

are. In a lifetime of teaching and writing on Judaism, I noted, I have never encountered a single normative statement in three thousand years of Jewish writing that asserts that man is basically good.[2]

The reaction from liberal Jewish readers was so negative that nearly an entire page of the newspaper was devoted to letters attacking me.[3]

How is this to be explained? Why would liberals react so strongly against someone who wrote that people are not basically good? In my original article, I offered one explanation: Since the Enlightenment, the secular world has had to believe in man (or "humanity") because if you don't believe in God and you don't believe in humanity, you will despair.

But one critic opened my eyes to a deeper psychological reason. This is what he wrote:

"What a sad world it would be if we all believed as Dennis Prager that mankind is inherently evil."

My response:

"I did not write that man is inherently evil. I wrote that he is not basically good. And, yes, that does make the world sad. So do disease, earthquakes, death and all the unjust suffering in the world. But sad facts remain facts. . . . A distinguishing characteristic of liberals and leftists," I concluded, "is their aversion to acknowledging sad facts."

No one likes pain, but people on the Left are more prone to avoiding painful realizations and denying painful behavior. That's why they prefer to deny real evil (for example, Communism in its heyday, and Islamism today) and therefore avoid confronting evil (hence the flirtation with pacifism and proclivity to appease evil); why they believe that evil can be negotiated with; why they think people are basically good; and why they maintain that men and women have similar natures and want the same things. The list of Leftist wishful thinking is extensive. Avoidance of pain is probably a major reason the Left dislikes capitalism and free markets. Free markets create winners and losers, and the Left does not like the painful fact that some people lose and some win.

This reluctance to accept anyone losing expresses itself on the micro-level as well. Many liberal educators and parents oppose children playing in competitive sports because they can lose, sometimes by a big score. Many schools now emphasize "cooperation instead of competition" since they do not want children to experience the pain of losing. That is also why liberals introduced the foolish and destructive idea of giving sports trophies to all children who play, win or lose: If only the winners receive trophies, the players who didn't win may experience pain.

Human nature not being basically good is only one of many facts of life denied by Leftism because of the pain they cause. Another such fact is that men and women are inherently different. Many on the Left have rejected this idea because some of the differences are too emotionally upsetting to accept. For example, the fact that men are generally more driven to variety in sexual partners is emotionally upsetting (especially, and understandably, to women). It is also feared that this excuses married men who have affairs. Therefore, it is widely denied.

The fact that black males disproportionately commit violent crime in America is usually ignored by the Left. When it is noted, the Leftist reaction to this painful fact is to label those who do note it racist and/or to argue that there are too many black males in prison because of American racism, thereby shifting the blame from the black criminals onto American society.

It is generally believed that as people grow older, they reject much of the liberalism they believed in when they were young. This is true, and one reason is relevant here: As we get older, we tend to make peace with painful facts of life.

Good Intentions Are What Matter Most

FOR THE LEFT, intentions are all-important. Leftists are certain they mean well—that it is they who care for the poor, the downtrodden, the oppressed, and minorities, and they are the ones who want a peaceful world. This certitude regarding intentions is enough to legitimize Leftists' policies in their eyes—and, at least as important, to delegitimize their opponents' motives.

Since conservatives also believe they mean well, what distinguishes Leftists is that for the Left intentions trump results. As this book demonstrates, nearly everywhere that distinctive Leftist policies have prevailed, the results have been destructive. If people on the Left judged their beliefs by their results, few people would remain on the Left.

That is a major reason far more people leave the Left than the Right as they get older; they have had the time to look at life and see the results of their ideas. Conversely, it also helps explain why far more young people are on the Left; when one is young and more naive, intentions are what matter most.

The worst aspect of intentions-based assessments is that if one assesses intentions more than results, one's opponents must be judged as having bad intentions. As we shall see, that is what the Left does—it is as certain of the bad intentions of conservatives as it is of its own good intentions.

WHEN GOOD PEOPLE DO BAD THINGS

In 1981, Rabbi Harold Kushner wrote *When Bad Things Happen to Good People*, a perennial bestselling book that propelled the author to international renown. Today we need another book that uses the words of Rabbi Kushner's classic title, but addresses a different issue: When Good People Do Bad Things.

We need such a book because of the disheartening fact that much, perhaps even most, evil does not emanate from particularly evil people or even from the bad or self-centered parts of human nature, but from the good and idealistic parts. Most evil is not committed as a result of unbridled lust or greed; and the sadistic monster who revels in inflicting pain on other people is rare.

The Left has a history of many decent people supporting many bad people doing great harm. Good intentions cause most of the world's great evils.

Take Communism, for example. The greatest mass-murdering ideology in history, the greatest destroyer of elementary human rights, was an ideology supported by millions of people who cared deeply about progress and human equality. It took Stalin's peace pact with Hitler to awaken many Western Leftists to how evil Communism was. And still, vast numbers of Westerners went on to support Stalin, Mao, Ho, Castro, and other Communist murderers and tyrants. Were all these Westerners bad people? If a bad person is defined as one who revels in the suffering of others, of course not.

Were all the Koreans who supported the North Korean monster Kim Il Sung bad people? Were all the Russians who wept at Stalin's funeral supporters of torture and mass murder? Of course not. For that matter, few Germans who voted for Hitler and the Nazis were voting for the extermination of the Jews.[4] Aside from the core Nazi Party leadership and early true-believing members—who were Jew-haters above all—most German voters for Hitler were preoccupied with reviving Germany after World War I.

Let me restate the major lesson to be learned from all this in the words of the late Rabbi Wolfe Kelman, head of America's Conservative rabbinate for many years. As a young man, I sought advice from him, and he offered this piece of wisdom: "I pretty much have my bad inclination [*yetzer hara* was the well-known Hebrew term he used] under control; it's my good inclination [*yetzer hatov*] that always gets me into trouble."

When it comes to personal relations and, even more so, to formulating social policy, intending to do good is completely insufficient. In order to do good in both the personal and social spheres, people also need wisdom, common sense, and a moral value system.

THE UNIMPORTANCE OF WISDOM

Because the Left relies heavily on feelings and intentions, wisdom and preexisting moral value systems do not count for much. This attitude was encapsulated in the famous Left-wing baby boomer admonition, "Never trust anyone over thirty." With that sentence, the 1960s and '70s youth announced that there was nothing to be learned about leading a good life—the purpose of all wisdom teaching since Athens and Jerusalem—from anyone older than the baby boomers, let alone anyone who lived long ago. It was enough to rely on one's own feelings for such insights.

The Left-wing adulation of youth was part of this rejection of wisdom. One can revere youth or wisdom, but not both. Thus, the 1960s and '70s in America saw the end of required courses at universities: Eighteen- and nineteen-year-olds would choose what to study.

Western universities have an abundance of professors with intellect, men and women who possess a vast repository of knowledge (though often in increasingly narrow areas of study), who are certain that they mean well and that they know better than others. Yet the Western university has been morally wrong on nearly every disputed great moral issue—support for Marxist ideas and causes, nuclear disarmament during the Cold War, belief that America was as responsible as the Soviet Union for the Cold War, sympathetic views of Communist tyrants such as Mao, Ho, and Castro, the portrayal of the United States and Israel as international villains, support for pacifism, and so forth.

Why? One reason is that it lacks wisdom. The university relies on the good, the "progressive," intentions of its professors, not on the accumulated wisdom of the ages, for solutions to society's problems. That is why, in the Left's view, the American Founding Fathers, the Constitution, and in particular the Bible have little or nothing to teach people today. The Bible is deemed completely out of touch—its being rooted in belief in God is enough to invalidate it; the Constitution is antiquated, written by slaveholding, affluent white males who were therefore morally flawed, men of their time who could not have anticipated the complex world of the twentieth and twenty-first centuries. In order to be relevant to today's America, the Constitution means whatever the contemporary progressive says it means.

Those of us who grew up in religious Jewish and Christian schools were taught early in life that our heart is an awful guide to doing what is right, that the human being is essentially flawed, that human nature needs to be constantly controlled, and that the greatest moral insights preceded our birth. For this reason many Americans who studied at traditional Jewish and Christian high schools have more wisdom (though, of course, less knowledge) than many professors, artists, and editorial page writers.

For example, unlike the Left, those who value wisdom know that when you give people something for nothing, you produce ungrateful people; that when you obscure the differences between men and women, you end up with many aimless men and angry women; that when you give children "self-esteem" without their earning it, you produce narcissists who enter adulthood often incapable of empathy and of handling life; that if you do not destroy evil, it will proliferate; and that if you are kind to the cruel, you will end up being cruel to the kind.

If you really want goodness to prevail, wisdom is a key to unlocking it. The heart is not. That's why we have a minimum voting age and a minimum age for running for public office. As good as a young person may be, personal goodness is not enough to be competent to choose society's leaders or to be one.

So, why do otherwise good people do bad things? In large part, because they lack wisdom.

STAGE ONE THINKING

The Left-wing reliance on good intentions is the major reason for what one of this generation's greatest thinkers, Stanford professor Thomas Sowell, has called "Stage One Thinking."

Think of a problem and ask what policies would be suggested by good intentions alone—that is, not taking into account other factors such as what works, what is responsible, and what the costs and the consequences might be—and you will understand how most Left-wing policies are devised.

Let's take two examples.

Societal Problem: There are disproportionately fewer blacks than whites or Asians on college campuses.

Solution Suggested by Good Intentions Alone: Lower the admissions standards so as to enable more blacks to enter colleges they would otherwise not have been admitted to.

The Consequences: Blacks who were not ready for colleges that lowered standards for them dropped out of college at higher rates than other students. Liberal defenders of affirmative action dispute this by pointing out that blacks admitted to the most elite universities do not drop out at particularly higher rates. But, as Sowell points out, that is irrelevant. Harvard has no need to lower standards to admit any group. Blacks who are admitted to Harvard have very similar SAT scores to other Harvard students. What matters here is how well or poorly blacks do when admitted to universities that did lower their admissions standards in order to admit them.

Here is Sowell:

> The real issue, however, is not how highly ranked the institutions are, but how big the racial difference in admissions standards has been. This they [the defenders of affirmative action] never tell us, despite mountains of statistics on everything else. From other studies, however, it is clear that racial differences in SAT scores, for example, are much smaller at Harvard (95 points) than at Duke (184 points) or Rice (271 points).
>
> In other words, where the racial preferences in admissions are not as great, the differences in graduation rates are not as great. The critics of affirmative action were right: *Racial preferences reduce the prospects of black students graduating.* Other data tell the same story.
>
> Compare racial preferences in Colorado, for example.

At the flagship University of Colorado at Boulder, test score differences between black and white students have been more than 200 points—and only 39 percent of the black students graduated, compared to 72 percent of white students. Meanwhile, at the University of Colorado at Denver, where the SAT score difference was a negligible 30 points, there was also a negligible difference in graduation rates—50 percent for blacks and 48 percent for whites. (emphasis added)[5]

Having to drop out of a college for which they were unprepared was not the only negative effect that affirmative action programs had on black students. The other was walking through campus day after day thinking that other students wondered if you were there because you merited it or because you were black. It is difficult to overstate the humiliating impact of such thinking.

Left-wing defenders respond that any suspicions on the part of white or other students regarding the academic worthiness of black students emanate from racism. This argument is classic Leftism—since Left-wing policies come from good people (progressives), those who oppose such policies must be bad people.

Liberals further respond by asking why no one suspects the academic abilities of white students who are beneficiaries of a different type of affirmative action—those admitted to a college because their parents were alumni of, or big donors to, the college.

The answer is that other students cannot identify the white students who were admitted because of their parents. Blacks are immediately identifiable, but these students are not. If every white student admitted thanks to Mom or Dad wore a sign saying, "My parents gave a lot of money to this university," they would walk around campus under the same cloud of doubt.

Societal Problem: Millions of citizens live under the poverty line.

Solution Suggested by Good Intentions Alone: Spend trillions of dollars on the poor.

The Consequences: Massive governmental spending has affected societies adversely. Among the many terrible consequences are a great number of citizens who come to rely on the state rather than on themselves and on their families and neighbors, the creation of an entitlement mentality that chips away at the moral foundations of society, and the rendering of the individual increasingly less significant.

Fear of the Right

FINALLY, MANY PEOPLE SUPPORT the Left, not because they necessarily affirm Leftist doctrines, but because they fear the Right. It is fair to say that the Left has succeeded in demonizing the Right more than it has succeeded in any other area of life. This is discussed in detail in the next chapter. But it must be stressed here that vast numbers of people on the Left have convinced themselves or been convinced by others that the Right is essentially fascistic, not to mention sexist, intolerant, xenophobic, homophobic, Islamophobic, racist, bigoted, small-minded, anti-science, anti-reason, and anti-intellectual. Once one believes all this, it becomes morally compulsory to be on the Left. One does not have to seriously think through the issues. All one has to know is that he or she is against whatever positions fascistic, bigoted, anti-intellectual haters hold.

If only people who considered themselves Leftists held Left-wing views, Leftism would be far weaker. This is especially true in America where, according to Gallup 2010, only 20 percent of the population self-identifies as "liberal or very liberal." Yet Left-wing ideas are dominant in many institutions and are held by many individuals who do not think of themselves as Leftist. Why has that happened?

Why the Left Succeeds

WHY HAS LEFT-WING THINKING succeeded in most of the non-Muslim world? Why, in particular, do Left-wing candidates so often win elections in center-Right America?

There are many reasons. Understanding them unravels the mystery of the appeal of something that has poisoned so many areas of life—the arts, the universities, religion, the family, the fight against tyrannies; that, in its extreme forms, has murdered more people than any idea in modern history; and that has led to the near bankrupting of the Western world's democracies through the welfare state incurring unsustainable debt.

1. Leftism Venerates Feelings

ONE MUST FIRST RECOGNIZE that the Left is animated largely by feelings. Though it prides itself as intellectual (and most intellectuals are on the Left), Leftism primarily appeals to emotions, sometimes noble emotions (such as compassion).

That is one reason Leftist positions are young people's "default" positions. Young people are guided by feelings, they trust their feelings, and they have neither had the time nor the inclination to think issues through. If one only emotes—for example, feels for the poor, loves peace, hates war, despises racism, yearns for equality—without sustained reflection, one is going to hold Leftist positions. It often takes many years of rethinking one's original Leftist views to realize that if one hates poverty, loves justice, hates war, loves peace—and most important, hates evil—one will reject Leftism.

Of course, people on the Left see themselves and Leftism as the opposite of feelings-based. They see themselves as rational, as the heirs of the Enlightenment, and as intellectual. It is their ideological opponents whom they deem, and routinely label, irrational, anti-intellectual, and worst of all, as hostages to religion, the ultimate irrationality.

Before presenting the case for the Left as primarily feelings-based, it is important to emphasize that the claim that most Leftist thinking is feelings-based is not only a *critique* of the Left; it is also a *defense* of the Left in that it does not ascribe nefarious motives to all Leftists. There are, as I repeatedly note, many well-intentioned people on the Left, especially among liberals, just as there exist mean-spirited individuals on the Right.

WHY LIBERALS SO OFTEN FEEL "OFFENDED"

The feelings-based nature of liberalism helps explain a liberal and Left phenomenon—how much more likely people on the Left are to say that they feel "offended" when confronted with views with which they differ. Where other people would say, "I disagree," many on the Left will say, "I am offended." This is a key to understanding Leftist thinking. After all, when are people offended? When their feelings are hurt. A pro-choice woman is far more likely to say that she is "offended" when encountering a pro-life position than is an equally fervent pro-life woman when she encounters a pro-choice position. Why? Because the pro-choice position is nearly always feelings-based: A mother's feelings, not the objective worth of a human fetus, determine whether a human fetus has any intrinsic worth.

So, too, the concept of "political correctness" revolves around not offending people's feelings—which almost always means Left-leaning people's feelings since there is essentially no Right-wing political correctness. Suggest that women's brains may not be as wired for math or engineering as men's brains are, and liberal women (and many liberal men) are offended. The question that political correctness poses is "Does this statement or position hurt anyone's feelings (especially anyone on the Left)?" That, not "Is the statement true?" is what matters to the feelings-based.

LEFT-WING POSITIONS ARE EMOTION-BASED

Name a Left-wing position and the chances are that it is based on feelings more than reason. Take, for example, the Hollywood film industry. It is dominated by Leftists who advocate increases in taxes; yet these very same film producers routinely leave California to make films in states and countries with lower tax rates than California. In other words, they act in accord with reason—avoiding high taxes that reduce both profits and employment—but they support, with tens of millions of dollars in donations, candidates who advocate increasing taxes that reduce employment. How do they reconcile their pro-tax stands with their anti-tax behavior? They don't (in large measure because the media never challenge them), because they can't. They have to come to their liberal positions on taxes from emotion—compassion for the poor and resentment of the income divide—not from reason.

Of the Left's emotions, compassion is one of the strongest—compassion for the poor, the weak, the "disenfranchised," the minority, the hungry, the animal, and often even the criminal.

I recall being a guest on the CNN show *Larry King Live* the night before a convicted American murderer, Stanley "Tookie" Williams III, was to be executed. As one who supports the death penalty, I argued that despite his having written children's books while on death row, Williams should be executed. Representing the other side was a well-known American actor, Mike Farrell, who was attending a vigil on behalf of Williams at the prison where Williams was to be executed. Farrell shouted at me, accusing me, among other things, of "salivating" at the thought of bloodshed.

Even many opponents of capital punishment would acknowledge that he offered emotions, not rational arguments. Now, of course, one could argue that this was atypical. And, indeed, in terms of raw emotion, it was atypical; I have debated articulate and calm abolitionists on my radio show. Nevertheless I believe that anti-capital-punishment positions are nearly always emotion-based: Many people simply recoil at the thought of the state taking the life of a murderer, and many Americans opposed to capital punishment are embarrassed by the fact that their country is among the only Western democracies to enforce the death penalty for murder. (It would be interesting to see what would happen to the abolitionist movement in America if nearly all European countries reinstated capital punishment.)

The one argument against capital punishment that appears reason-based is that a mistake may be made and an innocent person put to death. This is a rational position—and there are rational counterarguments. But this argument is often a rational cover for emotion-based opposition to capital punishment. One proof is that most people who offer the innocent-may-be-killed argument oppose the taking of any murderer's life, even a murderer whose guilt is beyond doubt. Nearly all opponents of capital punishment believe that Israel was morally wrong in executing Adolf Eichmann, the man who directed much of the Holocaust and as such was the murderer of millions of men, women, and children.

As for the minority of opponents of the death penalty who, like the Israeli government, argue that only murderers such as Eichmann—mass murderers—should be executed, that argument is also entirely emotion-based. The position that mass murderers should be put to death but murderers of "only" one or two—or dozens of—people should not is pure emotion. It also happens to be immoral in that it cheapens the infinite value of the individual human.

LEFT-WING SLOGANS

The most popular slogans of the Left provide additional examples of the emotion- and feelings-based nature of Left-wing positions. We all recognize that a slogan can only rarely encapsulate all nuances of an idea, but a one-sentence slogan can still be true, rational, and even deep. "Life is not a dress rehearsal" would be such an example. But the most popular Left-wing slogans are none of these.

*"A woman has the right to do what
she wants with her own body."*

This famous slogan is the decades-old liberal defense of a woman's right to have an abortion for any reason and at any time. On its face, the statement is neither rationally nor morally objectionable—though, seemingly ironically, the people who most deny women the right to do what they want with their bodies are the very people who promote this slogan. It was Leftists, not conservatives, who sought to deny women the right to obtain silicone breast implants.

But as regards abortion, this statement is both rationally and morally untenable. It is a non sequitur. The statement has nothing to do with abortion. The human fetus, the baby, the unborn—readers can pick their own term—is not her body; it is in her body. That is why no one asks a pregnant woman, "How's your body?" Pregnant women are asked, "How's the baby?"

"War is not the answer."

"War is not the answer" if the question is, let us say, "What is the square root of eleven?" But if the question is "How do we stop enormous evils in the world?" the answer is, unfortunately, quite frequently "War." Nazi and Japanese racist genocide were ended by soldiers shooting people, and by bombers bombing people, not by people who believed "war is not the answer." Moreover, the slogan is disingenuous because those who place this bumper sticker on their car really mean to say that war is *never* the answer. They dare not say what they mean, however, because that would alienate the vast majority of people who understand that forswearing war means that the evil will prevail.

"Coexist."

Another popular liberal bumper sticker reads "Coexist," in which each of the letters is drawn to represent a religion. The *C* is an Islamic crescent, the *x* is a Jewish star, the *t* is the Christian cross, and so on. The problem with this message is not its sentiment; no decent person can object to it. The problem is that in America it is an essentially pointless message. It is needed less in America than anywhere else in the world. Preaching to Americans to "coexist" with other religions is akin to preaching to the French to "enjoy wine."

No religion is persecuted in America, a fact that is all the more remarkable given that one religion, Christianity, has by far the largest percentage of adherents, and given what Muslims in the name of Islam have done to Americans. If Christians in the name of Christianity had slaughtered thousands of Muslims in a Muslim country, Christians living among Muslim majorities would have been massacred in far greater numbers than they are now. Yet after 9/11, even the Council on American-Islamic Relations (CAIR), the Islamist organization that is devoted to finding anti-Muslim behavior in America, found a total of one—needless to say, despicable—killing of someone for being perceived as Muslim (the poor man was a Sikh).

The message is morally unserious. Americans are the people who least need to be admonished to "coexist" with people of different faiths. Yes, the bumper sticker is needed, but not in America. Why then would some Americans communicate a largely irrelevant message to fellow Americans? The answer: For the Left, the combination of feeling good about oneself and denigrating America kills two birds with one stone.

"Vote no on H8."

"Vote no on H8" was the ubiquitous slogan directed against California's Proposition 8, the 2010 ballot proposition to retain the man-woman definition of marriage and make it part of California's constitution. Unlike the previous examples of liberal slogans that transcend any political moment, this one was specific to a certain time and place. But it represented the Left-wing tactic of indicting the motives of opponents. Indeed, what was hateful here was not the desire to keep the man-woman definition of marriage, but the accusation that this desire emanated solely from hate. More to the point, declaring the desire to keep marriage defined as man-woman as "hate" is pure emotion. In fact, it is actually puerile: "If you don't give me what I want, you hate me."

"If It Feels Good, Do It."

There is another aspect to the feelings-based attitudes of the Left. People who are guided by feelings do not develop into good people.

A good human being rarely acts on his feelings, but rather masters his feelings and acts in accord with values that transcend feelings. Since the 1960s, however, the opposite has been taught. One of the ideas ushered in by the baby boomer Left was that if you do not act in consonance with your feelings, you are inauthentic or, even worse, a hypocrite.

An example: I have devoted much of my life to studying, writing, and lecturing about the subject of happiness. In particular, I have advocated that people act as happy as possible even when they do not feel happy. This is, I believe, both a moral obligation to all those who are in our lives—it is unfair to others to inflict our bad moods on them—and a particularly effective way to increase our own happiness, since acting happy elevates one's mood. This is hardly controversial—in just about every area of life, human beings deeply influence how they feel by how they act.

As a rule, those who object to this idea of acting contrary to how one feels are people on the Left—because on the Left, feelings are sacrosanct.

One can only imagine, then, Left-wing reactions to two columns I wrote titled "When a Woman Is Not in the Mood." I suggested that a woman who is married to a good and loving man might choose to have sex with him even on some occasions when she is not in the mood, given how loved most men feel when their wife says "yes" to sex. Across the Left-wing spectrum, I was not only attacked and personally ridiculed, but I was accused of advocating marital rape. Never mind that the entire premise was based on the wife agreeing to have sex. The mere suggestion that a woman not be guided solely by her feelings when it comes to having sex with her husband meant I was advocating marital rape. Perhaps the biggest Left-wing website, the *Daily Kos*, actually ran the headline: "Dennis Prager Endorses Marital Rape."[1]

Why was I so attacked? Because I violated three Left-wing taboos. I advocated that people not act on their feelings; addressed this to women—a group the Left has labeled "victim" and therefore not to be the object of any demands; and did so regarding sex, an area in which women's feelings are viewed as particularly inviolable.

The Leftist belief that feelings must be expressed was exemplified on July 1, 2008, in Denver, Colorado—on the occasion of the mayor's annual State of the City address. As in previous years, the day was to begin with the singing of the National Anthem, an honor given to a black jazz singer, Rene Marie. But Marie had, by her own admission, long had other plans. Instead of the National Anthem, she sang a different song, "Lift Ev'ry Voice and Sing," a song often referred to as the "Black National Anthem."

According to traditional moral norms, Marie deceived the mayor of Denver (a Democrat, as it happened) and all others present when she agreed to sing the National Anthem. But that was of no consequence to her. She defended her deception by noting her feelings: "I want to express how I feel about living in the United States as a black woman, as a black person," she explained.

Asked on her website, "Wasn't this dishonest?" she responded with an additional Left-wing belief—the artist is above conventional morality: "I can see how it may be perceived that way. But I looked at it a different way: I am an artist. I cannot apologize for that. It goes with the risky territory of being an artist."

She later added: "I don't think it is necessary for artists to ask permission to express themselves artistically."

Not having to ask permission to express one's feelings publicly is why the Left also venerates graffiti, or what the arts establishment calls "street art." In 2011, the prestigious Museum of Contemporary Art, Los Angeles featured a major exhibition titled "Art in the Streets" honoring fifty such "artists," people who are known to the non-Left as vandals.[2]

AN ACHE TO BE LOVED

Another aspect of the centrality of emotion and feelings to Leftism is an ache to be loved.

The desire to be loved has the capacity to do enormous harm in both the macro- and micro-spheres. In the macro-sphere, a leader who yearns to be loved cannot be a good leader. That is why the Left's desire that America be loved by the world would mean that America cannot lead. If the United States were to be primarily motivated by a desire to be loved, that desire would obviously have to trump its desire to do good, and the consequences to the world would be terrifying.

This desire is also destructive in the micro-realm. A good general rule is that one should seek to be loved by one's peers—one's spouse and one's friends are the best examples—but beyond that, one should first seek to be respected. Seeking to be loved is almost always destructive to non-peer relationships. Teachers, for example, should seek to be respected by their students, not loved. Likewise parents, when raising their children, should not seek to be loved; they need to do too much that may not elicit love in order to raise good and, ironically, loving children.

In the liberal world in America, the roles of parents and teachers shifted from authority figures to peers. The results have not been good for children or for society. When one seeks to be loved by those over whom one must exercise authority, one compromises the values necessary to do a proper job.

SELF-ESTEEM

It makes perfect sense that the Left would have created the very influential (and very destructive) self-esteem movement. First, the Left places great emphasis on feelings, and the self-esteem movement is about how one feels about oneself. Second, the Left has extremely high self-esteem. The Left knows it is brighter, kinder, finer, more sophisticated, more enlightened, more selfless, and more intellectual than anyone else.

The self-esteem movement is just one more way in which the Left's emphasis on feelings has hurt society.

In 1984, the California legislature voted to fund a "Task Force on Self-Esteem and Social Responsibility." It was initiated by a liberal Democratic state senator, John Vasconcellos, who, having worked his way from poor self-esteem as a young person to higher self-esteem as an adult, came to believe in self-esteem's singular importance.[3] He attributed his becoming a better person to this increased self-esteem, achieved through years of psychological therapy entered into well into adulthood (he explained this to me personally in an interview I conducted with him). Vasconcellos applied the therapeutic model to society,[4] something the Left frequently does, and deduced that raising young people's self-esteem would lower society's rates of social pathology such as crime, drugs, and out-of-wedlock births.*

But self-esteem for its own sake turns out to be much worse than merely reinforcing unearned positive feelings about oneself. Not only does high self-esteem (especially when unearned) not increase "social responsibility"; it decreases it. The criminologist and sociologist Roy Baumeister, a professor of psychology at Florida State University who has spent a lifetime studying violent criminals, notes that the great majority of criminals have higher self-esteem

---

* It is rather important to note that throughout his youth and early adulthood, while Vasconcellos was allegedly suffering under the low self-esteem imposed on him by the restrictive religious environment in which he said he was raised, he was not engaging in any socially pathological behaviors. On the contrary, he was working hard to become the very productive and successful adult that he became—well before gaining the self-esteem he attributes to his therapy.

than noncriminals. You need high self-esteem to think that rules apply to others but not to you.[5]

A well-known study further illustrates the lack of correlation between high self-esteem and accomplishment. As reported by, among others, Paul Vitz, professor emeritus of psychology at New York University: "A 1989 study of mathematical skills compared students in eight different countries. American students ranked lowest in mathematical competence and Korean students ranked highest. But the researchers also asked students to rate how good they were at mathematics. The Americans ranked highest in self-judged mathematical ability, while the Koreans ranked lowest. Mathematical self-esteem had an inverse relation to mathematical accomplishment."[6]

As frequently happens, after great damage has been done by Left-wing positions and policies, a few on the Left begin to acknowledge this damage. Thus, a quarter of a century after the birth of the self-esteem movement, the *Atlantic* published a devastating article on self-esteem and children by a liberal writer, Lori Gottlieb. The title says it all: "How to Land Your Kid in Therapy." Some excerpts:

"Rates of narcissism among college students have increased right along with self-esteem."

"Rates of anxiety and depression have also risen in tandem with self-esteem."

"People who feel like they're unusually special end up alienating those around them."[7]

But Lori Gottlieb and a few others on the Left notwithstanding, it is unlikely that the Left will forgo emphasizing the importance of self-esteem. Feelings in general and self-esteem in particular are simply too important to the Left.

If the Left came to believe that behavior is more important than feelings (for example, maybe it is a good idea to make love to one's husband sometimes even when not in the mood); if the Left abandoned reliance on feelings and substituted objective moral standards (for example, maybe the worth of a human fetus should not to be determined by the mother's feelings but by a moral code); if the Left

were more concerned with good outcomes than with good intentions (from the welfare state to race-based affirmative action); if the
Left ceased to feel superior in every way and regarded many of those
who oppose the Left as just as bright and just as kind as Leftists believe they themselves are, the Left would more or less cease to exist.

Feelings of self-esteem play a role in the world of the Left in a
darker way. Because holding Leftist positions leads to self-esteem,
many people on the Left—not all, but more than a few—have used
Left-wing positions as a moral mask to hide personally immoral
behavior. If one is decent just for holding "social justice" and environmental positions, one can easily view oneself as having been
given a license to act however one wants in one's personal life. The
personal lives of many leading Left-wing intellectuals have borne
testimony to this danger.[8]

FEEL-GOOD TEXTBOOKS

Feeling good about oneself is so central to Leftism that it is a higher
value than truth. The Left has changed a generation's worth of
American school textbooks from books attempting to convey history to books attempting to make women and members of select
minorities feel good about themselves. Wherever it can, Left-wing,
that is, Democratic, lawmakers pass laws demanding that textbooks
be rewritten to include more blacks, Latinos, women, and other
Democratic Party blocs so that students who belong to those groups
feel good about themselves. The Democratic legislature in the largest textbook-buying state, California, passed a law that all history
textbooks used in that state beginning in first grade include gays,
lesbians, bisexuals, and transgendered people. In an Orwellian moment, the Democratic governor of the state, Jerry Brown, signed the
bill and announced, "History should be honest."[9]

2. The Left-Wing Brainwash

How IS ONE TO EXPLAIN the support for Leftist ideas nearly throughout the world? One possible answer is that Left-wing ideas are logi-
cally and morally compelling and that the Left-wing understanding
of the world is self-evidently accurate. But this explanation is most
unlikely since the Leftist understanding of the world is, as shown
repeatedly in this book, usually wrong both morally and as policy.
Support for Communist and other Left-wing tyrannies, creation
of economically unsustainable and frequently character-destroying
welfare states, the disastrous self-esteem movement, the undermining of Western military strength, policies that have constantly
lowered the level of public education, the politicization of the universities and the arts—these are among the Left's many failures.

How is one to explain that the record of the more radical elements of the Left, the most murderous record in history, is so widely
ignored?* And how is one to explain that, according to opinion
polls around the world, America and Israel, two particularly humane, free, liberal countries, are widely regarded as the greatest
threats to the world? How is such a moral inversion possible?

The support of so many people around the world for the Left
and its positions is overwhelmingly a result of the influence of the
Left-wing orientation that pervades school and university curricula, the news media, and other media such as film and television.
In other words, Leftism is the only way in which vast numbers of
people around the world are taught to view the world.

Leftism is so pervasive that if applied to any other way of looking at life, it would be widely recognized as a form of brainwash-
ing. Imagine a person who attended only fundamentalist Christian

---

* Leftists always cite the Crusades and the Spanish Inquisition in assessing Christianity's moral
record—even though one occurred a thousand years ago and the other more than five hundred years
ago. Yet they rarely confront, and strongly object to citing, the uniquely large numbers of people
slaughtered and enslaved by radical Left-wing regimes in China, the Soviet Union, and elsewhere in
the twentieth century.

schools from preschool through graduate school, who never saw a secular, let alone an anti-Christian, film, and who only read religious books. Most people would say this person had been "brainwashed." Why, then, would we not use the same term to describe an individual who only attended secular liberal schools from kindergarten through college, watched and listened to only Left-of-center television, movies, and music, and had essentially no exposure to religious or conservative ideas?

I have confronted many individuals on the Left with this comparison, but they reject any equivalence. They acknowledge that an education consisting solely of Christian schooling combined with a life consisting of virtually no exposure to secular or liberal ideas constitutes a brainwash. But an equally liberal-Leftist life does not. Why not? Because, they tell me, the very definition of a liberal is to be open-minded. Therefore, "brainwashed liberal" is an oxymoron.

The irony here is that this denial shows how effective the Left-wing brainwash is. Most religious Christians (or Jews) who have rarely been exposed to secular ideas and values would readily acknowledge they are not open-minded to secularism or to other religions. They know they have been given one worldview. But those on the Left fool themselves into thinking that they have been exposed to all points of view or that there is no other view worth exploring.

This is one reason it has become increasingly apparent that the most closed-minded people in American and European society today are more likely to be on the Left than in the religious world or on the Right. The majority of fundamentalist Christians are exposed to much more secular and Left-wing thought and behavior than secular liberals are to religious and conservative thought and behavior. Virtually all religious Christians and Jews study secular subjects, have been taught by secular teachers, read secular-liberal books, and have watched secular-liberal films and television. Substitute "conservative" for "religious" and the same holds true. Virtually every conservative reads liberal newspapers, watches liberal TV shows and movies, reads liberal magazines, and has been taught in liberal schools by liberal professors. On the other hand, few liberals read conservative newspapers or magazines, listen to conservative talk radio, have studied in conservative schools, or been taught by conservative professors.

The distinguished late professor Allan Bloom, of the University of Chicago, wrote his bestselling *The Closing of the American Mind*, not about religious or conservative America but about liberal America as embodied by the university.

"WORLD OPINION" AS LEFT-WING OPINION

Another aspect of the Left-wing brainwash is the identification of "world opinion" with Left-wing opinion. It is probably impossible to name any difference between what the media refer to as "world opinion" and Left-wing opinion.

Examples of Left-wing positions portrayed as world opinion include: contempt for conservative American presidents and admiration for liberal ones; opposition to almost all American military endeavors and attributing them to nefarious motives (for example, the invasion of Iraq was for oil); viewing Israel, not those who wish to destroy it, as the major obstacle to peace in the Middle East; judging the American free enterprise system as morally inferior to Europe's welfare-state systems; and deeming capital punishment "barbaric" (the term *New York Times* editorials use) even though majorities in almost every country that abolished capital punishment were for capital punishment when it was banned.[10]

Why are "world opinion" and Left-wing positions essentially all the same? The most obvious answer is that much of the world is Leftist in its views. But that only restates the question: Why are world and Left-wing opinion usually the same?

A major reason is that the world's news media, which are Leftist in their politics, both define "world opinion" and shape it.

Of course, there are other institutions in the world—primary and secondary schools, universities, entertainment media, and religions—that shape public opinion. But except for some religious institutions, virtually none of them contravenes the Left's views. Even Islamic institutions, which in many areas differ with the Left, and which shape the opinions of the majority of the world's 1.3 billion Muslims, agree with the Left on international issues such as the villainy of Israel, support for the United Nations, and weakening American influence around the world.

Another influential non-Leftist institution is the Roman Catholic Church. But its differences from Leftist positions nearly always concern personal matters—same-sex marriage, abortion, sex education in schools—not social and political issues. The United States Conference of Catholic Bishops—and frequently the Vatican itself—holds Left-wing views on redistribution of wealth, capital punishment, expansion of the welfare state, reduction of American expenditures on defense, and other social issues.

UNIVERSITIES

Western universities have become Left-wing seminaries. They are to Leftism what a Christian seminary is to Christianity. The biggest difference between them, aside from curriculum, is that Christian seminaries acknowledge their purpose, to produce committed Christians, while universities deny their purpose, to produce committed secular Leftists. They portray themselves as having no political agenda.

The purpose of a university education should be to search for and teach truth, and, in art and literature, to teach the best that humans have produced. While some professors still cling to these goals, most do not. Many deny there is such a thing as truth. Rather they claim that race, gender, class—the Left-wing trinity—render objective truth impossible to determine. There is white truth and non-white truth, male truth and female truth, and poor people's and rich people's truth. In the arts and literature, they deny the notion of greatness because they deem it entirely subjective.

On occasion, college presidents admit they have an agenda other than truth and excellence. For example, one of the founders of progressivism in America, Woodrow Wilson, president of Princeton University before becoming president of the United States, said in a speech in 1914, "I have often said that the use of a university is to make young gentlemen as unlike their fathers as possible."[11] In 1996, in his commencement address to the graduating seniors of Dartmouth College, the then president of the college, James O. Freedman, cited the Wilson quote favorably. And in 2002, in another commencement address, Freedman said that "the purpose of a college education is to question your father's values."

For Wilson, Freedman, and countless other university presidents and professors, the purpose of a college education is to question one's father's values, not to seek truth. Fathers represented traditional American values. The university is there to undermine them.

Here is a sampling of the Left-wing values that permeate American and other Western universities:

- The United States is no better than any other country, and in many areas worse than many. On the world stage, America is an imperialist country, and domestically it mistreats its minorities and neglects its poor, while discriminating against non-whites.
- There is no better and worse in literature and the arts. The reason universities in the past taught Shakespeare, Michelangelo, and Bach rather than, let us say, Guatemalan poets, Sri Lankan musicians, and Native American storytellers was "Eurocentrism."
- God is at best a non-issue, and at worst, a foolish and dangerous belief.
- Christianity is largely a history of inquisitions, crusades, oppression, and anti-intellectualism. Islam, on the other hand, is "a religion of peace." Therefore, criticism of Christianity is enlightened, while criticism of Islam is Islamophobia.
- Israel is a racist state, morally no different from apartheid South Africa.

- Big government is the only humane way to govern a country.
- The South votes Republican because it is still racist and the Republican Party caters to racists.
- Mothers and fathers are interchangeable. Claims that married mothers and fathers are the parental ideal and bring unique things to a child are heterosexist and homophobic.
- Whites can be racist; non-whites cannot be (because whites have power and the powerless cannot be racist).
- The great world and societal battles are not between good and evil, but between rich and poor and the powerful and the powerless.
- *Patriotism* is usually a euphemism for chauvinism.
- War is ignoble. Pacifism is noble.
- Human beings are animals. They differ from "other animals" primarily in having better brains.
- We live in a patriarchal society, which is injurious to women.
- Women are victims of men.
- Blacks are victims of whites.
- Latinos are victims of Anglos.
- Muslims are victims of non-Muslim Americans.
- Gays are victims of straights.
- Big corporations are bad. Big unions are good.
- There is no objective meaning to a text. Every text only means what the reader perceives it to mean.
- The American Founders were sexist, racist slaveholders whose primary concern was preserving their wealthy status.
- The Constitution says what progressives think it should say.
- The American dropping of the atom bomb on Hiroshima was an act of racism and a war crime.

- The wealthy have stacked the capitalist system to maintain their power and economic benefits.
- The wealthy Western nations became wealthy by exploiting Third World nations through colonialism and imperialism.

The behavior of universities reflects the Leftism they espouse.

Northwestern University School of Law kept an unrepentant radical ex-terrorist on its faculty, former Weather Underground leader Bernardine Dohrn. As the *Wall Street Journal* commented, Dohrn "could not pass a character and fitness test and could not be admitted to the bar," but she teaches at a law school.[12] Needless to say, an unrepentant ex-terrorist member of the Ku Klux Klan would find no employment at an American law school.

In 2006, a black stripper accused—falsely, it was soon revealed— white members of the Duke University lacrosse team of gang-raping her. The university (and most of the liberal media) immediately assumed that the accusations were true and went into a frenzy about white racism at Duke and other elite campuses. Eighty-eight members of the Duke faculty signed a letter strongly suggesting the lacrosse players were guilty and accusing the university of widespread racism. Those who signed this now infamous letter included 80 percent of the African and African-American Studies Department, 72 percent of the Women's Studies faculty, 60 percent of the Cultural Anthropology Department, 45 percent of the Romance Studies faculty, 41 percent of the Literature, 32.2 percent of the English, 31 percent of the Art and Art History, and 25 percent of the History Department faculty.

In 2009, Yale University Press published a book on the Danish Muhammad cartoons that led to worldwide Muslim riots. Right before publication of the book, *The Cartoons That Shook the World*, Yale announced that the book would not contain pictures of the cartoons nor would it allow any picture of Muhammad, even those painted or drawn by Muslims through the ages. As the shocked author, Jytte Klausen, a Danish-born professor of politics at Brandeis

University, pointed out, even "Muslim friends, leaders and activists thought that . . . the cartoons needed to be reprinted so we could have a discussion about it."[13]

The author went on to note that Reza Aslan, a well-known Iranian-American scholar of Islam, was so incensed with Yale that he withdrew the supportive blurb that he had supplied for the book. "To not include the actual cartoons is to me, frankly, idiotic," he said. But it was not idiotic. It was cowardly—and the greater the influence of the Left in universities, the greater their cowardice. This has become one of the dominant features of modern universities, which should be the first line of defense of liberal Western civilization and freedom of speech.

The extent to which universities influence students in a leftward direction extends to personal sexual practices. An example was an article written by a female student in the McGill University newspaper. She wrote: "It's hard to go through four years of a Humanities B.A. reading [Michel] Foucault [a major French 'postmodern' philosopher] and [Judith] Butler [a prominent 'gender theorist' at the University of California, Berkeley] and watching 'The L Word' [a popular TV drama about glamorous lesbians] and keep your rigid heterosexuality intact. I don't know when it happened exactly, but it seems I no longer have the easy certainty of pinning my sexual desire to one gender and never the other."

I interviewed the twenty-two-year-old woman on the radio. She verified that prior to attending McGill, she only wanted to be with males sexually, but the university had taught her how limiting, how heterosexist, that was. Therefore, she was now sexually involved with both men and women.[14]

Another student whose life was turned around by Left-wing professors attended UCLA. At the time of Israel's Independence Day in May 2003, she wrote a blistering attack on Israel's origins in the UCLA newspaper, the *Daily Bruin*. I was particularly intrigued by the column because the author's last name sounded Jewish. So I invited her onto my radio show. She confirmed that not only was she a Jew, but that she had been raised in Britain in a Zionist home, had visited Israel on a number of occasions, and had had a Jewish education.

"So what happened?" I asked, somewhat incredulous at the 180-degree change in her views on Israel.

"I attended university," she responded.

From a Zionist upbringing to writing in a university newspaper about Israeli Jews' "annihilation of Palestinian society," "ethnic cleansing," "rape," "war crimes," and "Israeli terror"—all thanks to the university. There are many like her.

Universities are the most anti-Israel mainstream institutions in America. And anti-Israel campus rallies, demonstrations, and classes not infrequently express anti-Semitism. As Harvard president Lawrence Summers said in a 2002 address to the Harvard community: "Where anti-Semitism and views that are profoundly anti-Israeli have traditionally been the primary preserve of poorly educated right-wing populists, profoundly anti-Israel views are increasingly finding support in progressive intellectual communities. Serious and thoughtful people are advocating and taking actions that are anti-Semitic in their effect if not their intent."[15]

Many in the university are not even intellectually open in the natural sciences if an idea may clash with Left-wing opinion. In a talk before fellow economists, the same Lawrence Summers, when he was president of Harvard University (he had been secretary of the Treasury under President Bill Clinton), addressed the issue of why there were so many fewer women than men in some areas of science, in math, and in engineering. He suggested that among other reasons, one might be that women's brains are less suited to these subjects than men's brains. More than one hundred Harvard professors signed a petition against President Summers, Left-wing alumni threatened not to give any more money to Harvard, and the vast majority of Harvard's professors kept a cowardly silence while their colleagues sought to suppress completely respectable intellectual inquiry. Consequently, President Summers felt forced to apologize. In the year 2005, nearly four centuries after Galileo was forced by the then-dominant Catholic Church to recant observable scientific facts about our solar system, the president of Harvard University, an institution whose motto is *Veritas* ("Truth"), was forced by the now-dominant Left to recant observable facts about men and women.

On February 21, 2011, the six hundred Northwestern University students enrolled in the popular Human Sexuality course taught by Professor John Michael Bailey were told that if they wished to stay after class, they would see a live demonstration of female ejaculation, the subject of that day's class. A naked young woman would demonstrate the use of a motorized sex toy to orgasm in front of the students. About 120 of them stayed. When word got out about this, Northwestern's official spokesman, Al Cubbage, released this statement: "Northwestern University faculty members engage in teaching and research on a wide variety of topics, some of them controversial and at the leading edge of their respective disciplines. The university supports the efforts of its faculty to further the advancement of knowledge." [16]

It is very difficult for many people to acknowledge the low intellectual and moral level to which many professors and universities have sunk. The belief that the university—like, for example, the United Nations—is necessarily a force for good dies hard. But the breaking of a functioning moral compass at Western universities did not begin with the baby boomer Left—though that generation has radicalized the universities beyond anything that preceded it. Like most other bad ideas, the Left-wing ideas of the universities came originally from the European universities. Europe's post-Christian, thoroughly secularized universities regularly incubated nihilistic ideas. According to Professor Michael Mann—whose book, *Fascists*, published by Cambridge University Press in 2004, was declared by the *American Historical Review* to be "by far the best comparative study of interwar fascisms"—"All fascist movements during the interwar period appealed disproportionately to the well-educated, 'to students in high schools and universities and to the most highly educated middle-class strata.'"

In other words, if you were well educated, not only were you more likely than the less educated to support Communism, but you were more likely to support the various fascisms as well. And, contrary to what many people believe about Nazi atrocities—that they were perpetrated overwhelmingly by rural ignoramuses—they were in fact led and perpetrated by the well educated. To cite one of many such examples, of the four *Einsatzgruppen*—mobile murder units of the SS—sent into Russia, "Three of the four commanders held a doctorate, whilst one was a double Ph.D." [17] These Nazi mass murderers "included many high-ranking officers, intellectuals and lawyers. Otto Ohlendorf, who commanded Einsatzgruppe D, had earned degrees from three universities and achieved a doctorate in jurisprudence." [18]

If you are a serious student, you can learn a great deal at a university. But its primary purpose remains graduating secular Leftists. As the Left-wing takeover of the universities continues, this agenda overshadows all other university concerns. Take the University of California, San Diego. Instead of hiring people to actually teach, it spends millions of dollars a year on promoting "diversity." This one university campus has allocated millions to fund:

The vice chancellor for equity, diversity, and inclusion
The Chancellor's Diversity Office
The associate vice chancellor for faculty equity
The assistant vice chancellor for diversity
Faculty equity advisors
The graduate diversity coordinators
The staff diversity liaison
The undergraduate student diversity liaison
The graduate student diversity liaison
The chief diversity officer
The director of development for diversity initiatives
The Office of Academic Diversity and Equal Opportunity
The Committee on Gender Identity and Sexual Orientation Issues

The Committee on the Status of Women
The Campus Council on Climate, Culture, and Inclusion
The Diversity Council
The Cross-Cultural Center
The Lesbian Gay Bisexual Transgender Resource Center
The Women's Center

That is a Left-wing seminary, not a university.

Examples of Left-wing damage to learning, to moral inquiry, to historical truth—in short, to every noble goal of the university—abound. Yet, like the damage done by the Left just about everywhere else, it goes largely unnoticed—except when a professor has a young woman masturbate in front of students, and then the media pay it attention for a day or two. After all, who will point out the terrible impact of the Left on academia—the Left-wing media, nearly all of whose members spent their formative years at these universities?

THE MEDIA

A Morally Upside-down World

In 1982, Madame Tussauds Wax Museum in London held a vote for the most hated people of all time. The winners: Hitler, Margaret Thatcher, Ronald Reagan, and Dracula.[19]

How is that possible?

In 2003, the Europe edition of *Time* magazine asked readers which of three countries was the greatest threat to world peace—North Korea, Iran, or the United States. Seven hundred thousand people responded, of which 86.9 percent voted that the United States was the most dangerous in the world.

How is that possible?

In the same year, as reported in the *Guardian*, "Israel has been described as the top threat to world peace, ahead of North Korea, Afghanistan and Iran, by an unpublished European Commission poll of 7,500 Europeans, sparking an international row. The survey [was] conducted in October, of 500 people from each of the EU's member nations . . ."[20]

How is that possible?

In 2004, "BBC World asked 1,500 viewers of its news and international channel for the biggest problems in the world with 52% saying the US and globalisation. Respondents from Europe, Asia, North and South America, the Middle East, Africa and Australasia, ranked the power of the US and large corporations as the biggest worry (52.3%)."[21]

In 2005, "A poll released . . . in Australia, long known for friendly relations with America, found that only 58 percent of the population had a positive view of the United States. That put the United States behind China (69 percent positive), and not even in the overall Top 10 countries, regions or groups that Australians respect. They have a more positive opinion of . . . the United Nations . . ."[22]

In another 2005 poll, a "survey was carried out by polling group GlobeScan and the University of Maryland with some questions provided by the BBC World Service. Of the 23,518 people polled, 47% said the US had a negative effect on the world, with US neighbours and allied countries being among its biggest critics. Overall, 15 of the 23 countries surveyed said the US had a negative influence in the world. Disapproval for the US was highest in Argentina, Germany, Russia, Turkey, Canada and Mexico."[23]

According to a 2005 U.S. State Department report, "For what can be heard around the world, in the wake of the invasion of Iraq, the prisoner abuse scandal at Abu Ghraib, and the controversy over the handling of detainees at Bagram [Afghanistan] and Guantanamo Bay, is that America is less a beacon of hope than a dangerous force to be countered."[24]

In 2006, 87 percent of British voters believed that Osama bin Laden was a great or moderate danger to peace, while 75 percent believed this of President George W. Bush.[25]

"CanWest News Services, owners of several Canadian news-

papers including the *National Post* . . . commissioned a series of polls
to determine how young people feel about the issues that were facing the country's voters. . . . In one telephone poll of teens between
the ages of 14 and 18, over 40 per cent of the respondents described
the United States as being 'evil.' That number rose to 64 percent for
French Canadian youth."[26]

"British voters see George Bush as a greater danger to world
peace than either the North Korean leader, Kim Jong-il, or the Iranian president, Mahmoud Ahmadinejad."[27]

How are all these possible? How could the greatest force for
good in the world, the protector of the free world, the United States
of America, be so widely perceived—in friendly democratic countries, no less—as evil?

The answer is, largely, the world's media.

People perceive the world as the world is reported to them. How
could they do otherwise? And the reporting is Left-wing. It is not
a conspiracy. But it is a fact. The world's news media—newspapers,
newsmagazines, radio, and TV news—are, with few exceptions, Left-
wing. The greatest producer of films that are seen around the world is
Hollywood, which is almost uniformly Left-wing. Therefore, to cite
two of countless examples, America and Israel are almost relentlessly
portrayed negatively. Their flaws are exaggerated and their decency
ignored or minimized. That explains the polls cited above.

One only has to recall the months-long fixation of the world's
media on the rogue U.S. soldiers who sexually humiliated Iraqi
prisoners at the Abu Ghraib prison in Baghdad. Or the media's cov-
erage of Israel's attack on Palestinian terrorists in Jenin in the West
Bank in 2002, which the BBC so hyped that it labeled it—falsely, it
soon turned out—"the Jenin massacre."

BBC News headline, April 18, 2002: "Jenin 'massacre evidence
growing'"

BBC News headline, April 18, 2002: "Jenin camp 'horrific beyond belief'"

BBC News headline, August 1, 2002: "UN says no massacre in
Jenin"

Favored Groups Are Rarely to Blame

While the media are quick to blame America and Israel and seek to focus as much negative attention on them as possible, they do the opposite vis-à-vis violent members of groups with whom the Left has more sympathy. The media routinely try to deflect attention from their crimes—either by ignoring the crime or by equally blaming the victims of their crimes—and when that is impossible, to deny that their being a member of the Left-favored group played a role in their crime. The examples are dramatic and compelling.

First, some Islamic examples: The world's liberal media regularly attempt to minimize Muslim responsibility for violence.

In 2002, there was widespread Nigerian Muslim opposition to the Miss World pageant scheduled to take place that year in Lagos, the Nigerian capital. In defense of the pageant, a young Nigerian female reporter wrote a column in which she said that not only are the contestants not whores, as alleged by the Muslim protestors, but they are such fine women that "Muhammad would probably have taken one of the contestants for a wife."

That one sentence led to Muslim rioting, the beating and killing of Christians, the burning of churches, and the razing of the newspaper's offices.

This is how the *New York Times* article reported the events:

First the headline: "Fiery Zealotry Leaves Nigeria in Ashes Again."

Notice that no group is identified as responsible. Reading the headline one would have no idea that it was Muslims who burned churches, killed Christian bystanders, and razed newspaper offices. But putting the moral responsibility on the Muslims who actually started the rioting would violate the media doctrines of moral neutrality between good and evil *when the evil is anti-Western*. Therefore, for the *New York Times* headline writer the culprit is "fiery zealotry," not murderous Muslims.

It gets worse. The article then begins:

"KADUNA, Nigeria, Nov. 28—The beauty queens are gone now, chased from Nigeria by the chaos in Kaduna."

If this is not a direct lie, it surely is an indirect one. The beauty queens were not chased out of Nigeria by "chaos," but by Muslim rioters. Would the *New York Times* write that American Indians were often chased from their homes by "chaos" or by white Americans?

Lest the reader miss the point that no group is morally responsible, the article's next sentence develops this idea: "But there are no celebrations in this deeply troubled town, which has become a symbol of the difficulty in Nigeria—and throughout Africa—of reconciling people who worship separately."

So, the problem is not Islamic intolerance and violence in Nigeria, nor is it Islamists attempting to violently spread Islamic religious law (as in sentencing a *non-Muslim* Nigerian woman to death by stoning for giving birth out of wedlock). No, the *Times* assures us, what happened in Kaduna is merely another example of Africa's "difficulty in reconciling people who worship separately."

Nigeria's and Africa's Christians and Muslims are equally guilty, as the next sentence makes clear: "Kaduna is too occupied burying its dead, some of whom followed Jesus and others Muhammad . . ."

Two paragraphs later the paper moves on to the one thing—religion—the paper can blame: Nigeria's population "has shown itself to be devoutly religious but also quick to kill." Fanatical Muslims are not the killers— "devoutly religious" people are.

Everyone-is-responsible is the trademark of virtually all reporting from the Middle East. Take this typical Reuters report: "A suspected Palestinian militant tried to ram a car laden with explosives into a crowded Tel Aviv nightclub Friday. . . . The apparent suicide attack was the latest in a fresh cycle of tit-for-tat violence . . ."[28]

"Cycle of violence" is the culprit—meaning that Israel is just as responsible for violence as are the terrorists. Moreover, as in this Reuters report, Westerns journalists nearly always use *militant* or *gunman* to describe Islamist terrorists. For Reuters, BBC, the Associated Press, CNN, and nearly all newspapers, it violates moral neutrality to label even a man attempting to smash a bomb-laden car into a nightclub a terrorist.

On the other hand, when Israel unsuccessfully attempted to assassinate Hamas leader Khaled Meshal in Jordan, after a series of Hamas-directed terror attacks against Israeli civilians, a *Washington Post* editorial did use that word—*to describe Israel*: "[Israel] is revealed again as a practitioner of cross-border state terrorism."[29]

And, of course, virtually every news source lists the greater number of Palestinians killed in Arab-Israeli wars in order to depict the Israelis as guilty (of "disproportionate response"). Had similar reporting taken place during World War II, the Western Allies would have been deemed the villains since Germany and Japan lost far more civilians than America or Britain.

It is one thing to argue that Islamist terror has no basis in normative Islam. But Western and Muslim defenders of Islam also frequently argue that Islam plays no role in Islamists' actions.

In 2009, commentators on the Left told Americans that we could not know the motive or motives of Nidal Malik Hasan, the U.S. Army major who fired more than one hundred shots at fellow American soldiers at Fort Hood, Texas—while yelling, *"Allahu Akbar!"* He ended up murdering thirteen people, but government and army spokesmen (also infected by the Left-wing politically correct virus) and the mainstream media claimed that they could not figure out why Hasan did this. They were only certain that it was not an act of terrorism.

Following the shootings, the Sunday *New York Times* "Week in Review" article about Nidal Hasan was titled "When Soldiers Snap." The gist of the article was that Major Hasan had snapped. Even though he had never been in combat, he snapped in advance of going into combat. A mere two sentences of the article were devoted to the possibility that his motives were in any way relatable to his Muslim faith.

NPR correspondent Tom Gjelten echoed this novel "snapped-in-advance" explanation. Though Hasan had never been in combat, Gjelten opined that Hasan may have suffered from "pre-traumatic stress disorder" because he anticipated having traumatic distress: "Was he an example of these soldiers who are literally freaked out by what they are likely to face when they are deployed?" Listeners to Gjelten on NPR's *Morning Edition* were also reassured that "we know he was a devout Muslim, took his faith very seriously. We can't say, of course, that that was relevant, here."[30]

Likewise, the liberal TV commentator Chris Matthews said, "It's unclear if religion was a factor in this shooting." For Matthews, not only was it unclear if Hasan's Islamic faith was *the* factor; it was unclear if it was *a* factor. And on FoxNews, correspondent Geraldo Rivera—not every commentator or correspondent on FoxNews is a conservative—said, "I don't know what motivates him. . . . As far as I know . . . he's a sociopath; he's a criminal. He could have had a toothache and gone off because of that."

In 2010, after the Pakistani-American terrorist Faisal Shahzad tried to mass-murder people in New York's Times Square, *Washington Post* blogger Ezra Klein wrote: "You of course don't want to speculate on why someone 'really' did something. The hearts of men are opaque, and motives are complex. But it's a reminder that foreclosures [on homes] generate an enormous amount of misery and anxiety and depression that can tip people into all sorts of dangerous behaviors . . ."

Widely ridiculed—in the comments section of the *Washington Post* itself—for what he wrote, the next day, Klein tried to undo the damage to his credibility: "In case there's actual confusion . . . I do not believe that foreclosure leads to terrorism."

Most observers would argue that the "actual confusion" was on Klein's part. But, in any event, even in his explanatory column, he made no reference to Shahzad's religious beliefs as a possible motivation for the Muslim terrorist's attempted act of terror. Instead, he re-emphasized that it was impossible to even speculate what Shahzad's motive might be: "Speculating about why a terrorist commits a terrorist act is a mug's game. . . . People who desire the murder of innocents qualify, I think, as pretty disturbed."

Evan Thomas, editor at large at *Newsweek*, said on PBS's *Inside Washington*, "I think he's probably just a nut case. But with that label [Muslim] attached to him, it will get the right wing going . . ."

In 2004, a young American businessman was kidnapped by Islamists in Iraq and slowly beheaded on video, a video that much of the world was able to see on the Internet. The monsters who did this claimed that they were avenging the American army abuses at Abu Ghraib prison. As beheading innocent people is a way of life for Islamist killers, who would believe that revenge was the reason for the ritual murder?

The Left did and reported it as such.

The vast majority of America's and the world's news media reported the claim of Nick Berg's murderers that they were avenging American abuses in the Abu Ghraib prison as if it were a fact:

"American beheaded in revenge for abuses"
—*Atlanta Journal-Constitution*

"Grisly Vengeance"
—*Hartford Courant*

"Militants avenge abuse with taped beheading"
—*Des Moines Register*

"Vengeance on Video"
—*Arizona Republic*

"With a Vengeance"
—*Newsday* (Long Island)

To prove the point that this was Left-wing reporting, contrast those headlines with the headlines of the few nonliberal newspapers in America. They made no mention of the "revenge" claim, and called the act what it was:

"Terrorists Behead American"
—*New York Sun*

"Pure Evil"
—*New York Daily News*

"Savages"

—*New York Post*

"Bastards"

—*Philadelphia Daily News*

In Canada, too, the headline in the liberal *Globe and Mail* was "Murderous revenge: U.S. hostage dies in wake of Iraq prison abuse," while the headline in the conservative *National Post* was "Al-Qaeda Beheads American."

Revenge? Islamists slaughtering innocents is not revenge. Was the slaughter of *Wall Street Journal* reporter Daniel Pearl in Pakistan "revenge"? The terrorists called Berg's murder "revenge" in order to justify their savagery and because they know that the world press is so malleable and so anti-American that it will print their justification.

The denial or rationalization of Muslim violence against non-Muslims is not the only example of the predominantly Left-wing media filtering news and commentary to defend select groups. They do this with regard to black violence against whites as well, since the only American racism the Left acknowledges—and wildly exaggerates—is white racism.

In the summer of 1991, in the Crown Heights section of Brooklyn, New York, the seven-year-old child of Guyanese immigrants was killed when a car driven by a Hasidic Jewish driver accidentally hit him. The driver, who had left his car to try to save the child (and the boy's cousin, who survived), was immediately set upon by four blacks who beat him.

Days of black-on-Jew rioting ensued during which a young Hasidic Jew was stabbed to death, many Jews were injured, and mobs of blacks screamed, "Heil Hitler!" and "Death to the Jews!" and carried signs that featured messages such as "Hitler didn't finish the job." A Brandeis University historian who wrote a book on the events characterized them as "the most serious anti-Semitic incident in American history."[31]

Yet the *New York Times* refused to characterize the riots as anti-Jewish, let alone as a modern-day pogrom. As Ari Goldman, a *New York Times* reporter who covered the riots, wrote twenty years later, "Journalists framed the story as a 'racial' conflict and failed to see the anti-Semitism inherent in the riots"—just as Muslim riots against Christians are "interreligious" conflicts.

Now a professor of journalism at Columbia University, Goldman wrote, "When I picked up the paper, the article I read was not the story I had reported. I saw headlines that described the riots in terms solely of race. 'Two Deaths Ignite Racial Clash in Tense Brooklyn Neighborhood,' the *Times* headline said. And, worse, I read an opening paragraph, what journalists call a 'lead,' that was simply untrue: 'Hasidim and blacks clashed in the Crown Heights section of Brooklyn through the day and into the night yesterday.'

"In all my reporting during the riots," Goldman continues, "I never saw—or heard of—any violence by Jews against blacks. But the *Times* was dedicated to this version of events: blacks and Jews clashing amid racial tensions."[32]

And the *New York Times* editorial followed suit: "The violence following an auto accident in Crown Heights reminds all New Yorkers that the city's race relations remain dangerously strained."

This is how the mainstream media report news: few outright lies, just filtered to support the Leftist view of reality.

On August 3, 2010, in Manchester, Connecticut, a black man murdered eight whites at his place of work because they were white.

The *New York Times* headline later that day read: "Troubles Preceded Connecticut Workplace Killing," and in the second paragraph, the *Times* reported: "He might also have had cause to be angry: he had complained to his girlfriend of being racially harassed at work, the woman's mother said, and lamented that his grievances had gone unaddressed."

Four days later, the *Washington Post* headline read, "Beer warehouse shooter long complained of racism." The same day, the Associated Press report, reprinted in the *Washington Post* and throughout America, read in part:

To those closest to him, Omar Thornton was caring, quiet and soft-spoken. . . . But underneath, Thornton seethed with a sense of racial injustice for years that culminated in a shooting rampage Tuesday in which the Connecticut man killed eight and wounded two others at his job at Hartford Distributors in Manchester before killing himself. . . . "I know what pushed him over the edge was all the racial stuff that was happening at work," said his girlfriend, Kristi Hannah. . . . "He always felt like he was being discriminated (against) because he was black," said Jessica Anne Brocuglio, his former girlfriend. "Basically they wouldn't give him pay raises. He never felt like they accepted him as a hard working person . . ." "Thornton changed jobs a few times because he was not getting raises," Brocuglio said.

The mainstream media all focused on the murderer being a victim of whites. But the one indisputable, and the most pertinent, pre-murder fact was that Thornton had been fired for stealing. There was video proof of him doing so. But this fact got lost within the larger context of the media reporting Thornton's defenders, who claimed he had been a victim of white racism. Just as leading liberals would not ascribe Islamist motives to Muslim attacks on Americans—until there was no possibility of denying those motives—no major liberal media in America called these Connecticut murders what they were: racist.

Finally, nine months later, on May 13, 2011, the Associated Press reported, "There is no evidence to support a man's claim that he was a victim of racism before he fatally shot eight co-workers at a beer distribution company last year, police said Thursday."

Needless to say, the police report's conclusion was not widely published, and no liberal media apologized for their original reporting.

In August 2011, at the Wisconsin State Fair, mobs of black teens attacked whites, including pulling some whites out of their cars and beating them. As far as the mainstream media were concerned, these racist mob attacks never happened. Only local news and conservative news sources reported them. The only exceptions I could find were the *Christian Science Monitor*, which covered the topic accurately, and NPR, which headlined the attacks this way: "Wis. State Fair Latest Target Of Violent Flash Mobs."

One more example was the kid-gloves treatment Bill Moyers of PBS gave the anti-American, anti-white, anti-Jewish black clergyman, the Reverend Jeremiah Wright, who had been the longtime pastor and friend of Barack Obama. This was after, among other revelations about the reverend, the recordings of his "God damn America" sermon were released and the public became aware of his charges that the American government had deliberately developed the AIDS virus and inflicted it on blacks.

But beyond one line in his introduction about "Wright repeating the canard heard often in black communities that the U.S. government spread HIV in those communities," Moyers never raised the subject. However, Moyers did ask Wright these questions:

"When did you hear the call to ministry? How did it come?"

"What does the church service on Sunday morning mean in general to the black community?"

And this is how Moyers dealt with Wright's "God damn America, God damn America!" sermon: "One of the most controversial sermons that you preach is the sermon you preach that ended up being that sound bite about God damn America."

Wright's response was to deliver a three-hundred-word indictment of America for its violence against the world.

How did Moyers respond?

"What did you mean when you said that?"

To which Wright then delivered another, 174-word indictment of America for its evils. But instead of challenging Wright or defending America, Moyers's third question was:

"Well, you can be almost crucified for saying what you've said here in this country."

Moyers transformed Wright, the racist America-hating giver of the "God damn America" sermon, into Wright, a black victim of America. For the Left-wing media and the Left-wing generally, the only blacks who may be portrayed negatively are black conservatives, whom it is permissible to degrade, humiliate, and vilify—as was done to Justice Clarence Thomas.*

While black racists are almost never labeled racist, the Left and the media depict whites as racist when they are not. Conservative attacks on President Barack Obama were frequently labeled racist, and the Tea Party—as well as conservatism generally—was routinely presumed to be animated by racism.

Quite understandably, vast numbers of people believe media news reports. Only when one knows the truth—from the New York City black attacks on Jews to the Wisconsin State Fair to the lack of racism in conservative America—can one begin to appreciate how profound the Left-wing brainwash has been.

America's Poor Health Care System

If you are an American who believes that America has a poor health care system, it is probably not because you have experienced inferior heath care, but because the Left and the Left-wing media have repeatedly told you that America has inferior health care.

Here are major news media headlines on this subject from the last week of June 2010:

Reuters: "U.S. scores dead last again in healthcare study."

Los Angeles Times: "U.S. is No. 1 in a key area of healthcare. Guess which one . . ." (The answer was spending.)

NPR: "US Spends The Most On Health Care, Yet Gets Least."

The Week: "US health care system: Worst in the world?"

Now let's delve into one of these examples, the widely reported headline as written by Reuters. For those who rely on a headline to get their news—and we all do sometimes—the issue was clear: America is rated as having the worst health care "again." For those

---

* The liberal media and the Democratic Party's treatment of Clarence Thomas when he was nominated to the U.S. Supreme Court was the cruelest noncriminal behavior I have witnessed in my lifetime. And the reason is that no Americans are as hated by the Left as are black conservatives. An example of that hatred was expressed by San Francisco mayor Willie Brown in a speech to the Association of Black Sociologists: Thomas "must not be allowed any comfort from any of us. . . . He should be reduced to talking to only white conservatives. He must be shut out."

who read a sentence or two, an even more common practice, the Reuters report begins this way: "Americans spend twice as much as residents of other developed countries on healthcare, but get lower quality, less efficiency and have the least equitable system, according to a report released on Wednesday. The United States ranked last when compared to six other countries—Britain, Canada, Germany, Netherlands, Australia and New Zealand, the Commonwealth Fund report found."

The claim of the headline and of the first two sentences is then commented upon by the head of the group that conducted the study: "'As an American it just bothers me that with all of our know-how, all of our wealth, that we are not assuring that people who need healthcare can get it,' Commonwealth Fund president Karen Davis told reporters . . ."

Only later in the Reuters report is the discerning reader given a clue as to how agenda-driven this woman, this organization, this study, and therefore this Reuters report are: The otherwise un-identified Karen Davis, president of the never-identified Common-wealth Fund, is quoted as saying how important it was that America pass President Obama's health care bill.

Could it be that Davis and the Commonwealth Fund are Left-wing?

Of course they are, but Reuters, which is also on the Left, never lets you know. The study is reported as if it is fact, rather than an agenda-driven report by an agenda-driven organization. How agenda-driven? Here is how the Commonwealth Fund's 2009 re-port from Davis, its president, begins: "The Commonwealth Fund marshaled its resources this year to produce timely and rigorous work that helped lay the groundwork for the historic Affordable Care Act, signed by President Obama in March 2010."

In addition to marshaling her group's resources to help pass what became known as "ObamaCare," Karen Davis had served as deputy assistant secretary for health policy during all four years of Jimmy Carter's presidency. And in 1993, speaking to new members of Congress, she advocated a single-payer approach to health care.

Yet I could not find any mainstream news report about this study that identified the politics of Karen Davis or the Commonwealth Fund. If they had, the headlines would have looked something like this: "Liberal think tank, headed by single-payer advocate, Obama-Care activist, and former Carter official, says America has worst health care."

How would the average American have then reacted to a news story about how inferior American health care is?

We have here four major developments of the last fifty years:

1. The Left dominates the news media in America; and outside of America, Left-wing media are often the only major news media.
2. The media report most news in the light of their Left-wing values.
3. Most people understandably believe what they read, watch, or listen to.
4. This is one major reason more and more people hold Left-wing positions. They have been given a lifetime of Leftist perceptions of the world (especially when one includes higher education) and therefore regard what they believe about the world as reality rather than as a Leftist take on reality.

The same thing happened in 2000 when the world press reported that the United Nations World Health Organization (WHO) ranked America thirty-seventh in health care, behind such countries as Morocco, Costa Rica, Colombia, and Greece. This WHO assessment was reported throughout the world and regularly cited by critics of American health care. Yet few people were told that the UN report ranked Cuba thirty-ninth—essentially tied with the United States.

But who in his right mind thinks Americans and Cubans have equivalent levels of health care? How many world leaders travel to Greece or Morocco instead of to the United States for health care? The answer is that WHO, like the Left generally, doesn't assess health care *quality*; it assesses health care *equality*. And since the world's and America's news media are on the Left, they report a Leftist bogus assessment of American health care as true.

Imagine if the headlines around the world read: "World Health Organization declares America and Cuba tied in health care." Of course, only Leftists would believe that. But since non-Leftists would realize how absurd the claim was, that is not what anyone was told. Instead, the world and American media all announced, "America rated 37th in health care by World Health Organization."

These two reports illustrate why so many people in America and around the world think America's health care is inferior and why they support movement toward nationalized health care.

These reports are examples of the larger problem—the world's thinking is morally confused because it is informed by the morally confused.

3. Demonization of the Right

AS IMPORTANT TO THE LEFT'S SUCCESS as any other factor—and often the single most important factor—is its ability to demonize ideas and especially people it opposes. From Stalin's labeling Leon Trotsky, the father of Russian Bolshevism, a "fascist" and continuing right up through to the present day, the Left has labeled its opponents as evil. And when you control nearly all news media and schools, that labeling works.

When I was in high school, one of the first books I bought was titled "Danger on the Right." While I was never pro-Left, I stayed a Democrat until the 1980s because of how effective liberal and Left-wing demonization of the Right was. However much harm the Left did, I and multitudes of other non-Leftists were certain about there being a "danger on the Right."

For the past fifty years there has been almost no conservative leader who has not been labeled by the Left—by universities, on television, in newspapers and magazines, by Hollywood, and by Left-dominated professional organizations—as stupid, mentally imbalanced, quasi-fascistic, mean-spirited, a tool of big business, dangerous, and worse.

In 1950, four professors at the University of California, Berkeley, published what became a highly influential book, *The Authoritarian Personality*. Its primary message was that to be on the Left is to be mentally healthy and to be on the Right is to have a pathologic authoritarian personality.

This equation by psychologists and other professionals of Right-wing with psychopathology reached its nadir in 1964 when a Left-wing magazine published a survey in which 2,417 psychiatrists declared the Republican presidential candidate for president, Arizona senator Barry Goldwater, psychologically unfit to be president of the United States. Though not one of the psychiatrists had ever treated Senator Goldwater, they nevertheless assessed him as having a severely paranoid personality.*

In 1963, following the assassination of President John F. Kennedy, the Left attributed the assassination to the Right-wing racism and hate that, the Left alleged, permeated Texas specifically and America generally. Even though Lee Harvey Oswald was a pro-Soviet, pro-Castro Marxist, the Left used the assassination to demonize the Right. The Left learned an important lesson: With its dominance in the media, every crisis makes it possible to demonize the Right.†

---

* This is an excellent example of two important characteristics of Leftism: its damaging effects on nearly anything it influences—in this case the psychiatric profession—and that Leftists are committed to Leftism more than they are to any other identity or value system. In this case Leftism trumped two fundamental moral principles of psychiatry: to make evaluations only of patients and to keep those evaluations private. In other words, these thousands of psychiatrists were more committed to Leftism than to psychiatry, just as the black Left is more committed to Leftism than to black progress (see the example of the Congressional Black Caucus refusing to meet with the leading black dissident in Cuba); Left-wing Jews and Christians derive their values from Leftism more so than from Judaism and Christianity; and so on.

† To measure how successful the Left was in demonizing the Right over an act committed by a Leftist, ask any college student if he or she thinks John F. Kennedy was assassinated by a Left-winger or Right-winger.

A generation later, in 2011, in Tucson, Arizona, a man named Jared Loughner attempted to kill Congresswoman Gabrielle Giffords, and he did in fact kill six people. The entire world of the Left immediately announced that the murders were a result of Republican and conservative hate-filled rhetoric. The day after the shootings, *New York Times* columnist Paul Krugman already knew it was Right-wing hate that had provoked Loughner to murder: "It's the saturation of our political discourse—and especially our airwaves—with eliminationist rhetoric that lies behind the rising tide of violence. Where's that toxic rhetoric coming from? Let's not make a false pretense of balance: it's coming, overwhelmingly, from the right. . . . So will the Arizona massacre make our discourse less toxic? It's really up to G.O.P. leaders. Will they accept the reality of what's happening to America, and take a stand against eliminationist rhetoric? Or will they try to dismiss the massacre as the mere act of a deranged individual, and go on as before?"

As it turned out, the Tucson massacre was entirely "the mere act of a deranged individual." But the Left, beginning with a *New York Times* columnist, used the tragedy to demonize the Right, as it did with the Kennedy assassination.

Krugman and the *New York Times* blaming the Right for Loughner was so premature and so wrong that, in a rare moment in American journalism, one major newspaper attacked the morality of another. The *Wall Street Journal* attacked the *New York Times* under the heading "The New York Times has crossed a moral line." And Pulitzer Prize–winning *Washington Post* columnist Charles Krauthammer responded to Krugman in a column titled "Massacre, then libel," with this sentence: "The origins of Loughner's delusions are clear: mental illness. What are the origins of Krugman's?"

The same Left—led by the *New York Times*—that had warned against making any quick assumptions that Islam had played any role in Major Nidal Hasan's murder of thirteen people and wounding of thirty others at Fort Hood now immediately made the assumption that the Arizona murders were a result of a "climate of hate" induced by former Republican vice presidential candidate Sarah Palin and other conservatives.

It is a seminal contributor to Left-wing success: The only way the Left can succeed—anywhere, but especially in America, which is a center-Right country—is by libeling the Right. Only 20 percent of Americans label themselves liberal, let alone Left. How, then, do Leftists get elected? The answer is that, through its dominance of the news media, entertainment media, and educational institutions, the Left is able to successfully demonize the Right. The Left rarely convinces Americans to adopt its views. Rather, it creates a fear of the Right.

For example, at least until 2012, wherever it was put to a vote, most Americans, even in liberal California, voted to retain the man-woman definition of marriage. The Left was not able to convince the voters of any state to redefine marriage to include members of the same sex. So what the Left did was demonize as "haters" all those who merely sought to retain the man-woman definition of marriage.

Granting for exceptions that all generalizations allow for, conservatives believe that those on the Left are wrong (and foolish and naive and therefore destructive). But those on the Left believe that those on the Right are evil.

Examples are innumerable.

Howard Dean, the former head of the Democratic Party, on Republicans: "In contradistinction to the Republicans, we [Democrats] don't believe kids ought to go to bed hungry at night."[33]

Princeton professor Cornel West: ". . . a morally insensitive period from Reagan to the second Bush, when it was fashionable to be indifferent to the suffering of the most vulnerable."[34]

Former Florida Democratic congressman Alan Grayson: "I want to say a few words about what it means to be a Democrat. It's very simple: We have a conscience."[35]

In an interview in 2001, retiring *New York Times* columnist Anthony Lewis lumped then attorney general John Ashcroft, a conservative Republican, together with Osama bin Laden: "Certainty is the enemy of decency and humanity in people who are sure they are right, like Osama bin Laden and John Ashcroft."[36]

Have conservative spokesmen of the same stature as these liberals ever said anything analogous about Democrats not caring about the suffering of children or not having a conscience? I am not familiar with any.

Why this liberal belief in the demonic nature of conservatives?

One reason is that Leftism, as we have seen, is largely based on good intentions. The Left is certain that it has good intentions—compassion, love of social justice, concern for the environment, and so on. Therefore, its opponents must have bad intentions—they must, by definition, lack compassion, not care about social justice, and not care about clean air and clean water, the poor, or the downtrodden.

A second reason is that when you don't confront real evil, you hate those who do. During the 1980s, the Left expressed far more loathing of Ronald Reagan than of any Soviet Communist dictator. Those who refused to confront Communism hated those on the Right who did. They called the latter "warmongers," "hawks," "cold warriors," charged them with "missile envy," and with loving war.

The Left has had similar contempt for those who take a hard line on Islamism. The liberal and Left-wing media routinely place quotation marks around the phrase "War on Terror." Indeed, the Obama administration actually forbade use of the term "Islamic terror." America was at war with a nameless enemy.

Third, fulfillment of the Left's utopian visions is prevented by the Right. How could a utopian not hate a conservative? To put it another way, the famous 1960s Left-wing motto "Make love, not war" expressed the problem as the Left sees it: The Left makes love and the Right makes war. How could one not hate the Right? The Right, with its belief in the need for a strong military; its opposition to the nurturing state; lack of faith in the United Nations; and in its policy of punishing criminals is the anti-Love, the Leftist equivalent of the Antichrist.

Demonization of their opponents is, therefore, not just a Leftist tactic. It is a bedrock Leftist belief. Given that those on the Left are certain that they are kinder, finer, smarter, and more compassionate than those on the Right, demonization of conservatives, for a Leftist, is merely describing reality.

LABELING OPPONENTS "RACIST"

With regard to any issue that involves blacks, or even non-race-based conservative-liberal differences, the Left will label the Right "racist."

- When he was Senate minority leader, Democratic senator Harry Reid called a Senate bill that would make English "the national language" of the United States "racist."
- A Capitol police officer who stopped Cynthia McKinney, a black member of Congress, to verify her ID as she entered the Capitol was called racist (and punched by McKinney).
- In 2011, a black Democratic congressman, Andre Carson, said of his Republican colleagues, "Some of them in Congress right now with this Tea Party movement would love to see you and me . . . hanging on a tree."[37]
- Former president Jimmy Carter: "I think an overwhelming portion of the intensely demonstrated animosity toward President Barack Obama is based on the fact that he is a black man, that he's African-American."[38]
- Jack Cafferty of CNN on why opinion polls in September 2008 showed Barack Obama and John McCain nearly tied: "The polls remain close. Doesn't make sense . . . unless it's race."[39]

- Jacob Weisberg of *Newsweek* offered the same reason:
  "The reason Obama isn't ahead right now is . . . the
  color of his skin . . ."[40]
- According to *New York Times* columnist Charles M.
  Blow, things not only did not improve for blacks after
  the election of a black president, but white racism actually increased. "We are now inundated with examples
  of overt racism on a scale to which we are unaccustomed."[41]

What were Blow's examples? He provided two. The first and
presumably most important was that "racially offensive images of
the first couple are so prolific online that Google now runs an apologetic ad with the results of image searches of them."

Having never seen a racially offensive image of the first couple, I
was curious what Blow was referring to. I had somehow missed this
alleged flood of racist images on the Web. Luckily, Blow provided
a URL, an Internet link. I clicked on the link, and I came upon a
statement by Google titled "An explanation of our search results,"
in which Google noted, "Sometimes Google search results from
the Internet can include disturbing content, even from innocuous
queries. We assure you that the views expressed by such sites are not
in any way endorsed by Google."

The statement continued along those lines, but there was not a
word about racism, blacks, the first couple, or anything related. It was
a generic apology, and one that I had never in fact encountered. So
not having had any luck corroborating Blow's accusation of "overt
racism on a scale to which we are unaccustomed" on the Internet,
I searched "first couple," clicked on "images," making sure that the
Google filter was turned off. All I saw were hundreds of beautiful
images of what was in fact a handsome-looking first couple and first
family. I then searched on "Michelle and Barack Obama pictures"
and got similar results. One must conclude that Blow wildly exaggerated, if not made it all up, when he wrote that America is "inundated" with "overt racism" on the Internet (or anywhere else).

His second proof of an increasingly racist America: "And it's not all words and images; it's actions as well. According to the Federal Bureau of Investigation's 2008 hate crimes data released last week, anti-black hate crimes rose 4 percent from 2007 . . ."

A 4 percent increase in anti-black hate crime: Was that an indication of a major increase in anti-black racism in America? According to the FBI hate crime statistics, in 2007, 3,434 blacks were victims of a hate crime, and in 2008, the number rose to 3,596—an increase of 162. Given that there are about 40 million blacks in America and about 260 million non-blacks, to charge America with ever-increasing racism based on an increase of 162 incidents of racism is as morally indefensible as it is absurd. To put it statistically, the increase, as a proportion of the black population, was .0004 percent.

Moreover, the number itself, 3,434, is negligible for such a large population. And we should bear in mind two additional factors: We have no way of knowing how many of those 3,434 incidents were committed by whites and how many by non-whites (such as Latinos). Moreover, of those 3,434 hate crimes, one was for murder, not one was a rape, a tiny 386 were aggravated assaults, and 1,257 were "acts of intimidation," not acts of violence.

Only to blacks and whites on the Left do these statistics describe a racist, let alone an increasingly racist, society. What they really describe is the least racist multiethnic, multiracial society in human history.

The fact is that there is much more racism on the Left than on the Right. The very notion that race is a significant human characteristic—a basic Left-wing tenet—is racist. The notion that whites and blacks should not be judged by identical moral standards—or even taught similarly—is also racist. Yet both are basic liberal attitudes. Take, for example, a widely used 2011 teachers' manual, *The Cultural Proficiency Journey: Moving Beyond Ethical Barriers Toward Profound School Change*. It asserts that teachers must "reject the 'color-blind' approach to teaching," in which teachers treat all children the same. A teacher who teaches students of all colors in the same color-blind manner is condemned by the Leftists who administer America's schools.

The very existence of the Congressional Black Caucus (or any other race-based caucus) is also racist. The CBC is so color-based that even a congressman who represents a majority-black district, unless he or she is black, is not allowed to be a member. Democratic representative Steve Cohen of Tennessee, representing a majority-black district, applied for membership and was refused solely because he is white.

The myriad professional black-only associations are racist (and, of course, Leftist). Why is there a National Association of Black Social Workers? This organization is so race-preoccupied that it made national headlines when it condemned white adoption of black children as "cultural genocide." Why is there an Association of Black Psychologists? Or a National Association of Black Journalists? Aside from its implied racism, is such an association good for journalism? If there is any profession that should be free of racial and other biases, shouldn't it be journalism?

LABELING OPPONENTS "HOMOPHOBIC"

The Left declares "homophobic" anyone who believes that marriage should continue to be defined as the union of a man and a woman. Indeed, any difference with the Left on any matter concerning gays is ascribed to conservative "homophobia" and bigotry. In 2010, during a national debate over whether to drop the "Don't Ask, Don't Tell" (DADT) policy regarding gays in the military, *New York Times* columnist Frank Rich wrote a column titled "Smoke the Bigots Out of the Closet." As the title proclaimed, anyone who was for continuing DADT was a bigot.

The article contained seventy-one sentences. Twelve of them contained an insult of conservatives.

Some examples:

Conservative spokesmen expressed "old homophobic clichés."

"Such arguments . . . are mere fig leaves to disguise the phobia that can no longer dare speak its name. . . . [T]he flimsy rhetorical camouflage must be stripped away to expose the prejudice that lies beneath."

"Those opposing same-sex marriage are just as eager to mask their bigotry."

"The more bigotry pushed out of the closet for all voters to see . . ."

". . . the deep prejudice at the root of their [Republicans'] arguments."

Conservatives who oppose repeal of DADT are "attack dogs."

Likewise, anyone who supported California Proposition 8—to amend the California Constitution to define marriage as the union of a man and a woman—was not only homophobic but a "hater."

To those on the Left, one cannot be a decent person and oppose redefining marriage—in a way no civilization has ever defined it, one might add.

Marc Shaiman, the Tony Award–winning composer of the film and stage musical *Hairspray*, composed a three-minute musical piece against California Proposition 8. Viewed more than 2 million times on the Internet, it featured major Hollywood talents playing the roles (through song) of two groups on a beach—gay men and women in beach clothes and a stuffy, formally dressed church group. Its message begins with a religious man and woman reacting to the cheerful gay group by singing these words:

> *Look! Nobody's watching*
> *It's time to spread some hate*
> *And put it in the constitution*
> *Now, how? Proposition Hate!*
> *Great!*

The "hate" consisted of this one sentence: "Only marriage between a man and a woman is valid or recognized in California."

As is usually the case, nearly all the hate on the marriage definition issue came from Left-wing activists like Shaiman.

"Jesus, doesn't the Bible say these people are an abomination?"
Jesus responds, "Yeah."

It was quite audacious to put a falsehood into the mouth of Jesus. The fact is that nowhere in the Bible are homosexuals called "an abomination"—male-male intercourse is labeled an abomination, not those who engage in it, let alone gays who do not. Nor has any normative conservative spokesman referred to gays as "abominations."

Shaiman and his fellow Left-wing activists could not acknowledge what conservatives regularly acknowledge, namely that there are good people on both sides of this issue. Why not? Because once the Left acknowledges that their opponents can be decent people, the Leftist edifice crumbles. Leftism is based on the Left's self-image of moral superiority.

LABELING OPPONENTS "ANTI-WORKER"

From Greece to the United States, suffocating government debt is, aside from entitlements, in large measure a result of governments hiring far too many employees. In the United States, more than 20 million people work for federal, state, and local governments. That is about one in seven workers in America, and their salaries and benefits total approximately $1.5 trillion of taxpayer funds each year—about 10 percent of gross domestic product. Yet any Republican or conservative who wishes to decrease the number of federal, state, and municipal employees is labeled "anti-worker," among other awful things. For example, in August 2011 it was reported that "House Minority Leader Nancy Pelosi (D-Calif.) on Monday hammered Republicans for what she labeled their 'anti-worker agenda.' . . ."[42]

Conservatives are not depicted as opposing policies, but rather as opposing people—blacks, workers, teachers, women, Muslims, etc.

LABELING OPPONENTS "ANTI-EDUCATION"

According to the Organisation for Economic Co-operation and Development, the United States spends an average of $91,700 per student between the ages of six and fifteen. That is the second most in the world, and by far the most for a large country. Only Switzerland, a country of 7.6 million people, spends more. The United States population is over 313 million, forty-one times larger than Switzerland. Moreover, the results are worse than many of the countries that spend far less, and since President Jimmy Carter created the Department of Education in 1979, the costs have soared while the results have declined. Consequently, many Americans believe that vast sums of money are wasted on education—especially on the federal and state bureaucracies that have become a deeply entrenched part of the education system. What does the Department of Education do, exactly? But to the Left, such a position is "anti-education" and "anti-teacher." As one newspaper headline put it, "Democratic Video portrays GOP as anti-education." [43] And any attempt to weaken teachers unions' control of education is depicted as "anti-teacher."

LABELING OPPONENTS "FASCISTS" AND "NAZIS"

From *The Authoritarian Personality* to today, the equation of conservatives with fascism or even Nazism has been a recurring theme on the highest levels of the Left.

The argument that spokesmen on the Right call people on the Left fascists and Nazis just as often is not true. It is not true in frequency nor, more important, in the stature of the accusers. Pulitzer Prize–winning *New York Times* reporter Chris Hedges wrote a book titled *American Fascists: The Christian Right and the War on America*, one of many books by Left-wing writers whose theme is that conservative Christians are fascists. The *New York Times* reviewer of the book began his review with these words: "Of course there are Christian fascists in America." [44]

Representative Steve Cohen of Tennessee said on the House floor on January 19, 2011: "[Republicans] say it's a government take-over of health care, a big lie just like Goebbels. You say it enough, you repeat the lie, you repeat the lie, you repeat the lie and eventually, people believe it. . . . That's the same kind of thing the Germans said enough about the Jews and the people believed it—and you had the Holocaust."

Frank Rich of the *New York Times* wrote that Tea Partiers engaged in a "small-scale mimicry of Kristallnacht."[45] Kristallnacht, the "Night of the Broken Glass," is considered the opening act of the Holocaust. In November 1938, in the course of two days, tens of thousands of German Jews were arrested and deported to concentration camps; scores of Jews were beaten to death; 267 synagogues were destroyed; and thousands of Jewish-owned businesses were vandalized—often by having their windows smashed. Had an equally prominent conservative columnist written the same thing about a large group of Democrats, he would have been forced to resign, given how intense the attacks by Jewish defense organizations and liberal media would have been.

Democratic Georgia congressman John Lewis, on the floor of the House on March 21, 1995, paraphrased the anti-Nazi pastor Martin Niemoller's timeless speech about the Nazi takeover: "They came first for the Communists, and I didn't speak up because I wasn't a Communist. Then they came for the Jews . . . trade unionists . . . Catholics . . . Protestants . . ." And then he said, "Read the Republican contract. They are coming for the children. They are coming for the poor. They are coming for the sick, the elderly, and the disabled."

Not only was there no outcry from the news media, which largely ignored Lewis's comments, but when reported, they were related in an almost sympathetic manner. The next day on ABC's *Good Morning America*, ABC correspondent Bob Zelnick emphasized the social programs the Republican wished to cut, and then cited the Lewis comments this way: "At times, the floor debate became emotional—one Democrat invoking the memory of Nazi Germany . . ."

Jesse Jackson on the newly elected Republican Congress in December 1994: "In South Africa, we call it apartheid. In Nazi Germany, we'd call it fascism. Here in the United States, we call it conservatism."[46]

Jesse Jackson on Republican plans to repeal the Obama health care bill: "A kind of creeping genocide."[47]

Julian Bond at the NAACP convention said of President Bush: "He has selected nominees from the Taliban wing of American politics, appeased the wretched appetites of the extreme right wing, and chosen Cabinet officials whose devotion to the confederacy is nearly canine in its uncritical affection."

And, finally, longtime *Boston Globe* columnist Ellen Goodman wrote: "Let's just say that global warming deniers are now on a par with Holocaust deniers . . ."

LABELING OPPONENTS "SEXIST"

For decades any person who suggested that men and women are basically different—psychologically and mentally, not just physically—was labeled sexist. Though some on the Left now acknowledge some inherent differences between the sexes, when a man makes this claim, he is still dismissed as sexist.

Arguing that, in general, men derive more satisfaction and more self-worth from a career than women do is sexist.

Advocating all-girls schools is progressive. Advocating all-boys schools is sexist.

Opposition to any aspect of feminism is sexist.

And, of course, opposition to abortion is not morality-based; it, too, is labeled sexist.

LABELING OPPONENTS "ISLAMOPHOBIC"

Why is it that one can criticize every religion—and mock as well as criticize Christianity—except Islam? Because the Left sets the rules of discourse in America and much of the rest of the world. There is no other reason.

Take, for example, how the Left treated all opposition to a Muslim leader's plans to build a $100 million Islamic center in New York City within blocks of Ground Zero, where nearly three thousand Americans were killed on September 11, 2011, by Muslims acting in the name of Islam. All opposition was labeled Islamophobic. I did not come across a mainstream Leftist description of opponents of the mosque/Islamic center who did not describe all opponents as hate-filled, intolerant, bigoted, xenophobic, or, most of all, Islamophobic.

Michael Kinsley, editor at large, the *Atlantic*: "Is there any reason to oppose the mosque that isn't bigoted, or demagogic, or unconstitutional? None that I've heard or read."

Roger Ebert, *Chicago Sun-Times*: "The far right wing has seized on the issue as an occasion for fanning hatred against Muslims."

Peter Beinart, associate professor of journalism and political science at City University of New York: "Republicans are clawing over each other to demonize Muslims." And he warned "fellow Jews" who opposed the building of the mosque near Ground Zero: "It's never crossed your mind that the religious hatred you have helped unleash could turn once again against us."

New York Times editorial: "Republican ideologues, predictably . . . spew more of their intolerant rhetoric. . . . Too many Republican leaders are determined to whip up as much false controversy and anguish as they can . . ."

Glenn Greenwald, a former constitutional lawyer, columnist at Salon.com, and the author of *Great American Hypocrites: Toppling the Big Myths of Republican Politics*: "The argument against the proposed Park51 community center is necessarily and definitively grounded in bigotry. . . . The right-wing campaign . . . is a classic case of that warped mentality; indeed, this campaign is one of the ugliest this country has seen in some time. . . . toxic demagoguery . . ."[48]

James Zogby, president of the Arab American Institute: "Shame. Your bigoted appeals to fear and intolerance disgrace us all and put our country at risk in the world."

In the *Huffington Post*, foreign policy analyst Michael Hughes: "Even more hideous is the way in which these bigots try to hide their overt prejudice in the emotional guise of love and caring, purportedly because they believe we must be 'sensitive' to the families of the victims of 9/11."

New York Times columnist Nicholas D. Kristof: Republican opponents of the mosque are "just like the Saudi officials who ban churches, and even confiscate Bibles, out of sensitivity to local feelings. . . . Today's crusaders against the Islamic community center are promoting a similar paranoid intolerance."

New York Times columnist Frank Rich: "This month's incessant and indiscriminate orgy of Muslim-bashing. . . . . So virulent is the Islamophobic hysteria of the neocon and Fox News right—abetted by the useful idiocy of the Anti-Defamation League. . . . The Islamophobia command center, Murdoch's News Corporation . . ."

Responding to these attacks on opponents of the mosque, *Washington Post* conservative columnist Charles Krauthammer wrote: "Ground Zero is the site of the most lethal attack of that worldwide movement, which consists entirely of Muslims, acts in the name of Islam and is deeply embedded within the Islamic world. These are regrettable facts, but facts they are."[49]

Presumably Krauthammer, too, is Islamophobic.

As in virtually every instance of Left-Right difference, the Left demonized the Right. In this case, however, it was particularly ugly. Even the relatives of men and women who were incinerated on 9/11 and who opposed a giant mosque and Islamic center two blocks away were demonized. On the other hand, virtually every conservative acknowledged that there were good people on both sides of this issue.

No one escapes the Left's demonization of critics of Islam. Not even Ayaan Hirsi Ali, who, as an African woman who fights for women and gays, should be a Left-wing hero. *Newsweek* senior writer Lorraine Ali reviewed Ayaan Hirsi Ali's autobiography, *Infidel*. It is the extraordinary story of Hirsi Ali, born and raised a Muslim in Somalia, who fled to the West, where she learned Dutch and mastered a new civilization so well that she was elected to the Dutch Parliament, and then eventually moved to America. But to *Newsweek*'s Lorraine Ali, Ayaan Hirsi Ali is a "bombthrower," and her book is "reactionary," written to appease "right-wingers."

To characterize Hirsi Ali, rather than the bomb-wearing people she is fighting at the risk of her life, as a "bombthrower" is to truly invert morality and reality. As is Lorraine Ali's use of the words *right-wing* and *reactionary* to describe Hirsi Ali, a feminist, atheist, pro-gay activist who combats the greatest religious extremism of our time.

THE CHARGE THAT "BUSH LIED, PEOPLE DIED"

For most, if not nearly all, Americans on the Left, the invasion of Iraq to depose Saddam Hussein was explained in four words: "Bush lied, people died."

But Bush did not lie. At worst, he was mistaken about weapons of mass destruction (WMD) in Iraq and about invading Iraq and deposing Saddam Hussein. At the time of the American and allied invasion of Iraq, leading Democrats,[50] most Western intelligence services, and the British prime minister, Tony Blair—of the Labor Party—also believed that Saddam Hussein was hiding weapons of mass destruction. That is why Britain was America's strong ally, sending the next-largest commitment of troops to Iraq after America's. It is highly unlikely that a British prime minister—especially one from the Labor Party—would have sent forty-five thousand British soldiers to war unless his own intelligence agencies had independently assessed a very serious, perhaps imminent, threat. As the prominent liberal commentator, Fareed Zakaria of CNN, wrote at the time, "We cannot abandon our policy of containing Saddam Hussein. He is building weapons of mass destruction."[51]

Did Zakaria lie?

In good conscience, along with many others, with good reason (Saddam Hussein had already used WMD against his own people), George W. Bush believed that Saddam Hussein had or was building such weapons. But saying Bush was mistaken violates the Left-wing need to demonize its opponents. Bush had to be portrayed as lying, and doing so for another liberal characterization of conservatives: greed. This time for oil and in order to enrich his friends at defense contractors such as Halliburton.

NOTHING BETTER SUMMARIZES THE Left-wing demonization of conservatives than a question posed to the father of modern conservatism, the late William F. Buckley Jr., in an interview with the *New York Times Magazine* on the occasion of Buckley's taking leave from *National Review*, the magazine he founded fifty years earlier. Given the Left-wing views of the *New York Times* and its interviewer, the questions were nearly all challenging. But nothing quite prepared a reader for this one: "You seem indifferent to suffering. Have you ever suffered yourself?"[52]

That one statement summed up the liberal view of conservatives: "indifferent to suffering."

4. The Left's Manufacture and Use of Crises

WITHOUT CONSTANT CRISES, the Left has no raison d'être, and, even worse, is not needed. The Left needs crises; and crises need the Left to solve them.

The Left is both prone to hysteria—expressing exaggerated and/or irrational fears—and to producing hysteria for tactical reasons. As the list below—which is not exhaustive—shows, for the Left there is always an imminent calamity, a looming great disaster. Additionally, those threats must be solved immediately and they must be solved by government action.

These are the means by which hysteria and fabricated crises work for the Left:

1. The Left identifies—usually meaning exaggerates or invents—some serious threat.
2. The threat is rarely a great evil.
3. The threat will be determined more by emotion than by reason, and therefore is frequently not an actual threat.
4. The news media will repeat how dire the threat is.
5. The threat must be solved immediately.
6. The solution will involve enlarging government by passing new laws and/or appropriating additional tax dollars.

Let's start with a nonpolitical issue—bullying.

Every normal, not to mention decent, person decries bullying in schools (or anywhere else). Therefore, given that there are more conservative parents than liberal ones (because more Americans identify as conservative than liberal), and no parent wants his or her child bullied, one would assume that conservatives would be equally if not more represented among politicians, educators, and parents in clamoring for something to be done about the alleged epidemic of school bullying.

Yet, as the following Associated Press report in March 2011 shows, that is not the case. Indeed, this story provides a fine example of nearly each element in Left-wing hysteria:

> BISMARCK, N.D.—North Dakota senators on Thursday approved requiring schools to take new steps to prevent bullying, despite arguments that the effort was a time-wasting example of the "nanny state . . ."
> The measure, which the Senate approved, 36–10, mandates that school districts adopt anti-bullying policies by July

2012, and make training available to teachers and school aides in bullying prevention.

North Dakota is one of only a handful of states that doesn't have an anti-bullying law for public schools, said Sen. Richard Marcellais, D–Belcourt.

Sens. Oley Larsen, R–Minot, and Margaret Sitte, R–Bismarck, spoke against the measure.

Larsen said children need to be taught how to handle bullying, rather than ordering schools to focus on bullying prevention. The legislation "rewards kids for thinking and acting like victims. It will promote a victim mentality and handicap kids for life, not just after the school bell rings," Larsen said.

Sitte said anti-bullying instruction and training would waste valuable school time and called it "just another example of nanny-state government run amok."

"From the beginning of time, people have picked on each other. Call it bullying, call it what you will," Sitte said. "People do need to learn to stand up for themselves."

A reader of this news story will readily note that the most vocal voices against the bill were those of Republican, presumably conservative Republican, legislators. Their concerns, typical conservative concerns, were that preoccupation with bullying and the outlawing of it by the state were (1) an example of the "nanny state" and (2) would create a sense of victimhood among many students.

On the other hand, Democratic state senator Marcellais was perturbed that North Dakota was one of only a handful of states that did not have an anti-bullying law. To the liberal mind, knowing that any other state (or country) has banned something undesirable while one's own state or country has not is a moral failing.

When I was a summer camp counselor at an eight-week sleep-away camp, there was no bullying in my cabin of eight thirteen-year-old boys. The major reason was that my campers knew from day one that, if necessary, I would have physically overpowered a bully. In those days, counselors, like teachers, could use physical force if necessary. Thanks to the Left, that is now considered child abuse and therefore illegal. In the Left's view, it is better for a young student to be taken away by the state police in handcuffs to jail (see the story on page 144 about the young boys in an Oregon school who "butt-slapped" a girl) than to be smacked by a teacher or a camp counselor—or by a parent.

As the Left has undermined teacher and parental authority, it has increasingly transferred such authority to the state. Thus, according to the North Dakota bill, "School districts would need to involve parents, school employees, volunteers, students, law enforcement, domestic violence and sexual assault organizations and community representatives when developing the policy." One wonders why the fire department was not involved.

School bullying and the North Dakota legislators' reaction provide an excellent example of Left-wing hysteria because the Left and the Right both detest bullies and because parents on both sides equally love their children. Yet, their views about what should be done about it—and even whether this is an epidemic—completely differ.

FRIGHTENED CHILDREN AT THE DEMOCRATIC CONVENTION

The Democratic National Convention in 2000 provided an example of the primacy of its hysteria, and of its desire to instill its irrational fears in others—especially children, whose innocence Leftism often robs for ideological purposes.

On August 16, 2000, the third day of the convention, the Democrats introduced five young people—by my best guess, from five to eleven years of age: "Ladies and gentlemen," the convention's official voice announced, "we are pleased to welcome five special young people . . . for 'When I Grow Up.'"

First child: "When I grow up, I wonder if people will be more afraid to cry than they are to die. Will I be able to see a rainbow in a smog-filled sky? Will there be any trees alive? If not, how will the planet survive? Will the Internet have a website at www .lifetime-air-supply?"

Second child: "When I grow up, if I got bored, and had nothing to do, and me and my son build a canoe, would water that used to be blue be so polluted it would give us the flu? Will a thousand dollars be enough for a shoe? Will I have to be like you—letting money make every decision for everything that I do?"

Third child: "When I grow up, will the existence of dolphins and whales just be a story I tell—starting with 'Once upon a time . . . ,' ending with 'Where did we fail?' Will adults be the hammer and nail? Will schools be next door to jails? Will the truth be illegal to sell?"

Fourth child: "When I grow up, will anyone be on the news for anything besides killing? Will those drug dealers still be standing in front of my building? Will they ever learn how to love, or stay afraid of the feeling? Will TV and music videos still raise America's children?"

Fifth child: "When I grow up, will innocent kids still be wrongfully touched? Will students go home from school in a bulletproof bus? What if children don't have anyone to trust? That would hurt me so much. And I want to be happy . . . when I grow up."

Kids who should have been playing ball or taking a summer trip with their family or church group were instead reciting lines expressing (adult liberals') fears of growing up in an America that might choke them environmentally or abuse them sexually—lines written for them by America's Left-wing party.

SEXUAL HARASSMENT

According to the Left, the great majority of girls and women in America frequently experience a nightmare of sexual harassment. While sexual harassment is real and sometimes truly vile, this has largely been another example of Left-wing hysteria, resulting, as always, in far more laws, far bigger government, and therefore less liberty for Americans.

On the *CBS Evening News* on May 29, 2008, anchorwoman Katie Couric reported this alarming news:

"A new study on teens and sexual harassment should give every parent pause. Most teenage girls report they've been sexually harassed. . . . In a study that appeared in the journal *Child Development*, 90 percent of teen girls say they've been harassed at least once."

Millions of American parents and their daughters were told on one of the most widely watched evening newscasts that nine out of every ten American girls aged twelve to eighteen are sexually harassed. Suspecting that at least two elements of Leftism were at play here—hysteria and Left-wing feminist victim ideology—far more than some real crisis of sexual harassment, I decided to take a closer look at the report cited by Couric.

There was a summary of the report on the *Ms.* magazine website:

A study released this month reports that 90 percent of girls between the ages of 12 and 18 reported experiencing sexual harassment. The study found that girls who had a better understanding of feminism from the media, their parents, or teachers were more likely to recognize sexual harassment.

Campbell Leaper, professor of psychology at the University of California, Santa Cruz, and one of the authors of the study, said in a press release, "Sexism remains pervasive in the lives of adolescent girls. Most girls have experienced all three types of sexism—sexual harassment, sexist comments about their academic abilities, and sexist comments about their athletic abilities."

Science Daily reports that the study found Latina and Asian American girls reported less sexual harassment than the other girls who participated in the study. The most commonly reported forms of sexual harassment were unwanted romantic attention, demeaning gender-related comments, teasing based on their appearance, and unwanted physical contact.

This confirmed my suspicions.

First, "The study found that girls who had a better understanding of feminism were more likely to recognize sexual harassment."

There is no question that this is true. Girls subjected to feminist indoctrination are undoubtedly more likely to interpret largely innocuous behavior as sexual harassment. In order for the American Left to achieve its political goals, and because many on the Left sincerely believe it, virtually every group in America except white, male, heterosexual Christians must be portrayed as—and constantly told it is—oppressed. Women are oppressed by men. Blacks and Hispanics are oppressed by whites. Gays are oppressed by straights. Non-Christians are oppressed by Christians. The poor are oppressed by the wealthy. This helps the Left gain and retain these groups' votes and it is also part of the Left's race-gender-class explanation of how the world works.

American women have more opportunity and more equality than just about any women in the world today and certainly ever in history. In fact, if either sex is more "oppressed" today, it is more likely to be males. If women were incarcerated, let alone murdered, as disproportionately as men are; if only 40 percent of those getting a bachelor's degree were female; if girls dropped out of high school at the rate males do; if females committed suicide as often as—let alone considerably more often than—males do, there would be a national outcry. But for feminists, academics, and CBS News, it is women who are "oppressed." And that is what they are taught in high school and college by feminist-oriented teachers.

Second, "sexual harassment" is a term that includes utterly trivial acts and non-acts: "Sexist comments about their academic abilities, sexist comments about their athletic abilities, unwanted romantic attention, demeaning gender-related comments, teasing based on their appearance, and unwanted physical contact."

If a girl's bra is snapped in elementary, junior high, or high school; if a girl is told she should learn to throw a ball "like a guy"; if a boy pursues a girl and doesn't know exactly when to stop pursuing her—these are all instances of sexism and sexual harassment. This leads to—as acknowledged by the *Ms.* report itself—girls and women seeing themselves as victims of sexual harassment.[53]

If you deem all these things sexual harassment, there really is a plague of sexual harassment. And if there is a plague of sexual harassment, then the Left is not only vindicated; it is empowered—because only an expanded state guided by the Left can cure it.

Thanks to the Left's hysteria about sexual harassment, little boys are now deemed sex offenders for doing what little boys have done since little boys were first invented.

In Woodbridge, Virginia, officials at an elementary school called in police to arrest a six-year-old boy for slapping a six-year-old girl on her bottom. The boy was then labeled a sex offender, a charge that will permanently remain in his school records. And he was hardly alone among elementary school students. As related in the *Washington Post*: "The Virginia Department of Education reported that 255 elementary students were suspended last year for offensive sexual touching, or 'improper physical contact against a student.' In Maryland, 166 elementary school children were suspended last year for sexual harassment, including three preschoolers, 16 kindergartners and 22 first-graders, according to the State Department of Education."[54]

Another example, in which my radio show and I came to be directly involved: At Patton Middle School in McMinnville, Oregon, students started something called "slap butt day." On one such day in February 2007, according to the *Oregonian*: "Two boys tore down the hall of Patton Middle School after lunch, swatting the bottoms of girls as they ran—what some kids later said was a common form of greeting. But bottom-slapping is against policy in McMinnville Public Schools. So a teacher's aide sent the gawky seventh-graders to the office, where the vice principal and a police officer stationed at the school soon interrogated them."[55]

A police officer interrogated them.

"After hours of interviews with students," the *Oregonian* continued, "the day of the February incident, the officer read the boys their Miranda rights and hauled them off in handcuffs to juvenile jail, where they spent the next five days."

Two seventh graders were read their Miranda rights. And hauled off to jail. And kept in jail for five days. For butt-swatting.

It gets worse. The seventh graders were not permitted contact with their parents for twenty-four hours, they were brought into court in shackles and jail garb, and they were strip-searched four times during the course of their incarceration. All because the Yamhill County district attorney, Bradley Berry, brought felony sex charges against the two boys. When he finally explained himself under pressure from the media, Berry told the *Oregonian*, "From our perspective and the perspective of the victims, this was not just horseplay."

Berry's explanation was not only absurd— it was false. The girls involved did regard it as horseplay, and they claimed virtually from the outset that they had been pressured into making a case against the boys.

I appealed to my radio show listeners to donate to a legal fund for the boys, and due to the legal help they received the charges against them were eventually dropped.

There is real sexual harassment. And there is real hysteria about sexual harassment, which has the usual benefits for the Left: a victim group, more laws, which in turn mean more lawsuits and bigger government, and the Left as savior.

NUCLEAR POWER

Though strongly opposed to fossil-based sources of energy, the Left in America has been just as opposed to clean nuclear energy. The stated reasons? Nuclear energy is not safe because it can leak radiation and because we do not know how to safely dispose of nuclear waste.

This is another Left-wing hysteria that emanates from Leftists being prone to excessive fears and/or making up such fears in order to push a different agenda—in this case "green" energy such as windmills and solar panels.

The Left has made a meltdown at Three Mile Island in Pennsylvania in March 1979 synonymous with terrible danger from nuclear reactors. As coincidence would have it, the nuclear-power-is-dangerous film *The China Syndrome*, starring Jane Fonda and Jack Lemmon, was released just days before the Three Mile Island accident. The film, the news media, and Fonda's antinuclear activism all created a fear of nuclear power among many Americans.

The antinuclear Left rapidly organized demonstrations throughout America. In May 1979, sixty-five thousand people, including California governor Jerry Brown, attended a march and rally against nuclear power in Washington, D.C. In September, the largest demonstration was held in New York City, where two hundred thousand people listened to anti-nuclear-power speeches given by Jane Fonda and Ralph Nader. The rally was held in conjunction with a series of nightly "No Nukes" concerts given at Madison Square Garden from September 19 to 23 by Musicians United for Safe Energy. And, of course, various companies had to pay out tens of millions of dollars thanks to class-action suits.

The number of reactors under construction in the United States consequently declined every year from 1980 to 1998. And between 1980 and 1984, orders for fifty-one American nuclear reactors were canceled.

Why did all this happen?

Solely because of Leftist hysteria and activism.

Not one person died as a result of Three Mile Island; in fact, exposure to radiation was next to zero. According to the Nuclear Regulatory Commission, "Estimates are that the average dose to about 2 million people in the area was only about 1 millirem. To put this into context, exposure from a chest x-ray is about 6 millirem. Compared to the natural radioactive background dose of about 100–125 millirem per year for the area, the collective dose to the community from the accident was very small. The maximum dose to a person at the site boundary would have been less than 100 millirem. . . . Comprehensive investigations and assessments by several well-respected organizations have concluded that in spite of serious damage to the reactor, most of the radiation was contained and that the actual release had negligible effects on the physical health of individuals or the environment."[56]

Even the worst nuclear power disaster in history, the 1986 Chernobyl nuclear reactor disaster in Ukraine, which was entirely a result of Soviet incompetence and lack of concern for its citizens, was far less injurious than the drama around it suggested. As of 2006, twenty years after the disaster, according to the United Nations Scientific Committee on the Effects of Atomic Radiation:

> There is no scientific evidence of increases in overall cancer incidence or mortality rates or in rates of non-malignant disorders that could be related to radiation exposure. The incidence of leukemia in the general population, one of the main concerns owing to the shorter time expected between exposure and its occurrence compared with solid cancers, does not appear to be elevated. Although those most highly exposed individuals are at an increased risk of radiation-associated effects, the great majority of the population is not likely to experience serious health consequences as a result of radiation from the Chernobyl accident. . . .
>
> For the most part, they were exposed to radiation levels comparable to or a few times higher than annual levels of natural background, and future exposures continue to slowly diminish as the radionuclides decay. Lives have been seriously disrupted by the Chernobyl accident, but from the radiological point of view, generally positive prospects for the future health of most individuals should prevail.[57]

Regarding deaths from Chernobyl, as of twenty-four years later, the *Guardian* reported the "UN's World Health Organisation

[WHO] and the International Atomic Energy Agency claim that only 56 people have died as a direct result of the radiation released at Chernobyl . . ."[58]

The article also notes that WHO predicts that "about 4,000 will die from it eventually." But "Michael Repacholi, director of the UN Chernobyl forum until 2006, has claimed that even 4,000 eventual deaths could be too high."[59]

Each of the fifty-six deaths is a human tragedy (as well as negligent homicide on the part of the Soviet government). But fifty-six is not the number that anyone would have expected given the amount of attention and the severity of nuclear radiation released—four hundred times more radioactive material, according to the International Atomic Energy Agency, than from the atomic bomb in Hiroshima.[60]

As for the Left, such numbers are unacceptably small. They do not lead to hysteria and therefore do not lead to sufficient antinuclear sentiment. Thus the Left-wing environmentalist group Greenpeace rejected the United Nations numbers and released a report at the same time declaring that many tens of thousands of people will have died from the Chernobyl accident.[61]

For much of the world's media, Greenpeace is the source to go to for such figures. The Associated Press began its report on April 18, 2006: "Greenpeace said Tuesday in a new report that more than 90,000 people were likely to die of cancers caused by radiation from the Chernobyl nuclear disaster, countering a United Nations report that predicted the death toll would be around 4,000."

And Greenpeace is acting responsibly here compared to the world's best-known antinuclear activist, Dr. Helen Caldicott, who said in 2011 that "nearly a million" people were killed by Chernobyl.[62]

Nuclear power, after Three Mile Island, after Chernobyl, and after the 2011 earthquake and tsunami in Japan, remains extraordinarily safe.

ANOREXIA

Two prominent feminist writers, Gloria Steinem and Naomi Wolf, wrote in their bestselling books, *Revolution from Within* and *The Beauty Myth*, respectively—and the news media reported—that 150,000 girls and women die every year from anorexia nervosa.

According to the Centers for Disease Control and Prevention (CDC), in 1991, the year before the Steinem book was published, fifty-four American girls and women died of anorexia. Steinem and Wolf, two feminist icons, exaggerated by a factor of 30,000. Moreover, the impossibility of the number the two authors gave is easily demonstrated. In 2009, fewer than 50,000 females between the ages fifteen and forty-four died in America *of all causes.*

Why did they write something so mendacious? First, because of the animus against men that has pervaded Left-wing feminism. As Wolf put it, every female who dies from anorexia is killed not by nature, but by men. And second, if the true numbers are given, there is no crisis. And the Left without a crisis is like a fish without water.

SECONDHAND SMOKE

My brother and I grew up with two parents who regularly smoked inside the house. My mother (who lived in excellent health until her death at age eighty-nine) smoked cigarettes and my father (who is in excellent health at age ninety-three) smoked cigars. My brother and I have been blessed with excellent health all our lives. Our generation of baby boomers has been the longest-living, healthiest generation in American, if not world, history, and most of us grew up with daily secondhand smoke. Yet much of this generation has bought the notion that secondhand smoke is a major killer. Or, to be more precise, those Left of center have bought it, just as those Left of center have sold it.

The genesis of this hysteria is easy to identify. Antismoking activists—people for whom abolishing tobacco use (cigars and pipes as well as cigarettes) is a religious calling—saw that Americans did not respond as the activists wished they would. No matter how much the activists attempted to strike fear in smokers' hearts, many people continued to smoke. So they devised a far more effective tactic—they told nonsmokers that smokers were killing them.

Of course, they could rarely point to people who died as a result of being exposed to what became known as secondhand smoke. So they used epidemiological studies—defined by the WHO as "the study of the distribution and determinants of health-related states or events including disease"—to "prove" their contention. Fifty thousand Americans a year, we are told, are killed by secondhand smoke. This is hysteria masquerading as science. First, because it is not science as much as it is interpreting statistics, and second, because it is animated in almost every case by an extrascientific impulse—the desire to end smoking. One highly regarded epidemiologist, Dr. James Enstrom of the UCLA School of Public Health, disputed the mainstream epidemiological studies on secondhand smoke. His findings, printed in the *British Medical Journal*, were that "[t]he results do not support a causal relation between environmental tobacco smoke and tobacco related mortality. . . . The association between exposure to environmental tobacco smoke and coronary heart disease and lung cancer may be considerably weaker than generally believed."[63]

As a result of his studies on secondhand smoke and other studies that went against the dominant positions of the Left that permeate even some of the sciences—especially public health—Enstrom was denied tenure at UCLA.[64] All the academic politics and virtually all the government funds for academics on this particular issue are devoted to "proving" secondhand smoke kills fifty thousand Americans a year.

Concerning the nonscientific basis of concern with outdoor smoke, Michael B. Siegel, a professor of community health sciences at the Boston University School of Public Health, wrote in a column published in the *New York Times*: "Not only can people move around and thus avoid intense exposure, but smoke quickly disperses in the open air. . . . [N]o evidence demonstrates that the duration of outdoor exposure—in places where people can move freely about—is long enough to cause substantial health damage. . . . [F]rom a public health perspective, [the outdoor ban is] pointless."

Siegel, a longtime proponent of indoor bans on smoking, concluded his column thus: "In trying to convince people that even transient exposure to secondhand smoke is a potentially deadly hazard, smoking opponents risk losing scientific credibility. . . . New York's ban on outdoor smoking seems to fulfill its opponents' charge that the movement is being driven instead by an unthinking hatred of tobacco smoke."[65]

Let me make clear that I do not deny that asthmatic children, for example, may well have an increase in asthmatic episodes as a result of being around secondhand smoke. And secondhand smoke may cause or exacerbate other conditions in some people. But that is far from the claim that secondhand smoke kills fifty thousand Americans a year.

Moreover, it is worth pondering—since presumably just as many individuals on the Right dislike smoke as do individuals on the Left—why people Left of center are so much more likely to believe that any exposure to secondhand smoke can seriously hurt their health and even kill them, and why it is that liberal cities governed by liberals are so much more likely to ban outdoor smoking, and even smoking in cigar shops, than conservative cities are.

There are actually three answers. One is that when people on the Left hear the words "studies show" or "experts say," they often cease thinking critically. They cease to live by their own motto to "question authority." The second is that they panic easily. The third is that they hate big companies, and none more than tobacco companies.

HETEROSEXUAL AIDS IN AMERICA

In the 1980s, American media featured cover articles about the looming epidemic of heterosexual AIDS in America. They made sure to feature white heterosexual women—members of the second-least-likely demographic group in America to contract AIDS (the least likely were lesbians)—in order to illustrate that, in the politically correct phrase of the day, "AIDS doesn't discriminate." Or as a *Life* magazine cover put it, "Now, No One Is Safe."

Though not true, the belief that heterosexual AIDS was developing into an epidemic in America was fostered by the Left, including more than a few physicians.* Why? One reason was that the Left desired to destigmatize AIDS by deflecting attention away from (male) homosexuals, who, along with intravenous drug users and their partners, were the largest groups of AIDS carriers. Another reason was to further increase spending on AIDS research. The Left believed, probably correctly, that if the American public associated AIDS almost exclusively with small subgroups, it would balk at spending enormous sums of money on AIDS research to the detriment of funding for other, much more prevalent, deadly diseases. But if the American public were led to believe that AIDS threatened all Americans equally, it would readily acquiesce to spending much more money on AIDS research.

SWINE FLU

In 2009, an outbreak of a strain of influenza called H1N1 that came to be popularly known as "swine flu" killed some people. The world's media and the United Nations picked up on this issue and, again, those on the Left were far more concerned than those on the Right. Emblematic was the reaction of the vice president of the United States, Joseph Biden, a liberal Democrat, who told the nation that he recommends that people not travel on any public mode of transportation such as an airplane because the person seated next to them might be a carrier and his or her sneeze could be fatal.

After the airline and other travel industries vehemently pro-

---

* Of course, in Africa heterosexual AIDS was and remains a very real problem—for reasons specific to Africa.

tested, the vice president took back his words. It is inconceivable that the previous vice president, the conservative Dick Cheney, would have said anything analogous.

SILICONE BREAST IMPLANTS

Another Left-led hysteria concerned alleged serious dangers of silicone breast implants to women's health. Feminist and other ideologically driven groups led a campaign to have the implants banned despite the lack of scientific evidence to substantiate their charges. The campaign was successful, as the Food and Drug Administration (FDA) banned the implants in 1992. As in all the other cases, nearly all the news media had been publishing articles and broadcasting about how dangerous the implants were. Typical was CBS News broadcaster Connie Chung, two years before the ban: "But what's shocking is that these devices have never been approved by the federal government. Only now is the government looking at the dangers. But for some women, it may be too late." The show featured four women who claimed to be sick as a result of the implants and a physician who supported their claims. No dissenting voice was heard on the show.[66]

Meanwhile, juries were awarding enormous sums of money to lawyers and their clients on the basis of their claims that silicone implants ruined their health. In 1991, a California jury awarded $7.3 million to a woman with mixed connective-tissue disease—despite the testimony of her doctor that she showed symptoms two years before getting implants.[67]

In June 1994, an epidemiologic study done at the Mayo Clinic was published in the *New England Journal of Medicine*. The study found no association between breast implants and the connective-tissue diseases and other disorders that were studied.[68]

In June 1995 another, very large, study was published, again in the *New England Journal of Medicine*. The study was conducted by epidemiologists and rheumatologists at Harvard Medical School,

Brigham and Women's Hospital, and the Harvard School of Public Health. It, too, found no association between silicone breast implants and connective-tissue diseases.[69]*

Such studies led Dr. Ed Uthman, a pathologist and adjunct professor of pathology at the University of Texas Health Science Center at Houston, to write in 1996: "Of my years in pathology, I have never seen such high-profile behavior and deliberately misleading literature from physicians as I have seen surrounding breast implants." Lest one think that Uthman was in the pay of silicone breast implant makers, it is worth noting that he was, in fact, an outspoken opponent of breast implants in women with normal breasts: "Any woman whose Significant Other wants her to undergo surgical breast enlargement needs to get a new Significant Other, not new breasts."[70]

In November 2006, the FDA finally approved silicone breast implants. But the liberal media continued its crusade against the product. Immediately after the approval, *NBC Nightly News* anchor Brian Williams announced, "Given the history of this product, I think a lot of people are going to have a hard time with the government blessing for this particular product, being a foreign substance being sewn inside the bodies of women."[71]

HOMELESSNESS IN AMERICA

During the Reagan era another crisis in America was announced by Left-wing activists. This time it was homelessness. Every homeless person is a tragedy, but, again, the Left created hysteria. The estimate of American homeless given at the time by the U.S. Department of Housing and Urban Development (HUD) was between 250,000 and 350,000. But the best-known spokesman for the cause, a man named Mitch Snyder, regularly announced that there were between two and three million homeless Americans. And the press repeat-

---

* Unfortunately, the studies came too late for U.S. company Dow Corning, manufacturer of silicone breast implants and other silicone-based products. As a result of multibillion dollar class action lawsuits brought against it by trial lawyers on behalf of thousands of women who were not harmed by its products, the company filed for bankruptcy in 1995.

edly cited these numbers as if they were accurate. It was the Left's way, among other things, of demonstrating how callous America is to its own people—especially under a Republican administration. The numbers, however, were beyond wildly exaggerated; they were made up. When finally questioned about his numbers by Ted Koppel on ABC's *Nightline*, Snyder admitted the numbers were invented. "Everybody said we want a number," Snyder told Koppel. "We got on the phone, we made a lot of calls, we talked to a lot of people, and we said, 'Okay, here are some numbers.' They have no meaning, no value."[72]

HUNGER IN AMERICA

After the massive homelessness issue was finally dismissed as hysteria, the Left focused attention on another alleged area of Americans' disdain for their fellow Americans—hunger. John Edwards, Democratic candidate for vice president of the United States in 2004, repeatedly proclaimed, "Thirty-five million Americans last year went hungry. . . . This [election] is about those 35 million people who are hungry every single year."

There was no truth to this charge. The only basis for it was a U.S. Department of Agriculture report that said that about 35 million Americans experienced "household food insecurity." That term does not, the USDA emphasized, mean hunger. It only means being forced to reduce "variety in their diets" or eat a "few basic foods" at various times of the year. If a country could sue for libel, America would have had cause to sue John Edwards and all those on the Left who repeat this falsehood.

PEANUTS

In 2005, according to the CDC, eleven Americans died of all food allergies—that is, adults as well as children, and from an allergy to any food, not just peanuts. Yet schools across America have banned peanuts and peanut butter, among the few protein-rich foods many children like to eat.[73] Compare this with about ten thousand children who are hospitalized each year for sports-related traumatic brain injuries. The hysteria has been led by school officials, the Asthma and Allergy Foundation of America, and *Consumer Reports*, a liberal magazine that helped stoke the hysteria about secondhand smoke. It is mind-boggling that schools have banned peanut butter. But in the Age of Hysteria, one child who might die suffices to ban a food for the millions of students who would benefit from it.

MAN-MADE GLOBAL WARMING

The most recent Left-wing induced crisis and hysteria appears to be over allegedly severe global warming caused by humans burning fossil fuels. Computer models suggest that the increased carbon dioxide in the earth's atmosphere will raise the earth's temperature so precipitously as to endanger much of civilization as we know it.

One must accept all of the following statements or the entire global warming edifice crumbles:

1. The earth is heating up at a dangerous rate.
2. The cause of that heating is mankind's burning of fossil fuels, releasing so much carbon dioxide into the atmosphere that it is the reason for the increase in the earth's temperature.
3. The final result of this heating of the earth's temperature will be catastrophe for mankind and the biosphere. For example, polar ice caps will melt, resulting in rising oceans that will drown coastal cities throughout the world and severe droughts will render drinking water so scarce, entire regions of the world will go to war over water.
4. Therefore, in order to avoid imminent worldwide disaster on an unprecedented scale, the industrialized world must significantly scale back its use of fossil fuels and

transfer trillions of dollars to poorer countries adversely affected by the affluent countries' warming of the globe.

If only one of the four propositions is incorrect, we have a new example of hysteria, and we have no reason to cause the Western world's economies to contract greatly enough to induce widespread unemployment and economic dislocation.

On statement 1: If the earth is not heating up dangerously, the entire issue is moot. There is some scientific dispute over whether the earth is heating up at all, and considerable dispute about whether it is doing so to world-endangering levels. Why else would the global warming alarmists have renamed "global warming" "climate change"?

Professor Mojib Latif, a climate expert at the Leibniz Institute at Kiel University in Germany and member of the UN Intergovernmental Panel on Climate Change (IPCC), the world's most significant organization arguing for the man-made global warming threat, said that recent fluctuations in ocean currents in the North Atlantic (Arctic oscillation) may signal cooler temperatures ahead, perhaps for the next thirty years (though he still believes that the even longer term trend is toward global warming).

In January 2012, sixteen eminent scientists published an article in the *Wall Street Journal* titled, "No Need to Panic About Global Warning." They included the president of the World Federation of Scientists, a Princeton University professor of physics, a Hebrew University professor of astrophysics, the former president of the New York Academy of Sciences, and others of similar stature:

In their column, they wrote, among other things:

The number of "scientific heretics" is growing with each passing year. The reason is a collection of stubborn scientific facts. . . .

Perhaps the most inconvenient fact is the lack of global warming for well over ten years now.

The lack of warming for more than a decade—indeed, the smaller-than-predicted warming over the twenty-two years in the UN's Intergovernmental Panel on Climate Change (IPCC) began issuing projections—suggests that computer models have greatly exaggerated how much warming additional CO_2 can cause.

On statement 2: If the earth is heating up, but there is a natural explanation for this—that is, if human beings burning fossil fuel is not the primary cause—the issue is moot. And this may be the case. After all, the earth experienced much hotter periods before there was any fossil fuel burning, and before there were any human beings.

Denis G. Rancourt, professor of physics and an environmental science researcher at the University of Ottawa, has written that "even doubling the present atmospheric CO_2 concentration, to the unattainable value of 800 ppm (parts per million) say, without changing anything else in the atmosphere, would have little discernable effect on global temperature or climate."[74]

Dr. Willie Soon, an astrophysicist at the Solar and Stellar Physics division of the Harvard-Smithsonian Center for Astrophysics, argues, "Saying the climate system is completely dominated by how much carbon dioxide we have in the system is crazy—completely wrong. . . . Carbon dioxide is not the major driver for the earth-climate system."[75]

So, too, the earth has been much colder, also having nothing to do with human beings. We know, for instance, that ice ages have come and gone throughout the earth's history. In fact, as recently as the 1970s, there were widespread scientific predictions of global cooling. George Will gathered some representative statements from scientific and liberal news, predicting global cooling:

In the 1970s, "a major cooling of the planet" was "widely considered inevitable" because it was "well established" that the Northern Hemisphere's climate "has been getting cooler

since about 1950" (The New York Times, May 21, 1975).
Although some disputed that the "cooling trend" could
result in "a return to another ice age" (the Times, Sept. 14,
1975), others anticipated "a full-blown 10,000-year ice age"
involving "extensive Northern Hemisphere glaciation" (Science
News, March 1, 1975, and Science magazine, Dec. 10, 1976,
respectively). The "continued rapid cooling of the Earth"
(Global Ecology, 1971) meant that "a new ice age must now
stand alongside nuclear war as a likely source of wholesale death
and misery" (International Wildlife, July 1975). "The world's
climatologists are agreed" that we must "prepare for the next
ice age" (Science Digest, February 1973). Because of "ominous
signs" that "the Earth's climate seems to be cooling down,"
meteorologists were "almost unanimous" that "the trend will
reduce agricultural productivity for the rest of the century,"
perhaps triggering catastrophic famines (Newsweek cover story,
"The Cooling World," April 28, 1975).[76]

On statement 3: If the earth's temperature does rise and this
does not lead to massive catastrophe—in other words, if we humans
can adapt to the warmer temperatures or if the warmer temperatures
are in fact good for us—the issue is, again, moot. Rancourt: "There
is no known case of a sustained warming alone having negatively
impacted an entire population. If it were not for the global green-
house effect, the planet would on average be 33 C colder and [un]
inhabitable. As a general rule, all life on Earth does better when it's
hotter: Compare ecological diversity and biotic density (or biomass)
at the poles and at the equator . . ."[77]

On statement 4: Even if one accepts the first three premises, the
economic dislocation of the proposed remedies would render the
cure far worse for humanity than the disease. This is Danish professor Bjorn Lomborg's thesis. A committed environmentalist, named
one of the "50 people who could save the planet" by the Left-wing
newspaper the Guardian, Lomborg does believe the globe is getting
warmer. But he believes that so much more good could be done for

humanity for so much less money (fighting AIDS, distributing mosquito nets, etc.) than it would take to combat global warming that such massive funds would be wasted and ultimately harm the world.

The media have ignored the global warming denials of Richard Lindzen, the scientist who may be America's leading climatologist. An atmospheric physicist who is Alfred P. Sloan Professor of Meteorology at the Massachusetts Institute of Technology (MIT), Lindzen wrote in the *Wall Street Journal* in 2009, "It is generally accepted that a doubling of CO_2 will only produce a change of about two degrees Fahrenheit if all else is held constant. This is unlikely to be much to worry about," and "The basis for the weak IPCC [UN Intergovernmental Panel on Climate Change] argument for anthropogenic [man-made] climate change was shown to be false."[78]

Even more irresponsible than ignoring Lindzen, the media constantly report that there is an overwhelming "scientific consensus," indeed "97 percent" of all scientists agree on the man-made global warming thesis—yet the media ignore a petition on the Internet signed by more than 31,000 scientists, including 9,029 PhDs, 7,157 with a master's of science, and 12,715 with a bachelor of science degree, all of whom dispute the global warming thesis. Here is a listing they provided of their fields of expertise:

1. Atmospheric, environmental, and Earth sciences includes 3,805 scientists trained in specialties directly related to the physical environment of the Earth and the past and current phenomena that affect that environment.

2. Computer and mathematical sciences includes 935 scientists trained in computer and mathematical methods. Since the human-caused global warming hypothesis rests upon mathematical computer projections and not upon empirical observations, these sciences are especially important in evaluating this hypothesis.

3. Physics and aerospace sciences include 5,812 scientists trained in the fundamental physical and molecular prop-

erties of gases, liquids, and solids, which are essential to understanding the physical properties of the atmosphere and Earth.

4. Chemistry includes 4,822 scientists trained in the molecular interactions and behaviors of the substances of which the atmosphere and Earth are composed.[79]

The scientist who organized this "Global Warming Petition Project" was Professor Frederick Seitz, one of America's most honored physicists. Seitz, who died in 2008, was president of the National Academy of Sciences, the highest honor a scientist in America can attain. He was also president of Rockefeller University. He received the National Medal of Science and numerous other awards, including honorary doctorates from thirty-two universities around the world. Seitz wrote on the home page of his Petition Project, "Research data on climate change do not show that human use of hydrocarbons is harmful."

The media have likewise ignored sixty Canadian scientists, all of whom are accredited experts in climate and related disciplines, who published an open letter to the Canadian prime minister in which they concluded: "Observational evidence does not support today's computer climate models."[80]

The media have ignored Claude Allegre of France, a member of both the French Academy of Sciences and the National Academy of Sciences, and a former French minister of education (Socialist Party). Allegre argues that the vast amount of money governments have thrown at scientists who advocate the man-made global warming theory has distorted science.

There are other scientists with impeccable reputations all over the world who have taken issue with the man-made-global-warming-leading-to-catastrophe hypothesis. But given the Left-wing bias of the world's news media, they are rarely given attention. In addition, the Left has done to these people what it normally does to opponents—demonize them. Anyone who is skeptical of any of the four propositions is labeled "anti-science," and any scientist who expresses skepticism is accused of being in the pay of energy companies despite the fact that the vast majority of global warming research money is made available only to scientists who have sided with the Left's view of the issue.

For the record, the previously mentioned professor Denis Rancourt, a major global warming expert, is a radical Leftist: "I argue that by far the most destructive force on the planet is power-driven financiers and profit-driven corporations and their cartels backed by military might; and that the global warming myth is a red herring that contributes to hiding this truth. In my opinion, activists who, using any justification, feed the global warming myth have effectively been co-opted, or at best neutralized."[81]

It is too early to state definitively that what we have here is another expression of Left-wing hysteria. We do know that if we enact the Left's prescriptions to dramatically slash carbon emissions, the Western world would experience a severe economic depression, government power would greatly expand, and individual liberty would contract.

So, both sides need to be honest: The vast majority of people who believe the man-made global warming leading to calamity prognosis know nothing about climate science, and the vast majority of skeptics also know nothing about climate science. On this issue, we all choose what to believe and, more important, what to do. I choose to join the skeptics because an extraordinary number of scientists—tens of thousands—consider the prognostications to be either outright wrong or greatly exaggerated; because I am not prepared to wreck the Western world's economy, which is already on the brink of debt-caused collapse; because computer models predicting what may happen in half a century are not compelling; because climate has always changed (sometimes dramatically) without any human influence; because climate is extremely complex and quite beyond anyone's current ability to predict with certitude; and because the people pushing this thesis have been wrong regarding every crisis and hysteria they have heretofore asked the rest of us to believe in.

When you cry wolf ten times, many people are not inclined to change their lives on the eleventh.

WHY THE NEED FOR CRISES?

What does the Left gain by making up or exaggerating crises—to the point of frightening children as it did at the Democratic National Convention and does in schools throughout America? And why do so many ordinary people Left of center believe these "crises"?

First, the more things one fears, the more one is likely to hold Left-wing positions. This is not an impressive characteristic, but it is not meant only as criticism. It is also a statement about the sincerity of Left-wing hysteria. Most people on the Left really do fear for the viability of the earth because of carbon emissions, really do believe that 35 million Americans go hungry, that 150,000 girls and women die from anorexia each year, that monkey bars and dodgeball and peanuts are too dangerous for children, that secondhand smoke is a major killer, and so on.

Second, since the wish to create a utopia is central to Leftism, there is little tolerance for risk. After all, "better safe than sorry"—so why allow anything that can hurt a child in schools?

Third, hysterias usually demand far more government intervention in people's lives. Leftism trusts the state—when run by the Left—not the individual.

And, finally, and most significantly, it seems to be a law of life that *those who do not confront the greatest evils will confront lesser ones.* Most humans know the world is morally disordered, and people therefore try to fight what they deem to be most responsible for that disorder. The Right tends to fight human evil; Communism and Islamism are two examples. The Left has generally avoided confronting such evils, but it does fight. And what it tends to fight are considerably lesser threats, often non-evils.

First and foremost the Left fights those who do fight the great evils. Anti-Communists were vilified and anyone who uses the term *Islamofascism* is likewise vilified.

The Left fights:

1. The Right
2. Judeo-Christian influence
3. Socioeconomic inequality
4. Environmental threats
5. Big businesses—such as "big oil," "big pharma," "big tobacco," and the "military-industrial complex" (while supporting "big law," "big labor," and "big government").

A good example of what the Left fights instead of great evils—or, if you will, what the Left defines as great evil—was stated on the cover of the first "Green Issue" of the popular Left-wing magazine *Vanity Fair*: "A Graver Threat than Terrorism: Global Warming."[82]

The notion that global warming is a graver threat than terrorism is astonishing. Human beings are incomparably more threatened, to cite one example, from the terror-sponsoring regime of Iran obtaining nuclear weapons than by carbon emissions.

The *Vanity Fair* cover reinforces the conviction that while fine people can have Left-wing views, individuals who think morally clearly will not have these views. To argue that global warming is a graver threat than terrorism is to betray a callousness to human suffering that has long characterized the affluent Western environmentalist Left. For example, it kept pushing for worldwide bans on the pesticide DDT despite the fact that these bans led to millions—yes, millions—of preventable deaths in Africa and elsewhere from malaria.

Conservatives are more concerned with human evil than with ever cleaner air, the fate of the three-inch delta smelt fish, or the possibility that fifty to a hundred years from now human carbon dioxide emissions may lead to the flooding of some coastal areas. So they hold the opposite view: that Islamic terror—and human evil in general—is a far graver threat than global warming.

A cover of *Time* magazine was even clearer in depicting the Left's substitution of fighting evil with fighting for the environment.

The cover took the iconic Joe Rosenthal photograph of American Marines raising the American flag on Iwo Jima and replaced the flag with a tree. The cover story called green "the new red, white and blue."[83]

Needless to say, American veterans groups thought the *Time* cover morally obscene. But for the Left, trees are their flag; environmentalists are their Marines; and carbon emissions (and the Right) are the enemy. It would be difficult to imagine a clearer indication that the Left avoids fighting the greatest evils and instead fights lesser ones.

5. *Creating, Then Protecting, Victims*

FROM MARX UNTIL TODAY, victim groups have played an indispensable role in Leftist success. Without victim groups, the Left cannot succeed. They enable the Left to play the role of savior—without us, groups A, B, and C would be devastated. And they enable the Left to villainize the Right—were it not for the Right, those groups would not be suffering.

In the United States, the Left identifies blacks, Latinos, women, gays, Muslims, and the poor as the primary victim groups. They are, in the Marxist vernacular, "oppressed" groups, victims, respectively, of racism, xenophobia, sexism, homophobia, Islamophobia, and "rapacious capitalism."

The harm done by the Left to individual members of most of these groups and to American society generally has been incalculable. Since the 1960s, the media, schools, and the Democratic Party have told black Americans that the United States is a racist society. Imagine being a black child in America constantly told that the white majority disdains you. It is difficult to overstate how harmful that is. Why work hard? The society is out make you fail. Why befriend whites? They can't be trusted and they have no desire to befriend you. And the harm done to blacks by affirmative action has already been described.

Moreover, it is a lie. The United States is the least racist multi-racial country in the world. It is probably the best place in the world for a black to live—which is why almost no black Americans have decided to leave America for anywhere, including black Africa; and it is why more black Africans have immigrated to America than were sent over as slaves.

But the day most blacks acknowledge how little racism there is in America is the day they stop automatically voting Democrat. It is impossible to deny the fact that the less that blacks, women, Latinos, gays, and Muslims see themselves as victims of America, the less the appeal of the Democratic Party. It would take a willingness to lose elections for the American Left to stop labeling these groups as victims. We therefore have a troubling situation—it is vital to the very survival of the Democratic Party to portray as many groups as possible as victims.

One of the many destructive consequences of the Left-wing labeling of white Americans as racist is that many white Americans stopped reacting normally to blacks out of fear that something they may say will be construed as racist. To cite an illustrative example, as a radio talk show host, I was shown a video of people reacting to radio talk shows. Organized by a firm that specializes in analyzing such shows, the members of the listening panel were carefully chosen to represent all major listening groups within American society. I quickly noticed something odd, however. There were no blacks among the selected listeners. I asked why. And the response was stunning.

Blacks had always been included in these listener test groups, I was told, but not anymore. This was not because the firm was uninterested in black listeners; on the contrary, blacks compose a significant segment of the radio audience. They were not invited because the company had discovered that almost no whites would publicly differ with the opinions of the blacks on the panel. Once a black listener spoke, whites stopped saying what they thought, if what they thought differed from what a black had said.

Left-wing political correctness has created an environment in which one who differs with a black is not perceived as merely disagreeing with him, but as "dissing" him. Former Harvard University president Lawrence Summers asked Professor Cornel West, a black academic superstar then still at Harvard, to engage in more scholarship and less rap music making and political activism (West had been a major figure in the Al Sharpton campaign for president). The result? West announced that Summers had shown him "disrespect," as if demanding more professional work from a black professor is disrespectful. The lesson was clear: Even a Harvard president doesn't tell a black professor what to do. West then went to Princeton, where he continued to do little worthwhile in the intellectual arena.

In sum, a combination of political necessity—we can't allow blacks to leave the Democratic Party—and white guilt has led the Left to pursue policies and foster attitudes that have done real damage to black America and to America generally. This is especially true of the Left's positions that blacks cannot be judged by the same standards as others—manifest from lowering standards of admission to universities and on civil service exams, to blaming whites for the high number of black men in prison for violent crimes, to denying black racism exists.[84]

So we now have, thanks to the Left, precisely the opposite situation from the one we sought—that blacks be treated just like anyone else, and certainly as any white would be.

The Left's Moral Record

T HE ENDURING MYTH OF modern life is that the Left has been the greatest force for good in the world since its inception. That it has done some good is undeniable, and we will address this issue. But the reason for the endurance of this myth is not that it is based on truth but that the Left's story is told . . . by the Left. It is related in almost all schools and in almost all the media of the Western world.

On balance, the Left's moral record is among the worst of any organized group or idea in history. In the relatively brief period of time it has existed it has brought more death and misery to more people in more places than any other doctrine.

Of course, the greatest of the Left's evils have been committed by the far Left, by Communists. But much of the non-Communist Left supported the far Left until its atrocities became too well-known to deny. Even excluding Communism, the Left's record is one of almost continual moral confusion.

Virtually everything Leftism has touched it has made worse— morals, religion, art, education from elementary school to university, and the economic condition of the welfare states it created. There is a very real question of whether Western Europe is viable—and it is a question largely because of what Leftism has wrought there.

Communism: One of History's Great Evils

NOTHING IN WORLD HISTORY has equaled in such a short period of time the suffering brought about by Communism. Listed below are the numbers of civilians murdered by Communists in the twentieth century. These are civilians, not military casualties; and they are not civilian casualties of war. They are innocent civilians murdered by Communist regimes. The statistics are taken from the work of French scholars who wrote *The Black Book of Communism*, first published in France in 1997 and two years later in the United States. For those who assume that the book was published by some Right-wing press, it should be noted that the American edition was published by Harvard University Press (though one wonders how many courses at Harvard or any other university assign this book).

The numbers are generally considered conservative:

Soviet Union:	20 million
China:	65 million
Vietnam:	1 million
North Korea:	2 million
Cambodia:	2 million
Eastern Europe:	1 million
Latin America:	150,000
Africa:	1.7 million
Afghanistan:	1.5 million

"The total approaches 100 million people killed."[1]

These figures do not include the civilians enslaved, tortured, and raped. And they certainly do not include the billion or so people whose lives were ruined by deprivation of basic necessities of life and of elementary human rights.

Some will object to including Communist totalitarianism and mass murder in a book on the Left. They will argue that the vast majority of people on the Left outside of Communist countries cannot fairly be saddled with the crimes of the Communists.

There are a number of responses to this objection:

First, I am not saddling all people on the Left with what Communism has done. There were always individuals on the democratic Left who were in the anti-Communist camp. But it is fair to hold Leftism responsible for Communism and what it has wrought because Communism is a direct, though not necessarily inevitable, product of Leftism. Were there no Left, there never would have been Communism. On the other hand, were there no Right, there still would have been Nazism. Nazism was produced by racism, nationalist chauvinism, and it was specific to Germany.

Second, while not all Leftists supported Communism, and some strongly opposed it, most Leftists supported it (unlike many liberals, who, until the Vietnam War, were strong anti-Communists). Very many leading artists, writers, professors, and other intellectuals in non-Communist countries admired Communist regimes. And among those who did not, very few were anti-Communist. The Left successfully demonized anti-Communism as a Right-wing movement—which, to the everlasting credit of the Right, turned out to be largely true.

Third, there is no Right-wing equivalent to Communism's record of enslavement and murder. The only competitor was Nazism, which murdered, according to the latest data compiled by Yale professor Timothy Snyder, about 12 million civilians.[2] Even if one labels Nazism "Right-wing"—and the truth is that it was neither Right-wing nor Left-wing; it was a uniquely German form of murderous racism—non-democratic Leftist regimes murdered about ten times as many innocents as non-democratic Rightist ones and enslaved hundreds of times more.

Fourth, while major figures on the Left supported Lenin, then Stalin, then Mao, then Castro and other Communist tyrants, there were virtually no conservative or Right-wing figures of any prominence who defended Nazism. And after World War II, there were no Nazi parties beyond a few cranks in some societies, while there remain vibrant Communist parties throughout the world.

The number of innocents killed by Leftist movements dwarfs

the numbers killed by any other movement in a comparable period of time at any time in history, and certainly in the modern world. The Church, a favorite target of the Left, hardly competes. For example, in its nearly five hundred years of existence the Inquisition killed approximately five thousand people. And that ended more than five hundred years ago, when barbarity was the norm.

WHY DOESN'T COMMUNISM HAVE AS BAD A NAME AS NAZISM?

Given the amount the human suffering Communists have caused, why is *Communist* so much less a term of revulsion than *Nazi*? When people describe particularly evil individuals or regimes, why do they use the terms *Nazi* or *fascist* but almost never *Communist*? And, unlike Hitler, Communist mass murderers are rarely used as examples of evil incarnate. Sometimes, in fact, they are used in a heroic or even entertaining way. There are "Mao" restaurants in various cities in the Western world. It is unlikely that there are any "Hitler" restaurants in the West. So, too, while Che Guevara T-shirts and posters are ubiquitous, there is nothing similar celebrating a Nazi, or fascist, or perhaps any non-Communist killer.

Here are some reasons:

1. Communists murdered their own people; the Nazis murdered others. Mao was responsible for the deaths of about 65 million people—*nearly every one in peacetime*—all of them Chinese. Likewise, the tens of millions of people that Stalin had killed were nearly all Soviet citizens. The Nazis, on the other hand, killed relatively few fellow Germans. Their victims were Jews, Slavs, and other "non-Aryan" groups.

"World opinion"—that vapid, amoral concept—deems the murder of members of one's group less noteworthy than the murder of outsiders. That is one reason blacks killing millions of fellow blacks in Congo elicits virtually no attention from "world opinion." Between 1998 and 2008, according to the International Rescue Committee, 5.4 million people in Congo were killed, and virtually no one in the world knows this.³ But if a few Iraqi prisoners are sexually humiliated in an American-run prison, or if one Palestinian dies at the hands of an Israeli soldier, the story is on the front pages of the world's newspapers.

2. Communism was based on altruistic-sounding theories while Nazism was based on heinous-sounding theories. Communism's words are far more intellectually and morally appealing than the unintellectual racism of Nazism. As a result, the monstrous evils of Communists and Marxists are dismissed as perversions of a beautiful doctrine.*

Nazi atrocities, on the other hand, have been perceived (correctly) as the logical and inevitable results of Nazi ideology.

3. There is widespread ignorance of Communist atrocities compared to those of the Nazis. As Barry Gewen, an editor of the *New York Times Book Review*, acknowledged, "We are all familiar with personal accounts of the Holocaust and the Gulag, less so with descriptions of the torture chamber that was Mao's China."⁴ Whereas both Right and Left loathe Nazism and teach its evils in detail, the Left's dominance of the teaching profession has meant that Communist atrocities are rarely taught.

Moreover, when Communist atrocities are taught, they are rarely labeled "Communist," let alone "Leftist." Soviet atrocities are attributed to "Stalin" or "Stalinism"; Chinese atrocities, when they are noted at all, are attributed to "Maoism"; Cambodia's genocide is attributed to Pol Pot, and North Korea's autogenocide through starvation and concentration camps is blamed on Kim Il Sung and his successors, never on Communism. Nazism, on the other hand, is blamed by name for its atrocities—rarely "Hitlerism"—and often

---

* It is important to note that the people who offer this excuse for Leftist doctrines never offer that excuse for Christians who committed evil in the name of Christianity. The Left attributes evil committed in Christendom to Christianity (though none of the immense good that has emanated from within the Christian world is attributed to Christianity), while the evils committed by Marxists in the name of Marxism are dismissed as perversions of Marxism, and the evils committed by Muslims in the name of Islam are dismissed as perversions of Islam. Only Christians, Americans, and capitalists who commit evil are true to their Christianity, true to their imperialist and racist doctrines, and true to capitalism.

labeled "fascism" so as to lump Nazism with Right-wing groups the Left labels "fascist."

Another reason for the relative ignorance of Communist atrocities is that Germany has thoroughly exposed the evils of Nazism, taken responsibility for them, and attempted to atone for them. Russians have not done anything similar regarding Lenin's or Stalin's horrors. Indeed, an ex-KGB operative, Vladimir Putin, became the most powerful man in post-Soviet Russia; Lenin remained widely revered; and, in the words of University of London Russian historian Donald Rayfield, "people still deny by assertion or implication, Stalin's holocaust."[5] China is even worse. That country has thus far exposed no crimes of Mao and the Chinese Communist Party. The image of Mao is ubiquitous in China, and the greatest mass murderer and enslaver of all time remains officially revered in China. Until Russia and China—and the world's Left—do what Germany has done and acknowledge and report the monstrous evils they—and Cambodian, Vietnamese, and Cuban Communists—have committed, humanity will remain much less aware of Communism's evils than those of Nazism.

4. Communism won and Nazism lost World War II. The victors write history.

5. Nothing exactly matches the Holocaust. The rounding up of every possible man, woman, child, and baby of one ethnic/religious group and sending them to die is unparalleled. The Communists killed far more people than the Nazis did but did not match the Holocaust in the systematization of murder. The uniqueness of the Holocaust as well as the enormous attention paid to it since then has helped ensure that Nazism has a worse name than Communism.

6. Finally, in the view of the Left, which is the prevailing view in the Western world, the last "good war" America fought was World War II, the war against Nazism and against Japanese fascism. The Left does not regard America's wars against Communist regimes as good wars. The war against Vietnamese Communism is regarded as immoral and the war against Korean (and Chinese) Communism is largely ignored.

The Decline of Europe

SINCE 1960, THE LEFT has always pointed to Europe in order to prove how effective Left-wing policies are. The American Left has sought to transform America into the image of Western Europe. We are living, however, at precisely the time during which Left-wing European dreams are crumbling. The Left-wing assault on God and religion, specifically Christianity, has left Europe morally weakened—why fight for anything or for anyone?—and secularism has bred a crushing materialist ennui.

Moreover the Left-wing welfare state is financially unsustainable. The president of the European Council, Herman Van Rompuy, acknowledged in 2010, "We can't finance our social model."

European debt—the result of the welfare state and of far too many government employees—will either lead to the end of the European Union, the end of the welfare state, a depression, or all three.

And the third pillar of Left-wing Europe—multiculturalism—also failed. In 2011, the three major European leaders—British prime minister David Cameron, French president Nicolas Sarkozy, and German chancellor Angela Merkel—all declared multiculturalism a failure.

Cameron: "Under the doctrine of state multiculturalism, we have encouraged different cultures to live separate lives, apart from each other and the mainstream . . ."[6] "We have even tolerated these segregated communities behaving in ways that run counter to our values."[7]

Sarkozy: "'We have been too concerned about the identity of the person who was arriving and not enough about the identity of the country that was receiving him,' he [Sarkozy] said in a television interview in which he declared the concept [multiculturalism] a failure."[8]

Merkel: "The approach [to build] a multicultural [society] and to live side by side and to enjoy each other . . . has failed, utterly failed."[9]

Multiculturalism is a Left-wing-induced failure in the United

States as well. Here is a perfect example of where the American value system, with "E Pluribus Unum" as one of its pillars, is needed in every society.

All these Left-wing ideas have led to the decline of the great European civilization.

Outside of sports and popular entertainment, how many living Germans, French, Austrians, or even Brits can any outsiders name? Even well-informed people who love art and literature and who follow developments in science and medicine would be hard-pressed to come up with names. In terms of greatness in literature, art, music, the sciences, philosophy, and medical breakthroughs, Europe's creativity is a shadow of what it was less than a hundred years ago. If you asked anyone the same question then, a plethora of world-renowned names would have flowed. Obvious examples would include (in alphabetical order): Brecht, Buber, Cezanne, Chekhov, Curie, Debussy, Eiffel, Einstein, Freud, Hesse, Kafka, Mahler, Mann, Marconi, Pasteur, Picasso, Proust, Strauss, Stravinsky, Tolstoy, Zeppelin, Zola. Not to mention the European immortals who lived in the century before them: Beethoven, Darwin, Dostoyevsky, Hugo, Kierkegaard, Manet, Monet, Mozart, and Van Gogh, to name only a few.

What happened?

What happened is that Europe, with a few exceptions, has lost its sense of purpose, and therefore largely lost its creativity, intellectual excitement, industrial innovation, and risk taking. Europe's creative energy has been largely sapped. Europeans are marrying less and less and are having so few children that most European countries' populations are in decline. There are many noble European individuals, but there aren't many creative, dynamic, or entrepreneurial ones—and many of them have chosen to live in America. The issues that preoccupy most Europeans are overwhelmingly material and self-centered: How many hours per week will I have to work? How much annual vacation time will I have? How many social benefits can I preserve (or increase)? How early can I retire? How can my country avoid fighting against anyone or for anyone?

This happened thanks to secularism, the big and powerful welfare state, and the war against national identity and culture. Any one of them alone is destructive to society. Together they are lethal. Even if one holds that religion is false, only a dogmatic and irrational secularist can deny that it was religion in the Western world that provided the impetus or backdrop for nearly all the great artistic, literary, political, economic, and even scientific advances of the West.

Religion in the West raised all the great questions of life: Why are we here? Is there purpose to existence? Were we deliberately made? Is there something after death? Are morals objective or only a matter of personal preference? Do rights come from the state or from the Creator? And religion gave positive responses: We are here because a benevolent God made us. There is, therefore, ultimate purpose to life. Good and evil are real. Death is not the end. Human rights are inherent since they come from God. And so on.

Secularism drains all this out of life. No one made us. Death is the end. We are no more significant than any other creatures. We are the result of chance. Make up your own meaning (existentialism) because life has none. Good and evil are ultimately euphemisms for "I like" and "I dislike."

When religion dies, creativity begins to die. Take Russia, for example. Christian Russia was backward in many ways, but it gave the world Dostoyevsky, Chekhov, Tolstoy, Pushkin, and Tchaikovsky. Once Christianity was suppressed, if not killed, Russia became a cultural wasteland (with a few exceptions like Shostakovich and Solzhenitsyn, the latter a devout Christian). This was largely the result of Lenin, Stalin, and Communism, but even where Communism did not take over, the decline of religion in Europe meant a decline in human creativity—except for nihilistic and/or absurd isms, which have greatly increased. As G. K. Chesterton noted at the end of the nineteenth century, when people stop believing in God they don't believe in nothing, they believe in anything. One not only thinks of the violent isms—Marxism, Marxism-Leninism, fascism, Maoism, and Nazism—but of all the non-violent isms that have become substitute religions, such as feminism, environmental-ism, and socialism.

The state saps creativity and dynamism just as much as secular-ism does. Why do anything for yourself when the state will do it for you? Why take care of others when the state will do it for you? Why have ambition when the state is there to ensure that few or no indi-viduals are rewarded more than others? America has been the center of energy and creativity in almost every area of life because it has remained far more religious than any other industrialized Western democracy and because enough of its citizens, until recently at least, have rejected the welfare state model and its mentality.

The Left argues that the state is essential to artistic excellence, but if this were the case, we would be living in a golden age of art. We aren't.

EUROPE'S NON-AMERICAN VALUES

The Large Welfare State

Europe believes in socialism—meaning the large welfare state, not pure socialism, which very few people believe in and which, in its pure definition, differs little from Communism—while America believes in free market capitalism. That is why Left-wing parties in Europe are nearly all named "Socialist" or "Social Democrat"—not because they advocate pure socialism, but because they advocate the welfare state in which the state is by far the most powerful force in society. The Left in America, and especially the Democratic Party, take offense when called or compared to socialists, but the critique is not meant literally. It refers to the way Western Europeans use the term. The proof is that one would be hard-pressed to name a single significant position about which the socialist parties of Europe and the Democratic Party in America differ.

Most Western Europeans believe in socialism as fervently as religious Christians, Jews, and Muslims believe in their respective religions. To many Americans, socialism may be only an economic system, but for Western Europeans and for the Left in America, it has largely replaced Christianity as their faith. That is why George Will calls Britain's National Health Service "the established religion" of Britain. How could it not be? It became, as he notes, the sixth-largest employer in the world—behind the Chinese army, Walmart, China National Petroleum, China State Grid Corporation, and Indian Railways.[10]

The United States not only rejects socialism, but it has been the chief obstacle to its spread—because of its power culturally, militarily, religiously, and economically.

Opposition to Nationalism

As a result of the massive bloodshed of the nationalism-based world wars, Western Europeans concluded that the abolition of national identities is a moral necessity. Europe's elite decided to believe in Europe and in the United Nations rather than in their individual nations. An English protestor quoted in the *Los Angeles Times* explained his protest of the war in Iraq in terms of support of the United Nations, not Britain: "[British prime minister Tony Blair] has totally misjudged how dangerous this has been to the United Nations. And we believe in the United Nations."[11]

While Europeans were losing faith in their national identities, Americans continued to affirm their faith in their national identity as vigorously as ever. While Europeans and the American Left have more faith in the moral judgment of the United Nations—where Libya under Qaddafi chaired the Human Rights Commission and where dictatorships like Syria and China vote in the Security Council—most Americans have more faith in America.

Pacifism

In Europe, another major ideological consequence of the two world wars was widespread belief that war is wrong. America, on the other hand, believes that morality often demands fighting evil.

The German example is particularly telling. Given how much the Germans, to their credit, have faced up to their terrible past—

specifically the Holocaust and World War II—one would assume that Germany had learned great lessons from that past. But it seems that with all their knowledge about Nazism, Germans have learned little about good and evil. They cannot confront and often cannot even recognize evil. A nation that saw Nazism defeated solely by armies has essentially embraced pacifism. A nation that saw what appeasement of evil leads to has come to embrace appeasement.

After 1945, one would have expected German leaders to stand up and say, "My fellow Germans, we know a Hitler when we see one; therefore all decent people must confront Leonid Brezhnev, or Saddam Hussein, or the Ayatollah Khomeini." But no German leader stood up to say this. Instead, a German minister of justice compared an American president to Hitler.[12] So, too, we would have expected German leaders to stand up and say, "My fellow Germans, we know genocidal anti-Semitism when we see it, and we see it in the Arab world." But no German leader stood up to say this, either.

Instead of learning to fight evil, Germans concluded that to fight is evil.

Unlike the United States, where members of the military are highly esteemed, German troops, when they return home, are warned not to wear their army uniform in public lest somebody beat them up:

"A staff sergeant, who had been risking his life almost daily outside Kunduz [Afghanistan], recalled a trip to Berlin during which he was wearing his uniform at a train stop. He was told to make himself scarce or he would be beaten up. 'It was shocking,' said the sergeant, Marcel B., who, according to German military rules, could not be fully identified. 'We're looked down on. With American soldiers, they tell me how they receive recognition, how people just come up to them and say they're doing good.' . . . Reinhold Robbe, the German Parliament's military commissioner, said he remained impressed by the memory of seeing on trips to Tampa and Washington and El Paso that 'complete strangers are buying soldiers beer.'"[13]

Secularism

European values affirm secularism and a godless life, while America remains the most religious among the industrialized democracies. That is a major reason that the predominance of America, a religious country that affirms the religion the European elites have rejected, infuriates many Europeans. One consequence of Europeans' secularism is a disdain for moral absolutes and moral judgments. Whether it was President Reagan calling the Soviet Union an "evil empire" or President Bush labeling North Korea, Iran, and Iraq an "axis of evil," most Europeans (and the American Left) found such moral labeling contemptible.

Thomas Jefferson and Benjamin Franklin suggested that the Great Seal of the United States depict the Israelites' exodus from Egypt. Just as the Israelites needed to leave Egypt, they and the other Founders knew that America had to separate from Europe. It is truer now than ever.

The Left's Moral Confusion

> *Someone who does not know the difference between good and evil*
> *is worth nothing.*
> —Miecyslaw Kasprzyk, Polish rescuer of Jews during the Holocaust [14]

It took a Polish rescuer of Jews in the Holocaust, cited sixty years after the liberation of the Auschwitz concentration and death camp, to best describe those people who cannot recognize, or refuse to acknowledge, the difference between good and evil.

Since the 1960s, with few exceptions, on the greatest questions of good and evil, the world's Left has been supportive of, or opposed to the opponents of, great evils. Though not necessarily pro-Communist, the Left was overwhelmingly anti-anti-Communist. Much of the Left would not identify Communist regimes as evil, and leading Leftists would offer strong support for Left-wing dictators from Ho to Castro to Chavez; have supported the terror-supporting, corrupt Palestinian Authority against the liberal democracy of Israel; and opposed the war against the Islamist-Baathist terrorists in post-Saddam Iraq. Within the United States, the Left has undermined the religious bases of American society, damaged universities, nearly ruined public education, and come close to bankrupting many local and state governments. As for Europe, as noted above, that once-great continent may simply not survive what the Left has done to it.

Leftists were morally confused when they admired Communist tyrants; when they condemned American arms as the greatest threat to world peace during and after the Cold War; when they condemned Israel's destruction of Saddam Hussein's Osirak nuclear reactor; and on and on. The Left frequently does "not know the difference between good and evil."

One reason is naïveté. From Communist evil to the evil of Islamism to the evil of violent criminals, naïveté about evil has been the key ingredient of Left-wing moral confusion. The day after Hamas, the Palestinian organization committed to Israel's destruction, won an electoral landslide in Gaza, the *Los Angeles Times* editorialized, "Most Palestinians, like most Israelis, want peace." [15]

That was wishful thinking. Most Palestinians have not wanted peace with Israel; they have not even recognized Israel as a Jewish state. To the extent they want peace, they have wanted peace without the Jewish State of Israel. In the words of an Israeli ambassador to the United States:

> Two Israeli peace proposals, in 2000 and 2008 . . . met virtually all of the Palestinians' demands for a sovereign state in the areas won by Israel in the 1967 war—in the West Bank, Gaza and even East Jerusalem. But Palestinian President Yasser Arafat rejected the first offer and Abbas ignored the second, for the very same reason their predecessors spurned the 1947 Partition Plan.
>
> Each time, accepting a Palestinian State meant accepting the Jewish State, a concession the Palestinians were unwilling to make.

That is the issue. Not settlements. Not boundaries. The Palestinians, like most of their fellow Arabs and like many Muslims elsewhere, have never acknowledged that the Jews came home to Israel because they have never acknowledged that the Jews ever had a national home there. And they don't even acknowledge that the Jews are a people.[16]

In September 2011, in Ramallah, the de facto capital of the Palestinian Authority, I interviewed Ghassan Khatib, director of government media for the Palestinian Authority and the spokesman for Palestinian president Mahmoud Abbas. He reiterated the same point: There is no Jewish people (only a religion called Judaism) and therefore there should be no Jewish state.[17]

But to the naive Left, "Most Palestinians, like most Israelis, want peace."

Another example of the Left's morally confused worldview is its tendency to blame many of the victims of Islamic terror.

After the 9/11 terror attacks, one widespread reaction among academics and in the media was to ask, "Why do they hate us?"—the implication being that America had done bad things to Muslims to arouse such hatred. The Left's response was not to absolve the terrorists from all moral blame, but to have America share it.

Was the Danish newspaper at least partially at fault for the deadly Muslim riots that followed its printing of cartoons depicting Muhammad? On the Left, the answer was yes. To fully blame the Muslim mobs who killed and burned and maimed would be to engage in Islamophobia.

Was Israel partially responsible for the terror unleashed against it? For many on the Left, the answer has been yes: Given the fact that Palestinians have no conventional weapons, what else are they supposed to do to rid themselves of Israeli occupation?

Was Spain at least partially responsible for the Islamist terror attacks on Madrid trains, killing 191 people and injuring 1,500 others? That is what the Spanish Left argued—that the attacks were

THE LEFT'S MORAL RECORD

the result of Spain sending troops into Iraq—and the argument led them to electoral victory and to removing all Spanish troops from Iraq.

Was France at least partially responsible for the mostly Muslim rioters who burned and looted for a month in 2005? For the Left, the answer was, of course. As the BBC reported on November 5, 2005, then interior minister "Sarkozy's much-quoted description of urban vandals as 'rabble' a few days before the riots began is said by many to have already created tension." Calling rabble "rabble" caused them to act like to rabble.

A man named Michael Berg, a Green Party candidate for Congress from Delaware, provides an excellent example of Left-wing moral thinking. Like many others on the Left, Berg expressed more antipathy toward President George W. Bush than toward the Islamist murderers Bush was fighting. Indeed, in Berg's view President Bush was "more of a terrorist than Zarqawi," the leading terrorist in Iraq at the time.

What makes Berg's opinion noteworthy is that Zarqawi had slit the throat of his son, Nick Berg, on an infamous Internet video. Berg's Left-wing worldview led him to say, "Zarqawi felt my son's breath on his hand as [he] held the knife against his throat. Zarqawi had to look in his eyes when he did it. George Bush sits there glassy-eyed in his office with pieces of paper and condemns people to death. That to me is a real terrorist."

When asked two years later on CNN about his reaction to the death of Zarqawi, his son's torturer and murderer, Berg responded: "Well, my reaction is I'm sorry whenever any human being dies. Zarqawi is a human being."

The incredulous CNN interviewer, Soledad O'Brien, then asked Berg, "At some point, one would think, is there a moment when you say, 'I'm glad he's dead, the man who killed my son'?" Berg responded: "No. How can a human being be glad that another human being is dead?"

One might add, as a postscript to the upside-down moral world of pacifism, another awful doctrine that appeals to the Left, talk-show host Michael Medved asked Berg if he would have killed Zar-qawi as the terrorist was about to cut his son's throat. Berg said he would instead have thrown his body in front of the knife. As Medved noted, that would have only ensured that two innocent people would be murdered.

Like other Left-wing international and domestic groups dedi-cated to human or civil rights, Amnesty International (AI), which was founded largely to combat torture, devolved into another pre-dictably anti-American, morally confused organization. That devo-lution was made apparent when Amnesty listed the United States as a major violator of human rights. On what grounds did the orga-nization label the United States, perhaps the freest country in the world, with major protections of civil and human rights, a violator of human rights? On the grounds that the United States executes murderers.

To the world's Left, every murderer has a human right not to be executed. Therefore a country that executes a mass mur-derer is in the same moral league as countries that execute political dissidents.

Whenever Amnesty International takes a position that is also held by the Left, it is likely to be morally confused, as occurred in 2005 when the then secretary general of the organization, Irene Khan, branded the U.S. prison camp at Guantánamo Bay "the gulag of our times." After moral outrage in the United States and presum-ably among survivors of the Soviet Gulag, Amnesty International defended Khan. Among her defenders was the American head of AI, William Schultz, who said on the television show *Hardball* that there is a difference only "in scale" between Gulag and Guantá-namo, but otherwise the comparison is apt.

Here is the scale. Is the comparison apt? At Guantánamo at that time, there were about 520 prisoners, the vast majority, if not all, of whom were rounded up in antiterror warfare. They were deemed nonuniformed terrorists and therefore not subject to Geneva con-vention rules on prisoners. But they were, as even Schultz acknowledged, provided with medical care, with a fine diet that honored their religious codes, and allowed to practice their religion.

On the other hand, the 20 to 30 million prisoners sent to the string of camps across the Soviet Union known as the Gulag Archipelago were innocent of any crime, obtained no medical care, were served portions of food often inadequate to human survival, and were frozen and worked to death in the millions. Every prisoner of the Gulag would have given anything to be a prisoner in Guantánamo.

Comparing Guantánamo to "Gulag" smeared America and trivialized the suffering and death of tens of millions of people. But smearing America and trivializing evil are characteristics of the Left. The *New York Times* editorial page defended AI's Gulag-Guantánamo comparison, and I found no major Left-wing media, other than the *Washington Post*, that denounced it. The reason the *Post* condemned Amnesty International was that Anne Applebaum, author of a definitive work on the Gulag, sat on the newspaper's editorial board. She knew how immoral the comparison was. She actually knew what happened in the Gulag. I believe that most members of the press do not, given the ignorance of Communist atrocities among most of the world's journalists. Proof? An Associated Press report printed in the *Washington Post* and countless other newspapers described the Gulag this way: "Thousands of prisoners of the so-called gulags died from hunger, cold, harsh treatment and overwork." [18]

"Thousands"? Having graduates of universities that rarely teach about Communist mass murder, it is understandable that the Associated Press would write of "thousands of prisoners of the so-called gulags." Imagine, however, if a mainstream media organization had written about "thousands of Jewish prisoners of so-called Nazi concentration camps died from hunger, cold, harsh treatment, and overwork."

For the record, here are some comparisons between the Gulag and Guantánamo as compiled from Applebaum's book by David Bosco. [19]

Individuals detained: Gulag—20 million. Guantánamo—750 total.

Number of camps: Gulag—476 separate camp complexes comprising thousands of individual camps. Guantánamo—five small camps on the U.S. military base in Cuba.

Reasons for imprisonment: Gulag—Hiding grain; owning too many cows; need for slave labor; being Jewish; being Finnish; being religious; being middle class; having had contact with foreigners; refusing to sleep with the head of Soviet counterintelligence; telling a joke about Stalin. Guantánamo—Fighting for the Taliban in Afghanistan; being suspected of links to Al Qaeda and other terrorist groups.

Red Cross visits: Gulag—none that Bosco could find. Guantánamo—regular visits from January 2002.

Deaths as a result of poor treatment: Gulag—at least 2–3 million (Bosco inexplicably understates). Guantánamo—no reports of prisoner deaths.

Irene Khan's comparison of Guantánamo to Gulag was morally grotesque. But it was not grotesque to Amnesty International, the *New York Times*, or others on the Left.

Another example of Left-wing moral confusion was its reaction to a lecture given by Pope Benedict XVI on September 12, 2006, at the University of Regensburg, in Germany. In the course of the lecture on the subject of faith and reason, Pope Benedict cited the Byzantine emperor Manuel II Paleologus (1350–1425). The emperor had some critical things to say about Islam, specifically about the relative unimportance of reason in Islam and the spread of Islam via the sword.

The speech resulted in riots in parts of the Islamic world and intense criticism of the pope by the world's Left. The same people who have charged that Pope Pius XII was too silent about the evils of his time (specifically, the Nazi annihilation of European Jewry) took Benedict to task for even suggesting that something was morally awry within the Islamic world.

The *New York Times* editorial page argued that Benedict will create only more anti-Western Muslim violence. But that was exactly the excuse defenders of Pius XII offered for why Pius XII did not speak out more forcefully—that he was afraid it would engender only more Nazi violence against the Jews and others. Yet Pius's critics understandably dismissed that excuse out of hand.

Karen Armstrong, a widely read scholar of religion as well as a former nun, wrote of Pius XII that his "apparent failure to condemn the Nazis has become a notorious scandal." Moral and logical consistency suggest that she would welcome a pope who did confront today's greatest evils. But she joined those condemning Pope Benedict. She wrote (putting these arguments in the mouths of affronted Muslims with whom she sympathized): "The Catholic Church is ill-placed to condemn violent jihad when it has itself . . . under Pope Pius XII, tacitly condoned the Nazi Holocaust."

The argument can only be explained by the Left's desire to condemn the Catholic Church and to defend Islam. How do you condemn the silence of one pope when confronted with evil in his time and condemn another pope when confronting evil in his time? And, if indeed the Church is guilty of condoning evil in the past, why does that render it "hypocritical" to confront evil in the present? If my grandfather was a murderer, am I a hypocrite for condemning murder?

John Cornwell, the author of a scathingly critical book about Pius XII, *Hitler's Pope*, also condemned Pope Benedict. He described the pope's words about Muhammad and Islamic violence as "incendiary" and "abrasive" (calling Pius XII "Hitler's Pope" was not incendiary and abrasive?), and he criticized Benedict for "having said that dialogue with Islam was difficult."

Another illustration of the Left's inverted moral universe concerns Cuba.

For example, in April 2009, seven members of the Congressional Black Caucus[20] visited Cuba, where they met with the dictators of Cuba, Fidel and Raul Castro. They were impressed with Fidel

Castro, the longest-reigning dictator in the world, the man who deprived generations of Cubans of the most fundamental human rights.

Representative Laura Richardson: "He looked right into my eyes and said, 'How can we help you? How can we help President Obama?'"

Representative Bobby Rush: "I think that what really surprised me, but also endeared me to him was his keen sense of humor, his sense of history and his basic human qualities. . . . He drank water, we drank water, nothing else was served, but that was just fine! I was, after all, in the presence of history. . . . In my household, I told Castro, he is known as the ultimate survivor."

Regarding this last comment, columnist Mona Charen pithily noted: "Funny how easy it is to survive when you don't hold elections."[21]

But most egregious was that these black members of Congress would not even meet with the leading black dissident in Cuba, who was on a hunger strike at the very time the CBC members visited.[22]

On its website, the Congressional Black Caucus calls itself "the conscience of the Congress since 1971." Another good example of Left-wing self-esteem.

The number of Leftists in the arts who visited and praised Castro was probably as proportionately large as the number of Leftists in politics who did so. Hollywood director Steven Spielberg, known for his noble work outside of filmmaking as well as for his morally significant films such as *Schindler's List* and *Saving Private Ryan*, visited Fidel Castro in November 2002. According to Cuban news media, he described his meeting as "the eight most important hours of my life."[23] Spielberg's visit is an example of good men being misled because of their Leftism.*

---

* This is a significant arena of Leftist damage. Leftism morally confuses otherwise decent people. How else is one to explain Spielberg's long and laudatory visit? How else can one explain *New York Times* columnist Thomas Friedman writing that the only reason the members of Congress gave Israel's prime minister Benjamin Netanyahu standing ovations was that they were "bought and paid for by the Israel lobby"? Why would a self-identifying Jew write an out-and-out anti-Semitic statement? Because of Leftism. Leftism not only poisons institutions; it poisons individuals.

The Left and Israel is another area where the Left confuses moral norms.

Just as anti-Americanism finds a home on the Left, so does hostility to Israel. Virtually every Left-wing group in the Western world has been active in undermining Israel's security, economy, and often even its legitimacy as a Jewish state. This is true of Left-wing labor unions (outside the United States), political parties (other than the Democratic Party in the United States), religious groups, media, and professors, as well as feminist, gay rights, and civil rights groups. Even the American Library Association has sponsored anti-Israel events.

Here is a small list of the many boycotts of Israel and/or economic divestment from Israel. All are Left-wing organizations.

- In 2004, the General Assembly of the Presbyterian Church (U.S.A.) voted to "initiate a process of phased selective divestment in multinational corporations operating in Israel."[24]
- In 2005, a major regional council of Norway passed a motion calling for a comprehensive boycott of Israeli goods. The council, Sør-Trøndelag, includes Trondheim, Norway's third-largest city.[25]
- In 2006, the Ontario division of Canada's largest union, the Canadian Union of Public Employees, voted to support an international campaign to boycott Israel.[26]
- Shortly thereafter the Congress of South African Trade Unions published a letter expressing their support for the Canadian union's boycott of Israel.[27]
- In 2006, the Church of England's General Synod overwhelmingly voted to divest from companies whose products are used by Israel in the Palestinian territories. The Archbishop of Canterbury voted for divestment.[28]
- In 2007, Britain's biggest journalists union, the forty-thousand-member National Union of Journalists, voted

in favor of "a boycott of Israeli goods similar to those boycotts in the struggles against apartheid South Africa led by trade unions, and to demand sanctions be imposed on Israel by the British government."[29]

- In 2008, Ireland's largest public sector and services trade union, the Irish Municipal, Public, and Civil Trade Union, endorsed a boycott of Israeli goods and services.[30]

- In 2009, Britain's 6.5-million member labor federation the Trade Union Congress called for a consumer-led boycott and sanctions campaign against Israel. The Fire Brigade Union, Britain's largest trade union, Unite, and the largest public sector union, Unison, all called for a complete boycott of all Israeli products.[31]

- Professors and students in most universities in the Western world regularly sponsor anti-Israel days, anti-Israel weeks, divestment seminars, etc.

The power of Leftist ideas such as hostility to Israel is so great that some of the most anti-Israel and anti-Jewish Leftist voices are those of Left-wing Jews.

Norman Finkelstein is one such example. The son of Holocaust survivors, he is a former assistant professor at DePaul University who has devoted his life to attacking Israel—which he has called, among other things, a "lunatic state" and a "vandal state"—and to attacking the "Holocaust industry," the title of one of his books and his term for Elie Wiesel's work and for Jewish organizations and individuals that are professionally involved with the Holocaust. He has written that Jewish organizations "steal, and I do use the word with intent, 95 percent of the monies earmarked for victims of Nazi persecution."[32]

Jews, he says, "are not Zionist by conviction, they are Zionist because it is useful for their political and more recently financial self-interest."[33]

In a lecture delivered in Beirut, Lebanon, Finkelstein likened

Israeli actions to "Nazi practices" during World War II, albeit with some added "novelties to the Nazi experiments."[34]

The best-known example of an anti-Israel Jewish Leftist is MIT professor Noam Chomsky. He, too, has devoted his life to attacking America and Israel; he is alienated from, and vilifies, the two identities into which he was born, American and Jewish. In the late 1970s, Chomsky even signed a petition defending a Holocaust-denying French academic named Robert Faurisson. The petition contained this statement about Faurisson: He "has been conducting extensive research into the 'Holocaust' question."

Note the quotation marks around the word *Holocaust*, and the use of word *research*. The latter refers to statements of Faurisson such as his denial of use of gas to murder Jews: "so-called gassings [are a] gigantic politico-financial swindle whose beneficiaries are the state of Israel and international Zionism." Other Faurisson research has been devoted to "proving" that the diary of Anne Frank was a fraud.[35]

In 2006, Chomsky traveled to Lebanon to appear with Sayyed Nasrallah, the leader of Hezbollah, in order to lend his support to that group, which is committed to the annihilation of Israel and listed as a terrorist organization by the United States.

A third example of a Left-wing Jew who has devoted much of his life to weakening Israel (and the United States) is George Soros, the immensely wealthy financier. He, too, was born to Jewish parents, but affirms no Jewish identity. He is one of the many Left-wing Jews who do great harm to the Jewish people, even though not personally anti-Semitic.[36] As described by Martin Peretz, editor in chief of the *New Republic*, "George Soros is ostentatiously indifferent to his own Jewishness. He is not a believer. He has no Jewish communal ties. He certainly isn't a Zionist. He told Connie Bruck in the *New Yorker*—testily, she recounted—that 'I don't deny the Jews their right to a national existence—but I don't want to be part of it.'"

Writing in the *Wall Street Journal*, Joshua Muravchik reported that Soros has publicly likened Israel to the Nazis.[37] Though opposed to Jewish nationalism, Soros does support Palestinian nationalism. That is a consistent position of the Left: American nationalism and Jewish nationalism are bad; anti-Jewish and anti-American nationalisms are good.

He and others are what are called "non-Jewish Jews," a term attributed to the Jewish historian Isaac Deutscher, who wrote an essay with that title in 1954. It describes the individual who, though born a Jew (Judaism consists of a national/peoplehood identity as well as a religious one), identifies only as a citizen of the world (therefore the appeal of Leftism), not as a Jew, either nationally or religiously.

There have been many non-Jewish Jews since Jews were allowed to leave their European ghettos and assimilate. But a small though significant percentage of them became radicalized. In effect substituting Leftism for Judaism, they came to loathe "bourgeois," that is, traditional middle-class, values and Judeo-Christian society, Western national identities, and particularly loathed Jewish religious and national identity.

Karl Marx, the grandson of two Orthodox rabbis, wrote one of the most significant anti-Semitic essays of the nineteenth century: "On the Jewish Question" (1844). In it he wrote that "[m]oney is the jealous god of Israel, beside which no other god may exist. . . . The god of the Jews has been secularized and has become the god of the world. . . . The social emancipation of Jewry is the emancipation of society from Jewry."

Leon Trotsky, born Lev Bronstein, was the ideological father of Russian, later Soviet, Communism; along with Stalin and three others, he fought to succeed Lenin as leader of the Communist Party after Lenin's death in 1924. In 1920, when Trotsky was head of the Red Army, Moscow's chief rabbi, Rabbi Jacob Mazeh, asked him to use the army to protect the Jews from widespread anti-Semitic attacks (beatings, rapes, and murders of Jews). Trotsky is reported to have responded, "Why do you come to me? I am not a Jew." To which Rabbi Mazeh answered: "That's the tragedy. It's the Trotskys who make revolutions, and it's the Bronsteins who pay the price."

How to explain Jews such as these? People without a strong, let alone any, national or religious identity will often seek to undermine the national and religious identity of others, especially those who affirm an identity they have abandoned. That explains, for example, the special animosity some ex-Catholics have toward the Church. Likewise more than a few Jews with no religious or national identity dislike Jews who have those identities, just as Americans who have become world citizens do not much care for Americans who wave the American flag.

In 2009, a thousand people from around the world went on a hunger strike and solidarity march on behalf of Hamas-controlled Gaza. Among them, as reported by the *New York Times*, was a Holocaust survivor named Hedy Epstein.[38] For a Holocaust survivor to go on a hunger strike on behalf of a regime that calls for another Holocaust takes a real commitment—to Leftism.

Support for Leftism among Jews has a long and unfortunate history. A Yiddish scholar, Professor Gennady Estraikh of New York University, has written, "It is hardly an overstatement to define Yiddish literature of the 1920s as the most pro-Soviet literature in the world."[39] Two of the three leaders of the Polish Communist Party at the end of World War II were Jews (Hilary Minc and Jakub Berman). The leading radical in Weimar Germany was Rosa Luxemburg. Other examples of Jews supporting Communism and similar expressions of radical Left-wing evil are legion. And to this day, many Jews cannot bring themselves to believe that the Left is far more a danger to them and to society than is the Right.

Why so many Jews have so long supported the Left is a subject beyond the scope of this book. It is also highly complex, since it is a mixture of moral idealism emanating from the Hebrew prophets and fears—of the Right, of nationalism, and of Christianity. And, for all their secularism, Jews may be one of the most religious groups in the world—but for most, their religion is no longer Judaism; it is socialism, feminism, environmentalism, scientism, Marxism, secularism, and any other ism on the Left. On the other hand, Jews who do believe in God and in the Torah as revealed text—that is, in traditional Judaism—are overwhelmingly not on the Left: They have a religion—Judaism.

Another revealing example of the moral confusion of the Left has been its support for the Palestinians in their conflict with Israel. Why does the Left support the Palestinians against Israel?

The question is rarely asked. It is simply taken for granted. (To be clear, I am referring to support for the Palestinians against Israel, not support for a Palestinian state.) But the question should be asked because support for the Palestinians is inconsistent with the Left's professed values. Just about every value the Left claims to uphold Israel upholds and its enemies, including the Palestinians, do not.

The Left speaks about its passion for democracy. Yet it is Israel that is a fully functioning democracy, as opposed to its Arab and Muslim enemies, including the Palestinians who have been led largely by terrorists, from Yasser Arafat to Hamas.

The Left claims to have a particular concern for women's rights. Yet it is Israel that has as highly developed a feminist movement as that of any Western country. It is Israel that conscripted women into its armed forces before almost any Western country did. At the same time, the state of women's rights among Israel's Muslim enemies is perhaps the lowest in the world.

The Left's greatest current preoccupation is with gay rights. Yet it is Israel that has annual gay pride days, while Arab and Muslim countries persecute homosexuals.

It is Israel that has an independent (and liberal) judiciary. It is Israel that has a Left-wing press. It is Israel that has been governed by Leftist, even socialist, parties. Israel's enemies have none of this.

So, why isn't the Left leading pro-Israel demonstrations?

Perhaps because women's equality, independent judiciaries, liberty, gays, and a free press are not the primary concerns of the anti-Israel Left. The causes the Left speaks for are often noble-sounding covers for deeper concerns such as the weakening of Western, especially American, power in the world, the weakening of Judeo-

Christian religions, the weakening of free market capitalism, and support for the "underdog."

The Left tends to divide the world into rich and poor, strong and weak, and favorite and underdog rather than good and evil or right and wrong. Support for the "underdog" is the reason given by Richard Falk, a leading Left-wing anti-Israel (and anti-American) activist, who, owing to his support for the Palestinians, was appointed the United Nations special rapporteur to the Palestinian territories: "In reality, Falk told the *Forward*, his criticism of Israel is [due to] . . . his posture as an American leftist, perennially dedicated to history's underdogs—in his eyes, the Palestinians." [40]

In order not to recognize Israel's moral superiority to its enemies, one must use a different moral yardstick. The Left does.

Two weeks after the July 2005 terror bombings in London that killed fifty-two and injured seven hundred civilians, the then mayor of London, Ken Livingstone, a prominent Leftist, defended the Palestinian use of suicide bombers. "In an unfair balance, that's what people use," he said. [41]

ONE FINAL EXAMPLE OF the Left's morally upside-down world: If something is good for America, aside from a good economy during a Democratic presidency, it is probably bad for the Left and the Democratic Party.

- If black Americans come to believe that America is a land of opportunity in which racism has been largely conquered, it would be catastrophic for the Democrats. The day that most black Americans no longer view America the way the Left and the Democratic Party portray it—as an essentially racist society—will be the day Democrats lose almost all hope of winning a national election.
- If women marry, it is bad for the Democratic Party. Single women are an essential component of any Democratic victory. To cite a close election, in 2004, unmar-

ried women voted for the Democrat John Kerry by a
25-point margin (62–37), while married women voted
for President Bush by an 11-point margin (55–44). After
women marry, they are more likely to abandon Leftist
views and to vote Republican. And if they then have
children, they will vote Republican in even more lop-
sided numbers. When Americans marry, it is bad for the
Democratic Party; when they marry and make families,
it is disastrous for the Democrats. (On the other hand,
when women have children without marrying, it is
great for the Democrats.)

- If immigrants assimilate, it is not good for Democrats.
The Democratic Party is invested in Latino separatism.
The more Latino immigrants come to feel fully American, the less likely they are to vote Democrat. The liberal notion of multiculturalism helps Democrats, while
adoption of the American ideal of E Pluribus Unum
helps Republicans.

Aside from the state of the economy—which, when bad, always benefits the party out of power—there is no equivalent list
of bad things happening to America that benefits Republicans. All
these examples of good things happening to America being bad for
a party are unique to the Democrats and the Left.

Does Leftism Make Good People?

ANY DOCTRINE, RELIGION, OR IDEOLOGY that seeks to make a better world must first have a way to make good individuals. Making
good people is the single most important project any civilization,
doctrine, or religion must engage in. In this regard, Leftism must
be judged a failure—not because its methods of doing so are flawed,
or because of its poor moral record. Nor is it because there are no
people of good character with Leftist values; there certainly are. It is

because inculcating moral character in individuals is not how Leftism believes a better world is made.

Religions such as Judaism and Christianity have emphasized character development because they see sinful human character as the primary source of evil. But the Left has always believed that evil—to the extent that the Left addresses evil as opposed to socio-economic inequality—emanates first and foremost from material inequality and what the Left regards as its sources: big business, capitalist competition, and Western imperialism. *Leftism is concerned with materially transforming society, not with morally transforming individuals.*

This is one reason violent crime is attributed not to the moral defects of the violent criminal's character but to poverty, environment, etc. Likewise white-collar crime is attributed to the flaws of capitalism that produce greed and a dog-eat-dog mentality, not to the moral defects of the white-collar criminal. As a result, there is no mechanism in Leftism for inculcating moral character in people.

Of course, any given individual Leftist may be an individual of great personal integrity and generosity. But it is not Leftism that has inculcated these noble traits in him. Leftism has no mechanism for doing so.

In truth, Leftism is more likely to promote narcissism than altruism. It has taught billions of people around the world to expect to be taken care of, and thereby bred a worldwide epidemic of self-centered entitlement. That is why millions of Frenchmen demonstrate, to the point of shutting down much of their society, against raising their retirement age by a mere two years; or half a million Brits take to the streets to protest proposals that college students pay more for their education. "What will others—the 'rich' and the state—do for me?" That is the attitude Leftism inculcates.

THE LEFT DESTROYS STANDARDS AND STANDARDS-BASED INSTITUTIONS

Leftism not only does not address the issue of character development; it disparages and weakens values and institutions that do inculcate moral character, most obviously religion-based institutions, which have been the primary carrier of moral and ethical instruction in America and Europe.

The ostensible reason for Left-wing opposition to religious standards governing people's lives in America has been to protect the "separation of church and state," a phrase found in no official document of the United States: not in the Constitution, the Declaration of Independence, or the Bill of Rights. The real reasons for the Left's war against religion, especially Christianity, are that Leftism has always been an antireligious doctrine (though there is a religious Left, which is Leftism in values coupled with Christian or Jewish religious rhetoric) and that the Left understands that the more religious a Christian or Jew, the more likely the person is to oppose Leftism.

In America, the modern Left's war against religion can be said to have begun with the 1962 U.S. Supreme Court ruling that all school prayer is unconstitutional. The specific prayer the court ruled on was a tepid, nondenominational, school prayer said *voluntarily* in New York state schools: "Almighty God, we acknowledge our dependence upon Thee, and we beg Thy blessings upon us, our parents, our teachers and our Country."

To rule such a prayer unconstitutional was truly an expression of secular extremism. And the results have been devastating. Within one generation, schoolchildren went from asking God's blessing on their teachers to a level of disrespect for teachers that is unprecedented. Whether the end of praying for teachers led to the cursing of teachers can be debated, but what is clear is that the Left has successfully removed religious expression from nearly all of public life in America. Just to cite one more example, in 2011 the liberal governor of Rhode Island renamed the state Christmas tree, a "holiday tree."

Given the indispensable role that religion has played in American history in forming character, the decline of religion has led to what one would expect—the deterioration of the moral character of many Americans. When added to the Left's war on the Boy Scouts—ostensibly because the Boy Scouts did not allow openly gay boys or men to be in the Scouts—there was no institution outside of the home except for church and similar religious groups to teach young Americans character.

CURSING*

At a Democratic Party fund-raiser in 2003 before two thousand people for then governor Howard Dean of Vermont, who was seeking the Democratic nomination for president, MoveOn.org, a leading Left-wing organization, featured a series of entertainers whose presentations were laced with obscenities. As described by the *New York Post*'s Washington bureau chief: "Pro-Dean comics . . . competed to see how often they could use the F-word in the same sentence."

Two examples: "Comic Judy Gold dissed President Bush as 'this piece of living, breathing shit' and Janeane Garofalo ridiculed the Medicare prescription-drug bill that Bush had just signed as the 'you can go fuck yourself, Grandma' bill."

The reporter also noted, "Just a few days before, rival [Democratic Massachusetts senator] John Kerry had used the F-word to attack Bush in *Rolling Stone* magazine in an apparent bid to sound hip."[42]

Most Americans regard public and deliberate cursing (as opposed to using expletives in private or in a public slip of the tongue) as a sign of a civilization in decline. But to the Left, cursing is "hip," and opposition to it is a conservative hang-up.†

The ACLU threatened Southwest Airlines with a lawsuit after the airline ordered a passenger off a flight for refusing to cover her T-shirt on which was printed "Fuckers," referring to President George W. Bush, Vice President Dick Cheney, and Secretary of

---

* In this chapter, I have decided to spell out the actual expletives. I do not think that the effect of the words is nearly as great if they are not spelled out. I ask readers who object for their forgiveness.

† President George W. Bush used the word *asshole* to describe a *New York Times* reporter in a private remark to Vice President Dick Cheney. He assumed that nearby microphones were not on. There is no moral equivalence between using an expletive when you think no one can hear you and when you want the world to hear you.

State Condoleezza Rice. The ACLU position was not surprising. It had previously defended a high school student whose school had prohibited him from wearing to class a T-shirt that read "Big Pecker."

During the George W. Bush presidency innumerable cars in liberal areas of the country sported a bumper sticker that read, "Buck Fush." Given that there were many on the Right who strongly disliked former president Bill Clinton, to the best of my knowledge, no Clinton-hater put a "Cluck Finton" bumper sticker on a car.

In 2007, the editorial board of the Colorado State University student newspaper published an editorial containing just four words: "Taser this . . . Fuck Bush."*

In its special fortieth anniversary issue in 2007, *Rolling Stone* featured interviews with people the magazine considered some of America's leading cultural and political figures. Examples included Al Gore, Jon Stewart, Bruce Springsteen, Cornel West, Paul Krugman, Kanye West, Bill Maher, and George Clooney.

Most of the interviewees used curse words in their considered responses.

Some examples:

Comedian Chris Rock:

"Bush fucked up."

"That's a major fuckup."

"I say some harsh shit."

Novelist William Gibson:

"The shit you've been doing for the past four hundred years . . ."

Actor George Clooney:

"My sister and I were quizzed on shit."

"Now you're going to hear about all this shit."

"What the fuck's wrong with you?"

"[China] doesn't give a shit . . ."

---

* September 21, 2007. "Taser" referred to police who had used a stun gun on a student at the University of Florida who refused to relinquish the microphone at a speech given by Senator John Kerry. How George Bush was connected to the use of a Taser on a Left-wing student interrupting a speech by a Left-wing senator was not explained by the editor.

"I don't give a shit."

"This war is bullshit."

Rock musician Billie Joe Armstrong:

"What the fuck are you doing?"

"When you say, 'Fuck George Bush' in a packed arena in Texas, that's an accomplishment."

"I don't have a fucking clue what they're talking about."

"All the fucked-up problems we have."

"This girl was fucked-up."

"Why did I worry so much about this shit?"

The Daily Show host Jon Stewart:

"We have a shitload of guns."

"That fucked up everything."

"We fucking declared war on 'em."

"The whole fucking thing's ours."

"Two vandals . . . can fuck up your way of life."

"I'll take those odds every fucking day."

Musician Eddie Vedder:

"Why the fuck is he doing that?"

Author and atheist activist Sam Harris:

"Any religious bullshit."

Actress Meryl Streep:

"Oh, fuck, why me?"

Actor Tom Hanks:

"People have stopped giving a shit."

"Where the fuck have you people been?"

Politically Incorrect's Bill Maher (on Republicans and global warming):

"They're selfish pricks by nature: 'I've got my own air. What do I give a shit?'"

AMONG THE FIVE NOMINEES for the 2011 Grammy Awards Record of the Year was a song titled "Fuck You."

Here are the song's opening lyrics:

I see you driving 'round town
With the girl I love and I'm like,
Fuck you!
Oo, oo, ooo
I guess the change in my pocket
Wasn't enough, I'm like,
Fuck you!
And fuck her, too!

It is also worth noting that the video of this song included children who appeared to be under twelve years of age, and all the performers are black—another example of how the Left undermines black life. The nomination of "Fuck You" as Song of the Year was no aberration. Two of the other four nominees were rap "songs" with similar lyrics.

Here are typical lyrics from Eminem's nominated "Love the Way You Lie":

And I love it the more that I suffer
I suffocate
And right before I'm about to drown
She resuscitates me
She fucking hates me
And I love it.

How deep is the decay in the music industry? According to the *Los Angeles Times*, these Grammy nominees were "decided on by about 12,000 voting members of the Recording Academy."

THE ARTS

The Left's record in the arts has been as destructive as elsewhere. It has largely taken over the arts and denigrated greatness in favor of diversity, political correctness, hostility to middle-class norms, and promoting Left-wing positions.

As Yale University professor David Gelernter has written, "Modern museums are devoted to diversity as opposed to greatness."

"Stop any person on the street," he wrote, "and ask them to name a living poet, a living painter, or a living composer. There will be complete silence. When I was a child, artists were heroes. Everyday people knew Robert Frost's poems, and not only people like me, a respected Yale professor. Classical music was moving closer to the middle class, Leonard Bernstein concerts were broadcast on television. It was a marvelous thing to have poets, novelists, painters, and musicians representing the middle and working classes and giving them greater and greater artistic depth. All of this was killed or at least dealt a very serious blow by the encroachment of the universities." [43]

The general approach has been that if the middle class likes something, it is bad art. There is a snobbishness on the Left that is rarely noted but is one of the most significant animators of Leftism: a contempt for the middle class, and for middle America, that is essential to Left-wing identity. The Left sees itself as far superior to the churchgoing, Norman Rockwell–loving, flag-waving, Pledge of Allegiance–reciting American. So, if the average guy likes it, there must be something wrong with it.

Most Americans would be horrified to know that an opera was written about terrorists murdering a crippled man, which aimed to show, in the composer's words, that "neither side is beyond reproach." Yet that opera, *The Death of Klinghoffer*, by Pulitzer Prize–winning composer John Adams, was revered by the musical elite. How could it not be? It features a chorus of Palestinian terrorists who in 1985 hijacked the *Achille Lauro* cruise ship, murdered American Jewish passenger Leon Klinghoffer, and threw him overboard in his wheelchair.

In museums, works of scatological "art" are common. In Germany in 2010 a sculpture of a squatting policewoman urinating was awarded a thousand-euro prize by the prestigious Leinemann Foundation for Fine Arts. As described by the Agence France-Presse, "It depicts a young female police officer in full riot gear crouching to pee, with exposed buttocks and a small gelatin 'puddle' affixed to the floor of the gallery at the Academy of Fine Arts in Dresden."[44]

The amount of junk masquerading as "art" is immeasurable. In 2011, the Museum of Contemporary Art in Los Angeles featured a work by "performance artist" Marina Abramovic. As described by the *Los Angeles Times*, people sat around a dinner table for eight, for three hours. At the table performers poke their head "up through a hole in the center of the table and spin around extremely slowly on a Lazy Susan and quietly gaze with intention but no particular emotion at the seated dinner guests."

Patrons of the museum paid $2,500 per person to see the performance art.

The year before, Abramovic had created "her Museum of Modern Art retrospective, 'The Artist Is Present.' . . . The show revisited some of the artist's early extreme-sport-style hits in a range of media, including photographs of her 1974 performance in which she laid [*sic*] inside a burning sculpture of a star (she lost consciousness) and a re-enactment of the 1977 'Imponderabilia' in which originally she and her then-lover/collaborator Ulay faced off, naked, within the frame of a doorway, leaving little room for people to squeeze by."[45]

Leonard Bernstein

The arts have been dominated by brilliant Leftists for nearly a century. Let's begin with the foremost American musician of his time, Leonard Bernstein. With all his goodwill and charm, his moral compass was broken, another example of a decent man morally poisoned by Leftism.

On January 14, 1970, in his Manhattan penthouse, Bernstein threw what became probably the most infamous private fund-raiser in American history—for the violent, racist, America-hating Black Panther Party. Here is how Panther leader "Field Marshall" Don Cox began the evening:

"We call [the police] pigs. . . . We recognize that this country is the most oppressive country in the world, maybe in the history of the world. The pigs have the weapons and they are ready to use them on the people. . . . They are ready to commit genocide against those who stand up against them."[46]

Bernstein did not express a word of protest, let alone end the fund-raiser, after hearing police labeled "pigs" and America labeled "the most oppressive country in the world."

Clarence B. Jones, speechwriter and counsel to Martin Luther King Jr., began the public contributions to the Panther Defense Fund with a donation of $7,500. Bernstein himself followed by pledging his entire fee for conducting the opera *Cavalleria Rusticana*. The film director Otto Preminger followed with a pledge of a thousand dollars. Smaller contributions came from lyricist Sheldon Harnick (*Fiddler on the Roof*), lyricist and composer Burton Lane (*Finian's Rainbow*), actor Harry Belafonte, and renowned art dealer Richard Feigen.[47]

Norman Mailer

Another man of the Left was perhaps the most honored American writer of his generation, Pulitzer Prize–winning author Norman Mailer. His nonliterary legacy included working successfully to get a convicted murderer, Jack Henry Abbott, out of prison. Abbott was a self-proclaimed Communist, who corresponded with Mailer while in prison.

Mailer—along with much, if not all, of the literary Left—was quite taken with Abbott's writing. That they were smitten by a man who described his own murder of a man says a lot about the literary Left. Here is an excerpt from Abbott's book, *The Belly in the Beast*, a series of letters about prison life from Abbott to Mailer. It is important to remember that Abbott was in prison for doing exactly what it described—stabbing a fellow prisoner to death:

> Here is how it is: You are both alone in his cell. You've slipped out a knife (eight- to ten-inch blade, double-edged). You're holding it beside your leg so he can't see it. The enemy is smiling and chattering away about something. You see his eyes:

Green-blue, liquid. He thinks you're his fool: he trusts you. You see the spot. It's a target between the second and third button on his shirt. As you calmly talk and smile, you move your left foot to the side to step across his right-side body length. A light pivot toward him with your right shoulder and the world turns upside down: you have sunk the knife to its hilt into the middle of his chest. Slowly he begins to struggle for his life. As he sinks, you will have to kill him fast or get caught. He will say "Why?" Or "No!" Nothing else. You can feel his life trembling through the knife in your hand. . . .

Thanks to Mailer's efforts, Abbott was paroled. Six weeks later, Abbott stabbed to death twenty-two-year-old Richard Adan, an aspiring New York City writer who was working as a waiter. Adan had told Abbott that the restaurant's men's room was for employees only. They argued and Abbott stabbed him. "'As Adan lay dying,' [eyewitness Wayne] Larsen said, the 'taller figure' [Abbott] stood over him and taunted him 'very sadistically.'"[48]

Eight years after the murder, two Hollywood celebrities on the Left, Susan Sarandon and Tim Robbins, named their son after Abbott (Jack Henry Robbins, born 1989).

The morally foolish Left has taken over the arts.

The Left's Totalitarian DNA

ANOTHER MAJOR CONTRIBUTOR to Leftism's moral problems is its embedded temptation toward totalitarianism. *Virtually every totalitarian regime has been a Leftist one.*

This needs to be explained. There have been many non-Leftist dictatorships, but there have been few non-Leftist totalitarian regimes. The only ones that come to mind are the Nazi regime and Islamist states such as Iran's under the ayatollahs and Afghanistan under the Taliban.

With regard to Nazism, it is not intellectually honest to label Nazism either Right-wing or Left-wing. Nazism was sui generis in its race-based totalitarianism. However, Leftists have effectively labeled Nazism Right-wing since Hitler invaded the center of Leftism, the Soviet Union, and that label has stuck. The Left labels its enemies "Right" or "far Right" even when its enemies are on the Left, as many individuals on the democratic Left were in the 1930s and 1940s. This branding of Nazism as Right-wing has immeasurably helped the Left. It has made people fear the Right.

Nor were the handful of fascist regimes—Italy and Spain specifically—Right-wing in any meaningful way. Jonah Goldberg, in his book *Liberal Fascism*, has documented how many progressives saw the Mussolini regime in Italy as a progressive, not a Rightwing, regime.

The key difference between Leftist and Rightist non-democratic regimes is the difference between totalitarianism and authoritarianism. It was President Ronald Reagan's ambassador to the United Nations, Jeane Kirkpatrick, in a famous *Commentary* magazine article, who best clarified the distinction between the two types of dictatorships. *Totalitarian* comes from the word *total*. The totalitarian regime seeks to control the total life of its citizens. The individual's life is controlled in virtually every way.

In the typical authoritarian state, however, the citizen's life is controlled almost only in the political realm. One can lead a life relatively uncontrolled by the authoritarian state so long as one does nothing to oppose the dictatorship. It is then that the evil nature of an authoritarian regime becomes manifest. Outspoken opponents are often imprisoned, tortured, and/or executed. Otherwise, the citizen in an authoritarian society is relatively free to do many things forbidden in a totalitarian state: practice one's religion, travel both within his country and, if he has the funds, even abroad; live more or less wherever he wants; join all sorts of nonpolitical organizations with little or no government controls; and read what he wants, except for antigovernment writings.

The citizen in a totalitarian state can do none of those things. He cannot freely practice his religion; he cannot live anywhere in his own country without government permission; he cannot travel abroad; he cannot form or join any nongovernment-sponsored organization; and he can only read what the state allows.

A personal example: I visited authoritarian fascist Spain and the totalitarian Soviet Union in the same year, 1969. There was no comparison between the two. For example, in Spain, I was allowed to stay at any hotel I wanted, and to receive Spanish guests (though they had to leave by midnight). In the Soviet Union I was told what hotels to stay at, and no Soviet citizen (except for Soviet officials) was allowed inside the hotel. In Spain, I could purchase and read publicly just about any foreign newspaper. In the Soviet Union I could purchase and read only Soviet and other Communist Party newspapers. The list of differences between life in fascist Spain and life in the Soviet Union is endless.

Why is totalitarianism a Left-wing rather than a Right-wing phenomenon?

The most obvious reason is that Leftism is based on the principle of a big state; and the bigger the state, the more it controls. American and conservative values, on the other hand, are based on having as small a state as possible. Obviously, a doctrine predicated on having less power will be less likely to control others' lives—and less desirous of doing so.

Another reason is that Leftism is close to all-encompassing. If the Left had its way, the citizens of the state would be told how to live in almost every way: what to drive and when; what lightbulbs to use; what temperature to keep their homes; what men would be permitted to say to women; what school textbooks must include; when God could be mentioned, and when not; how much of their earnings people may keep; what art would be funded and what art would not; what food children could be fed; how enthusiastically to cheer girls' sports teams (see page 211); and much more. The list of Left-wing controls over our lives is ever expanding.

Committed Leftists are certain that they know better than others how people should live their lives. As I demonstrate repeatedly in this book, Leftists know that they are smarter, kinder, finer, more compassionate people than others—precisely because they are Leftists. Therefore, they have every right—indeed a duty—to control society.

Finally, Leftism is rooted in secularism, and the more secular a society, the more laws it needs to pass in order to keep its citizens from hurting one another. When more people feel accountable to God and to moral religion—as in the American value system—society can get by with fewer laws. The American Founders knew that a country with the amount of individual freedom Americans would have would be viable only if its citizens were individuals of integrity—an integrity they believed was dependent on affirming God-based morality, moral accountability to God, and religion that emphasized these values.

AIRBRUSHING HISTORY

In the Soviet Union, a famous dissident joke stated: "In the Soviet Union the future is known; it's the past that is always changing."

The reference was to the Communists' constant rewriting of history. Under Stalin, for example, all references to Leon Trotsky's seminal role in the Bolshevik Revolution and in the founding of the Communist Party were removed, as were all photographs of him. There is a photo of the early Bolsheviks in which Soviet censors removed Trotsky, but failed to airbrush his shoes, from the photo. One sees Stalin standing next to a pair of shoes.

The practice of rewriting history by doctoring photos has been taken up by the politically correct Left in the contemporary West. To cite just one example, photos featuring famous persons smoking:

- In 2003, the cigarette in Paul McCartney's hand was airbrushed out of the famous Beatles *Abbey Road* album cover.

- In 1994, a U.S. postage stamp commemorating blues guitarist Robert Johnson removed the cigarette from the musician's mouth.
- In the 2000 rerelease of the 1948 film *Melody Time*, the Disney Company removed the cigarette from the cartoon character Pecos Bill. (Instead of a cigarette in his mouth, kids now see him holding a gun by his mouth.)
- In 1999, the U.S. Postal Service removed a cigarette from a photograph of the artist Jackson Pollock.
- On the cover of the 2006 release of the Beatles album *The Capitol Albums, Volume 2*, EMI was pressured to remove images of band members smoking. The clumsy censors also removed two of drummer Ringo Starr's fingers.
- In 2006, the BBC reported, "Children's TV channel *Boomerang* is to edit scenes from *Tom and Jerry* cartoons where characters are shown smoking."[49]
- As reported by George Will: "A London museum, advertising its exhibit about Britain at war, used a picture of Winston Churchill with an oddly twisted mouth: The health fascists had airbrushed away his cigar."[50]
- In 2002, there were so many protests about the James Bond character smoking in *Die Another Day* that it was the last Bond film in which he smoked. (Bond films did continue to show murder, torture, semi-nudity, and drinking.)
- And not only tobacco: In 2008 the U.S. Postal Service released a Bette Davis stamp. Michael Deas, the stamp's designer, acknowledged that he changed Davis's coat from mink to velvet to avoid a protest from People for the Ethical Treatment of Animals.

Health issues frequently bring out the totalitarian instincts of the Left. In 2002, a New York Supreme Court justice, Robert F. Julian, banned a divorced mother from smoking when her son stayed with her. The thirteen-year-old boy, who lived with his father and grandparents, had overnight visits with his mother, but she was told that if she smoked while he was there, she would lose the right to have her son visit her. As reported by the *New York Law Journal*, Justice Julian himself said "he was unable to find any decision ordering parents to maintain a smoke-free environment absent an underlying diagnosis of asthma, allergy or another disorder."[51]

Justice Julian simply expanded judicial power over parents by having the court assume the role of *parens patriae* ("government as parent"). It should be noted that the mother smoked only in the bathroom when her son visited. But to an activist liberal judge, it is better for a child not to visit his mother than to be in her home when she smoked.

CONTROLLING PEOPLE'S BEHAVIOR

Federal education officials, citing Title IX, the civil rights law that mandates equal athletic opportunities for both sexes, ordered that American high school cheerleaders cheer for girls' teams as often as they do for boys' teams. As reported in the *New York Times*, almost no one directly involved wanted this—not the cheerleaders, not the fans, not the boys' teams, and not even the girls' teams. But in true totalitarian fashion, the Left-wing education officials even mandated the level of enthusiasm the cheerleaders must express: "A statewide group of physical education teachers in California called for cheerleaders to attend girls' and boys' games 'in the same number, and with equal enthusiasm.'"[52]

In the name of gender equality, the Left has also forced school districts in America to end male-male wrestling and force high school males to wrestle girls.

If the contention that the Left has totalitarian DNA is true, the institution most controlled by the Left ought to exhibit the most restrictions on personal liberty. The university is that institution, and indeed there is no non-religious mainstream institution in America with as stringent rules governing speech, or where personal liberty is as restricted. Universities are probably the least free major institutions in the United States. Nearly all of them have instituted "hate speech codes," which prohibit, among other things: "Discriminatory harassment which includes conduct (oral, written, graphic or physical) directed against any person or group of persons because of their race, color, national origin, religion, sex, sexual orientation, age, disability, or veteran's status and that has the purpose or reasonably foreseeable effect of creating an offensive, demeaning, intimidating, or hostile environment for that person or group of persons." [53]

In many colleges, incoming freshmen must attend sensitivity training seminars. These are extensive sessions on how to act and speak according to the latest rules of the Left. They are reminiscent of totalitarian regimes' "reeducation" camps.

Harassment Laws

All reasonable men and women acknowledge that it is morally wrong for an employer to say to an employee, "Sleep with me or you will be fired." That was the original meaning of sexual harassment and laws passed to ban such conduct were widely accepted. The Left has stretched the meaning of sexual harassment to such an extent that anything that *might offend one* person (usually, but not necessarily, a woman) is illegal.

The totalitarian temptation inherent in such laws should be obvious. Before providing examples, let us take a moment to analyze three words: *might*, *offend*, and *one*.

Might: Something does not have to actually offend anyone in the workplace. Some behavior or speech can be illegal solely because it *might* offend someone.

Offend: This is one of the most important words in the Left's vocabulary. As noted elsewhere, the notion that a person feels offended is enough to render an act illegal because feelings are the basis of Leftism.

One: A hundred women might find nothing objectionable in a joke placed on the office bulletin board. But if one woman does, it is enough to render the joke impermissible or even illegal. Since it is likely that one such person works in just about every office setting, jokes, especially those with the slightest sexual content, cannot be told or posted at work.

The Left has ensured passage of laws banning harassment in the workplace based on race, sex, sexual orientation, gender identification, age, religion, national origin, disability, military membership or veteran status, marital status, political affiliation, criminal record, occupation, citizenship status, personal appearance, receipt of public assistance, and more. The result is that the American workplace is, with regard to speech, visual displays, and other personal expressions, an authoritarian place with totalitarian characteristics. I have often noted on my radio show that at my radio station, when I speak on the radio I have freedom of speech and the moment the microphone is turned off, I lose it.

Thanks to the Left, "emotional distress" is a legal category. And causing but one person to experience it can lead to the prosecution of an entire business. The banning of whatever will cause "emotional distress" again illustrates two major characteristics of the Left: its totalitarian temptation and its fear of life's pains. Of course, the two are related. The Left yearns for a pain-free world, and it does whatever it can to achieve it.

- In 1995, a Los Angeles police officer was suspended for five days for saying, "Hi, babe" to a female police officer. When, *two years later*, the suspension was overturned, "women's groups assailed" the decision.[54]
- Courts have ruled that use of job titles such as "foreman" and "draftsman" may constitute sexual harassment.[55]
- A Kentucky human rights agency ordered a company to change its "Men Working" signs (at a cost of over thirty-five thousand dollars) arguing that the signs "perpetuat[e] a discriminatory work environment and

could be deemed unlawful under the Kentucky Civil Rights Act."

- The Montana Human Rights Commission ruled that a workplace constituted a "hostile work environment" based solely on off-color jokes and cartoons displayed in the workplace. None of the jokes were said specifically to the women who complained; none referred to them; the cartoons were distributed by men and women alike, apparently once or twice a month over several years; and the cartoons weren't even sexist or misogynistic.

- The Iowa Civil Rights Commission has warned that "jokes of a sexual nature and cartoons, drawings, or caricatures of a sexual nature" are examples of potentially harassing actions.

Freedom of speech has generally been considered to be the quintessential American value. To this day, there is more freedom of speech in America than in Western Europe. But America is catching up; the Left, after all, has governed Western Europe for a longer period of time. Preventing hurt feelings is one of the many considerations that the Left deems more important than liberty.

Schools Banned from Inviting Clergy Who Advocate Man-Woman Marriage

The Connecticut branch of the ACLU, the Connecticut Civil Liberties Union, "informed the Windsor Locks School District that it would face [legal] action if education officials chose to allow a presentation by clergy at Windsor Locks High School on homosexuality and related topics."[56] The high school had previously invited a gay activist organization, the Stonewall Speakers, to address students on homosexuality and same-sex marriage. In order to attempt to present an alternate view, the school then invited clergy to speak to the students.

Because "the clergy was supposed to offer a view based on religious scripture," Annette Lamoreaux, a legal director of the CCLU, "reported that the clergy presentation could violate the Establishment Clause of the United States Constitution and the Connecticut Gay Rights Law, which prohibits discrimination based upon sexual orientation. . . . She added that it would have violated the rights of gay and lesbian students to equal protection."

Aside from illustrating the Left's controlling nature, this story also illustrates the secular and Leftist brainwash most American children receive throughout their school life. For no defensible educational reason—especially given the poor general education that so many American students receive—a public school may use precious school time to have gay activists address students on behalf of same-sex marriage. But clergy defending man-woman marriage are not allowed to address the students.

THE COURTS

In keeping with its controlling tendencies, the Left pays particular attention to using courts to achieve its goals. This was forthrightly acknowledged by leading Democrat William A. Galston, a former senior aide to President Bill Clinton and an adviser to the Al Gore presidential campaign. "Beginning in the 1950s," Galston noted, "the Democratic Party convinced itself that, especially on social issues, the principal vehicle of advance would be the court."[57]

Whereas the Judeo-Christian and traditional Western understanding of the role of the court was that it be blind to everything but rendering a just verdict, the Left-wing view is that the court should be a vehicle for obtaining not justice, but "social justice"—the Left's term for all social policies it seeks, especially the elimination of material inequality. As a Democratic senator, Herb Kohl, put it, in objecting to the confirmation of conservative judge Samuel Alito to the Supreme Court: "The neutral approach, that of the judge just applying the law, is very often inadequate to ensure social progress . . ."[58]

Democratic senator Ted Kennedy acknowledged the same thing

at the same Senate hearing: Average Americans "have had a hard time getting a fair shake in his [Alito's] courtroom."[59]

And so did Democratic senator Richard Durbin: "I find this as a recurring pattern, and it raises the question in my mind whether the average person, the dispossessed person, the poor person who finally has their day in court . . . are going to be subject to the crushing hand of fate when it comes to your decisions."[60]

The prime Democratic objection to confirming Judge Samuel Alito to the U.S. Supreme Court was that he does not rule in favor of the Average Joe in his courtroom. But the purpose of a judge is not to rule in favor of the Average Joe. It is to rule justly.

SQUASHING LIFE'S LITTLE PLEASURES

Totalitarians hate joy. Totalitarian regimes attempt, often successfully, to extinguish as many of life's little pleasures as possible. If the democratic Left possesses a totalitarian temptation, we would expect to find a similar killjoy mentality there. And indeed we do. The finding of actions, including life's little joys, to condemn and ultimately ban is so pervasive on the Left that one never knows what the next joy to be banned will be.

Humor

Take activists' reactions to a national television ad for the fast-food chain Burger King. The ad featured the company's royal mascot running through a building, knocking a person over, and crashing through a glass window to deliver its newest food at the time, the Steakhouse XT burger. Called "crazy" by those present, the King was finally tackled by men in white coats. "The king's insane," the ad announced, for "offering so much beef for $3.99."

The ad was innocuous and innocent. Under threats to life and limb, almost no viewer of this ad could imagine what could be offensive. But the Left, in every field from library science to mental health, is always vigilant, looking for offenses to decry and eventually ban. Consequently, the ad triggered a storm of criticism from mental health activists (*activist* is a term that, unless otherwise specified, almost always refers to someone on the Left). The *Washington Post* ran the headline, "Burger King ad featuring its mascot as crazy offends mental health organizations."[61] (*Offends*, as noted, is another giveaway as to the Left-wing nature of the opposition.)

Michael Fitzpatrick, executive director of the National Alliance on Mental Illness, said the ad was "blatantly offensive . . . I was stunned. Absolutely stunned and appalled." David Shern, president and chief executive of Mental Health America, echoed this assessment. And, of course, reporters from the Associated Press to the *Washington Post* all agreed.

They should read what a Los Angeles listener to my radio show wrote to me: "I am a father of a 24 year old son with a mental health issue. I am particularly tuned to protecting my son's self-image. My son and I have both seen the Burger King Ad that you have referred to. It did not occur to either of us that the Burger King Ad was offensive in any way. Why would I raise my son to be hyper-sensitive about his disability? My objective as a parent is to strengthen him. Making him hyper-sensitive would have the opposite effect." Obviously, this father was not a man of the Left.

This labeling of a good-natured, silly burger ad as "offensive" is typical of the Left's squelching of life's little joys in the name of the endless list of causes the Left pushes. Myriad joys (except regarding sex and drugs), not to mention opinions, are "offensive" to the Left—and ultimately, hopefully, banned.

The Automobile and the Home

For most Americans, the car is not only a source of much pleasure; it is also identified with individual liberty. But to the extent the Left is able, it will tell you what kind of car you can drive and, whenever possible, get you out of your car and into mass transit or onto a bicycle.

So, too, on the Left, a home is not a man's castle; it is another place of too many joys—or, since Leftism is also a religion, too many sins. And the Left would like to exorcise them.

One such joy of the American home has always been the family fireplace. But in California, the state most controlled by the Left, environmentalist activists have succeeded in banning wood-burning fireplaces from all new homes. Another house-based pleasure is setting one's home at the temperature one prefers and is willing to pay for. If the Left has its way, however, the temperature of every home would be set by a central authority.

The Left has abolished another pleasure: the way we light our homes. It has banned the incandescent lightbulb. Though most people prefer to continue illuminating their homes with it, the Left has pushed for national laws mandating that people use alternatives such as compact fluorescent lamps (CFLs). These bulbs contain mercury, give a fair number of people headaches, emit less pleasant light in the view of many, are initially much more expensive, and if broken, they necessitate opening windows even in winter, and people and pets leaving the area. In fact, the Environmental Protection Agency has issued a sixteen-point procedure to follow if a CFL bulb breaks.

School Games

Schoolchildren have also been increasingly deprived of many of the little joys American schoolchildren have experienced for generations.

Virtually every game that previous generations of American children played during school recess has been banned because activist organizations such as the National Program for Playground Safety deem as too dangerous all games in which kids are "running into each other." Recess has even been ended in some American schools because the students may get hurt by running around too much.

Nor is the possibility of a player getting physically hurt necessary to ban a game. True to the Left's preoccupation with feelings, if a player can feel bad, there is a good chance that that game, too, has been banned. In many schools that means no more dodgeball or ring-a-levio, or the possibility of losing a baseball or soccer game by large margins. "We consider it inappropriate to use children as human targets," said Mary Marks, physical education supervisor for Fairfax County, Virginia, concerning dodgeball. Also, it may hurt the feelings of kids who are eliminated. For the same reason—potential hurt feelings of those eliminated—musical chairs is prohibited in many schools.

Smoking

One of life's great little pleasures is tobacco. Just watch old war footage to see the serenity and joy a cigarette brought to a wounded soldier. Though I do not smoke cigarettes, I have been smoking cigars and a pipe since I was in high school (as I noted earlier, my father still smokes cigars daily at age ninety-three), and it would be difficult to overstate how much I enjoy both.

No rational person could oppose educating the public about the dangers of cigarette smoking. Cigarette smoking shortens the lives of up to a third of smokers, often in terrible ways, and that is what public health organizations should be saying. But the battle against smoking has become a religious crusade for antismoking activists, who are usually on the Left.

As a result, smoking has been banned in entire cities, outdoors as well as in, even though outdoor bans have no scientific basis. In Burbank, California, and other cities where Leftist politics predominate, one cannot even smoke in a cigar store. That the Left has contempt for Prohibition reveals a startling lack of self-awareness.

If the Left hated Hugo Chavez or Fidel Castro as much as it hates "big tobacco," the world would be a better place.

THE LEFT, ABORTION, AND SEX

The Left, as repeatedly shown here, wishes to control as much of people's lives as possible. There are, however, two noteworthy exceptions—abortion and sex. In these two areas of human conduct the Left wants people to be left alone.

With regard to abortion, the Leftist view is that the human fetus has no rights at any point in its development. The mother has complete freedom to destroy it at any time for any reason. Not only does the Left oppose any legal bans on abortion, but pro-choice activists will not even morally condemn any abortion. If an affluent and married woman wishes to abort because she does not want another child, that is not morally wrong. If a woman wishes to abort one fetus of two she is carrying because she wants only one more child, that is not morally wrong. If a woman wants a boy and aborts a female fetus, that is not morally wrong.

For the Left, aborting human fetuses at any time for any reason is an absolute right over which society should have no authority. On the other hand, in almost every other area of life, as documented above, the Left seeks more and more governmental authority over the individual.

As regards sexual matters, the Left eschews making judgments regarding any consensual sexual behavior and opposes government involvement in such matters—a position that most conservatives also hold. But the Left goes further. For example, Europeans, who have adopted Left-wing values much more than most Americans have, did not understand Americans' objections to President Bill Clinton's extramarital affair with a young female intern in the White House. As an editorial in France's most prestigious newspaper, *Le Monde*, put it at the time, "We have a very French way of looking at things. We think a president who has affairs is charming."[62]

And the ACLU has gone to court arguing against porn filters in the computers of public libraries. To the objection of parents who do not want their minor children to see porn in the local public library, the ACLU responds, "Explicit sex information and even pornography do not themselves cause psychological harm to minors of any age."[63] The American Library Association has a similar position on porn displayed on library computers.

Given the Left's lack of standards regarding most sexual matters, it should not be surprising that, as documented in the chapter on universities, a Northwestern University professor would have a naked girl come to a postclass presentation in which she used a sex toy to bring herself to orgasm. Nor should it be surprising that the *Chicago Sun-Times* deputy editorial page editor wrote a column defending the professor. "The demonstration *was not a mistake nor does it degrade a Northwestern education in any way*," she wrote. "The demonstration which featured a sex toy used on a naked woman fell well within the bounds of the academic freedom vital to any university worth its salt. Under that rubric, professors are free to generate controversy, to push students to question what they think they know, so long as there is an educational purpose. . . . I'm still standing behind [Professor] Bailey . . . because *it is his right—and obligation*—to provoke, as long as it has an educational purpose . . ." (emphasis added)[64]

What About All the Good the Left Has Done?

THIS BOOK DELINEATES with scores of examples the toxic impact Left-wing thought and actions have had on civilization. From the far Left—with its virtually unparalleled mass murders and totalitarianism—to the democratic Left, nearly every area of life that the Left has influenced has been adversely affected. The culture has been debased, from the fine arts with their scatological exhibits and contempt for beauty and excellence, to the popular culture's nearly omnipresent vulgarity. Education has been corrupted, with students learning less and propagandized more. Economies have been wrecked by the irresponsible accumulation of debt, almost entirely a result of government expansion and entitlement programs. Masculinity and femininity have been rendered archaic concepts. The will to fight evil has been almost eradicated in the Western world outside of the United States. The moral character of great numbers of people has been negatively affected for reasons noted in the chapter detailing the effects of the welfare state on the character of citizens. And in the United States, the Left has marshaled its influence in schools and universities, labor unions, news media, entertainment media, and the arts to undermine the bases of Americanism—liberty, small government, God-based ethics, and E Pluribus Unum.

Nevertheless, hasn't the Left done some good?

The answer is that yes, of course, the Left has done good things. Most people acknowledge the good that social programs such as Social Security, Medicare, and Medicaid have achieved, and the role the Left played in pushing for them. So, too, the Left was the primary advocate for laws improving safety in the workplace, child labor laws, clean air and water legislation, and the like.

There is one huge problem, however, with some of these achievements: The entitlement programs are financially unsustainable. After all, any program that hands out trillions of dollars to its citizens will "work" for a period of time. Such programs take no effort and no thought: Just have younger workers pay for the retirement of older citizens, tax all other wage earners, and print money—then you can do all the good you want. What counts for success is the long-term viability of a program.

Then there is the perhaps unanswerable question of whether without liberal intervention America would have devised alternate ways of enabling the vast majority of its citizens to obtain good health care. I am certain it would have. And while that is not provable, America and most other countries will have no choice but to devise such alternate ways of providing affordable health care, now that these liberal programs have brought countries into near insolvency.

Beyond these unsustainable entitlement programs, the list of Left-wing achievements is short—unless, of course, one agrees with all, or nearly all, of what the Left has done to education, the arts, the tort bar, and in the unprecedented expansion of the state and government power.

What should not be put on the list of achievements is the identification of the Left with women's suffrage or with civil rights legislation and concern for black America.

Regarding women's suffrage, it was a Republican who introduced into Congress what became the Nineteenth Amendment to the Constitution, giving women the right to vote. In addition, the 1919 vote in the House of Representatives approving the amendment was made possible only because Republicans had retaken control of the House in the previous election (prior attempts to get it passed through Democrat-controlled Congresses had failed). The Senate vote was approved only after a Democratic filibuster; and 82 percent of the Republican senators voted for it, while only 54 percent of the Democrats did so. Only 18 percent of the Republicans voted against the amendment, while 46 percent of the Democrats did so. Moreover, twenty-six of the thirty-six states that ratified the Nineteenth Amendment had Republican-controlled legislatures.

As regards to working for civil rights for blacks, ever since the antislavery Republican Party was founded, it has been Republicans, not Democrats, who have overwhelmingly led the cause of black equality.

Every vote against the 1960 Civil Rights Act came from Democrats; and in the House, even the future Left-wing Democratic candidate for president, then-congressman George McGovern—of South Dakota (not a southern state)—merely voted "present." As regards the better-known 1964 Civil Rights Act, 82 percent of the Republican senators voted for the act, and only 66 percent of the Democrats did so. And in the House of Representatives, 80 percent of the Republicans and only 63 percent of the Democrats voted for the act.

The Left's response? All the Democrats who voted against all these civil rights bills were conservatives.

This argument is entirely self-serving. For one thing, even putting aside the issue of southern Democrats, how does one explain the fact that nearly every Republican voted for women's suffrage and for civil rights bills? Were the Republican all liberals? Of course not. They were nearly all conservatives. And while a handful of conservatives may have been racist, there is no racism in conservative ideology.

Even most of those Republicans who voted against the Civil Rights Act of 1964 did so solely on constitutional and liberty-related grounds. For example, Senator Barry Goldwater, the conservative Republican nominee for president that year, opposed two of the seven key provisions of the bill—those that interfered with property rights (by creating rules for privately owned housing) and those controlling public accommodations (he declined to vote for any legislation that, in his words, "tampers with the rights of assembly, the freedom of speech, freedom of religion, and the freedom of property").[65] But unlike the Democrats who opposed the bill, Goldwater was no racist. He was, in fact, a pro-black activist. He founded the NAACP in Arizona, donated large sums of money to the organization, and integrated the Arizona National Guard (even before President Truman integrated the armed forces).

In addition, the liberal argument that all the Democrats who opposed civil right laws were conservative means, among other things, that Senator J. William Fulbright, one of the most far-Left senators in the postwar period, was really a conservative.[66]

The fact is that virtually the entire history of antislavery and other pro-black activity in America was lopsidedly Republican. The notion, taught to virtually every American college student, that Democrats have been the anti-racism party and Republicans the pro-racism party, is as false as the depiction of the Kennedy assassination as a product of Right-wing hate in Texas even though the assassin, Lee Harvey Oswald, was a Communist.[67]

But whatever one's interpretation of civil rights legislation, all the good, real or alleged, that the Left has done pales in significance to all the damage it has done.

Moreover, whatever good it has done does not change the evaluation. There is no mass movement in the modern world, perhaps in all of history, that hasn't done good. Even evil movements and ideologies, incomparably worse than the democratic Left, have all done some good. That is why we do not morally assess a political or social or religious ideology by whether it did any good. If we did, no ideology could be assessed as bad or evil, since every ideology has done some good. What we need to assess is the totality of any movement or ideology: What is the net gain or loss to humanity because of its existence?

As we have seen, the most popular Left-wing historian, Howard Zinn, whose American history texts are the most widely used in American schools, believed that America "probably did more bad than good." I believe, and this book provides the evidence and arguments to sustain this judgment, that the Left has done more bad than good. In other words, had Leftism never arisen, whatever good it did would have happened sooner or later (rarely much later); but much of the bad it did might never have taken place, and that bad dwarfs the good it has done.

Unfortunately, a great many people do not evaluate movements or ideologies on moral grounds, that is, on how much good or evil it did. They place a higher value on things other than good and evil—material equality, social programs, and national prestige are three common examples. This explains, for example, why, according to a 2009 poll, nearly 60 percent of the Russian people would like to see the Soviet Union reestablished. The Soviet genocide in Ukraine, the Soviet creation of the world's largest concentration camp complex (the Gulag Archipelago), the tens of millions of Russian and other innocent Soviet civilians murdered, the peace pact with Hitler that helped bring about World War II, the support of foreign genocidal Communist regimes, the utter lack of freedom, and the violent suppression of religion in the Soviet Union—none of those evils matter to most Russians compared to the empire, the prestige, the social programs, and the appearance of material equality of the Soviet Union. As reported by the *Christian Science Monitor*, "Many [Russians] say they also miss being citizens of a huge, sprawling multiethnic superpower that seemed to command respect in the world." And "[o]lder Russians invariably recall the Soviet era as a time of stability and social security."[68]

So, if your primary concerns are expansion of the state, material equality, reduction of American power in the world, making America and Europe secular societies, removal of Judeo-Christian influence, substitution of internationalism for nationalism, and making ethnicity and race important values, the Left has been a wild success.

On the other hand, if your primary concerns are fighting evil, making people nobler, morally elevating societies, and creating conditions for prosperity, the Left has been a failure.

Epilogue: Why Conservatives Are Happier Than Liberals

ACCORDING TO POLLS such as those of the Pew Research Center and the National Science Foundation, conservative Americans are happier than liberal Americans.

Liberals respond that they are less happy because they "ruminate" more on serious issues than conservatives do and because they are troubled more by the existence of inequality. These are the explanations, offered, for example, by two psychology professors, Jaime Napier of Yale University and John T. Jost of New York University, in their academic paper, "Why Are Conservatives Happier Than Liberals?"

Needless to say, both explanations are self-serving. The first is another example of Left-wing self-esteem and Left-wing contempt for conservatives. Moreover, given how feelings-based Leftism is, it is difficult to ascribe "more thinking" to the Left. If the Left thought more, its track record in virtually every area of life would not be nearly as destructive as it has been. Spending governments into unsustainable debt, granting more and more citizens more and more entitlements, believing that "war is not the answer," or that the worth of a human fetus is solely determined by a mother, or any of the other Left-wing positions cited in this book are not products of deep thought nearly as much as they are products of deep feelings.

The second explanation has more truth to it but does not explain why liberals are less happy than conservatives. It is entirely true that the Left is more disturbed by inequality than is the Right. Indeed, the Left is more disturbed, as I have tried to show, by material inequality than by anything else, including evil. But this doesn't explain the happiness difference, because the Right is more disturbed than the Left about other issues—evil, for example, and the expansion of the state and the degradation of the culture.

Furthermore, while the Left may be more disturbed by inequality, conservatives are the ones who do more to alleviate it in their personal lives. Syracuse University professor Arthur Brooks, published these data in his book, *Who Really Cares: The Surprising Truth About Compassionate Conservatism*:

- Although liberal families' incomes average 6 percent higher than those of conservative families, conservative-headed households give, on average, 30 percent more to charity than the average liberal-headed household ($1,600 per year vs. $1,227).
- Conservatives also donate more time and give more blood.
- Residents of the states that voted for John Kerry in 2004 gave smaller percentages of their incomes to charity than did residents of states that voted for George Bush.
- George W. Bush carried 24 of the 25 states where charitable giving was above average.
- In the 10 most conservative states, i.e, those in which Bush got more than 60 percent majorities, the average percentage of personal income donated to charity was 3.5. Residents of the bluest states, which gave Bush less than 40 percent, donated 1.9 percent.
- People who reject the idea that "government has a responsibility to reduce income inequality" give an average of *four times more* than people who accept that proposition.[69]

Apparently, if one is to judge people by their behavior rather than by their political positions, the argument that liberals are less happy than conservatives because they care more about those poorer than themselves has no validity.

So, let's consider some other explanations.

One is that perhaps we are posing the question backward when we ask why liberals are less happy than conservatives. The question implies that liberalism causes unhappiness. And while this is probably true, it may be equally or more true to say that unhappy people are more likely to adopt Leftist positions.

Take black Americans, for example. A black American who is essentially happy is going to be less attracted to the Left. People who see themselves as victims cannot be happy, and liberal blacks view themselves as victims of a racist America. Black Americans who are conservative—meaning, among other things, that they do not see themselves as victims, and do not regard their country as racist— are going to be considerably happier. For all intents and purposes, a black American might consider abandoning liberalism in order to be a happier person. It is very hard, if not impossible, to be a happy person while believing that society is out to hurt you. So the unhappy black will gravitate to liberalism, and liberalism will in turn make him unhappier by reinforcing his view that he is a victim.

The unhappy of all races will gravitate toward the Left for a second reason. Life is hard—for liberals and for conservatives alike. But conservatives assume that life will always be hard. Liberals, on the other hand, have utopian dreams. And utopians will always be less happy than those who know that suffering is inherent to human existence. Furthermore, the utopian compares America with utopia and finds it terribly wanting. The conservative compares America with every other civilization that has ever existed and walks around wondering how he got so lucky to be born or naturalized an American.

One upshot of all this is that there is a simple way to produce fewer Leftists: Raise children who are grateful in general and grateful to be American in particular (or grateful to be the citizen of any decent country), who don't complain much, who learn to handle losing, and who are guided by values, not feelings. In other words, teach them how to be happy adults. That, more than any one other thing, will produce fewer Leftists—and a better world. Because the happy make the world better and the unhappy make it worse.

Part II

ISLAM AND
ISLAMISM

On Evaluating Religions

BEFORE DISCUSSING ISLAM, it is necessary to discuss the acceptability of critiquing a religion.

At the present time in the Western world, people are free to morally assess and critique any ideology, and to morally assess, critique, or even mock any denomination of Christianity. But any moral assessment of Islam that is not entirely positive is unacceptable. In parts of Europe it is actually illegal. And if the Organization of the Islamic Conference (OIC) has its way, criticism of Islam will be illegal throughout the world. In 2009, at the urging of the OIC, the largest bloc of nations in the United Nations, the UN Human Rights Council, passed a resolution condemning "defamation of religion"—with special attention to defamation of Islam—as a human rights violation.[1]

Even the European countries, some of them containing large populations of Muslims, and many of them fearful of Islamist retaliation, voted against the resolution. But just about everywhere, criticism of Islam is taboo, and sometimes life-threatening. One only has to compare the ease with which Christianity is criticized to appreciate how difficult it is to criticize Islam. An American "artist," Andres Serrano, placed a crucifix in a glass jar filled with his urine, certain that he would not be harmed by even a single one of the world's two billion Christians. Indeed Serrano's work *Piss Christ* won an arts competition, funded in part by the National Endowment for the Arts.[2]

Were anyone anywhere to do to a Koran or to a picture of Muhammad what Serrano did to a crucifix, that person would in all likelihood be murdered, as the Dutch filmmaker Theo van Gogh (for his film about the plight of Muslim women) and others have been; and violent demonstrations, probably involving fatalities, would take place in various parts of the Muslim world.

And that understates the problem. One need not place a sacred Muslim object in urine in order to incur violent retribution. One only needs to write that Muhammad would take for a wife one of the women who compete in the Miss World contest, or publish cartoon images of Muhammad.

Why, then, can one criticize, even mock, Christianity—not to mention Zionism, the Jewish (and Christian) religious-national movement to reestablish the Jewish state in Israel—and, of course, every other ideology and movement in the world, but not Islam? For that matter, why is there a word—*Islamophobia*—that pathologizes any critique of Islam, no matter how fair, but no word for the most rabid hatred of Christianity and Christians?

There are three answers: the Left, Muslim wealth, and fear.

First, the Left, which dominates the media, the arts, and most of intellectual life in the West, has rendered criticism of Christianity and Zionism acceptable, even laudable, but criticism of Islam unacceptable. Why has the Left done this? Because the enemy (radical Islam) of my enemy (America and Israel) is my friend, and because the Muslim world is regarded as the underdog vis-à-vis powerful America and Israel, and the Left supports what it perceives as the underdog.

A second reason for Islam's protection from criticism is money. Muslim nations have paid for a number of important professorial chairs and institutes at Western universities (such as Harvard and Georgetown). Those professors are unlikely to write or say anything critical of Islam, and they are likely to attack critics of anything Muslim. Meanwhile, it is very difficult for a scholarly critic of Islam to earn a living in academia.

Third, there is a legitimate fear of antagonizing Muslims. People who criticize Islam fear for their safety—even when they may have little reason to. That is the reason Yale University Press would not even print the Danish Muhammad cartoons in a book it published in 2010 about the Danish Muhammad cartoons. Yale forthrightly conceded that the reason was fear for its staff.

Regarding criticizing Islam, from 9/11 to this day, callers to my syndicated radio show have asked, "Is Islam a religion of violence?"

And since that day, I have responded: "I don't judge religions; I judge practitioners."

It is easy to dismiss this response as a politically correct cop-out, but there were valid reasons for this response.

First, in medieval Europe, many people would have asked, "Is Christianity a religion of violence?" And 2,500 years ago, people might have asked, "Is Judaism a religion of violence?"

Second, the question is often impossible to answer because practitioners of religions are rarely unified in their values (and often not even in their theology). For example, most evangelical Christians share a belief in the Christian Trinity with fellow Christians of the National Council of Churches (NCC), but they share almost no values. Most evangelical Christians share far more values with traditional Catholics, Orthodox Jews, and practicing Mormons than with fellow Protestant Christians of the NCC or of the Anglican Church in the United Kingdom. And liberal Jews (not only secular ones, but many Conservative and Reform Jews) share more values with liberal Christians and liberal atheists than with Orthodox Jews. So when assessing Christianity or Judaism, whose Christianity and which Judaism are we assessing? And when we assess Islam, are we assessing the Islam of most Indonesian, Indian, and American Muslims or of most Arab Muslims, or of Islamists within and outside the Arab world?

Third, when groups are violent, how much of their violence is directly caused by their religion—or by their irreligion? Alongside Hitler, who believed in no religion, Stalin and Mao were history's greatest mass murderers, and they were atheists who attempted to destroy organized religion. Could one have asked, "Is atheism a violent ideology?" As for religious evildoers, did medieval European Christians who persecuted Jews do so because of, or despite, their Christianity?

Fourth, even when a group does attribute its violence to its religion, as in the case of Muslim terrorists, does that mean the religion preaches violence to its adherents?

Nevertheless, despite these arguments for assessing adherents rather than religions, the amount of violence that has historically been committed, and that is committed at the present time, in the name of Islam makes some assessment of Islam necessary and inevitable. Even if there were little or no Islamic violence, such an assessment would be mandatory—because Islam offers itself as the best answer to humanity's problems.

How could a book purporting to evaluate competing ideas for humanity's improvement not evaluate Islam, an intensely proselytizing religion with over a billion adherents? And how could one of the world's most popular doctrines—one that offers itself as incomparably superior to all other ways of life, secular or religious—not expect to be evaluated?

Of course, many people, and probably nearly all believing Muslims, might object to such an evaluation on the grounds that evaluating any religion—and especially Islam in light of the emotions it evokes at the present time—is an inherently biased, even bigoted, exercise. Muslim institutions also argue that outsiders have no right—and certainly no ability—to judge others' religions.

But these objections simply place religion in the unique position of being above criticism. We judge secular ideologies all the time. Why would we not similarly assess religions? People on the Left regularly criticize conservatives and conservatism and people on the Right regularly criticize the Left. Why is that permissible and even expected but it is not permissible to assess a religion? Likewise, one could fill a library with books critiquing the Bible and Christianity. Why not the Koran and Islam?

It is true that many of those who judge or criticize a religion are prejudiced. This is frequently the case when one's agenda is to prove one's own religion true and all others false, when one simply hates members of another faith (anti-Semites, for example), or when one hates all religions (such as many of the popular atheist writers). But none of these apply here. Not only do I have no interest in proving Islam "false"; I believe that all people, including believing Muslims, who do good because they believe God commands them to do so are practicing a form of true religion. I believe that whatever rewards God will have for good members of my faith await the good people of all faiths (and of no faith, for that matter).

In any event, the existence of bigoted writing on religion hardly argues against all writing on religion other than praises by admirers and adherents. People should be allowed to evaluate religion just as they are allowed to assess anything else. Judaism and Jews have been the targets of a morally indefensible hatred. But not every critique of Judaism is anti-Semitic. Likewise, many contemporary attacks on Christianity and Christians are bigoted—such as when Christian fundamentalists are likened to Islamist terrorists. There are no Christian groups comparable to the Islamist groups that murder innocents or seek to violently impose Islamic law on both Muslims and non-Muslims. But not every criticism of Christians or Christianity emanates from anti-Christian bigotry. And one need not be prejudiced against Islam or Muslims to ask challenging questions about Muslims and/or their religion.*

---

* Readers who insist on identifying some religious prejudice here should be assured that I apply the same standard to my own religion. I do not want any one religion—not Christianity, not Judaism, not Islam, nor any other—to govern the world. I want mankind to adopt ethical monotheism—belief in the One God who wants people to be good and who judges individuals and nations—and to express that through whatever religious tradition they choose.

Why Islam Is Included

IF ISLAM WERE NOT as powerful a force as it is and if it did not seek to make the world Muslim, it might not be necessary to include Islam or Islamism in a book on the alternatives available for humanity at the present time. But from its inception, its primary aim has been to bring humanity to Islam. There is no normative version of Islam that does not have as its ideal the conversion of mankind to Islam. Muslims may differ at times as to how to attain this goal, but there is no mainstream Muslim movement that does not hold that the world must accept Allah as the one God, Muhammad as his final and most authoritative Messenger, and the Koran as that perfect message. The creedal sentence of Islam, known as the Shahada, states: "There is no God but Allah and Muhammad is his Messenger"; the other part of the Islamic creed is that the Koran is the one perfect and final revelation from God.

Yes, Christianity, too, seeks to have the world accept Christ. But there are at least four significant differences between these two religions that seek to convert the world.

First, and most obvious, Christians do not pose a threat to non-Christians. Non-Christians who live among Christians are not only not threatened—they are lucky. On the other hand, virtually all non-Muslim communities living among Muslim majorities live in fear for their safety. There is, therefore, all the difference in the world between a religion that wishes to be universally adopted, none of whose adherents threaten outsiders, and a religion that wishes to be universally adopted, many of whose adherents threaten others.

Second, Christianity not only accepts a separation of religious and secular authority; it essentially founded the idea with the New Testament statement, "Render unto Caesar the things which are Caesar's, and unto God the things that are God's" (Matthew 22:21). The concept of separation of church and state is alien to Islam, where the ideal has always been a Sharia-based government.

Third, Christianity does not seek to impose life-controlling religious laws on all Christians, let alone on non-Christians living in their midst. Christianity does not have an analogous body of religious laws in any way comparable to the Sharia (Islamic law). The Sharia is, as believing Muslims proudly explain, an all-encompassing code of conduct. It instructs the Muslim how often to pray, when to arise each day, when and what he may eat, what he may not drink, how to dress, and among stricter Muslims, what music may be listened to, prohibits almost any contact between unrelated men and women, directs women regarding where and how they may be seen in public, what subjects, if any, they may study, and much more. In addition, what we call Islamism seeks to create Islamic states that impose Sharia on all Muslims, and some of those laws on non-Muslims who live in Muslim-majority states.

Fourth, having written a book on anti-Semitism and taught Jewish history at the college level, I am well aware of Christian maltreatment of Jews in Europe during the Middle Ages in particular. But whatever sins Christians engaged in the past, and they were extensive, the fact is that the most humane and decent countries in the world nearly all have Christian origins. That is not true of states that grew out of Islam.

For these reasons, one cannot honestly liken the Christian desire for a Christian world to the Muslim desire for a Muslim world.

When fears concerning Islam are expressed, those who dismiss such fears argue that Islam had a golden period when it surpassed the Christian West in learning, art, and morality. That is true. The Muslim world transmitted the Greek philosophers, Muslim explorers were navigating much of the known world, Muslim math and science surpassed the West's, and social organization exceeded the West's.

But as the great scholar of Islam Professor Gustave E. von Grunebaum, after whom the Center for Near Eastern Studies at UCLA is named, wrote, Islamic science developed for a while despite, not because of, traditional Islamic beliefs: "Those accomplishments of Islamic mathematical and medical science which continue to compel our admiration were developed in areas and in periods where the elites were willing to go beyond and possibly against the basic strains of orthodox thought and feeling."[3]

In addition, the existence of a golden period well into the past does not signify much regarding the present or the future. There is hardly a civilization that has not had a golden period. The Chinese, Mongolian, Korean, Portuguese, Spanish, Dutch, Aztec, French, Vietnamese, and Indian civilizations all had golden eras when they surpassed much of the world in many areas. But no one would argue that because any of these had a golden period, the culture should be assessed only by that period, let alone that it should lead the world today.

This does not constitute a criticism of any of these civilizations, and it does not constitute a criticism of Islam. Every civilization goes into a decline after its golden age. Indeed, one reason for this book is the fear that American civilization will decline if its core values are abandoned.

Why Islamism *and Not Only* Islam

THIS BOOK DESCRIBES the competition between American, Leftist, and Islamist values and argues that the world needs American values to prevail. The use of the term *Islamist* rather than only *Islam*, *Islamic*, or *Muslim* is deliberate and needs to be explained.

What renders one an Islamist as described in this book is holding the belief that not only should all mankind be converted to Islam—something a non-Islamist Muslim can wish for—but that all Muslim societies (and eventually the world) be governed by the Sharia. An Islamist does not necessarily advocate violence to achieve this goal. "Islamist" does not mean "Muslim terrorist." But given Islamists' belief that true Islam is only practiced in a Sharia-led Islamic state, it is almost inevitable that this belief will lead some Islamists to religious violence.

Both Islamists and most critics of Islam would argue that there is no meaningful difference between Islam and Islamism. And the truth is that for much of Muslim history there has not been a great difference. Islam was largely spread by the sword—more so than other religions; normative Islam never held that non-Muslims were to be treated as equals; and great numbers of non-Muslims—with the partial exception of Jews and Christians (known as *dhimmi*)—were either enslaved or slaughtered. Jews and Christians were sometimes killed or enslaved, but when they were allowed to live, they were treated as humiliated inferiors.

I believe that Islam can evolve into a non-Islamist, that is, non-theocratic, religion. It would not entail overthrowing the Koran or abandoning the Shahada, the Islamic creed—"there is no god but Allah, and Muhammad is the messenger of Allah." It would essentially entail "individualizing" Islam—living an observant, even a Sharia-based, life—without seeking to establish an Islamic state that would impose Sharia law on anyone, Muslim or non-Muslim.

There are noble religious Muslim voices advocating that ideal. But those voices are rare and they are drowned out by more normative/traditional Muslim voices. If anything, Islamists constitute a more influential model and powerful force in the Muslim world today than they have in the past few centuries, when much of the Muslim world was politically, economically, and militarily weak, and largely dominated by outside forces.

Such an evolution within Islam will be possible only if non-Muslims support the Muslim reformers and if non-Muslims pressure the Islamic world to practice the same norms of tolerance and peaceful coexistence demanded of the rest of the world.

Finally, some personal notes concerning Islam.

First, as noted at the beginning of the book, it should go without saying—but in our time where any critical remarks about any group (other than Americans, Israelis, and Christians) are frequently declared to be bigoted by definition—I fully recognize that there are hundreds of millions of Muslims who lead lives morally indistinguishable from much of the rest of mankind.

Second, whatever critical comments are made in this section are not intended to hurt, and are written accordingly. But it helps no one, least of all the many decent Muslims who suffer at the hands of Islamists and Islamist regimes, to deny what is problematic about Islam and/or the Islamic world.

Third, in thirty years of radio broadcasting, writing, and lecturing, I do not recall ever having made an unfair, let alone bigoted, statement about Muslims or Islam.* For many years, in fact, I was so respected and trusted by the Muslim community in Southern California that I was invited to speak at one of the largest mosques in America, the Southern California Islamic Center. This was because I was among the only individuals in mainstream American media who routinely invited Muslim spokesmen to appear on a major radio show—in my case on a widely listened-to show on the ABC Radio station in Los Angeles. Moreover, I did not invite them to discuss terrorism or to defend Islam or Muslims. They were invited as equal partners along with Jewish, Protestant, Catholic, Mormon, Buddhist, and other representatives of virtually every religion in the world. I also invited Muslim spokesmen to appear at Jewish institutions in order to foster goodwill between Jews and Muslims.

One of the credos of my life is taken from Viktor Frankl, a Jewish survivor of Nazi concentration camps, who was a psychiatrist and author. In his highly influential book, *Man's Search for Meaning*, he related that after the war someone asked him if he "hated the German race." He responded that he did not because in his view,

---

* In my long career in public life, I was once charged publicly with engaging in "Islamophobia." The charge emanated from a column I wrote in which I wrongly argued against the first American Muslim congressman taking his symbolic oath of office on a Koran. It was wrong because an elected official should be allowed to choose the holy book with which he wants to take his oath of office. But as my column explicitly noted, it was not the Koran I objected to. I objected to what would have been the first deliberate removal of the Bible and use of another holy text in a swearing-in of any American elected to a national office. I wrote that I would have objected just as strenuously to a Mormon elected official substituting the Book of Mormon for the Bible—and I have enormous admiration for Mormons. My concern was about the further denial of the Judeo-Christian bases of American values. I hoped that the congressman, Keith Ellison of Minnesota, would bring both a Bible and a Koran to his symbolic swearing-in just as a Muslim American had done at his actual swearing-in as American ambassador to Bangladesh. In any event, in the halls of Congress some time later, I apologized to Congressman Ellison for any hurt I caused him, in the presence of Representative David Dreier of California. Congressman Ellison not only graciously accepted my apology but told me that his mother listens to my radio show every day in Detroit and that "she is your biggest fan." Only in America.

"There are only two races, the decent and the indecent." That is how I divide the world. Not between Muslim and non-Muslim, black and white, or American and non-American, but between the decent and indecent. The issues I raise about Islam are not about the decency of Muslims, but about whether Islam in its traditional Islamist configuration is more or less likely than the American value system to produce good societies.

If this book were written in the Middle Ages, I would have addressed moral problems in Christendom—its anti-Semitism, its intolerance, its inquisitions, its theocratic tendencies. But this is the twenty-first century, not the fifteenth. And Christianity has been a major force for good for some time, most especially, though not only, in its American incarnation. The abolitionist movement—the movement to end slavery—was overwhelmingly a Christian movement; the civil rights movement in America was led by a Christian pastor, the Reverend Dr. Martin Luther King Jr., largely in the name of God and Christianity;[4] great numbers of Christians have gone to the poorest and most remote places on earth to build hospitals, teach children, and care for the dying; and Judeo-based Christians founded the United States of America, the most successful experiment in large-scale social decency ever conducted.

With those introductory comments as background, we can proceed with a discussion of Islam and Islamism.

The Moral Record of Islam

THERE ARE A NUMBER of serious moral problems within the Muslim world: the lack of liberty, the treatment of women, the imposition of Sharia on Muslims and non-Muslims, the use of violent punishments for non-violent offenses, and an abandonment of reason, among others. Any one of these would seem to disqualify Islamism—meaning Sharia-based society, the traditional Islamic ideal—as a solution, let alone the best solution, to the problem of evil.

1. Islam and Liberty

LET'S BEGIN WITH LIBERTY, the central value of the American value system. Individual liberty as understood in the West has never been an important value in the Muslim world—or, for that matter, almost anywhere else (outside of England) before the American Revolution. But it is not important within Islam today either. One result is that there are essentially no free Muslim countries.[1]

Of the forty-seven Muslim-majority countries, the Freedom House 2010 survey ranked two as free, eighteen partly free, and twenty-seven not free.

How is one to explain this?

There are three widely offered exculpating explanations. One is that outside of Western civilization, liberty has not been a primary value in almost any culture. Another is that Muslim countries were colonized by Western nations and therefore stymied in their development. And a third is that, particularly in the Arab part of the Muslim world, many features of Bedouin Arab life remain strong.

Even if valid, none of these explanations recommends Sharia-based Islam to those who seek liberty. But they are not valid. Regarding the lack of liberty outside the Western world, that was true until the modern era. But there are many non-Western societies that have embraced liberty—certainly to a greater extent than the Muslim world has. As regards the vestiges of pre-Islamic culture in Arab-Muslim society and culture, isn't the primary goal of religion to improve on the moral culture it replaced? If Jews had many of the same moral values and practices that Canaanites had, one would speak of Judaism as having failed morally. If Christendom still retained the practices and values of the Roman Empire, what possible moral argument could be made on behalf of Christianity? As for Arab and other Muslim countries having been colonized by the West, India, too, was colonized and ruled by British imperialists—and emerged a robust democracy. More on this later.

That liberty has been absent in the Arab part of the Muslim world demands further explanation. No part of the Muslim world is as steeped in Islam as is the Arab. Muhammad was Arab, the Arabs spread Islam, the Koran is in Arabic, the Muslim holy sites are in Arabia, and every Muslim is expected to make a pilgrimage to Arabia. Why, then, has the Arab world, which has been Muslim longer than any other part of the Muslim world, been the least free?

According to many observers of the Middle East, the lack of liberty in the Arab world begins in the Arab family. In the words of Brian Whitaker, Middle East editor for the *Guardian*, "To understand Arab society, and indeed its politics, we have to understand Arab concepts of the family. The family is the basic molecule of society and, in many ways, a microcosm of the Arab state. It is the primary mechanism for social control—or, put another way, the point where liberty begins to be constrained."[2]

This view is affirmed by an Arab sociologist: "Rulers and political leaders," Halim Barakat says, "are cast in the image of the father, while citizens are cast in the image of children. God, the father, and the ruler thus have many characteristics in common. They are the shepherds, and the people are the sheep: citizens of Arab countries are often referred to as ra'iyyah (the flock)."[3]

Moreover, it is not only a lack of individual liberty that characterizes the Arab world. The Arab Human Development Report of 2003, written by Arab scholars and published by the United Nations Development Programme, was devastating in its description of Arab countries.

Take, for example, their lack of interest in the non-Muslim world: "The total number of books translated into Arabic in the last 1,000 years is fewer than those translated in Spain in one year. Greece, with a population of fewer than 11 million, translates five times as many books from abroad into Greek annually as the 22 Arab countries combined, with a total population of more than 300 million, translated into Arabic."[4]

In addition, "Of the Arab League's 22 members, not a single one is a stable and fully fledged democracy. . . . Even sub-Saharan Africa has a better record of electoral freedom."[5]

It is difficult to avoid concluding that Islam is a cause of the Arab world's backwardness. As Professor Samuel Huntington put it when interviewed in an Islamic magazine—proving, one should note, that many Muslims are quite capable of handling critical comments— "Islamic culture explains, in large part, the failure of democracy to emerge in much of the Muslim world."[6]

At worst, it is the primary cause. At best, it has done little in over a thousand years to elevate the Arab world.

2. Islam and Violence

EVERY RELIGION, every culture, every ethnic group, and every nation has engaged in violence. Islam is hardly alone in this regard. However, among major world religions, Islam has stood out. Islam's origins are more violent than those of the two other monotheistic religions, Judaism and Christianity.

After the Jews conquered Canaan following the exodus from Egypt in about 1200 BC, the early Jewish kingdoms were involved in wars with other nations—and fought each other. But they never sought to increase their numbers through conquest, and did not seek to convert those they conquered or establish Jewish hegemony beyond the limited biblical borders. Judaism always welcomed converts, but unlike Muslims and Christians, Jews were under no theological compulsion to make converts. There was, therefore, nothing analogous within Judaism to Islam's conquering vast numbers of non-Muslims and converting them.

As for Christianity, the violence that accompanied Christianity's origins was directed against Christians, not committed by Christians, who constituted a small and weak minority in the Roman Empire. It took more than three hundred years—after the Roman Empire adopted Christianity as the state religion—for Christians to begin to wage war.

Beyond Islam's first few members, its original converts were largely converted through warfare. Until stopped by hostile forces centuries later, Islam never ceased conquering new areas to spread Islam.

When confronted with the violence perpetrated in spreading Islam, a favored response offered by defenders of Islam is to cite the verse in the Koran that says, "In matters of faith there shall be no compulsion" (Sura 2:256). This verse is of particular significance to defenders of Islam because it provides a Koranic basis for arguing that Islam forbids religious violence and because it suggests that Islam was not allowed to accept forced conversions.

In response, one would point out that there are approximately a hundred verses in the Koran that direct the Muslim in the other direction. Some examples:

> *"If anyone desires a religion other than Islam, never will it be accepted of him."* (Sura 3:85)

> *"I will cast terror into the hearts of those who disbelieve. Therefore strike off their heads and strike off every fingertip of them."* (Sura 8:12)

> *"Fight those who believe not in Allah nor the Last Day, nor hold that forbidden which hath been forbidden by Allah and His Messenger, nor acknowledge the religion of Truth . . ."* (Sura 9:29)

> *"O you who believe! Fight those of the unbelievers who are near to you and let them find in you firmness."* (Sura 9:123)

These verses are not cited to judge the Koran. They are cited to counter the argument that the verse that promotes religious tolerance is representative of the Koran.

Moreover, the issue here is not what any given verse in the Koran advocates. It is what Muslims did in the name of Islam.

Verses are open to interpretation; historical facts are not. Either many millions of non-Muslims were killed in spreading Islam, and either vast numbers of non-Muslims were given a choice of Islam or death, or not. Arguing that a Koranic verse advocating religious tolerance means that Islam was not often spread by the sword is analogous to arguing that because Jesus advocated loving one's enemies, the Church never persecuted anyone. In Muhammad's lifetime, the Arabian Peninsula became Muslim. After his death in 632:

Persia was conquered between 633 and 651.
Syria in 636–37.
Armenia in 639.

Egypt in 639.

The rest of North Africa between 652 and 665.

Cyprus in 654.

Central Asia (modern-day Uzbekistan, Tajikistan, and part
   of Kazakhstan) between 662 and 709.

India beginning in 664–712.

Iberia (modern-day Spain and Portugal) between 711
   and 718.

Constantinople (modern-day Turkey) by 718.

Georgia in 736.

Crete in 820.

Southern Italy in 827.

From its inception, Islam went to war to conquer and convert people in countries from the Atlantic Ocean to Western China. As Muhammad said in what is called his farewell address, "I was ordered to fight all men until they say, 'There is no God but Allah.'"

In the words of a leading scholar of Islam, Professor Efraim Karsh of the University of London: "Within a decade of Muhammad's death a vast empire, stretching from Iran to Egypt and from Yemen to northern Syria, had come into being under the banner of Islam in one of the most remarkable examples of empire-building in world history."[7]

It is also worth noting these wars were rarely, if ever, defensive wars. None of the conquered countries threatened Muslim Arabia. The purpose was to bring mankind to Islam.

Does this mean that Islam is inherently violent? Religions can evolve, and a religious Muslim can, if he chooses to, find in the Koran a basis for tolerance and nonviolence. But from its inception until the present, Islam has been violent, and traditionally religious Muslims believed that their religion countenanced that violence.

If a movement engages in violence for much of its 1,500-year history, if that violence is rarely in defense of self or of others, and if there are few recorded instances of voices from within that movement objecting to that violence, it would seem fair to deem that movement violent, though not inevitably so.

The leading Muslim theological and scholarly voices that are recorded sanctioned religious violence. Indeed, the Muslim success in conquering, killing, and enslaving of non-Muslims—specifically those who were neither Jews nor Christians—was deemed to be proof of God's approval of the killing and enslavement, and of course, of Islam.

To argue that Islam is inherently peaceful and tolerant, one would have to argue that most believing Muslims, including, especially, its most knowledgeable and most pious, from Muhammad's time forward, were violating their religion's basic tenets.

JIHAD

At the core of Islam's acceptance and prescription of religious violence is jihad, Islam's most distinguishing violent feature. *Jihad* is the Muslim term for holy war. Contemporary apologists for Islam argue that jihad can also mean struggle with oneself to become a better human being. That is true. But it is dishonest to argue that the latter definition has been the dominant one in Muslim history. Princeton University professor Bernard Lewis, generally considered, in the words of CNN and *Newsweek* commentator Fareed Zakaria, "the pre-eminent historian of Islam,"[8] has written that *in the large majority of cases in the Koran and the later hadith* (actions or statements attributed to Muhammad's doing or approving) *jihad refers to holy war.*[9]

Arguably the most important statement about holy war's central place in Islam was made by the man who is the most highly esteemed Muslim thinker to have ever lived, Ibn Khaldun (1332–1406). The work for which Ibn Khaldun is best known is *The Muqaddimah*, or "Introduction to History." This work was declared by the eminent Oxford historian Arnold Toynbee as "the greatest work of its kind that has ever been created by any mind in any time or place. . . . The most comprehensive and illuminating analysis of however human affairs work that has been made anywhere." It has been published in

English as one of Princeton University's Bollingen Series of world classics. In this work, Ibn Khaldun wrote, "In the Muslim community, the holy war is religious duty, because of the universalism of the Muslim mission and (the obligation to) convert everybody to Islam either by persuasion or by force." [10]

The most respected Muslim writer who ever lived is not only not apologetic about the fact that Islam demands holy war; he argues that this is one reason for Islam's superiority over all other religions: "The other religious groups did not have a universal mission, and the holy war was not a religious duty to them, save only for purposes of defense."

So, according to Ibn Khaldun:

a. Unlike all other religions, which demand war only in self-defense,
b. Islam demands jihad, holy war,
c. Muslims are therefore enjoined to wage jihad in order to make converts to Islam.

Even if one accepts that there are multiple meanings of the term *jihad*, and that other meanings can be moral and ennobling, that would have no bearing on the question of whether jihad as holy war is central to Islam. As Ibn Khaldun makes clear, jihad, meaning a holy war of aggression just as much as a holy war of defense, is central to Islam, and is Islam's distinguishing glory.

This does not mean that every believing Muslim today advocates jihad in order to make converts. Nor does it mean that every Muslim who supports jihad necessarily supports Islamist terror. Jihad is supported by all Muslim supporters of terror, but terror is not necessarily supported by every supporter of jihad. But violence in the name of Islam, whether for secular reasons such as acquiring power, wealth, and slaves, or in order to make converts to Islam—or, as was usually the case, for both—has been a normative part of Muslim history.

ISLAM AND TERROR

As of the second decade in the twenty-first century, nearly all acts of terror around the world (as opposed to acts of terror confined to one country, as in the case of the Tamil Tigers in Sri Lanka) have been committed by Muslims in the name of Islam. Of course the vast majority of Muslims are not terrorists. But this frequently noted fact is meaningless. The vast majority of Germans were not members of the Gestapo, nor were the vast majority of Russians members of the Communist Party, let alone the KGB.

Not only is international terror overwhelmingly Muslim, but there are virtually no terrorists committing terror in the name of Christianity, Judaism, Buddhism, Hinduism, or any other religion. Here is a typical Islamist act of terror that has no analogue in other religions: "In November 1997, 50 Swiss tourists rose early to visit the Valley of the Kings across the Nile from Luxor in Egypt. Suddenly from the hills came a group of Islamists. They shot, disemboweled and decapitated the tourists." [11]

No normative critic, conservative or otherwise, equates Islamic terrorism with all Muslims or with all of Islam. Rather, in Charles Krauthammer's words, "Radical Islam is not, by any means, a majority of Islam. But with its financiers, clerics, propagandists, trainers, leaders, operatives and sympathizers—according to a conservative estimate, it commands the allegiance of 7 percent of Muslims, that is, more than 80 million souls—it is a very powerful strain within Islam. It has changed the course of nations and affected the lives of millions. It is the reason every airport in the West is an armed camp and every land is on constant alert." [12]

One frequently offered explanation for Islamic terror is that countries and groups that have been attacked by Muslim terrorists have brought those attacks upon themselves. Those who offer this explanation always add that they do not condone terrorism; they are merely explaining it. This explanation is offered most often regarding terror against the United States and Israel. In the case of Israel, however, there is a particularly telling argument against this explanation. According to the 2009 *CIA World Factbook*, about 8 percent of Palestinians—about 167,000 people—living in the West Bank were Christian. If Israeli occupation, rather than something within Islam, has been the primary reason for Palestinian terror against Israel, why haven't there been Palestinian Christian suicide terrorists? After all, Christian Palestinians are no less occupied by Israel.

Some counter that there have been Palestinian Christian terrorists, that in fact the "godfather" of Palestinian terrorism, George Habash, founder of the Popular Front for the Liberation of Palestine, was a Christian. It is true that Habash was born a Christian, a faith he left when he became a Marxist, but he never went, and he never sent any Palestinians, on a suicide terror mission. As *Time* magazine put it when Habash died in 2008, "compared to the terrorists behind today's nihilistic suicide bombings and mass atrocities such as 9/11, Habash's commandos were almost softies. Before they blew up the three planes in Jordan in a spectacular, televised moment that was the 9/11 of its day, all of the 300 or so passengers were evacuated and quickly freed."[13]

The reason that Palestinian terror has been perpetrated by Muslim rather than Christian Palestinians seems clear. There is Palestinian Muslim terror largely for the same reasons there is non-Palestinian Muslim terror. A significant part of the Muslim world wishes to destroy those non-Muslims—Americans, Israelis, Filipinos, Nigerians, Sudanese, Christian Lebanese, and others—who prevent Islam from attaining power.

Muslim terror is caused by Muslims, not by the non-Muslims against whom it has been directed. In our morally confused world, Israel and America—and other victims of terror such as Spain, even after that country's socialists came to power promising to remove Spain's troops from Iraq—are often deemed largely responsible for having their men, women, and children blown up.

One of the most often asked questions posed after America was attacked on 9/11 was, "What has the United States done to arouse so much Muslim hatred?" The question, however, is on the same moral level as asking what German and other European Jews did to cause the Holocaust, or what blacks did to arouse the hatred among the American whites who lynched them.

The primary cause of Muslim terror is to be found within the Muslims who conduct the acts of terror and the Muslims who support them—not within the behavior of the victims or the victims' groups. What did the above-mentioned tourists in Egypt or their country (Switzerland) do to merit their being slaughtered?

As for terror against Israelis, Palestinian Muslim terror emanates from a desire to destroy Israel, not from Israel's conduct regarding Palestinians, whether occupation, settlements, or checkpoints. One proof is that the greatest amount of Palestinian terror against Israel was unleashed after Israel agreed to give up nearly all of the West Bank to the Palestinians at the end of 2000. Islamist terror against Israel is the result of Muslim, especially Arab Muslim, desires to annihilate the one non-Muslim state in the midst of the Arab world. For most Arab Muslims and for all Islamists, the Middle East is supposed to be under Muslim rule. There is no place for a Christian Lebanon or for a Jewish Israel, no matter what its borders. That Israel is Jewish is all the more an affront to many Muslims. Jews are supposed to have *dhimmi* status under Muslim rule, and no Muslim should be under Jewish rule.

Islamist terror in Algeria in the 1990s provides an important example of what Islamists will do to in order to install an Islamist regime in a country and of their willingness to murder fellow Muslims in order to achieve their goals. Islamist terrorists killed approximately one hundred thousand and injured approximately one million Algerians, nearly always innocent men, women, and children. Led by the Armed Islamic Group (GIA) of the Algerian Islamic Movement (MIA), the intention was to create an Islamist regime in Algeria. Here is a summary in a monograph sponsored by the Norwegian government, written by Algerian journalist M. Boudjemaa of the Algerian newspaper *Quotidien d'Oran*:

It is a movement that is genocidal in character, with no equivalent in Africa or the world, except perhaps the disastrous toll of the Khmer Rouge in Cambodia. A religious political movement, whose roots go deep down into the contemporary history of Algeria since independence, embodies this terrorist violence. . . .

Between 1992 and 1997, the GIA conducted a series of violent campaigns against an unarmed population and a security service that had never faced such a phenomenon. Their actions included bombings, purposeful criminal acts, the massacre of isolated citizens, sabotage, rape, mutilation, torture and the systematic liquidation of any Algerian citizen who refused to support the extremist fundamentalist solution. . . .

Through the assassination of foreigners, the terrorists have also targeted women and men of religions other than Islam, even those that preach tolerance and forgiveness. Catholics, Protestants, both monks (seven of whom belonged to the Trappist Order) and high dignitaries of the church, have been killed, such as Bishop Claverie, who was killed in a bomb attack in Oran in August 1995.[14]

MUSLIM ATTITUDES TOWARD TERROR

Many polls have been taken of Muslims living in Muslim countries and in the West. The polls reveal that at least 10 percent—and often far more—support Islamic terrorism. That would mean that, conservatively speaking, well over 100 million Muslims support suicide terror under various circumstances.

The polls also indicated that support for suicide bombings declined in various Muslim countries after 2002. If this is accurate, it is likely that the reason for the decline was the vast increase in suicide bombings directed against Muslims themselves, as opposed to earlier years when such acts of terrorism were directed primarily against non-Muslims, especially Americans and Israelis.

As of this writing, however, I could find no credible report of any significant Muslim demonstration against Islamic terrorism against non-Muslims anywhere in the world. The only major Muslim demonstration against Muslim terror that I could find took place in November 2005 in Jordan.

On November 9, 2005, there was a series of coordinated terrorist suicide bomber attacks on three hotels in Amman, Jordan. The attacks killed sixty people and injured 115 others. One of the attacks was during a wedding celebration and it killed the fathers of both the bride and the groom. Jordanians were so shocked that Muslim terrorists would blow up Jordanian families, including families celebrating a wedding, that Muslims publicly demonstrated against Islamic terror.

As long as Islamic terrorists blew up men, women, and children who were Jewish, Christian, Hindu, American, Australian, and black Sudanese, among others, there were no public protests in the Arab and larger Muslim worlds. In fact, Palestinians, who compose the majority of Jordan's population, celebrated when Jews were blown up at Passover seders and night clubs. And some took to the streets and cheered in the Palestinian fashion, handing out candy, when Americans were massacred on September 11, 2001.

There was widespread Jordanian condemnation of the man responsible for the Amman attack, Abu Musab al-Zarqawi, the Jordanian who headed Al Qaeda in Iraq. The London *Telegraph*, for example, reported that "Munder Moomeni, a 38-year-old former soldier who lives next to Zarqawi's house, 13 Ramzi Street, described his former neighbour as 'a bastard.' 'By killing Jordanians here in Jordan, civilian Jordanians going to a wedding, they did something that not even a Jew would do,' he said."[15]

That a neighbor in Zarqawi's formerly sympathetic hometown publicly acknowledged that Jews would not engage in such terror was significant. But over time the only real lesson learned was that Jordanian terrorists should not bomb fellow Jordanians.

3. Islam and Non-Muslims

FROM ISLAM'S INCEPTION, Muslims invaded every area of the world they could in order to conquer and/or convert the non-Muslims living there. There were rarely moral restraints on the treatment of those conquered; the conquering Muslims believed that non-Muslims (who were not Jews or Christians), that is, "nonbelievers," did not deserve to live. Therefore, in many cases they were given the choice of Islam or death, and in other cases they were either killed or enslaved. As a result, the number of non-Muslims killed in the name of Islam was in the tens of millions.

HINDUS

The largest number of these victims were Hindus. In 712 CE,[*] Muslims invaded India after conquering Persia and with the invasion by Mahmoud of Ghazni some three hundred years later, ultimately controlled much of the Indian subcontinent until about the middle of the eighteenth century—a period of approximately a thousand years. According to historian Will Durant, "The Mohammedan conquest of India is probably the bloodiest story in history."[16]

In the world prior to Communism and Nazism, Durant may have been right. In 1973, Indian professor K. S. Lal published *Growth of Muslim Population in Medieval India (1000–1800)*, in which he concluded that between 60 and 80 million Hindus died as a result of the Muslim invasions and rule over India in the years between 1000 and 1525.[†] That number cannot be precisely verified given the paucity of documents from that time and place. However, Lal (1920–2002)

---

[*] I use *CE* (Common Era) instead of *AD* (Anno Domini—"Year of Our Lord"), but I retain *BC* rather than *BCE*. I recognize that there is no consistency here. It is done because most readers recognize *BC*, while *AD* is more rarely used and *CE* is increasingly used.

[†] Whenever such statistics of death are cited, I think of the statement attributed (wrongly) to Joseph Stalin, "One death is a tragedy, a million is a statistic," and the line by the Polish poet Wislawa Szymborska, "History rounds off skeletons to zero."

was widely regarded both within and outside India as the preeminent historian of medieval India. He was professor of history at the University of Delhi and the chairman of the Indian Council for Historical Research.

Reading the descriptions of the Muslim invasions of Hindu areas over a thousand years and the genocidal killings involved, Lal's estimate and Durant's description seem plausible. There is also another—Muslim-based—argument that an enormous number of Hindu deaths occurred under Islamic conquest and rule. The Hindu Kush, the vast, 500-mile long, 150-mile wide mountain range stretching from Afghanistan to Pakistan, was populated by Hindus until the Muslim invasions beginning around 1000 CE. The Persian name *Hindu Kush* was proudly given by Muslims. It means "Hindu killer."

JEWS AND CHRISTIANS

Unlike Hindus or any of the other peoples conquered by Muslims, Jews and Christians had a special status in Islamic theology. Though they were often killed, mass killings of Jews and Christians were not common once Islamic rule was established. According to Islamic theology, Jews and Christians, being People of the Book (that is, the Old and New Testaments) were not to be slaughtered, but allowed to live under special rules.

Thus, Christians remained a large part of the North African countries ruled by Muslims since the seventh century. It was not until the fourteenth century—beginning in 1321, when Muslim mobs began destroying Coptic churches—that Christians and Jews in Egypt were killed in any numbers. In 1354, mobs were "attacking Christians and Jews in the streets, and throwing them into bonfires if they refused to pronounce the *shahadatayn* [Allah is the one true God and Muhammad is his messenger]."[17] By the end of that century, according to the contemporary Arab historian Muhammad al-Maqrizi (1364–1442): "[In] all the provinces of Egypt, both north and south, no church remained that had not been razed. . . . thus did Islam spread among the Christians of Egypt."[18]

Islam's view of the Jews emanating from Muhammad and the Koran were never favorable, and this led to harsh treatment of Jews, though rarely as harsh as the treatment Jews often experienced in Christian Europe. That fact, as we shall see, influenced the way major Western writers wrote about Muslim treatment of Christians and particularly of Jews.

Anti-Jewish sentiments began with Muhammad and the Koran and those origins have been cited to this day by Muslims as justification for maltreating Jews. Muhammad wanted the Jews of his time to accept him as God's final and authoritative prophet and to accept the Koran as the final divine revelation. Muhammad wanted all people to accept him and the Koran, but, as with Jesus six hundred years before, Jewish acclamation was more important than that of any other group. As Joseph Telushkin and I have written, "No group could validate Muhammad's religious claims as could the Jews, nor could any so seriously threaten to undermine them."[19]

Muhammad was deeply influenced by Judaism and the Torah, so much so that from the beginning of his prophetic vocation, he "had been trying to model the religious life of the *ummah* [Islamic community] on Judaism."[20] He originally fasted on the Jewish high holy day of Yom Kippur, he prayed toward Jerusalem, he modeled Islam's five-times-daily prayers after Judaism's three-times-daily prayers, and he made the Muslim version of the Jewish Sabbath on Fridays. After he gave up on the Jews accepting him as their prophet, he changed the Muslim fast from Yom Kippur to Ramadan and changed the direction of Muslim prayers from Jerusalem to Mecca.

As an eminent scholar of Jewish life under Islam, the late professor S. D. Goitein, founder of Hebrew University's School of Asian and African Studies, wrote: "It is only natural that Muhammad could not tolerate as a neighbor a large monotheistic community which categorically denied his claim as a prophet, and probably also ridiculed his inevitable blunders."[21] Therefore, alongside acknowledgment of the Jews having a special place in the divine scheme, of Moses as a Muslim prophet, and some other shared biblical beliefs, the Jews' rejection caused Muhammad to include severe accusations against the Jews in the Koran. Here is a sampling:

> "O you who believe! Do not take the Jews and the Christians for friends [some translations say "allies"]; they are friends of each other; and whoever amongst you takes them for a friend, then surely he is one of them; surely Allah does not guide the unjust people." (Sura 5:51)

> "Verily, you will find the Jews the greediest of mankind for life and even greedier than those who ascribe partners [other gods] to Allah." (Sura 2:96)

> "Those Jews who incurred the Curse of Allah and His Wrath, some of whom He has transformed into monkeys and swine . . ." (Sura 5:60)

> "And the Jews say: The hand of Allah is tied up! Their hands shall be shackled and they shall be cursed for what they say." (Sura 5:64)

> "And abasement and humiliation were brought down upon them, and they became deserving of Allah's wrath; this was so because they disbelieved in the communications of Allah and killed the prophets unjustly; this was so because they disobeyed and exceeded the limits." (Sura 2:61)

The guiding principle of Islam's treatment of Jews and Christians has been that Islam dominates and is not dominated. Therefore, while other non-Muslims were to be killed, enslaved, or converted, Jews and Christians were to be subservient and degraded.[22]

It is often argued that there was a golden age of Muslim tolerance (of Jews and Christians) between the years 700 and 1000 in Muslim-ruled Spain. This is offered as proof of Islam's inherent tolerance toward non-Muslims. Was it a golden age of tolerance? In answering this question, it is important to know that this idea was introduced largely by Protestant and Jewish historians in the eighteenth and nineteenth centuries. Examples included Edward Gibbon (1737–1794), the most prominent English historian of his era, author of *The Decline and Fall of the Roman Empire*, and Heinrich Graetz (1817–1891), the most prominent Jewish historian of the nineteenth century. They had the same agenda: to depict the Catholic Church in the most negative light possible (owing to its treatment of Protestants and Jews). It was therefore important to depict Islam, in comparison, as particularly beneficent to non-Muslims.

The truth is that compared with Christian Europe in the early Middle Ages, Islam in Spain did experience a golden age intellectually, scientifically, and in terms of tolerance toward Jews and Christians. However, though the Jews of Muslim Spain were not persecuted as much as the Jews and other non-Christians were in medieval Christian Europe, Jews and Christians were persecuted during this golden age. There was a Muslim legal code that prescribed the treatment of Jews and Christians (*dhimmis*)—the Pact of [the caliph] Umar, assumed to date from the late seventh or early eighth century. Among the rules that Jews and Christians had to obey:

"We shall show respect toward the Muslims, and we shall rise from our seats when they wish to sit.

"We shall not manifest our religion publicly nor convert anyone to it. We shall not prevent any of our kin from entering Islam if they wish it.

"We shall not mount on saddles . . ."[23]

The guiding principle for how to treat Jews and Christians was attributed to the Koran, Sura 9:29: "Fight against such of those who have been given the Scripture [that is, Jews and Christians] . . . who follow not the religion of truth [that is, Islam], until they pay the tribute readily, being brought low."

"Being brought low" meant humiliating *dhimmis*, especially

when they brought their tribute, their special *dhimmi* taxes, to Muslims. The rules for humiliating Jews and Christians were laid out explicitly:

"The dhimmi, Christian or Jew, goes on a fixed day in person to the emir, appointed to receive the poll tax, who occupies a high throne-like seat. The dhimmi stands before him, offering the poll tax on his open palm. The emir takes it so that his hand is on top and the dhimmi's underneath. Then the emir gives him a blow on the neck, and a guard, standing upright before the emir, drives him roughly away. The same procedure is followed with the second, third and the following taxpayers. The public is admitted to enjoy this show."[24]

Another law designed to humiliate *dhimmis* required them to wear distinguishing clothing so as to enable Muslims to immediately recognize a Jew or a Christian and in order to make Jews and Christians appear foolish. In 807, the Abbasid caliph Harun al-Rashid decreed that Jews must wear a yellow belt and a tall canonical hat. According to Holocaust historian Professor Raul Hilberg and in the view of Professor Bernard Lewis, this decree spread to the West and much later provided the model for the Nazi decree that Jews wear a yellow star.[25]

By the late eleventh century, the humiliation of Jews and Christians increased. According to a Jewish writer in Baghdad: "Each Jew had to have a stamp of lead . . . hang from his neck, on which the word *dhimmi* was inscribed. On women he [the Muslim vizier Abu Shuja] likewise imposed two distinguishing marks: the shoes worn by each woman had to be one red and one black. She also had to carry on her neck . . . a small brass bell. . . . And the Gentiles [Muslims] used to ridicule Jews, the mob and children often assaulting Jews in all the streets of Baghdad."[26]

Regarding Christians in the region that is modern day Iraq, in the words of BBC religious affairs reporter Edward Stourton, "Christians were persecuted and sometimes massacred during the turbulent period that lasted from the late 13th century until the early 16th century, and were forced to live as second-class citizens under the Ottomans."[27]

At the same time in Egypt, the Fatimid caliph Hakim ordered Christians to wear a cross with arms two feet long, while Jews had to wear around their necks balls weighing five pounds.[28]

Whatever one's assessment of the golden age, that era began to end in the eleventh century, when degradation of the Jews led to violence against them. In 1066, Muslim mobs massacred most of the Jews of Granada, and the Jewish vizier, Joseph ibn Naghrela, was crucified (crucifixion is one of the modes of execution prescribed in the Koran). The worst violence took place under the Almohades, a Berber Muslim dynasty that ruled Morocco and Spain in the twelfth and thirteenth centuries.

"At the beginning of the twelfth century, a Muslim jurist in Cordova [Spain] claimed to have found . . . a tradition, soon widely accepted in Morocco and Spain, that Muhammad's original decree of toleration of Jews had been limited to a period of five hundred years from the hegira [Muhammad's flight from Mecca]. If by that time the expected Jewish Messiah were not to arrive, the Jews were supposed to give up their religion and join the ranks of Islam. The time limit expired, of course, in 1107."[29]

On the basis of this new doctrine, in 1146, Abd al-Mu'min, the builder of the Almohad Empire in North Africa and Spain, gave the Jews the choice of Islam or death. When nearly all of them refused to convert, nearly every Jew in Fez, the capital of Morocco, was killed. As for those who converted, the Almohades put them under constant surveillance, and those whose conversions seemed insincere were executed, had their property confiscated, and their wives given to Muslims. In the words of S. D. Goitein, "All the horrors of the Spanish Inquisition were anticipated under Almohade rule."[30]

While the Almohades were distinguished by their violence, the humiliation of *dhimmis* was characteristic of Muslim rule generally. A good example is Yemen because it was the one Muslim country with a non-Muslim minority (Jews) that was never ruled by a

European power. It was therefore able to treat its Jews in a Muslim manner uninfluenced by non-Muslim domination. In 1679, Jews in most of Yemen were expelled from the cities and villages in which they lived. When allowed back, they were confined to special Jewish settlements outside of the cities, and the synagogue of San'a, the capital, was converted into a mosque, which still exists under the name Masjid al-Jala (the Mosque of the Expulsion).

The greatest recurrent suffering that Yemenite Jews experienced was the forced conversion to Islam of Jewish children whose fathers had died. This was practiced until the Jews of Yemen fled in 1948 to the newly established State of Israel. The justification for this practice was that Muhammad was believed to have said, "Everyone is born in a state of natural religion [Islam]. It is only his parents who make a Jew or Christian out of him." Accordingly, a fatherless Jew should grow up in "the natural religion" of Islam.

As a result, when a Jewish father died there was often a race between Jewish communal leaders who sought to place the man's children with Jewish parents and the Muslim authorities who sought to kidnap the children and place them in Muslim homes where they would be converted to Islam. Given the low status of women, the fact that the Jewish child still had a mother was of no significance to the Yemenis.

The Jews often lost this race. Goitein wrote that "many families arrived in Israel with one or more of their children lost to them, and I have heard of some widows who have been bereaved in this way of all their offspring." Yet, as persecuted as the Yemenite Jews were, they were also denied the right to leave the country.[31]

The purpose of these descriptions is not to offer a compendium of Muslim mistreatment of non-Muslims. It is to invalidate two arguments: that Islam's history reveals it to be a religion that has been tolerant of non-Muslims and that the anti-Semitism that has increasingly pervaded much of the Muslim world is solely a response to the existence of Israel (as if that were a moral defense).

Egypt provides another example.

In his authoritative book, *An Account of the Manners and Customs of the Modern Egyptians*, Edward Lane, a British Arabic scholar who lived most of his life in Egypt, wrote that, at the time of his study (1833–35), the Jews were living "under a less oppressive government in Egypt than in any other country of the Turkish Empire." Nevertheless, the Jews "are held in the utmost contempt and abhorrence by the Muslims in general."

Lane explained: "Not long ago, they used often to be jostled in the streets of Cairo, and sometimes beaten merely for passing on the right hand of a Muslim. At present, they are less oppressed; but still they scarcely ever dare to utter a word of abuse when reviled or beaten unjustly by the meanest Arab or Turk; for many a Jew has been put to death upon a false and malicious accusation of uttering disrespectful words against the Kur-an [*sic*] or the Prophet. It is common to hear an Arab abuse his jaded ass, and after applying to him various opprobrious epithets, end by calling the beast a Jew."[32]

That this was the Jews' situation in Egypt, "a less oppressive government" than elsewhere in the Muslim Arab world, obviously tells us a great deal about Muslim anti-Semitism in the nineteenth century—prior to Israel's existence and even prior to Zionism.

In Syria, in 1840, some French Catholics introduced into the Arab world the medieval Christian blood libel that Jews slaughter non-Jewish children in order to use their blood to bake Passover matzoh. After a Capuchin monk in Damascus vanished, the local French consul told police authorities that the Jews probably had murdered him to procure his blood for a religious ritual. Several Damascus Jews were then arrested, and under torture one "confessed" that leaders of the Jewish community had planned the monk's murder. Many other Jews were then arrested, and under torture more such confessions were extracted. French officials pressured Syria's ruler, Muhammad Ali, to try the arrested men, and only after an international protest organized by Jewish communities around the world were the Jews who survived their tortures released.[33]

The blood libel immediately became popular among Muslims,

who attacked Jews as drinkers of Muslim blood in Aleppo, Syria, in 1853; Damascus again, in 1848 and 1890; Cairo in 1844 and 1901–1902; and Alexandria in 1870 and 1881.[34]

In nineteenth-century Palestine, which was under Ottoman Muslim rule, Jews had to walk past Muslims on their left, as the left is identified with Satan, and they always had to yield the right of way to a Muslim by "stepping into the street and letting him pass." Failure to abide by these degrading customs often provoked a violent response.

In Palestine, where Jews had lived for thousands of years, synagogues could only be located in hidden, remote areas, and Jews could pray only in muted voices. In addition, despite widespread poverty, Palestinian Jews had to pay a host of protection taxes. For example, Jews paid one hundred pounds a year to the Muslim villagers of Siloam (just outside Jerusalem) not to disturb the graves in the Jewish cemetery on the Mount of Olives, and fifty pounds a year to the Ta'amra Arabs not to deface the Tomb of Rachel on the road to Bethlehem. They also had to pay ten pounds annually to Sheik Abu Gosh not to molest Jewish travelers on the road to Jerusalem, even though the Turkish authorities were already paying him to maintain order on that road.[35]

With regard to other Middle Eastern countries, the noted French-Jewish writer Albert Memmi, who grew up in North Africa, wrote:

In Morocco in 1907, a massacre of Jews took place in Casablanca, along with the usual embellishments—rape, women carried away into the mountains, hundreds of homes and shops burned, etc. . . . In 1912 a big massacre in Fez. . . . In Algeria in 1934, massacre in Constantine, twenty-four people killed, dozens and dozens of others seriously wounded. . . . In Aden in 1946 . . . over one hundred people dead and seventy-six wounded, and two thirds of the stores sacked and burned. . . . In June, 1941, in Iraq, six hundred people killed, one thousand seriously wounded, looting, rapes, arson, one thousand houses destroyed, six hundred stores looted. . . . [In Libya]: November

4th and 5th, 1945, massacre in Tripoli; November 6th and 7th in Zanzour, Zaouia, Foussaber, Ziltain, etc., girls and women raped in front of their families, the stomachs of pregnant women slashed open, the infants ripped out of them, children smashed with crowbars. . . . All this can be found in the newspapers of the time, including the local Arab papers.[36]

Memmi summarized the Jews' status under Islam in the twentieth century: "Roughly speaking and in the best of cases, the Jew is protected like a dog which is part of man's property, but if he raises his head or acts like a man, then he must be beaten so that he will always remember his status."[37]

Once the Jewish State of Israel was established, the anti-Semitism expressed throughout the Arab world, and among Islamists outside the Arab world, was and remains essentially the same as that of the Nazi regime. On an almost daily basis, magazine and newspaper articles have been written, films shown, books published, and television interviews conducted in which Jews—not only Israeli Jews, as if that would be morally defensible—have been depicted as subhumans worthy of death, as animals, and as sacrificers of children.

Of the tens of thousands of anti-Semitic statements regularly made in the Muslim world, we begin with three Saudi examples:

- Saudi Arabian delegate Marouf al-Dawalibi before the 1984 UN Human Rights Commission *Conference on Religious Tolerance* (emphasis added): "The Talmud says that if a Jew does not drink every year the blood of a non-Jewish man, he will be damned for eternity."[38]
- Saudi sheikh Abd al-Rahman al-Sudayyis, an imam and preacher at the Al-Haraam mosque—the most important mosque in Mecca—begged Allah to annihilate the Jews. He said Arabs should turn their backs on any peace initiatives because Jews are "the scum of the human race, the rats of the world, the violators of pacts

and agreements, the murderers of the prophets, and the offspring of apes and pigs."[39]

- An eighth-grade Saudi schoolbook: "They [Jews] are the people of the Sabbath, whose young people God turned into apes, and whose old people God turned into swine to punish them. As cited in Ibn Abbas [revered cousin of Muhammad]: The apes are Jews, the keepers of the Sabbath; while the swine are the Christian infidels of the communion of Jesus."[40]

Though mutually contradictory, both Holocaust denial and Holocaust celebration are normative features of Arab Muslim, and non-Arab Islamist, societies. Indeed, the Mufti (leading Muslim religious figure) of Jerusalem spent much of World War II in Berlin encouraging the Nazis in their extermination of the Jews, justifying it with citations from the Koran and other Islamic works. And in the European Union at the present time, half of the anti-Semitic incidents are committed by Muslims, even though Muslims make up only 3 to 4 percent of its population.[41]

The anti-Jewish rhetoric in some Muslim countries is genocidal in intent. The Iranian regime repeatedly calls for the annihilation of Israel, and the Palestinian media is saturated with Jew-hatred. Here are excerpts from a 2010 sermon given in a Palestinian mosque and *broadcast on Palestinian television*:

The Jews, the enemies of Allah and of His Messenger, the enemies of Allah and of His Messenger! Enemies of humanity in general, and of Palestinians in particular—they wage war against us using all kinds of crimes, and as you see—even the mosques are not spared their racism. . . . Our enmity with the Jews is a matter of faith; our enmity with the Jews is a matter of faith, more than an enmity owing to occupation and the land. . . .

Oh Muslims! The Jews are the Jews. The Jews are the Jews. Even if donkeys would cease to bray, dogs cease to bark, wolves cease to howl and snakes to bite, the Jews would not cease to harbor hatred towards Muslims. The Prophet said that if two Jews would be alone with a Muslim, they would think only of killing him. The Prophet says: "You shall fight the Jews and kill them, until the tree and the stone will speak and say: 'Oh Muslim, Oh servant of Allah'—the tree and the stone will say . . . 'Oh Muslim, Oh servant of Allah, there is a Jew behind me, come and kill him. . . .'" Thus, this land will be liberated only by means of Jihad.[42]

Christians Today

As we have seen, Christians living in the Muslim world were similarly treated. They have been spared only the genocidal rhetoric directed against Jews. But wherever Christians lived in countries conquered by Muslims, those communities were persecuted to the point of near or total disappearance. Once the center of the Christian world, the Middle East has been rendered virtually devoid of Christians. By the eleventh century Muslim invasions had largely annihilated Byzantine civilization.

The only remaining Middle Eastern Christian communities of any size are in Lebanon, Egypt, and Iraq.

In Lebanon, the Christian percentage of the population decreased from 54 percent in 1932 to 40 percent as of 2008.

In Egypt, the Christian Copts, who constituted the majority of Egyptians until the tenth century, now constitute 10 percent of the population. At the time of this writing, they are increasingly persecuted; they are beaten, murdered, and their churches are burned.

In Iraq, the Christian population, which also long predates the Muslim population, has so dwindled that Iraq may have almost no Christians in the near future. As reported in the *Telegraph* of London, "The campaign of violence against Christians is one of the most under-reported stories of Iraq since the [American] invasion of 2003. . . . By the time the dust finally settles on the chaotic current chapter of Iraq's history, the Christian community may have disappeared altogether—after 2,000 years as a significant presence. About 200,000 Iraqi Christians have already fled the country; they once made up three per cent of its population, and they now account for half of its refugees."[43]

Indonesia is the nation with the largest number of Muslims; they compose about 86 percent of Indonesia's population. Generally speaking, relations between Muslims and non-Muslims have been cordial. But it is worth noting that Indonesia was not invaded and Islamicized by Muslim armies, but became Muslim gradually, over centuries, beginning around the sixteenth—relatively late compared to other Muslim countries; and Indonesia was under Western European (Dutch) colonial rule for much of that time. Indonesia was never a Muslim state so much as an archipelago of islands with a Muslim majority (except for the island of Bali, which remains largely Hindu). At the present time, however, there are sporadic violent attacks against Christians and Christian churches. Such attacks have taken place a few times each year for over a decade. I offer only two examples:

In 2005 the BBC reported, "Three girls have been beheaded and another badly injured as they walked to a Christian school in [Sulawesi] Indonesia."[44] According to the *Australian*, the girls "were beheaded as a Ramadan 'trophy' by Indonesian militants who conceived the idea after a visit to Philippines jihadists."[45]

In 2011, "Hundreds of Muslims in central Java set fire to two churches and attacked a court, claiming that a five-year prison sentence given to a Christian who had allegedly blasphemed Islam was too lenient."[46]

In Pakistan, as of 2008, there were 2.8 million Christians, about 1.6 percent of the Pakistani population. Pakistan was founded to be a Muslim country, and its constitution prohibits Christians or any other non-Muslim from being president or prime minister and from holding a number of other leading positions in the country. Furthermore, the Federal Shariat Court has the power to strike down any law that it deems contrary to Sharia.

In the court's own words,[47] "The court is backed by powerful provisions of the Constitution. The preamble to the Constitution explicitly affirms that sovereignty over the entire universe belongs to Almighty Allah alone, and the authority to be exercised by the people of Pakistan within the limits prescribed by Him is a sacred trust. . . . Article 227 makes it incumbent that all existing laws shall be brought in conformity with the injunctions of Islam as laid down in the Holy Qur'an and the Sunnah of the Holy Prophet (peace be upon him), and Chapter 3-A . . . entrusts the court with the responsibility to examine and decide the question whether or not any law or provision of law is repugnant to the injunctions of Islam as laid down in the Holy Qur'an and the Sunnah of the Holy Prophet (peace be upon him)."

Pakistan has essentially become a Muslim theocracy, and Christians are therefore increasingly treated as second-class citizens. There are regular reports of Christians beaten and killed and churches burned. With the expansion of Pakistan's blasphemy laws beginning in the 1980s, Christians have been subject to additional avenues of persecution. According to the BBC, "Hundreds of Christians are among the accused—at least 12 of them were given the death sentence for blaspheming against the Prophet. . . . A large majority of Pakistani people support the idea that blasphemers should be punished."[48]

Christians in Nigeria

In November 2002, Muslims in Nigeria rioted, beating and killing Christians and torching churches. Why they did this is as important as what they did.

As mentioned earlier, Nigeria had been scheduled to host the Miss World pageant later that year, and many Nigerians were excited about having the pageant with its attendant world publicity. The Nigerian government hoped it would bolster trade, tourism, and international goodwill. However, many of Nigeria's Muslims, who make up about half of Nigeria's population, opposed the presence of the pageant. They condemned the pageant's "nudity" and its "encouraging of promiscuity."

On Saturday, November 16, 2002, the popular Nigerian newspaper *ThisDay*, almost half of whose staff was Muslim, published a piece responding to the Muslim opposition to the beauty pageant by one of its reporters, Isioma Daniel, a Christian in her midtwenties. In her article, she wrote, "The Muslims thought it was immoral to bring 92 women to Nigeria and ask them to revel in vanity. What would Muhammad think? In all honesty, he would probably have chosen a wife from one of them. The irony is that Algeria, an Islamic country, is one of the countries participating in the contest."

To most of us, this paragraph is utterly innocuous, insulting of no one and no faith. If anything, the article's citation of Muhammad was complimentary to both him and the contestants. To many Muslims, however, it was worse than insulting; it was "blasphemy."

Though the management and editor of *ThisDay* immediately profusely apologized in print, and did so day after day, Islamic fundamentalists, chanting "God is Great" burned cars, churches, houses, and the offices of *ThisDay*.

The Nigerian press reported, "Muslim youths chanting 'Allah Akhbar, Allah Akhbar' God is great, God is great, brandishing swords, cutlasses, knives, cudgels and other dangerous implements defaced some churches, hotels and other known Christian places of businesses which they razed."[49]

Christians counterattacked, and more than two hundred Nigerians died, some burned alive in gasoline-soaked tires.

Some Muslim leaders called for calm after accepting the newspaper's abject apologies. But many of those leaders made it clear that they considered the original article a grave insult to Islam, and compared the woman who wrote it to Salman Rushdie, the Muslim-born writer whose death sentence for writing a "blasphemous" novel they reaffirmed.

This story is a microcosm of much of what has been happening in significant parts of the Muslim world:

1. Nigerian Muslims murdered innocent Nigerians and burned down more than twenty churches because of an

innocuous sentence in a Nigerian newspaper. Murders of non-Muslims for "insulting Islam" have become a regular part of contemporary life.

2. Muslims killed non-Muslims and destroyed the newspaper's building. But it was the victims—the editors of the newspaper whose offices were razed—who were told to apologize. It is almost always the non-Muslim of whom apologies are demanded, including when the non-Muslim is the victim.

3. Nigerian Muslim leaders condemned as an "abomination" neither the murders, nor the riots, but rather the innocent sentence in a column defending the Miss World pageant.

4. The media chose to describe the Nigerian violence as "sectarian violence," thereby holding Nigerian Christians equally culpable. As we have seen, this is how Muslim–non-Muslim violence is almost always reported in the world's mainstream (that is, Left-wing) media.

Postscript: The young woman who wrote the sentence was immediately fired, fled Nigeria permanently, and finally settled in Norway, where she was granted asylum, and where she now lives.

In Nigeria since then, Christians have been killed and churches burned by Muslims on a regular basis, including an attack on a Catholic church on Christmas Day 2011, in which at least thirty-five people were killed and fifty-two wounded. Pope Benedict condemned the attack the following day. But beyond that, fears of antagonizing Muslims prevailed, and as far as the world was concerned, there was more "sectarian violence" in Nigeria.

Sudan

In Sudan, the Islamic government of that country engaged in mass murder—generally declared a genocide—through killing and starvation in the southern and western part of that country, particularly in the province of Darfur. Non-Muslim and non-Arab Sudanese

Muslims were targeted by the Islamic regime. Human Rights Watch released a report that the government of Sudan gave Arab gangs "a license to rape" non-Arab women and girls in Darfur.[50] And according to the United Nations Human Rights Council, "The genocide in Darfur has claimed 400,000 lives and displaced over 2,500,000 people."

BLASPHEMY—"INSULTING ISLAM"

In much of the Muslim world, "insulting Islam," most especially any reference to Muhammad deemed disrespectful by any Muslims, defines blasphemy, and the penalty is death. While other religions have the concept of blasphemy, there are two distinguishing aspects to blasphemy in Islam.

It takes only an "insult" to be considered blasphemy. And the definition of "insult" is entirely subjective. Anything anyone—usually a non-Muslim—says that any group of Muslims, a Muslim leader, or even one Muslim with access to the media finds insulting to Islam, the Koran, or Muhammad can be deemed blasphemy and worthy of death.

People are put to death for this religious offense to this day. Though in the Torah blaspheming God—understood as cursing God by name ("Jehovah")—is a capital offense, there is no record of a Jewish court executing a Jew or non-Jew for blasphemy in three thousand years. Within Christendom, the last execution of a blasphemer was in Britain in 1697.

But in numerous Muslim countries, non-Muslims are killed for this offense, as are Muslims who oppose blasphemy laws. As noted previously, Pakistan extended its blasphemy laws in 1982 and made blasphemy a capital offense in 1986. Attempts by liberal Pakistanis to repeal the country's blasphemy laws have been met with violent demonstrations and the killing of Pakistanis who support repeal.

One such courageous Muslim was Salmaan Taseer, the governor of Punjab province in Pakistan. A critic of the blasphemy laws,

Taseer publicly supported a Christian woman who was sentenced to death by a Pakistani court for allegedly making derogatory remarks against Muhammad. In January 2011, Taseer was shot dead by a member of his security detail. The assassin, Mumtaz Qadri, said he killed Taseer because of the governor's opposition to the blasphemy laws. Qadri became a hero in Pakistan, and was so widely supported by Pakistan's young lawyers that thousands of them volunteered to defend him. In addition, tens of thousands of Islamists demonstrated in Karachi in support of the blasphemy laws, while clerics threatened to kill anyone who challenged them. In the words of the *Wall Street Journal*, "The killing highlighted the extent to which extremist Islam has permeated Pakistan's middle class."[51]

Nearly every Muslim-majority country has blasphemy laws. Countries that use Sharia law as part of their legal system all have blasphemy laws. These include Malaysia and Indonesia, often cited as examples of tolerant and modern Muslim countries. In Iran, people have been imprisoned, tortured, and executed for violating the country's blasphemy laws. Twelve of Nigeria's thirty-six states have Sunni majorities and they all have Sharia courts that can execute a person for blasphemy.

Salmaan Taseer is an example of a proud and heroic Muslim. But he was not a practicing Muslim, and it is among practicing Muslims that both the problem and solution to Islamism lie.[52]

THE MUSLIM OBSESSION WITH ISRAEL

Much of the Islamic world and nearly the entire Arab world have been obsessed with destroying the Jewish State of Israel since its founding in 1948. The hatred of Israel is such that the anti-Jewish, anti-Israel, and anti-Zionist speeches, writings, television programs, and films that permeate the Arab and Islamist worlds rival the worst anti-Semitic propaganda in history.

It is critical to understand that it was not the creation of 760,000 Arab-Palestinian refugees that has created this hatred. It was this hatred that created the refugees. Had six Arab armies not attacked Israel to destroy it in 1948, there would not have been any refugees.

The Palestinian refugee problem could have easily been solved in 1948, just as virtually every other refugee problem in the world has been; and just as the refugee problem of the 800,000 Jews who fled Arab countries during and after 1948 was solved. But, since 1948, Arab countries have deliberately mistreated the Palestinian refugees by refusing to integrate them into their countries and by keeping them in refugee camps—the only refugees in the world to be kept in camps for three generations. The Arab countries did this so as to keep the world's attention focused on the plight of the Palestinian refugees and to use them as a way to defame and ultimately, they hope, delegitimize and de-Judaize Israel.

The dislocation of Palestinian refugees was among the least wrenching refugee crises in the world. Unlike virtually any of the other millions of refugees of the twentieth century, nearly all Palestinian refugees were dislocated within only a thirty-mile area, within the same culture and geography, among people in the same ethnic group, who spoke the same language and practiced the same religion.

Moreover, if the creation of refugees caused Palestinian terror or was the reason for the Palestinian/Muslim goal of destroying Israel, why didn't any of the world's other refugee problems create terror or the goal of destroying the refugee-producing state?

The Muslim country of Pakistan, for example, when it was created, just nine months before Israel was, produced approximately 14.5 million refugees: 7,276,000 Muslims fled to Pakistan from India and 7,249,000 Hindus and Sikhs fled to India from Pakistan. If creating refugees renders Israel illegitimate, Pakistan should be many times less legitimate than Israel. And unlike Israel, which existed twice before, there never had been a Pakistan—it was ripped out of India to make another Muslim state.

Then, in 1971, after years of neglect by the western half of Pakistan, the eastern half of Pakistan—what became Bangladesh—

seceded, and a bloody war unleashed by West Pakistan created about seven million additional Muslim refugees who fled to India (they knew they would be treated better by Hindus than by their fellow Muslims in western Pakistan). Yet those seven million Muslim refugees have been entirely ignored by the world—because the Muslim world has ignored them. Unlike the 760,000 Palestinian refugees of 1948, they serve no larger Islamic purpose. But if 760,000 Palestinian refugees render Israel illegitimate, why don't seven million Muslim refugees—or the seven million Hindu and Sikh refugees of 1947—render Pakistan illegitimate?

The bottom line is that Muslim nations, the Arab ones and Iran in particular, do not hate Israel because of concern over 760,000 Muslim refugees. The Muslim world has produced twenty times that number of refugees, many of them Muslim. And if Israel had not produced a single Arab refugee, the Arab world would still have sought its destruction. The Muslims who hate Israel do so because they cannot abide the fact that Jews have an independent state in their midst.

Judea Pearl, the father of murdered *Wall Street Journal* reporter Daniel Pearl, devoted his life in 2002, when Islamists in Pakistan murdered his son, to building bridges between Jews and Muslims. A secular liberal professor of computer science and statistics at UCLA, Judea Pearl had great hopes for this idealistic mission. He told me on my radio show in 2010, however, that he had come to the sad realization that "99.99 percent" of the Muslim world does not believe that Israel has the right to exist as a Jewish state.

The day the Arab and wider Muslim worlds accept the existence of a Jewish state—not merely sign a state of nonbelligerence treaty with Israel, as Egypt did—will mark the beginning of a moral and religious transformation within Islam that all people of goodwill yearn for.

4. Islam and Women

HONOR BEATINGS AND KILLINGS

In many parts of the Muslim world family members—usually females—are beaten or killed in order to preserve the family's "honor."

To cite one example, because of the prominence of the Muslim woman involved: In May 2010, at her father's home in Manchester, England, Afshan Azad, twenty-one, a Muslim actress who played the witch Padma Patil in four of the *Harry Potter* movies, was beaten, thrown across a room, and threatened with death by her father and brother. The reason? She was dating a Hindu actor.

"Locked in her room, Afshan escaped by climbing out through her bedroom window, reported the assault to the police and initially undertook to give evidence against her father and brother. But by the time the case came to trial, she refused to come to court so that the charges of attempted murder had to be dropped."[53]

To cite one more example:

"On May 31, 1994, Kifaya Husayn, a 16-year-old Jordanian girl, was lashed to a chair by her 32-year-old brother. He gave her a drink of water and told her to recite an Islamic prayer. Then he slashed her throat. Immediately afterward, he ran out into the street, waving the bloody knife and crying, 'I have killed my sister to cleanse my honor.' Kifaya's crime? She was raped by another brother, a 21-year-old man."[54]

Defenders of Islam's reputation argue that nothing in Islam calls for such atrocities and that the practices are cultural, not religious.

Even though the Koran calls for hitting a disobedient wife (Sura 4:34), I do not wish to argue against either claim. Christians and Jews have troubling verses in the Bible and they long ago found ways to remain religious believers without literally enacting those verses. And as regards cultural practices, there are indeed many cases in which culture is more influential than religious texts among other religious groups, not just Muslims.

What is troubling here are three additional facts.

First, even if cultural, the practice of honor killing is primarily found among Muslims. Moreover, it is not isolated to one or two Muslim countries, but exists in many of them, and persists among Muslims who migrate to Western Europe and America.

Second, few Muslim religious authorities have denounced honor killings, and whatever denunciations have been made pale in comparison to the intensity and frequency of Muslim denunciations of apostasy, blasphemy, and perceived insults to Muhammad among non-Muslims.

Third, and perhaps most problematic, Western Muslim groups deny that honor killings are a Muslim problem, since domestic violence occurs in all cultures. Thus honor killings are lumped together with all killing of female relatives for any reason. After Aqsa Parvez, a sixteen-year-old Muslim girl, was murdered by her father and brother in Ontario, Canada, for not wearing a hijab outside of their home, the editor of the *American Muslim* wrote, "This is not a Muslim problem because it crosses all religious lines."[55]

Far more common than honor killings are other manifestations of a lower status for women in many Islamic societies than elsewhere in the world. The ban on women traveling without a male relative as an escort, the requirement to wear a veil, or worse, an entire face-covering, and the Taliban ban on girls in Afghanistan attending school are a few examples of the suppression of women that are unique to Muslim society.

If Islam wishes to present itself as the best answer to humanity's problems, it will have to confront the real problem of the status of women in Muslim societies. So far, there is almost only denial that the problem exists.

5. The Rejection of Reason

UNLIKE THE WOMEN PROBLEM, what is almost unknown outside the Muslim world—and is perhaps not widely acknowledged within the Muslim world—is the rejection of reason that came to dominate Islamic theology beginning in the early Middle Ages. Christianity and Judaism have a long history of valuing reason. While both believe that certain faith claims can and must transcend reason—after all, if faith were only rational, *faith* would be a meaningless term—neither religion rejected, and both strongly affirmed, reason.

The most powerful example comes at the beginning of the Hebrew Bible, Judaism's only Bible, and one part of Christianity's Bible. Abraham, the first Hebrew, argues with God. When God informs Abraham of His intention to destroy the evil cities of Sodom and Gomorrah, Abraham immediately argues with God on behalf of the good people who might live in those cities: Why should they die along with the evil ones? Abraham's challenge (Genesis 18), "Will not the judge of all the earth act justly?" presupposes that God acts rationally, that is, in ways man can use reason to try to understand.

Such a scene—man arguing with God—is inconceivable in the Koran and in normative Islam. While *Israel* means "struggle with God," the term *Islam* means "submission" (to Allah). Allah's will is inscrutable, not subject to human beings' rational understanding.

The very fact that Abraham can question God's actions means that the Jewish understanding of God from the very beginning meant that there are humanly understandable moral and rational laws in the universe to which God Himself, the author of these laws, may be held accountable. As Islam developed, this notion became heresy, and Muslims who argued for it were eventually put to death. Allah is not understandable; Allah does what He wants; and the world works according to His will, which is neither subject to reason nor to laws, whether of morality or of nature, that man could in any way understand.

Allah alone runs the world; reason and nature have no say. When Muslims say "insha'allah," "if Allah wills it," which many do many times a day, it is not only meant as Jews or Christians mean it when they say "God willing." In Islam, "Allah's will" alone directs everything. To use a famous example, according to orthodox Muslim doctrine, whether or not an arrow hits a bull's-eye is not a result of the accuracy of the archer or of the prevailing wind pattern, because to claim that the shooter and the winds determined where the arrow would land limits Allah's power, and that constitutes heresy.

That is probably the primary reason why, after a certain date, science ceased to—most likely could not—develop in the Muslim world. Science studies the laws of nature. But if laws of nature dictate what happens in the universe, then, the thinking went, Allah's will is not the only thing that dictates what happens in the universe. And that cannot be. Therefore, traditional Islam came to deny reason and causality.

This also explains why the outlook of so many believing Muslims has been that there is nothing to be learned outside the Koran and of Islam as it developed. Everything non-Muslim is erroneous. The greatest Muslim writer, Ibn Khaldun, wrote, "When the Muslims conquered Persia, general Sa'd bin Abi Waqqas petitioned Caliph Omar for permission to distribute the huge quantity of captured books and scientific papers as booty. Caliph Omar wrote back: 'Throw them in the water. If what they contain is right guidance, God has given us better guidance. If it is error, God has protected us against it.'"[56]

In the words of Robert R. Reilly, former director of Voice of America and an expert on Middle Eastern history and culture, this denial of reason and causality and the ensuing neglect of the study of other cultures and religions "is the key to unlocking such puzzles as why the Arab world stands near the bottom of every measure of human development; [and] why scientific inquiry is nearly moribund in the Islamic world . . ."[57]

This was not always the case in Muslim theology. It became so between the ninth and thirteenth centuries because of the ascendance of what is known as the Ash'arite school of Muslim theology. Aside from the deleterious consequences to reason, science, intellectual curiosity, and culture, the ascendancy of the Ash'arite school created another terrible consequence. Just as reason is not applicable in the natural world, reason is not applicable in the moral realm. To a non-Muslim, people shouting *"Allahu akbar!"* "Allah is the greatest!" while slitting the throats of innocent men, women, and children or while blowing up people in trains, planes, schools, and pizza shops seems oxymoronic, since God is associated with normative moral standards. But to those who believe that human reason has no place in assessing right and wrong, murdering innocents while shouting *"Allahu Akbar"* is in no way absurd.

6. Theocracy

THE GOAL OF ISLAM is that the state and ultimately the world will be governed by Islam. This means Sharia law enforced by an Islamic government ruled by Islamic leaders. Islam without its theocratic goal would constitute a new form of Islam, one that, if enough Muslims wish to create, I believe can one day be created. But it has never existed and with few individual exceptions, does not now. The theocratic goal, probably more than any other factor, is why Islamist values are incompatible with liberty.

There is a Jewish parallel that may help illuminate the issue. Like Islam, the traditional Jewish ideal was also theocratic: a state run by and that enforced, Halakha, Jewish Law. This, too, would be incompatible with liberty.

There are, however, two critical differences between the traditional Jewish theocratic ideal and that of Islam.

First, mainstream Judaism, including mainstream Orthodox Judaism, long ago abandoned this goal (at least until a future Messianic Age). There is no normative Jewish movement that seeks to have the Israeli government impose Halakha (with a few exceptions such as kosher food in the Israeli army) on all Israeli Jews, let alone on Israeli non-Jews.*

---

* As noted, there is some government-legislated Halakha in Israel. Kosher food in the armed forces is a prominent example. There are also demands—sometimes honored—that the Israeli national airline not schedule flights on the Jewish Sabbath. In addition, there are Orthodox neighborhoods in Israel that ban traffic on the Sabbath. In general, laws in Israel governing public behavior on the Sabbath are reminiscent of American "blue laws" that were in force in America on Sundays. Neither resembles a Sharia-based state.

Second, and even more important, even if the Jewish ideal of a religious Jewish state that imposed Halakha on its Jewish citizens remained in force, it would only apply to one country (Israel). Judaism has never called for imposing Judaism on anyone outside Israel. Judaism doesn't even seek to make non-Jews Jewish, let alone impose Jewish law on them. It seeks only to make non-Jews ethical monotheists (that is, people who believe in the one God who demands ethical conduct—precisely what Washington, Jefferson, Franklin, and Lincoln believed, as we shall see).

The Islamist desire to have every human being governed by Sharia, which would be imposed by a religious Muslim state, has no analogue in the world. Traditional Christians yearn to see every human being come to belief in Christ. But just as with the Jewish theocratic ideal (which, to repeat, applied to Jews, and only in Israel), there is no similarity here. The only acceptable method of bringing people to faith in Christ is persuasion. There is nothing in Christianity today, whether Catholic, Protestant, or Orthodox, that believes in any form of coercion to impose Christianity. And there is no Christian religious law analogous to Sharia or Halakha. Therefore, there would be little that is uniquely Christian to impose. The argument that many Christians wish to impose a ban on abortion is also not analogous. There are many non-Christians, including atheists, Jews, and Buddhists, who believe that most abortions are immoral. But there is no non-Muslim community that believes that religious police should monitor women's clothing and other behaviors, or that a person who converts from one religion to another should be put to death.

Therefore, the Muslim desire to see the world governed by Sharia must be worrisome to non-Muslims—and to liberty-loving Muslims.

In December 2010, the Pew Research Center's Global Attitudes Project reported the results of its polling of Muslims in seven predominantly Muslim countries. Here are the responses to the question, "Is It Good or Bad that Islam Plays a Large Role in Politics?"[58]

Egypt: Good 95%; Bad 2%
Indonesia: Good 95%; Bad 4%
Pakistan: Good 88%; Bad 6%
Nigeria: Good 88%; Bad 7%
Lebanon: Good 72%; Bad 19%
Jordan: Good 53%; Bad 37%
Turkey: Good 45%; Bad 38%

As summarized by the Pew Center: "Muslims in Nigeria and in nearly all of the predominantly Muslim countries surveyed overwhelmingly welcome Islamic influence over their countries' politics."[59]

What does this mean? In real life, it means that the great majority of Muslims in the seven Muslim-majority countries polled—only three of which are Arab countries—want their countries to be governed by Sharia. How do we know this?

In Egypt, 82 percent of Muslims want adulterers stoned; in Jordan 70 percent; in Indonesia 42 percent; in Pakistan 82 percent; and in Nigeria 56 percent. Similar percentages of the Muslim populations of those countries want anyone who converts out of Islam to be put to death.

In response to such data, Muslim and Western apologists for the contemporary Islamic world point out that in all these countries (except Pakistan), a majority of the Muslims polled consider "democracy preferable to any other form of government." Therefore, the argument goes, the Muslim world differs little in its values from the Western world.

Unfortunately, this argument is misleading. While, of course, there are Muslims, especially the more secular ones, living in these Muslim countries, who yearn for Western-style democracy, the majority of respondents want democracy *under Islam*. They want to vote—for the religious Muslims who will govern them. It is not a preference for Western-style democracy in which non-Islamic or secular parties can govern. They want, in a nutshell, democracy more than liberty.

7. Islamic Law and Economics

SHARIA HAS ALSO BLOCKED Muslim economic development. A Turkish scholar, Timur Kuran, formerly King Faisal Professor of Islamic Law and Culture at the University of Southern California and presently professor of Islamic studies at Duke University, has written regarding the Arab world:

> The region as a whole has not yet come to terms with the reasons why it turned into an economic laggard. The idea that outsiders are somehow responsible for the Middle East's underdevelopment resonates with much of the population, including secularists who consider Islamic law backward and obsolete. In particular, the role of Islamic law in blocking organizational modernization and stultifying Middle Eastern, and particularly Muslim, enterprise is hardly understood. . . .
>
> It also sustains sterile debates about the virtues of embracing Islam for solutions to poverty, mismanagement, and powerlessness. . . . Not even the typical Islamist appreciates the limitations of Islamic law as a basis for social, economic, and political order in the twenty-first century.[60]

Islam, America, and the West

In the last 20–30 years America did not just respect Muslims, it bled for Muslims. We Americans engaged in five military campaigns on behalf of Muslims, each one resulting in the liberation of a Muslim people: Bosnia, Kosovo, Kuwait, Afghanistan and Iraq.

—Charles Krauthammer

Why Arab Anti-Americanism?

ACCORDING TO LEFTIST, Arab, and Islamic spokesmen, there are three reasons for anti-Americanism in the Arab world:

1. American support for non-democratic regimes in the Arab world—such as in Hosni Mubarak's Egypt and Saudi Arabia
2. American support of Israel
3. American presence on Muslim soil

The first argument assumes that those Arabs (and other Muslims) who hate America want open and free societies and hate America for aiding non-open regimes. But the least free and most repressive Arab governments were the least supported by America and most anti-American—Islamist Sudan, Assad's Syria, Saddam Hussein's Iraq, and Muammar Qaddafi's Libya. As corrupt and repressive as the Egyptian government under Mubarak was, Egypt was freer than any of those anti-American countries.

The Arabs and other Muslims who most hate America do not want a free and open society; they want a closed secular or closed Islamist one. And the small number of Arabs who are pro-American are the most desirous of a free society.

As for the second reason, American support of Israel has probably increased anti-Americanism in the Muslim world. But those Muslims most preoccupied with destroying Israel are precisely those Muslims who most loathe liberty and other American values, and who are either aligned with Islamist theocrats or secular totalitarians (such as the Baath Party). The obsession with eradicating Israel is a function of the Islamist goal of eradicating a Jewish state in the midst of the Muslim world. It is not as if these people would be lovers of liberty and America were it not for America's support of Israel.

As for the presence of American troops on Muslim soil—a favorite explanation for Osama bin Laden's hatred of America—this, too, avoids the greater and obvious question of why such a thing would produce such hatred. There have been American troops on German and Japanese soil since the end of World War II and on Korean soil since the 1950s. While Leftists in Germany, Japan, and South Korea periodically mount anti-American demonstrations against the American troops stationed in their respective countries, the presence of American troops in those countries doesn't elicit hatred remotely analogous to the anti-American hatred in parts of Arab and Muslim worlds.

America's and Israel's haters hate on a magnitude not seen since Nazi hatred. They want Israel gone, and they want a wounded— they hope fatally wounded—America. They say so publicly, and they say so in polls. Yet, the Israel and America haters of the West ignore all this and blame Israel for trying to live and America for enabling it to do so. If America abandoned Israel, Muslim haters of the Jewish state would rejoice, but they would not stop hating America. They would conclude only that terror and intimidation work, and that America will give in when the threats are great enough. One proof? Muslims who hate Israel and who live in European countries that are far less supportive of Israel continue to loathe Europe. Europe's relative abandonment of Israel has only convinced Muslims who loathe Israel and America that Europe has lost its nerve and is ripe for an Islamic takeover.

Muslims who hate America also do so because America—as well as, in the Middle East, Israel—prevents the expansion of Islamist rule. Expansionist totalitarian movements, whether Soviet Communism or Islamism, hate free societies, and America is the strongest free society. One of the most powerful statements against Muslim anti-Americanism was made by a Muslim writer, Professor Muqtedar Khan of the University of Delaware. Shortly after 9/11, in an open letter to American Muslims, he wrote:

> Muslims love to live in the US but also love to hate it. Many openly claim that the US is a terrorist state but they continue to live in it. Their decision to live here is testimony that they would rather live here than anywhere else. As an Indian Muslim, I know for sure that nowhere on earth, including India, will I get the same sense of dignity and respect that I have received in the US. No Muslim country will treat me as well as the US has. If what happened on September 11th had happened in India, the biggest democracy, thousands of Muslims would have been slaughtered in riots on mere suspicion and there would be another slaughter after confirmation. In patience and in tolerance ordinary Americans have demonstrated their extraordinary virtues. It is time that we acknowledge that the freedoms we enjoy in the US are more desirable to us than superficial solidarity with the Muslim World. If you disagree

than prove it by packing your bags and going to whichever Muslim country you identify with. If you do not leave and do not acknowledge that you would rather live here than anywhere else, know that you are being hypocritical.[1]

In the words of international affairs writer Peter Brownfeld, Muslims "have more opportunity in America to practice Islam than anywhere else in the world. . . . The chances of you being discriminated for your Muslim beliefs in the Muslim world is greater than it is in the United States . . ."[2]

Islamists in the West

THE ACTUAL NUMBER IS unknowable, but it is widely acknowledged that a significant percentage of Muslim immigrants to Europe have rejected Western social and moral values. In fact, some Muslims living in the West have actually become more insular, more radical, and more Islamist while living there.

British, not Middle Eastern, Muslims first raised the charge against the Indian Muslim writer Salman Rushdie that he insulted Islam and Muhammad in his novel *The Satanic Verses*. It was they who pushed the Iranian Islamists to issue the infamous fatwa (religious decree) calling on Muslims throughout the world to murder Rushdie. Ayatollah Khomeini's fatwa against Rushdie provided an early example of how radicalized many Muslims in the West had become. Few American or European Muslim leaders condemned the Rushdie fatwa; many supported it.

Ahmed Omar Saeed Sheikh, the head of Jaish-e-Mohammed (the Army of Mohammed), the Pakistani terror group that murdered American Jewish journalist Daniel Pearl of the *Wall Street Journal*, was born in England and educated at the London School of Economics.

The European failure to assimilate most Muslim immigrants has led the heads of some Western European countries to announce that multiculturalism has failed. It is difficult to overstate the significance of this admission on the part of Western Europeans. Multiculturalism has been a major Left-wing, therefore widely held cultural and political, value in Western Europe and the United States. Yet, in 2010–11, the heads of the United Kingdom, France, and Germany made this announcement.

In 2011, the *New York Times* reported that in Sweden, perhaps the European country most committed to multiculturalism, "Nearly a quarter of Sweden's population is now foreign born or has a foreign-born parent"—the country had begun to despair of assimilating most of its Muslim citizens.[3]

Part of the reason is that Muslim schools throughout the world, a large number of them funded by Saudi Arabia, teach millions of young Muslims the most xenophobic and insular expressions of Islam. Typically infidels, that is, non-Muslims, Americans and Jews in particular, are portrayed in a hate-filled way.

This even includes some Muslim schools in America. The *Washington Post* reported on Muslim elementary and high schools in America that teach religious bigotry: One "11th-grade textbook, for example, says one sign of the Day of Judgment will be that Muslims will fight and kill Jews, who will hide behind trees that say: 'Oh Muslim, Oh servant of God, here is a Jew hiding behind me. Come here and kill him.' Several students of different ages, all of whom asked not to be identified, said that in Islamic studies, they are taught that it is better to shun and even to dislike Christians, Jews and Shiite Muslims." In addition, "maps of the Middle East hang on classroom walls, but Israel is missing."[4]

Responses to Arguments on Behalf of Islam

1. Islam Is Not Monolithic

IT IS OFTEN ARGUED that only the ignorant assess Islam negatively, because Islam is not monolithic: There is no one Islam and Muslims are disunited among themselves. The Sunni-Shiite divide is an example of the former, while Arab Muslim fear of non-Arab Muslim Iran is an example of the latter.

But critics do not deny differences within Islam and among Muslims. It is just that those differences are irrelevant to the larger question of Islamist values. However significant Shiite-Sunni differences may be and however great the cultural differences between Arab and non-Arab Muslims, those differences do not change Muslim history, the treatment of non-Muslims, the role of Sharia, the Islamic theocratic ideal, or the diminished role of reason.

During the Cold War, opponents of anti-Communists offered the same argument—that anti-Communists exaggerated the threat of Communism because Communism was not monolithic; it, too, had a deep divide running through it—the Sino-Soviet split. Chinese and Soviet Communists hated one another and competed for support throughout the world. Therefore, it was argued, fears of Communism, given its lack of unity, were exaggerated and betrayed an ignorance of Communism.

The point here is not to equate Islam and Communism. The point here is that a movement's lack of unity or internal differences does not invalidate moral assessments of it.

In addition, the same people who argue against any negative assessments of Islam on the grounds that there is no one Islam offer glowingly positive assessments of Islam. But if Muslim disunity invalidates criticism, the same Muslim disunity should invalidate praise.

2. Every Bible Has Its Morally Troubling Verses

WHEN VERSES IN THE Koran are cited that call for the killing of nonbelievers, admonish a husband to hit a recalcitrant wife, depict Jews as animals, or call for the humiliation of Jews and Christians, defenders of the Koran note that every Bible has morally troubling verses as well as morally elevated ones. And they are right.

What troubles fair-minded people is that the most morally disturbing verses of the Koran are not found in the Bible. For example, there are no calls in the Old or New Testaments to kill nonbelievers, as there are in the Koran.* Therefore, Muslims who use violence against non-Muslims (especially those that are not *dhimmi*) can use more than a few verses in the Koran to legitimately defend their actions. At the same time, there are some, though considerably fewer, verses that warn Muslims against engaging in violence except in self-defense. And there are Muslims who emphasize those verses. These courageous individuals are the hope of Islam.

In any event, *the most humane societies in the world all emanate from*

---

* One seeming exception is the Israelite killing of the Canaanites in the conquering of the Holy Land. But it is not really an exception. First, it was a one-time event directed against one group three thousand years ago. There is no demand in the Old or New Testaments that nonbelievers be humiliated or put to death. Second, the Canaanites were not killed because they were nonbelievers but because they sacrificed children and engaged in other horrific acts; and the Jews are repeatedly warned in their Bible that if they act similarly, they will suffer the same fate the Canaanites did.

Judeo-Christian roots. No Koran-based societies have attained equivalent moral development, not to mention similar levels of liberty or tolerance. Perhaps one day Koran-based societies will compete in terms of human rights, tolerance of outsiders, and intellectual openness. All good people look forward to that day.

3. The Koran Has Many Uplifting Verses

THERE IS NO QUESTION that the Koran has morally uplifting verses. Perhaps the most widely cited example is "There shall be no coercion in matters of faith."[1] However, as previously noted, until the modern period, Muslim governments frequently offered the choice of Islam or death to non-*dhimmi* non-Muslims, and a subservient existence to *dhimmi* (Jews and Christians).

There are other morally elevated verses. Here are some concerning ultimate justice: "Whosoever does an evil deed shall be recompensed only with the like of it, but whosoever does a righteous deed, be it male or female, believing shall enter paradise, therein provided without reckoning" (40:40). Or, "Say, 'The Truth is from your Lord.' Let him who will, believe; and let him who will reject [it]" (18:29). Or, "Each soul earns but its own due" (6:164). Also: "And Allah created the heavens and the earth with truth, so that each soul might be recompensed according to what it has earned, with no one wronged" (45:22).

At the same time, two countervailing facts must be acknowledged. One is that morally compromised verses significantly outnumber and sometimes contradict the morally elevated ones. The second is that some moral demands and teachings that are central to the Bible are not found in the Koran. For example, the Torah, on three separate occasions, commands Jews to love the stranger, that is, the non-Jew. There is no command in the Koran to love the non-Muslim, and there are repeated commands to kill "nonbelievers."

The Koran is and always will be what Koran-based Muslims make it, just as the Bible is what Bible-believing Jews and Christians make it. The Bible has been used to justify evil (slavery and medieval anti-Semitism are the best-known examples) and it has been the basis for the best societies the world has known.

4. The Vast Majority of Muslims Are Peace-Loving People

PROBABLY THE MOST FREQUENTLY OFFERED argument on behalf of the contemporary Islamic world is that the vast majority of Muslims are peace-loving.

This argument is likely true. But it is irrelevant because, at least in modern times, it has been true of even the most violent societies. In what modern society has the majority of its citizens not been peace-loving? Germany in World War II? The Soviet Union? Contemporary Iran? It doesn't matter whether the majority of citizens in any given society or religion are peace-loving, because those people are not the ones who create wars of aggression or commit terror. A minority of Germans were members of the Nazi Party and an even smaller percentage of Soviet citizens were Communists. Yet those countries were murder machines.

According to a 2006 Gallup Poll of citizens of Muslim countries, the percentage of Muslims who "felt the terrorist attacks of Sept. 11, 2001, were 'completely justified' [was] 7% of the total population across the 10 countries included in the study." The poll, importantly, also concluded that these "political radicals were, on average, slightly more educated and more affluent than the moderates."[2]

So, about 100 million Muslims believe the 9/11 massacres of Americans were *completely* justified and these Islamists represent the more educated and more affluent strata of Muslim societies. As CNN's Fareed Zakaria, no conservative, wrote after 9/11, "The problem is not that Osama bin Laden believes that this is a religious war against America. It's that millions of people across the Islamic world seem to agree."[3]

5. Muslim Spain Was a "Golden Age" of Religious Tolerance

JUST ABOUT EVERY DEFENDER of the Islamic record cites Jews and Christians living under Muslim rule in Spain as an example of the inherently tolerant character of Islam. In the words of the religious historian Karen Armstrong, "We should also remember that until 1492, Jews and Christians lived peaceably and productively together in Muslim Spain—a coexistence that was impossible elsewhere in Europe."

Similarly, Fareed Zakaria wrote right after 9/11 that "[u]ntil the 1950s, for example, Jews and Christians lived peaceably under Muslim rule. In fact, Bernard Lewis has argued that for much of history religious minorities did better under Muslim rulers than they did under Christian ones."[4]

Both Armstrong and Lewis give their assessment of how Jews and Christians fared in Muslim Spain in comparison to how Jews fared in Christian Europe at the same time. This is, however, more of a statement of how oppressive Christian rule was at that time than a statement of how benevolent or tolerant Islam was then and there. Jews and Christians in Muslim Spain were oppressed, but rarely violently so, and fared better than Jews did in Christian Europe.

Nevertheless, as we have seen, Jews and Christians fared poorly throughout most of their sojourn in the Muslim world. Moreover, even if there was a golden age of Muslim tolerance—relative to Christianity—in Spain seven or eight hundred years ago, it is difficult to see the relevance of this to assessing Islamic rule elsewhere at that time, anywhere else at other times, or, most important, anywhere today. There has never been a model of non-Muslim equality under Muslim rule. And the situation of Christians under Muslim rule is worse today than at any time since the Turks' massacres of Armenian Christians during World War I.

6. Turkey Provides a Democratic Islamist Model

AFTER A CENTURY of forced de-Islamicization and secularization of Turkey, which rendered that country arguably the most modern and tolerant Muslim-majority country, the Turkish people voted into power the AK Party (Justice and Development Party) under the leadership of Prime Minister Recep Erdogan, a religious Muslim who has sought to create an Islamic democratic model in Turkey.

As a result, there have been major changes in Turkish foreign policy. Once the most pro-Western and pro-Israel Muslim country, Turkey has become pro-Iranian, less free, intensely hostile to Israel, and much more alienated from the West. Michael Rubin, senior lecturer at the Naval Postgraduate School's Center for Civil-Military Relations, and a senior editor of the *Middle East Quarterly*, wrote in 2010:

> Gone, and gone permanently, is secular Turkey, a unique Muslim country that straddled East and West and that even maintained a cooperative relationship with Israel. Today Turkey is an Islamic republic whose government saw fit to facilitate the May 31 flotilla raid on Israel's blockade of Gaza. Turkey is now more aligned to Iran than to the democracies of Europe. Whereas Iran's Islamic revolution shocked the world with its suddenness in 1979, Turkey's Islamic revolution has been so slow and deliberate as to pass almost unnoticed. Nevertheless, the Islamic Republic of Turkey is a reality—and a danger.[5]

In the words of Ayaan Hirsi Ali in that same year:

> True, there remain secularists in Istanbul who revere the legacy of Mustafa Kemal Ataturk, founder of the Republic of Turkey. But they have no hold over the key government ministries, and their grip over the army is slipping. Today the talk in

Istanbul is quite openly about an 'Ottoman alternative,' which harks back to the days when the Sultan ruled over an empire that stretched from North Africa to the Caucasus. . . .

A year ago Turkey's President Recep Erdogan congratulated Iran's Mahmoud Ahmadinejad on his re-election after he blatantly stole the presidency. Then Turkey joined forces with Brazil to try to dilute the American-led effort to tighten U.N. sanctions aimed at stopping Iran's nuclear arms program. Most recently, Turkey sponsored the "aid flotilla" designed to break Israel's blockade of Gaza and to hand Hamas a public relations victory.[6]

7. Muslim and Arab Countries Are Victims of Western Imperialism

IT IS FREQUENTLY SAID by Arab, Muslim, and Western defenders of the contemporary Arab and Islamic world's poor record regarding human rights, scientific and technological achievement, and economic vitality that this record originates in the fact that those countries were stymied in their moral and social development by Western colonialism.

This argument is easily countered.

First, Western control of Arab countries was rarely long.

- Syria was under French rule from 1920 until 1941 (or 1945 depending on how one reads the history). Otherwise the area in which modern Syria is located—Syria as a distinct modern nation was established after World War I—had been under Muslim rule since the beginnings of Islam.

- Egypt was invaded by Napoleon and was then under French control from 1798 to 1801 (four years) and much later fell under British rule—from 1882 to 1922 (forty years)—and stayed a British protectorate until 1952 (thirty years). If one counts the period of the protectorate, that is a total of about seventy-four years.

- Iraq was formed as a distinct modern nation after World War I, with the breakup of the Muslim Ottoman Empire. It remained under British control until 1932—about fifteen years.
- Libya was under Western control (Italian, French, British) for about forty years, from 1911 to 1951.

Second, contrast these countries with India, which was partially ruled by Westerners beginning in the sixteenth century, and was under complete British rule for nearly a hundred years, from about 1856 until 1947.

Third, Pakistan, increasingly Islamist, was never colonized. It was forcibly removed from India to create a *secular* Muslim-majority country the year India received its independence (1947).

Fourth, neither of the two most repressive Islamist countries, the Islamic Republic of Iran and Saudi Arabia, was ever colonized by a Western power.

If any national group has a right to claim victim status and use it to explain away its evils, it would be the Jews. They were under the rule of others for two thousand years, during most of which they endured mass murder in, and expulsions from, virtually every country in which they lived. Yet from the moment they were allowed independence, they created one of the freest, most liberal democracies in the world.

Western imperialism has virtually nothing to do with the problems that confront the Muslim world.

8. Muslims Did Not Impose Islam on Non-Muslims

PERHAPS THE MOST REMARKABLE DEFENSE of Islamic history is that of Karen Armstrong. She has said, for example, "The idea that Islam imposed itself by the sword is a Western fiction."[7]

There are few equivalents in mainstream Western historical writing to this rewriting of history. It is one thing to say that the early medieval world was a barbaric place, and one should not hastily judge violence in that period. But to deny that Muslims violently imposed Islam on Persia or India or significant parts of North Africa is, to use Armstrong's term, a fiction.

9. Criticism of Islam Is Islamophobic

THE MOST WIDELY OFFERED RESPONSE to criticisms of Islam is that they are Islamophobic.

Islamophobia is one of the most intimidating of all the politically correct epithets developed in the past generation. Whoever developed the term was quite brilliant. The term equates all criticism of Islam with anti-Semitism and racism. According to Western Islamic organizations, Western media, and the United Nations, they have everything in common. Anti-Semites hate all Jews, racists hate all members of a race, and Islamophobes hate all Muslims and Islam. The truth is that Islamophobia has virtually nothing in common with anti-Semitism or racism.

Note that the term is not *Muslim*-phobia or anti-*Muslim*; it is *Islamo*-phobia. There are two sleights of hand here. One is *phobia*, which of course means fear. But fear of Islam is not the same as hatred of Islam, let alone hatred of all Muslims. Fear and hatred are very different things. One can rightly or wrongly fear Islam, or more usually, aspects of Islam, and have absolutely no bias against Muslims, let alone be a racist.

The other sleight of hand is the equation of Islamophobia with racism, and that is particularly dishonest. Muslims come in every racial group, and Islam has no more to do with race than Christianity or Buddhism do. Nevertheless, mainstream Western media, Islamist groups calling themselves Muslim civil liberties organizations, and various liberal Western organizations repeatedly declare that Islamophobia is racism. To cite a typical example, the *Guardian* published a column titled "Islamophobia should be as unacceptable as racism."

Even granting that there are people who fear Islam, how does that in any way correlate with racism? If fear of an ideology renders one a racist, all those who fear conservatism or liberalism should be considered racists.

Some may respond that whereas conservatism and liberalism are ideas, Islam is a religion; one can attack ideas, but not a religion. It is, however, insulting to religions to deny that they are ideas. Religions are theological belief systems, but they are also ideas about how society should be run—and that is more so regarding Islam than perhaps any other religion, as religious Muslims proudly note. Islam, Christianity, Judaism, and Buddhism should be just as subject to criticism as are conservatism and liberalism.

However, the only religion about which criticism is ipso facto declared racist and immoral is Islam. People write books, give lectures, and conduct seminars on the falsity, and the alleged danger and absurdity, of Christian claims and about the immoral record of Christianity. No one attacks them for racism or bigotry, let alone attacks them physically. The B'nai B'rith Anti-Defamation League (ADL) released a report in 1994, *The Religious Right: The Assault on Tolerance and Pluralism in America*, declaring conservative Christians the most dangerous large group in America, in part because of their desire to Christianize America. Yet no one charged the ADL with racism or Christianophobia. However, anyone who argues that Muslims would like to Islamicize Europe or America is labeled an Islamophobe.

But there is no term for the fear of, let alone the loathing of, Christianity. Why not? Why is there Islamophobia but no Christianophobia or Americaphobia? If an artist places a crucifix in a jar of his urine, it is art. Howard Zinn, who devoted his life's work to portraying America as a largely vile society, became the bestselling American history author of his time. But if a person suggests that Islam has not appeared to be compatible with democracy or that the Islamic treatment of women is inferior to the West's, he is labeled a racist and Islamophobe.

One might counter that maligning people for criticism is not only true of those who criticize Islam; it is also true of critics of Israel and of America—the former, it is said, are labeled "anti-Semitic" and the latter "unpatriotic." Neither is true, however. No normative group or individual, conservative or otherwise, labels anyone anti-Semitic for merely criticizing Israel. People are sometimes labeled anti-Semitic for attempting to delegitimize Israel, thereby siding with those who wish to annihilate the Jewish state. And no one in any responsible capacity has called anyone "unpatriotic" just for criticizing America. Hillary Clinton claimed during a Democratic presidential debate that under President George W. Bush, the Defense Department called her "unpatriotic" for asking whether it has a plan to withdraw American troops from Iraq. There was no truth to the charge.

The term *Islamophobic* has one purpose—to suppress any criticism, no matter how responsible, of Islam.

10. *There Is No Difference Between Fundamentalist Muslims and Fundamentalist Christians*

FINALLY, IT IS ARGUED (by the Left and by Islamist defense agencies) that there are fanatics in all religions and that there is no difference among them, especially between Christian and Muslim fundamentalists.

According to Karen Armstrong, "Christian fundamentalists in the United States have committed fewer acts of terror than the others for two main reasons: they live in a more peaceful society . . .

[and they] believe that the democratic federal government of the United States will collapse without their needing to take action: God will see to it."[8] Like Muslim fundamentalists, "American Christian fundamentalists are not in favour of democracy."[9]

PBS host Tavis Smiley interviewed Ayaan Hirsi Ali, the ex-Muslim Somali writer and activist for human and especially women's rights in Islamic countries. After mentioning American Muslim terrorist Major Nidal Hasan, who murdered thirteen and injured thirty fellow soldiers at Fort Hood, and Faisal Shahzad, who attempted to murder hundreds in Times Square, this dialogue ensued:

> Ayaan Hirsi Ali: Somehow, the idea got into their [Hasan's and Shahzad's] minds that to kill other people is a great thing to do and that they would be rewarded in the hereafter.
>
> Tavis Smiley: But Christians do that every single day in this country.
>
> Ali: Do they blow people up?
>
> Smiley: Yes. Oh, Christians, every day, people walk into post offices, they walk into schools, that's what Columbine is—I could do this all day long. . . . There are so many more examples, Ayaan, of Christians who do that than you could ever give me examples of Muslims who have done that inside this country, where you live and work.[10]

Michel Martin, an NPR host, in discussing whether the Islamic center and mosque planned for near Ground Zero should be moved, compared the Muslim identity of the 9/11 terrorists to the "Christian" identity of American terrorist Timothy McVeigh: "Did anybody move a Christian church after Timothy McVeigh" bombed the Murrah Federal Building in Oklahoma City in 1995?[11]

ABC News *20/20* anchor Chris Cuomo tweeted this to his nearly one million followers: "To all my christian brothers and sisters, especially catholics—before u condemn muslims for violence, remember the crusades. . . . [S]tudy them."[12]

How does a PBS anchor equate Muslims who murder in the name of Islam with American murderers, who, with almost no exceptions, do not commit their murders in the name of Christianity?

How does someone equate the thousands of Islamic terrorists around the world, all of whom are devout Muslims, with one American terrorist who, furthermore, professed no religion?

And how does a news broadcaster assert that, because of the Crusades, Christians cannot condemn Muslims for violence? The Crusades occurred a thousand years ago. One might as well argue that Jews cannot condemn anti-Semitic violence because Jews destroyed Canaanite communities 3,200 years ago. In addition, it is hardly a defense of Islam to have to go back a thousand years to find comparable Christian conduct. And even then there is little moral equivalence. The Crusades were waged in order to recapture lands that had been Christian for centuries until Muslim armies attacked them. (Some Crusaders also massacred whole Jewish communities in Germany on the way to the Holy Land, a grotesque evil that most Church officials condemned at the time.) Bernard Lewis, has written, "The Crusades could more accurately be described as a limited, belated and, in the last analysis, ineffectual response to the jihad—a failed attempt to recover by a Christian holy war what had been lost to a Muslim holy war." [13]

Two reasons for lumping Christian fundamentalists with Islamists are clear.

First, it is a way to demonize conservative Christians, the Left's most despised target. That is what Armstrong did in stating that the only reasons Christians don't commit as many acts of terror as Muslims are that America is a more peaceful society than the societies in which Muslim terrorists live and that America's Christians don't have to commit terrorism in order to achieve their goal of bringing down the government. Her third point is that neither fundamentalist Christians nor fundamentalist Muslims believe in democracy.

Not a word of what she said to liken the two groups is true. There is no evidence to back up her charge that fundamentalist Christians do not believe in democracy or wish to bring down the

American government. But without naming names or supplying evidence, it sounds persuasive.

Tavis Smiley's equating of Muslim terrorism with all the criminal killings in America and Michel Martin's claim that Timothy McVeigh engaged in his act of terror in the name of Christianity are what one regularly hears on liberal television and radio. Normal rules of truth telling are suspended for the greater good of giving conservative Christians a bad name and deflecting moral judgment from the Muslim world.

If truth and morality matter, one cannot make any moral comparison between Islamists and Christian fundamentalists.

The very fact that anyone living among Christians feels perfectly secure in attacking fundamentalist Christians and mainstream Christianity shows there is no comparison. No one feels secure in criticizing Islam. In most Muslim countries, it is a death warrant. Even in the West it is highly dangerous. That is why ex-Muslim critics of Islam or Islamists—such as Ayaan Hirsi Ali, the Somali woman who works for Muslim women's human rights—usually travel with bodyguards. And others, such as the brilliant ex-Muslim author "Ibn Warraq," write under a pen name.

Another telling difference between Christian and Muslim fundamentalists was pointed out by a Christian postal worker who called in to my radio show after I related two news stories:

One news item from the UK and Australia told of some fundamentalist Muslim taxi drivers who refused to pick up passengers who had a dog with them—even when the passenger was blind and the dog was a Seeing Eye dog—because many Muslims believe that Islam forbids them to come into contact with dogs.[14] The other news story was related. Many Muslim taxi drivers in Minneapolis, who make up a significant percentage of taxi drivers in that city, refuse to pick up passengers who have a bottle of wine or other alcoholic beverage with them because of the Muslim ban on drinking alcohol.[15]

The Christian mailman from Denver called in to say that despite his profound religious objections to pornography, he could not imagine objecting to delivering even the raunchiest pornographic journals to homes that ordered it.

This was highly instructive. Given that fundamentalist Christians object to pornography at least as strongly as fundamentalist Muslims object to dogs (and remember, the former is a religious/moral objection while the latter is only a cultural one), why would the Christian mail carrier deliver pornographic material and the Muslim taxi driver refuse a passenger with a dog or with a can of beer? One reason is that, completely contrary to what Karen Armstrong alleges, religious—yes, fundamentalist—Christians in America believe that liberty is a religious value. As much as God may dislike porn, He cherishes liberty. Second, Christians do not hold non-Christians bound by their religious practices, just as Jews do not hold non-Jews bound to Jewish religious law (it is difficult to believe that any Orthodox Jewish taxi driver in America would refuse to drive a passenger who was eating a ham sandwich).

Let us put it this way: One could only wish that fundamentalist Christians and Islamists were morally comparable. If Muslim fundamentalists had the same values, the same commitment to liberty, democracy, and secular government that America's fundamentalist Christians have, the world would be a far less violent place.

Moderate Muslims—Islam's and the World's Hope

THERE ARE TRULY MODERATE religious Muslims, as opposed to many of those declared "moderate" by naive Westerners. They are religious Muslims who wish to see Islamists condemned and Islam reformed. These courageous individuals offer real hope that the Islamic world can one day make significant moral contributions to humanity.

These Muslims can be identified in the following ways, none of which necessitates rejecting a belief in the divinity of the Koran, the revelation to Muhammad, or belief in Islam as the final revelation:

1. They honestly confront the Muslim moral record—the lack of liberty in Muslim nations, the killing and persecution of large numbers of non-Muslims, the lower status of women, etc.

2. They oppose incorporating Sharia into the law of a political state and the establishment of any Islamic theocracy (which is not, in any event, Koran-based, according to moderate Muslims).

3. They accept the existence of Israel as a Jewish state, acknowledge the Jews' ancient and religious ties to Israel, and distance themselves from the Muslim/Arab obsession with destroying Israel.

4. They publicly and unambiguously condemn all violence in the name of Islam, including violence against Israel.

5. They reject the Islamist notion of an America hostile to Muslims, and acknowledge America's superb treatment of both its Muslim citizens and of Muslim immigrants.

6. They affirm the primacy of the value of liberty.

Examples of such Muslim moderates include the aforementioned professor, Muqtedar Khan.

Regarding America, Khan has written, "American Muslims really have no reason to feel they are victims of anything." The Muslim American community is thriving, proof of "America's benevolence and tolerance of Islam . . ."[16]

And as for the Muslim obsession with Israel, Khan has written: "It is time the leaders of the American Muslim community woke up and realized that there is more to life than competing with the American Jewish lobby for power over US foreign policy. Islam is not about defeating Jews or conquering Jerusalem. It is about mercy, about virtue, about sacrifice and about duty. Above all it is the pursuit of moral perfection."[17]

Another moderate is Ahmed al-Rahim, a professor of religious studies at the University of Virginia, who has said: "The most im-

portant message is that we condemn all kinds of hate speech including anti-Semitism and anti-Americanism and that we come out as
boldly as possible against violence committed by Muslims in Iraq,
in Israel . . ."

In a clear criticism of the Council on American-Islamic Relations and similar Muslim rights organizations that perpetuate
Islamist thinking, al-Rahim wrote: "There was more concern with
hate crimes against Muslims, which I think were relatively low,
and there was more focus on that than actually looking at the violence and the hate speech that has been committed in the name of
Islam." [18]

Zainab al-Suwaij, executive director of the American Islamic
Congress, is another moderate. A religious Muslim and refugee
from Saddam Hussein's Iraq, she publicly declared that America
"has given Iraqis the most precious gift any nation has ever given
another—the gift of democracy and the freedom to determine its
own future."

One more Muslim American who is a source of hope regarding Islam's future is Dr. M. Zuhdi Jasser, a physician in Arizona
whose parents fled Syria in the 1960s. He is the founder and chairman of the board of the American Islamic Forum for Democracy.
A believing and practicing Muslim, Dr. Jasser advocates American
values, and promotes traditional Islam, but one that is never imposed on others. He is particularly courageous in confronting the
victimhood-embracing Muslim groups that the mainstream media
in the Western world have promoted as the spokesmen for Western
Muslims.

THIS CHAPTER ON ISLAM NOTWITHSTANDING, I am confident, almost
to the point of certainty, that one day Islam will undergo major
changes, as have Christianity, Judaism, Hinduism, and other world
religions. These changes may begin to take place in the lifetime of
young people today; they may begin much later than that. But even

now there are voices of believing Muslims arguing for an Islam that affirms liberty and human rights, and that eschews theocracy.

They are rare. But given the power of communication, they can be heard.

And when that time comes, Islam may well present a moral expression of the American value system. The purpose of this chapter was to make it clear that that day is not today.

And should that day come, it will likely be the Muslims of America who lead the way—because they will have benefited from and assimilated into Islam the American value system. In the words of Professor al-Rahim, the Muslim community in America is "one of the few communities, if not one of the only communities, that can occupy this place of leading the Muslim world. If you look at European Muslims, they are living in ghettoes. If you look at the Muslim world, there is very little freedom of expression. America has really given Muslims an opportunity to rethink and redefine their position in the world. If it's going to happen anywhere, it's going to happen here."

And that is the point of this book. If the world is going to get better, it will happen thanks to America and its values.

Part III

AMERICA AND ITS UNIQUE VALUES

Americans have the chance to "begin the world all over again."

—Thomas Paine, *Common Sense*

The American Trinity

THE UNITED STATES OF AMERICA is not merely a geographical location. And unlike most of the world's nations, Americans are not, and never have been, a race or an ethnicity. America is and has always regarded itself as an idea. That idea is a value system. And that value system—unique to America—can be called the American Trinity.

Ask most Americans what the American value system consists of and you will get many responses, many of them in conflict with each other. The truth is that most Americans do not know what America's distinctive values are. But two things will unite nearly all respondents.

First, they will not consider the question odd. Most Americans believe that America has a distinct value system. This itself is significant. Most people in other nations would not understand what the questioner was asking. Ask a Dutchman or Uruguayan, individuals who live in decent, well-functioning democracies: "What are distinctive Dutch or Uruguayan values?" and they will probably respond by asking, "What do you mean?" Few citizens of any other country think about whether their country has a distinctive value system, and even fewer would resonate to the concept of their country being an idea. Yet one of the leading American historians, Gordon S. Wood, has written a book titled *The Idea of America*, in which he argues the case that from the outset, Americans conceived America as being an idea. The second way in which almost all Americans would be united in their response to what constitute American values is that they would use the words *liberty* or *freedom*.

Beyond agreeing that America is an idea and identifying liberty as an American value, few Americans could identify a distinctive American value system. For much of my life I was one of them. I knew that America had values, and I knew that liberty was one of them. But I could not name any distinctive American value. After all, the French Revolution declared its values to be "Liberty, Equality, Fraternity," and it therefore seemed presumptuous, even sanctimonious, to argue that liberty was a distinctly American value.

Then one day, in the most routine of actions—emptying my pockets—I discovered what generations of Americans used to know, but did not successfully pass on to my or even to my parents' generation. On every American coin were inscribed the three primary values of America—"Liberty," "In God We Trust," and "E Pluribus Unum."

Those three values make up the value system I have come to call the American Trinity. No other society or nation has identified those three values as its core values.

I will explain each of these values, argue why they constitute the best system ever devised to govern a society, and clarify how Leftism seeks to replace each of them with a Left-wing value.

Liberty

LIBERTY IS THE ESSENCE OF THE AMERICAN IDEA

The United States was the world's first free country.

It was the country that most inspired other countries to be free.

It is the country that has been free the longest.

It is the country that has most protected other free countries.

It is the country that has most spread freedom to other countries.

This is all because the United States was founded on the value of liberty.

America, "sweet land of liberty," is how one of its most beloved national songs describes the country. And it ends, appropriately, with these words: "From every mountainside, let freedom ring."

The American national anthem ends with these words: "Oh say, does that star-spangled banner [the American flag] yet wave o'er *the land of the free* and the home of the brave?" That is why France built the Statue of Liberty as a gift to the American people. No other country has exemplified liberty as has America.

More people from more countries have immigrated to America in order to be free than to the rest of the world's countries put together.

More black Africans have immigrated to the United States voluntarily—looking for freedom and opportunity—than came to the United States involuntarily as slaves.[1]

And no country has ever the felt the obligation to spread liberty elsewhere as has America. People differ as to whether this is always—or ever—a good idea. But it is indisputable that this has been an animating American idea.

It animated Americans to die in the liberation of Europe in two world wars.

It animated Americans to die to keep half of the Korean peninsula from falling under the rule of Communist totalitarians.

It animated Americans to die trying to keep half of Vietnam from falling under Communist totalitarians.

It animated America to fly food into West Berlin in order to break the Soviet blockade of a free city located in the midst of totalitarian East Germany.

It animated America to intervene on behalf of Muslims in Kosovo and to aid Muslims in Afghanistan.

Has America also backed dictators? Yes, it has. But that in no way negates all of America's unique sacrifices on behalf of others' liberty.

And in nearly every case of America backing a non-democratically elected leader, the alternatives to that leader were deemed—usually correctly—to be morally worse for his people and for the cause of liberty. Those who call America hypocritical for backing non-freely elected leaders rarely cite the most blatant example—America's backing of Joseph Stalin in World War II. It would be hard to identify a more blood-soaked regime than Stalin's. Yet no one charges America with hypocrisy for backing Stalin during World War II. Anyone whose moral compass works understands that in order to stop Hitler and Nazism, supporting Stalin against Hitler was obligatory. Had the Soviet Union fallen to the Nazis, it is difficult to see how the Western democracies could have prevailed in World War II.

So, too, many of the dictators America supported during the Cold War were perceived as the only viable alternative to a Communist dictatorship, which would have resulted in more cruelty, less freedom, and more death. That was the case in Cuba, where all Cubans had much more freedom, had access to a plethora of independent newspapers and radio stations, and most had a higher standard of living under the dictator Fulgencio Batista than under the Communist tyrant who overthrew him, Fidel Castro. So, too, by virtually any measurement of quality of life, Iranians were far better off under the American-backed dictator, the Shah of Iran, than under his successors, the theocratic tyrants who came to rule the Islamic Republic of Iran.

The fact is that America has been the greatest model of liberty, the greatest spreader of liberty, and the greatest preserver of liberty the world has ever known. It believed that it was its mission to spread liberty. President John F. Kennedy famously expressed this belief in his inaugural address in 1961, proclaiming, "Let every nation know, whether it wishes us well or ill, that we shall pay any price, bear any burden, meet any hardship, support any friend, oppose any foe, in order to assure the survival and the success of liberty."

Regarding this pronouncement, it is important to note that it is unlikely that the inaugural address by the leader of any other country promised the world that his country would pay any price to assure the survival and the success of liberty elsewhere. It is also worth noting that few Americans—Republican or Democrat—found the Kennedy statement odd. Yet it would be very odd for, let us say, a Swedish prime minister to make a similar comment upon taking office.

From the beginning, liberty was the great animating impulse of the American colonies. Probably the best-remembered statement from America's founding is that of Patrick Henry, "Give me liberty or give me death."

We have here, in a nutshell, a major difference between America and Western Europe: Liberty animates America; economic equality and economic security animate Western Europe.

For this reason, among others, if the United States ceased to exist, liberty would be diminished, if not extinguished, nearly everywhere on earth.

WHAT LIBERTY MEANS

For Americans, liberty has meant:

- Political freedom—the freedom to elect whomever the citizens of the country want to elect, and the right to be governed with the consent of the people
- Religious freedom—the right to practice any or no religion
- Freedom from religious coercion—the state may not impose religious requirements. Though not known to most Americans today, this was most insisted upon by many of the most religious founding groups in America. "Separation of church and state would not exist if not for the efforts of eighteenth-century evangelicals."[2]
- Freedom of assembly—the right to gather and associate publicly and privately with whomever one chooses
- Freedom of speech—the right to say and write whatever one wants short of "shouting 'fire' in a crowded theater"

- Economic freedom—the right to start and maintain a business and the right to keep as much of what one has legally earned as is practically possible
- Freedom of the press—the right of newspapers and magazines and other media to advocate anything legal
- Freedom from the state—the ability of individuals to be as free as practically possible from governmental interference in their lives

This last right is the one that is most responsible for so many people around the world seeing America more than any other place on earth as a land of opportunity. This right also means that one must have the ability to fail. Without that possibility, success for either the individual or for society is rarely possible.

LIBERTY NECESSITATES SMALL GOVERNMENT

Individual liberty exists in inverse proportion to the size of the state. The bigger the government/state, the less liberty the individual has. *The bigger the government, the smaller the citizen.* Whatever the arguments for a big state—such as protecting citizens from economic hardship and providing a free education and health care—the bigger the state, the more it controls. And the more it controls, the less the individual controls.

That is one reason the Founders of the United States were adamant about keeping the federal government out of every area of American life except for those specifically enumerated in the Constitution. As the Tenth Amendment to the Constitution states: "The powers not delegated to the United States by the Constitution, nor prohibited by it to the States, are reserved to the States respectively, or to the people."

But for the Left, for whom abolishing material inequality is a higher ideal than individual liberty, the ideal of small government is really little more than a cover for preserving economic inequality. As one Left-wing think tank, the Institute for Policy Studies, has written: "Americans of a more progressive bent tend, of course, to consider all this solemnity around the 'principle of limited government' just so much mumbo-jumbo meant to keep the rich and powerful safe and secure from any challenge to their wealth and power."[3]

For this reason, people on the Left are perplexed by the fact that many non-rich Americans, even poor ones, hold conservative/American values and oppose big government. The Left-wing understanding of life is that the ultimate conflict is between rich and poor. So why would any poor person advocate small government when big government is the vehicle to material equality? The Left cannot quite fathom that many people are driven by values that transcend material considerations. For those who hold American values, liberty—which depends on keeping government small—greatly transcends economic equality as a value.

The Bigger the Government, the More the Abuse of Power

The Founders of the United States were adamant about limited government for another reason: They did not trust people with power. Professor of history Thomas Kidd explained: "Because of their doubts about the goodness of human nature, they saw centralized government power as dangerous."[4]

Unlike the Founders, those who seek big government do trust people (provided they are kindred spirits) with immense power and do not see "centralized government power as dangerous." They believe that putting enormous power in a few people's hands is a good thing because for Leftists big government is the vehicle to accomplishing their goals. The Left does not trust the individual to govern his life.

In fact, evil ideologies—fascism, Nazism, Communism, military dictatorships—depend on big government, and fail when state power contracts. It is overwhelmingly because of big government with its vast amount of corruption that countries in Africa, Asia, and Latin America are poor. Their poverty is not because of a lack of raw materials, nor a lack of smart and talented people, nor is it the residue of Western colonialism. Any African, Asian, or Latin American nation that embraced the American value system would produce both prosperity and liberty for its people.

The Bigger the Government, the Smaller the Citizen

The bigger the government, the smaller the citizen is in every way, the moral sphere included. In other words, as the government gets bigger, not only does the individual recede in significance but the character of the average citizen also gets smaller.

1. Moral Character Begins with Taking Responsibility for Oneself

Moral character begins with taking care of oneself, if one is able to. Conversely, it is a moral defect to rely on others when one does not have to. That said, there are times when people simply cannot take care of themselves and must rely on others. Life is tragic and some people, despite their best efforts and their commitment to being a responsible person, must have others support them. And the rest of us are morally obligated to support them.

Given that people taking care of themselves is a moral virtue, even those who believe that the ideal society is one in which the state takes care of as many of its citizens as possible must acknowledge that such a state exacts a moral price. The more the state takes care of its citizens, the more deleterious the effects are on most citizens' moral character.

Of course, some might argue that there is no relationship between moral character and taking responsibility for oneself. But to do so would mean turning the concept of character, as it has been understood throughout Judeo-Christian and Western history, on its head. A seminal teaching of Judaism, enunciated by Rabbi Hillel, the leading rabbi in the making of the Talmud, Judaism's holiest work after the Hebrew Bible, is: "If I am not for myself, who will be for me? But if I am only for myself, what am I?" and the

New Testament teaches, "If a man will not work, he shall not eat" (II Thessalonians 3:10). The essence of good character is to be a responsible person, meaning, first and foremost, taking responsibility for oneself. Then one assumes responsibility for one's family and then for others who cannot take care of themselves.

2. Reliance on the State Creates a Sense of Entitlement

The more people rely on government, the more they develop a sense of entitlement, an attitude characterized by the belief that one is owed whatever one receives—and often more than one receives. This is a second big-government blow to moral character; and it, in turn, has terrible consequences.

First, the more one feels entitled, the less one believes one has to work for anything. Why work hard if I can look to the state to give me much of what I need, and, increasingly, much of what I want? This is one reason that Americans esteem work more than Europeans do. Europeans have been raised by the Left-wing welfare state, and Leftism places little moral value on work. Leftism regards work as a necessary evil; Americanism regards work as ennobling. The ideal for the Left, and therefore for most Europeans, is to work as little as possible, enjoy as much vacation time as possible, and retire on a state pension as early as possible. This is why Europeans riot over vacation time.

Second, the more entitled one feels, the less grateful one feels. This is obvious: Why be grateful for getting what you are owed?

This is of supreme importance because gratitude is the most important human quality. It is the root of both happiness and goodness. The ungrateful cannot be happy people, and the ungrateful cannot be good people.[5]

The ingratitude induced by Leftism is, therefore, another reason people Left of center are less likely to be happy than people Right of center. And that's not all. The more entitled one feels, the angrier one is likely to be. People who do not get what they think they are entitled to become angry. Anger and ingratitude are a toxic brew that produces not only unhappy people, but destructive ones as well.

Third, if the welfare state teaches people not to take care of themselves, how much more so does it teach them not to take care of others? Smaller government, along with religion, has been the primary reason Americans give more charity and volunteer more time per capita than do Europeans living in welfare states. After all, why take care of your fellow citizen, or even your family, when the state will do it for you? This question alone makes a powerful moral case against the welfare state. In other words, while altruistic motives may have created the welfare state, the welfare state creates selfishness.

This lack of concern for others extends to other nations as well. I am not referring to foreign aid, which is often ineffective and even destructive when given, as it often is, to countries ruled by corrupt governments. Rather I am referring to a willingness to fight, and if necessary die, for other nations' liberty. In that regard, no country has been as willing as America to sacrifice for others. And it is the conservatives in America (though not its libertarian wing) who most support these efforts and who most volunteer to fight. Conservatives in other Western countries are also far more supportive of fighting for others than are Left-wing citizens and governments. Shortly after the Left won in Spain, they withdrew all their forces from Iraq. Apparently, the massacre of Iraqis that would have followed a withdrawal of all coalition troops from Iraq meant little to Spain's Left. So, too, the election of a center-Left government in Japan meant abandoning that country's war effort in Afghanistan.

There are fine individuals on the Left, and there are selfish individuals on the Right. But as a rule, bigger government increases the number of angry, ungrateful, lazy, spoiled, and self-centered individuals.[6]

The Smaller the Government, the More the Individual Is Needed

Among the things that Left and Right, religious and secular, agree on is that human beings have to feel needed. When we are not, life seems pointless.

Unfortunately, however, the larger the state the less its citizens feel needed and, therefore, the less they—especially men—feel significant. It is definitional. The more the state does, the less its citizens need to do. One well-known example is the way welfare robbed so many men of significance when women and their children came to depend financially on the state.

Before the expansion of the state, the average American had much more societal significance. A generation ago, the men of the local Rotary Club had more prestige and social importance. So did fathers. So did clergy. With the ascendance of the state, much of these individuals' societal significance has eroded. As the state expands further into health care, the same will happen to doctors as autonomy and prestige are transferred from them to the heads of dozens of new government health regulatory agencies. Over time, if the Left has its way and the state keeps expanding, the individual's significance will continue to decline. He will not be allowed to decide at what temperature to keep his house (Left-wing legislatures seek to have home thermostats regulated by local and state governments), and she will not be able to make the lunch she wants for her schoolchild (American schools increasingly ban food from home because it is deemed less healthy), among many other examples.

This is what the battle in America was about with regard to the government banning the incandescent lightbulb: liberty and individual significance—not lightbulbs per se. If I cannot even choose what lightbulbs I use in my own home, I lose some autonomy, some liberty, and some dignity.

This is why the Left opposes homeschooling—it grants the individual too much influence over his or her children. In big-government Europe, homeschooling is strongly discouraged, and in Germany it is illegal except in rare cases.

In short, as the state grows, the individual citizen will be needed essentially for one thing: to finance the one thing that is needed—the state.

· · ·

THERE ARE PRICES TO BE PAID for liberty, prices that Americanism is willing to pay, but which Leftism is not: economic inequality in particular, but also personal failure and hurt feelings. With liberty, some people will inevitably be much richer than others. Therefore, the more a society demands equality, the less liberty it will have. With liberty, people are freer to fail. And with liberty, children will experience the hurt of losing a game by many points, and all people will experience the hurt that free speech may produce. Reduce the chances of experiencing emotional pain and you reduce the amount of liberty in society.

Americans fought for liberty above everything else. Did they extend it to all Americans? No, they did not. Slavery blighted the American moral landscape until vast numbers of Americans killed one another over the issue.* However, slavery troubled the Founders and it troubled any American who believed in liberty. The glare of the discrepancy was simply too bright to avoid. And America eventually created the freest place on earth for a black person to live.†

In God We Trust

THERE IS, OF COURSE, one great risk to a society founded on liberty—anarchy. Since liberty means that the state will be too small to effectively morally constrain each individual, this presents a problem. If, as the Founders believed, people are not basically good, what or who will keep people from acting poorly? To whom will each citizen feel accountable for their actions if not a powerful state?

Or, to put it another way, if the Founders mistrusted big gov-

---

* There has been an effort on the part of some ideologically driven historians and others to deny that the American Civil War was fought because of slavery. That this was the reason is easily proved, however: Every Southern state, in its official statement of secession, gave Union opposition to slavery as its reason for secession. No slavery, no civil war. No opposition to slavery, no civil war.

† Keith Richburg, a writer for the *Washington Post* who is black, confronted this issue head-on and concluded that thanks to his ancestors' terrible suffering as slaves, he was blessed to live in America rather than Africa. He wrote this after years of covering Africa for the *Post*. See Keith Richburg, *Out of America: A Black Man Confronts Africa* (New York: Basic Books, 1997).

ernment because they knew that people were not basically good, why would they trust liberty? If inherently flawed people will inevitably abuse power, won't inherently flawed people inevitably abuse liberty?

The answer, of course, is yes.

And that is the reason for the second value of the American value system—God.

If people are not morally accountable to an all-powerful state or to a monarch and they are granted an amount of personal freedom that is unprecedented in the history of mankind, they need to be accountable either to themselves—that is, their own hearts and consciences—or to a God who is moral and who judges each individual (and nation).

The first alternative was out of the question for the Founders—and should be out of the question for anyone who doesn't romanticize human nature. The heart is an awful guide to good behavior and the conscience may be a fine guide but 1) it is easily overwhelmed by human nature (for example, appetites, lust, envy, greed, etc.) and 2) it can be easily overridden by rationalizing one's behavior ("it's not that bad," "everybody does it," "it's a big department store, not a mom-and-pop store"); and therefore 3) people need to believe they are accountable to, and will be judged by, something greater than themselves.

What the Founders did regarding God and liberty was as unique as it was brilliant: they substituted God (and moral religion) for a powerful secular or religious state and they tied liberty to God. Thomas Kidd summarized Alexis de Tocqueville, the great nineteenth-century French observer of America, on this matter: "The partnership of religion and liberty lay at the heart of America's political success. . . . Freedom by itself would inexorably degenerate into rabid selfishness, but religion nurtured the purposefulness of freedom."[7]

God is as central to the American value system as is liberty. It was so from the beginning.

America was founded by God-centered individuals and God-centered religious communities. Not one of those identified as the Founders—including the so-called deists—was an atheist; every one of them believed in a judging God, and that without God-based values, America could not survive.

John Adams, one of the most influential of the Founding Fathers and second president of the United States, wrote in a letter to officers of a Massachusetts militia, "Our Constitution was made only for *a moral and religious* people. It is wholly inadequate to the government of any other."[8] And on another occasion, he said, "Religion was the only thing that could tame our savage natures."[9]

George Washington, in his Farewell Address in 1796 made this point abundantly clear: "Of all the dispositions and habits which lead to political prosperity, religion and morality are indispensable supports. . . . Let us with caution indulge the supposition, that morality can be maintained without religion." Alexander Hamilton, James Madison, and John Jay, the authors of the Federalist Papers, all helped Washington write this address.

Those who wish to deny the God-centered roots of the American experiment frequently argue that many of the Founders did not hold Christian beliefs such as the Trinity or the divinity of Jesus. They are right, but the argument is irrelevant. Not all the Founders held specifically Christian beliefs, but all believed in God. And not in Aristotle's unmoved Mover, but in the God of the Hebrew Bible. Benjamin Franklin, widely considered a deist, was, like every one of the Founders, an ethical monotheist, who, moreover, "embraced a very non-deistic view that God intervened in the lives of human beings."[10]

Franklin proposed that each session of the struggling constitutional convention be opened with a prayer imploring the Almighty to intervene on the delegates' behalf: "I have lived, Sir, a long time and the longer I live, the more convincing proofs I see of this truth— that *God governs in the affairs of men.* And if a sparrow cannot fall to the ground without his notice, is it probable that an empire can rise without his aid? . . . I therefore beg leave to move—that henceforth prayers imploring the assistance of Heaven, and its blessings on our deliberations, be held in this Assembly every morning before we proceed to business . . ."[11]

The American experiment in liberty was inconceivable to the Founders—and should be inconceivable to everyone today—without God and without God-based, morality-teaching religion. Tocqueville summarized the American view of the dependence of liberty on faith: "Despotism may be able to do without faith, but freedom cannot."[12]

The American value system is predicated on the belief that a good society must be God-based and must have good religion to keep its citizens decent. One does not have to be American or to live in America in order to affirm this proposition. As the Russian novelist Fyodor Dostoyevsky wrote in the nineteenth century (in *The Brothers Karamazov*), "Where there is no God, all is permitted." America's Founders would have wholeheartedly agreed.

While it is true that George Washington, Thomas Jefferson, Benjamin Franklin, and James Madison—those widely regarded as the preeminent Founders of the United States of America—departed from some or all aspects of specifically Christian theology, each of them passionately advocated God-based religion, in their case Christianity, or, to use the more modern term, Judeo-Christian values. Steven Waldman summarized the Founders' views on the moral necessity of religion: "Each felt that religion was extremely important, at a minimum to encourage moral behavior and make the land safe for republican government."[13]

Benjamin Franklin put the need for God-based religion perfectly: "If Men are so wicked as we now see them *with Religion* what would they be *without it*?" (emphasis added)[14]

"As for John Adams," writes Waldman, "although he was personally inclined toward Unitarianism (which denied the Christian doctrine of the Trinity), he also affirmed the public value of religion."[15]

Waldman summarizes John Adams's views this way: "He disliked secular humanism and feared that a world without faith would lead to moral mayhem."[16]

The Left, in its determination to secularize society, distorts many of the Founders' views on religion. Waldman cites a particularly telling example with regard to Adams:

"The liberal magazine *The Nation* and the website www.deism .org both honed [*sic*] in on this comment from Adams: 'Twenty times in the course of my late reading, have I been upon the point of breaking out, "this would be the best of all possible worlds, if there were no religion in it." ' But in typical culture-war behavior neither *The Nation* nor deism.org included the rest of the quote, in which Adams explained that the negative sentiment *soon passed* and was replaced by his realization that 'Without religion this world would be something not fit to be mentioned in polite society, I mean hell.'"[17]

Adams is saying that as bad as the world has been with religion, it would be a living hell without (Bible-based) religion (we will see why this is so). Adams attended church regularly. And with all his criticisms and despite his rejection of Christian theology, he regarded Christianity as the embodiment of "the eternal, self-existent, independent, benevolent, all powerful, and all merciful creator, preserver and father of the universe, the first good, first perfect, and first fair." Christianity was so perfect in its essence that "[n]either savage nor civilized man, without a revelation, could ever have discovered or invented it."[18]

WHY GOD AND RELIGION ARE NECESSARY

The Founders of America understood that flawed man needs God to make a moral society, and that a free society, in particular, needs God.

The Left believes that people can be good without God (indeed, that the world would be better without God). Now, it is true that there are good individuals who do not believe in God or religion. By and large, however, these individuals (in the Western world, at least) have simply adopted the values bequeathed by centuries of Judeo-Christian values. They are living on what one author called "cutflower ethics." Flowers are nurtured in a certain soil, and, when cut from that soil, they can appear to survive for a certain amount of time. But, of course, they soon wither and die. So, too, Western societies' ethical values were nurtured in Judeo-Christian soil, and cut off from that soil they, too, will seem to survive, but eventually, like cut flowers, those values will wither and die.

Therefore, while there will always be some good individuals in all societies, including primitive ones, godless ones, and even evil societies, that is of little consequence. What matters is making a good society, with large numbers of good people, not merely some good individuals.

To put it another way, there are fine musicians who never took music lessons and never even learned how to read music. But no one would argue that just because there are some fine musicians who never studied music, we don't need to teach music. If we want to produce good musicians and a musically literate society, music must be taught. Likewise, if we want to produce good individuals and an ethical society, we need moral religion to teach morality and a moral God to believe in.

Finally, when Leftists make the argument that God and religion are unnecessary, they omit to note that this is only achievable with a strong state. According to Leftists themselves, men will not treat women decently without a vast number of laws prohibiting sexual harassment, creating a hostile work environment, etc. Nor will whites avoid hurting blacks without a vast array of civil rights laws and politically correct speech codes. So the Left implicitly admits that only a powerful state can ensure a decent society without God. Here we have another reason that both Islamism and Leftism believe in a strong state—to enforce either Sharia laws or Leftist laws.

The American value system is predicated on liberty and God, which together enable a much weaker state than either Islam or Leftism advocate.

WHAT GOD?

Given that "In God We Trust" is one of the three components of the American Trinity, it is important to explain who and what this God is.

Here are the essential characteristics:

1. This God Is the God Introduced by the Hebrew Bible

The "Creator" in the Declaration of Independence is the God of Genesis: "In the beginning God created the heavens and the earth."

Though this God is the Creator, He is not an uninvolved, disinterested, amoral deity. He acts in history, primarily through the lives of nations, and sometimes in the lives of individuals. As Kidd summarized it, for all the Founders, "God—or Providence, as deists and others might prefer to deem it—moved in and through nations."[19]

This God is the reason every human life is infinitely precious. This, too, is from the Bible: Man was created "in the image of God." This does not mean that like God, man is inherently good; it means that human life is sacred and that, like God (but unlike the animals, who are not created in God's image), man knows good and evil—and has the freedom to choose between them.

And of critical importance to making a good society, this God is the biblical God who commands, "Love your neighbor as yourself, I am God" (Leviticus 19:18).

Every Founder, no matter what his theology, was preoccupied with the Bible. Every great university founded before the eighteenth century, including Harvard, Princeton, and Yale, was founded by clergy, and these universities placed Bible study at the center of their curricula.

Dartmouth College was founded by a pastor and a missionary to the Oneida Indians, Eleazar Wheelock.[20]

Columbia's first provost was a Presbyterian pastor, John Mitchell Mason, who was so orthodox in his Christianity that he wrote *The Voice of Warning to Christians on the Ensuing Election*, attacking Thomas Jefferson for denying the Flood and other miracles.

Princeton, Waldman writes, "was an *evangelical* [emphasis in the

original] Christian school. It was founded by New Light Presby-
terians, the faction that had arisen during the Great Awakening to
emphasize adherence to the Bible and passionate evangelism—to
churn out evangelists. Its first president was Jonathan Edwards, the
Billy Graham of his day. . . . The school's curriculum melded evan-
gelicalism and science, scriptures and the classics."[21]

2. This God Is the Source of Morality

Without this God as the ultimate source of a standard of good and
evil, there is no objective good and evil, only personal or societal preferences about right and wrong. If God is not the author of
"Thou shall not steal," men might still come up with the idea that
stealing is wrong. Indeed, many will. But it would still be men's
opinions, not an objective moral truth. Moreover, when God says
something is wrong, it has infinitely more clout than when reason
or logic or opinion or feeling alone says it. Among other things it
means that one who steals will be accountable to this God.

3. This God Demands Moral Behavior from All People and All Nations (Ethical Monotheism)

God judges all individuals and all nations. One aspect of the revolution inaugurated by Jewish ethical monotheism was that one God
means one morality for all humanity. Morality is the same for the
Jew, the non-Jew, the American, and the non-American. Ethical monotheism was a moral earthquake in human history. Before
the Hebrew Bible, all gods acted capriciously; they did what they
wanted—they were no more than supermen—and what they did
was beyond good and evil.

The notion of God judging nations was instrumental to all of
the Founders' beliefs, and this notion very much included America itself. Kidd writes, "Even though Washington seems personally to have held rather a distant view of the deity, he still believed
that God was providentially active in human affairs. . . . [H]e believed that God, through acts of providence, would judge wicked
nations . . ."[22]

All of the American Founders, even Thomas Paine, who is considered the least religious and the most anti-Christian, believed in the afterlife. As Paine said: "I trouble not myself about the manner of future existence. I content myself with believing, even to positive conviction, that the power that gave me existence is able to continue it, in any form and manner he pleases, either with or without this body . . ."[23]

Not one of the Founders was a deist in the sense that term is erroneously understood today—belief in a creator who has no interest or involvement in his creation.[24] The one most identified as deist in the sense of not believing in Christianity, Paine was raised in a religious home by an Anglican mother and a Quaker father, and he kept their values while dropping their religion. Kidd tells us that Paine "apparently worked for a brief period as an evangelical Methodist preacher . . ."[25] And Waldman writes, "Although he once described himself as a Deist, at other times in his life he embraced the very non-Deistic view that God intervened in the lives of human beings."[26] Moreover, his extremely influential *Common Sense* was filled with religious language and biblical references.

George Washington, in Waldman's words, "wasn't a Deist. He believed in an omnipotent and constantly intervening God. . . . He issued many orders calling for days of prayer, was heard to pronounce or call for prayers at meals, and—most important—seemed to believe that God could be influenced by the prayers and behavior of men."[27]

4. *This God Is the Source of Liberty*

This God was the source of liberty. In the famous words of the Declaration of Independence, all men "are endowed by their Creator with certain unalienable Rights, that among these are Life, Liberty, and the pursuit of Happiness."

If God is not the source of liberty, what or who will be? A king, a dictator, the state? Only if men regard God as the source of liberty will it not be removed by men. The American experiment in God-based liberty was unique—and it, too, traced it roots to the

THE AMERICAN TRINITY 331

Hebrew Bible. A biblical verse concerning liberty is the one inscription on the Liberty Bell: "Proclaim liberty throughout the land to all the inhabitants thereof." [28] No other society except America's with its Judeo-based ethical monotheism made God the source of liberty and the one who demands that society be based on individual liberty.

ETHICAL MONOTHEISM, NOT NECESSARILY CHRISTIANITY OR JUDAISM

One does not have to be a believing Jew or Christian in order to affirm this God of the American value system. One can come from any religious background or even affirm no specific religion, providing one affirms Judeo-Christian values (as set forth below). One can be an ethical monotheist like Thomas Jefferson and Benjamin Franklin. According to Kidd, "Franklin did question the divinity of Jesus, and he believed that morality was the essence of true religion, not correct doctrine. . . . Nearing the end of his life, Franklin privately expressed doubts about Jesus's divinity, but he believed in Christ's ethical teachings and a God who answered human prayers." [29]

If one had to be a Jew or a Christian to affirm American values, those values could not be exported to non-Christians and non-Jews. But a major theme of this book and of Americanism is that Judeo-Christian values are applicable to virtually every society and individual, no matter what their religion, nationality, or ethnicity. It was not theology that concerned the Founders of the United States and those who made "In God We Trust" the country's motto. It was God-based morality. It was understood that, as night follows day, without a moral and judging God, mankind will devolve into moral chaos.

The Founders—specifically, George Washington, John Adams, Thomas Jefferson, Benjamin Franklin, James Madison, and Alexander Hamilton—believed as the Jewish prophets did, that God is most concerned with humans behaving decently toward one another. The prophet Micah summed it up this way: "What does the

Lord require of you? To act justly, to love mercy, and to walk humbly with your God."[30]

In his autobiography, Benjamin Franklin penned his core religious beliefs. It is one of the most succinct and eloquent descriptions of ethical monotheism ever offered:

"I never doubted the existence of a deity, that he made the world, and governed it by his providence; that the most acceptable service of God was the doing good to man; that our souls are immortal; and that all crimes will be punished, and virtue rewarded either here or hereafter; these I esteemed the essentials of every religion."

America Was Founded to Be a God-Based Country with a Nonsectarian Government

Contrary to what most Americans have been taught for at least two generations, America was designed to be a religious, that is a God-based, country; and from its inception it was.

From even before the United States was founded, Americans believed that America had a God-given purpose: to be a "City on a Hill," and later "the Second Israel."

Yale professor David Gelernter (who is a Jew, not a Christian) has expressed it perfectly:

"America is no secular republic; it's a biblical republic.

"Americanism is no civic religion; it's a biblical religion.

"'America' is one of the most beautiful religious concepts mankind has ever known."[31]

The religion of the vast majority of its inhabitants has been Christianity. But America was not founded to necessarily be a theologically Christian country, that is, one in which all its citizens affirm Christian theological doctrines (specifically, the Trinity and the divinity of Jesus). God is affirmed in the Declaration of Independence as the author of human rights, but the document does not mention Jesus or Christianity. And every American president has mentioned God in his inaugural address, but no president has mentioned Jesus or Christianity in his inaugural address.

None of this denigrates the central role of Christianity and Christians in creating and sustaining America and its values. On the contrary, it is to American Christians' everlasting credit that they were so preoccupied with God and morality that they invented a value system for America that did not necessitate acceptance of Christian theological beliefs. No other religious group has done that.*

What every Founder did believe was that America had to be a God-based society, that its citizens had to be God-fearing men and women, and that America had no chance of surviving, let alone surviving as a good country, without widespread belief in God and adherence to Bible-based morality, that is, ethical monotheism.

America was always a religious country, and it remains the most religious of industrialized Western democracies. America derived its strength from religion, not secularism. It is a rewriting of history to deny the religious origins and purposes of America, or to claim that America was founded to be a secular state. The British historian Paul Johnson, who wrote a magisterial history of the United States, has affirmed America's religious purpose. "In [George] Washington's eyes, at least," Johnson wrote, "America was in no sense a secular state," and "the American Revolution was in essence the political and military expression of a religious movement."[32]

The phrase "separation of church and state," which appears in no founding document (only in a letter written by Thomas Jefferson), means that America must never have a state religion, not that the state be indifferent to religion. On the contrary, Kidd writes, "Washington believed that the government should support the interests of general nonsectarian religion."[33]

Jefferson, too, appreciated the indispensable role religion played in American life. In his first inaugural address, he described Ameri-

---

* Except for the Jews, who never believed that all mankind has to believe in Judaism, but that mankind must come to ethical monotheism. That is the raison d'être of the Jews and Judaism. That is one reason Jews who believe in the Jewish role are allied with Christians in promoting ethical monotheism.

cans as possessing: "A chosen country . . . enlightened by a benign religion, professed, indeed, and practiced in various forms, yet all of them inculcating honesty, truth, temperance, gratitude, and the love of man; acknowledging and adoring an overruling Providence, which by all its dispensations proves that it delights in the happiness of man here and his greater happiness hereafter—with all these blessings, what more is necessary to make us a happy and a prosperous people?"[34]

Only in a deeply religious country would its leaders proclaim, as the Continental Congress did in 1774 and 1775, Days of Fasting, calling on all Americans to confess their sins and repent. To this day every session of Congress is opened by a member of the clergy invoking God's blessings.

The Jewish Roots

Both believing Christians and the Christian ethical monotheists who founded America regarded Americans as a chosen people. But unlike the Church in Europe, these Christians did not see themselves as replacing Israel's chosenness, but rather as being a "Second Israel." In that sense and in so many others, America has Jewish roots.

- America may be said to be the first Judeo-Christian country.
- Even the so-called deists, Jefferson and Franklin, were Judeo-centered. Jefferson and Franklin had a great seal of the United States designed, and on it was depicted the Jews leaving Egypt. Just as the Jews left Egypt, Americans left Europe.*
- Until the nineteenth century students at Harvard University were required to study Hebrew.

---

* Ironically, this remains entirely relevant. The battle within America today is between those who wish to return the country to Europe by emulating its values and those who wish it to retain distinctly American values.

- The inscription on the Liberty Bell is from the Torah.
- The insignia of Yale University is from the Torah, and it is in Hebrew. It appears on the breastplate worn by the Jewish high priest.
- George Washington, among many others, was a Mason and "Rituals firmly placed Jewish biblical tradition at the heart of all Masonry."[35]
- Abraham Lincoln referred to the United States as the "almost-chosen" people.

JUDEO-CHRISTIAN VALUES

America was founded on Judeo-Christian values. These are values originating in the Jewish scriptures (the Old Testament), especially the Torah (the Five Books of Moses), as applied to society by American Christians.

Before explaining these values, some preliminary observations:

First, in order to affirm or live by these values one does not have to be a Jew or Christian, or to affirm Jewish or Christian theology. These values do not demand that one forsake one's ethnic, religious, or national identity. The proof, as we have seen, is that the Founders of America themselves embraced Judeo-Christian values while frequently not holding Christian (and obviously not Jewish) theological beliefs. They were models of how these values can be held without being a religious Christian or Jew.

Second, the converse is also true. Just as one can hold Judeo-Christian values without holding specific Jewish or Christian religious beliefs, there are believing Christians and Jews who do not hold all or even most Judeo-Christian values. These Jews and Christians affirm Leftist *values* alongside their Christian and Jewish religious *beliefs*. But Judeo-Christian values are in deep conflict with Leftist values, which is why there has been such a concerted effort on the part of the Left to undo the influence of religion in America and other Western societies. It has largely succeeded in doing so in Western Europe, which has been almost thoroughly secularized and rendered Leftist in its values—so much so that many of the remaining religious Christian leaders, such as the Archbishop of Canterbury, the head of the Anglican Church, are indistinguishable from secular Leftists in their values.

Nevertheless, Left-wing Jews and Christians argue that they are not only committed to Judeo-Christian values, but that they are actually more committed to Judaism and Christianity than other Jews and Christians, since they care more about clothing the naked and feeding the hungry.

This argument is only another testimony to the high self-esteem in which the Left holds itself. Who, pray tell, is for leaving the naked unclothed and the hungry without food? Judaism, Christianity, Islam, and Buddhism advocated caring for the helpless millennia before Marx was born. So, when the Jewish, Christian, or secular Left tell us repeatedly that they are for clothing the naked, they really mean two other things: (1) Their opponents are not for feeding the hungry and clothing the naked and (2) Only those who affirm Left-wing policies are.

Third, as is the case with American values, most people who believe they hold Judeo-Christian values cannot identify—let alone advocate—many of them. These values, therefore need to be explained.

Fourth, a word about why we need values. It may seem obvious, and it should be. But in the present Age of Feelings, it isn't. If people were basically good, we wouldn't need values; we could rely on the human heart to always do the right thing. But the heart is not a moral compass; it is a generator of emotions. Values are there to overrule our heart, our emotions, our appetites, our weaknesses, and even our often flawed reasoning. I have noted one example of the substitution of feelings for values: the answer I have received for thirty years when asking American high school and college students whether they would first try to save their dog or a stranger if both were drowning. At most, one-third vote that they would try to save the human being first. Two-thirds consistently say either that they would save their pet first or they just don't know what to do.

Why do they not all vote to save the human? Because they love their dog or cat, they do not love the stranger, and they are guided by a feeling, love. And what is greater than love? In fact, however, there is something greater than love—namely, moral values. In this case that value is the greater worth of a human being.

The best-known animal-rights organization, People for the Ethical Treatment of Animals, funded by many of the best-educated individuals in our society, launched a campaign called "Holocaust on your plate," which equates barbecuing millions of chickens with cremating millions of Jews in the Holocaust. PETA believes that there is no difference between the value of chicken life and human life.

Only a morally confused age could produce so many people who do not recognize the immeasurable distance between human and animal worth. We live in that age. We do in large measure because values based on God and the Bible have been replaced by feelings and/or by Leftist values.

The moral record of Christian Europe is, to be sure, a mixed one, especially regarding the one continuous religious minority that lived in its midst—the Jews. One has to be quite naive to believe that faith in God guarantees moral clarity, let alone moral behavior. But Chesterton was right about people not believing in nothing but believing in anything with the death of belief in God. The collapse of Christianity in Europe led to the horrors of Nazism and Communism. And to the moral confusions of the present.

The oft-cited charge that belief in God and religion has led to more wars and evil than anything else is as untrue as it is widely believed. Secular movements in the twentieth century alone killed and enslaved more people than any other movement in any century in history.

In fact, it was a secular Jew, the great German poet Heinrich Heine, who understood that despite its anti-Semitism and other moral failings, Christianity in Europe prevented the wholesale slaughter of human beings. In 1832, 101 years before Hitler and the Nazis rose to power, in the concluding passage of his *Religion and Philosophy in Germany*, Heine prophesied:

Christianity—and that is its greatest merit—has somewhat mitigated that brutal German love of war, but it could
not destroy it. Should that subduing talisman, the cross, be
shattered, the frenzied madness of the ancient warriors, that
insane berserk rage of which Nordic bards have spoken and
sung so often, will once more burst into flame. . . . The old
stone gods will then rise from long ruins and rub the dust of
a thousand years from their eyes, and Thor will leap to life
with his giant hammer and smash the Gothic cathedral. . . .

Thought precedes action as lightning precedes thunder. German thunder . . . comes rolling somewhat slowly,
but . . . its crash . . . will be unlike anything before in the
history of the world. . . . At that uproar the eagles of the
air will drop dead, and lions in farthest Africa will draw in
their tails and slink away. . . . A play will be performed in
Germany which will make the French Revolution look like
an innocent idyll.[36]

When that "restraining talisman, the cross," was shattered, fifty
million people were slaughtered.

Judeo-Christian Values, Not Judeo-Christian Theology

Many people wonder how anyone can speak of Judeo-Christian values when Judaism and Christianity have different, sometimes mutually exclusive, beliefs.

The answer is that we speak only of Judeo-Christian values, not
Judeo-Christian theology. Religious beliefs and moral values are
not the same things.

Of course, Judaism and Christianity have differing beliefs. If
they had the same beliefs, they would be the same religion. Christianity believes in a Trinity that Judaism does not believe in, and
that is a major theological difference. But it has little or no relevance
to moral values. So, too, Christianity believes that the Messiah has
come, whereas Judaism believes that he has not yet come. This, too,
is a theological, not a moral values, issue.

Regarding essential values, both religions are based on the Old Testament, which Judaism and Christianity both hold to be divinely authored or divinely inspired. There are a few values differences between the Old and New Testaments—for example their views on the permissibility of divorce—but in general, conservative, traditional, believing Catholics, Evangelical Protestants, and Orthodox Jews have much the same views on moral issues. Another way to put it is that virtually all those who regard the Torah as divine (that would include Mormons as well) share moral values—values that are called, quite correctly, Judeo-Christian.

Judeo-Christian values are values that emanate from a Jewish scriptures–based Christianity. Christians always had the choice to reject the Jewish roots of Christianity, to ignore those roots, or to celebrate and embrace them. American Christians have, more than any other Christian group, embraced them. For much of Christian history, however, the majority of Christians either denied the Jewish origins of Christianity and/or ignored the Jewishness of Jesus and the Apostles.

The great achievement of Judeo-Christian values as developed in America is that they combined the best of both religions and cast aside some other aspects. For example, the Christian emphasis on faith above works led too often to faith without works. And, while most American Christians continue to hold that only faith in Christ saves, the Judeo-based American Christian has always emphasized good works in the here and now—as well as the need to work alongside non-Christians who affirm Judeo-Christian values.

As for Judaism, Judeo-Christian values helped universalize Jewish moral teachings in ways that religious Jews, historically preoccupied with Jewish survival and religious observance, had not done. Over the centuries, God-centered, Torah-believing Jews retreated from mainstream society. They did so because anti-Semitism forced Jews into ghettos and because Jewish ritual laws increasingly restricted contact with non-Jews. (On the other hand, though Jews were exiled from their homeland for thousands of years, most of them in hostile societies, it was Jewish rituals that kept Judaism and the Jews alive—while the abandonment of ritual, for example, Sabbath observance, has hurt Christianity.)

We now turn to the important task of defining some of the basic Judeo-Christian values.

Basic Judeo-Christian Values

1. People Are Not Basically Good

American values are predicated on the recognition that people are not born basically good, but morally flawed.

Thomas Kidd writes, "In promoting this God-centered idea of virtue, [the great eighteenth-century revivalist preacher Jonathan] Edwards was fighting against the tide of most eighteenth century philosophy associated with the Enlightenment, which asserted that people were naturally good . . ."[37]

The men who founded America were not seduced by Enlightenment fantasy about human nature. John Adams reflected on this in a letter to a friend: "When men are given up to the rule of their passions, they murder like weasels for the pleasure of murdering, like bulldogs and bloodhounds in a fold of sheep."[38]

James Madison wrote in the Federalist Papers, the seminal essays on behalf of the proposed U.S. Constitution, written by Madison, Alexander Hamilton, and John Jay: "What is government itself but the greatest of all reflections on human nature? If men were angels, no government would be necessary. If angels were to govern men, neither external nor internal controls on government would be necessary."[39]

Madison attended Princeton University when its president was the Reverend John Witherspoon. The reverend's outlook on human nature: "Nothing can be more absolutely necessary to true religion, than a clear and full conviction of the sinfulness of our nature and state."[40]

Those who believe people are born good argue that babies are born innocent. They are right. But people confuse innocence with goodness. Babies are born innocent, but not good. No culture—

including Judaism—prior to the Enlightenment held that human beings are naturally good.*

No issue has a greater influence on people's social and political views than whether they view human nature as basically good or not.

Blame Outside Forces, Not the Individual, for Evil

Those who believe that people are not basically good blame the evil that people do on individuals not controlling their flawed nature or on their holding beliefs that lead to evil. On the other hand, those who believe that people are born good attribute the evil that people do to forces outside the individual. They have no choice. If people are intrinsically good, evil must originate outside the individual.

One of the most widely cited external causes of evil is poverty. This has been so since Marx because of the materialist nature of Marxist and other Leftist thinking: Economics explains human behavior more than any one other thing. As a result, our secular liberal culture has usually attributed evil to poverty. This is true whether the evil are domestic criminals or international terrorists. A typical Left/liberal explanation for violent crime in America is unemployment and poverty in America and a typical Left/liberal explanation for international terrorism is unemployment and poverty in Muslim countries. Both explanations are wrong.

To take the terrorist example first, the nineteen Muslim terrorists who committed the 9/11 atrocities in the United States were all from middle- and upper-class families. So, too, Ahmed Saeed Omar Sheikh, better known as "Sheikh Omar," the man who was

---

* Many modern Jews believe that Judaism holds that people are basically good. They believe this because many Jews have adopted Left-wing values, because many Jews think that Judaism usually believes the opposite of Christianity, and because the revered Dutch-Jewish teenager Anne Frank wrote in her diary, the most famous piece of writing to come out of the Holocaust, that she believed people are basically good. But the Torah states that "every inclination of man's heart is evil from his youth" (Genesis 8:21), and all of Judaism and its laws are predicated on the notion that man needs constant self-discipline to be good.

sentenced to death in Pakistan in 2002 for the beheading murder of American journalist Daniel Pearl and suspected of links to the September 11, 2001, attacks, came from a privileged background. Born in Britain in the early 1970s, Omar was the son of a well-to-do wholesale clothes merchant, and he attended the London School of Economics. And Umar Farouk Abdulmutallab, the Nigerian Muslim who attempted to blow up a Northwest Airlines flight from London as it landed in Detroit, had been enrolled, at a cost of $25,000 a year, as a student at University College, London.[41]

The fact is that people who strap bombs to their bodies to blow up families at a Bar Mitzvah in Israel, plant bombs at a nightclub in Bali, or slit stewardesses' throats and ram airplanes filled with innocent Americans into office buildings do not do so for any reason related to poverty. They do so because they hold evil beliefs and have deformed consciences.

"Poverty causes crime" has been a credo of the Left since Marx. Abolish poverty, the thinking goes, and you will essentially end human evil.

Take the recession in America beginning in 2008, America's worst recession since the Great Depression. Just about every liberal and Leftist who has commented on this phenomenon expressed surprise that the crime rate actually declined during this period.

Tim Rutten, Left-wing columnist for the *Los Angeles Times*: "The *remarkable* thing is that the last 36 months of decline [in crime rates] have coincided with the worst period of economic distress since the Depression. . . . Serious historians and analysts *now* acknowledge that the reasons crime—and, particularly, homicide—waxes and wanes are complex . . ." (emphasis added)[42]

To this man of the Left, it is "remarkable" not only that increased poverty did not lead to increased crime but also that crime actually sank to its lowest level in half a century. And "serious" historians and analysts only *now* acknowledge that the reasons for crime are "complex," meaning not necessarily related to economics. Of course, everybody else has known this for thousands of years.

But by "serious," our liberal columnist means liberal. Only liberal historians and analysts are serious; and they all believed that since poverty causes crime, a recession will bring about a significant increase in crime.

Writing on the same subject—the plunging level of crime in Los Angeles—a *Los Angeles Times* editorial the day before the Rutten article acknowledged that "[s]ociologists and criminologists [that is, *liberal* sociologists and criminologists] once doubted that police could do much about violent crime," but, alas, they turned out to be wrong. Now, why would liberal sociologists and criminologists ever have thought such a foolish thing? Because they believed that poverty and socioeconomic circumstances determined violent crime rates much more than values and policing did.

Another example of an external factor widely blamed by the Left for violent crime is racism. This is particularly so in the United States, where blacks have accounted for a highly disproportionate amount of violent crime (which is directed mostly against fellow blacks, one might add). This is as false as the poverty explanation for violent crime.*

Finally, if poverty and racism are responsible for violent crime committed by poor and black criminals, how does one explain the great majority of poor people and blacks who do not commit robbery, rape, and murder? Do they react abnormally to their poverty and race? Or do they have better values and self-control?

---

* The 1992 riots in Los Angeles provided a perfect example. The Left did not blame the arson or the beatings and shootings of innocent non-blacks, especially Korean-Americans, on the blacks who committed these acts. They blamed white America and the allegedly racist police brutality they contended occurred during the arrest of a black man named Rodney King. The liberal news media were largely responsible for creating the frenzy, indeed the hysteria, in America, and especially in black America, that led to those riots. For weeks, national and local news shows repeatedly televised a tiny segment of a video showing white police officers beating a black man identified only as "a black motorist." The "black motorist" was in fact a convicted criminal who was finally caught by police after a long car chase at high speeds through residential neighborhoods. One part of the video never shown on American television showed King refusing police orders to exit his car or to lie down to be frisked. The members of the jury were among the only Americans to see the entire video, which is why they acquitted the police officers. And that acquittal was the ostensible reason for the riots, fires, beatings, and murders.

Goodness and Character Are Neglected in Raising Young People

A second reason the question of whether people are born good is so important is that when society and parents believe that people are born good, they do not stress character development in the raising of children. Why would they? The already good don't need to learn how to be good. Just give them love, the thinking goes.

In the past, when Americans understood that people are not born good, parents and schools emphasized the teaching of moral character. This was regarded as the primary task of education. After all, what is the worth of knowing literature, the arts, history, and the sciences if not to make a decent human being?

But now schools teach young people everything but character development. They are taught the alleged dangers of secondhand tobacco smoke, how to use condoms, how to avoid using plastic bags, and how to slow global warming. And they have been taught how to struggle against the alleged evils of American society, such as sexism, racism, xenophobia, and homophobia.

The struggle they have not been taught is the one they most need to wage: against their own natures. Arguably the greatest difference between a religious education and a secular one is that students in secular schools learn that their greatest struggles are with society, while the religious students are taught that the greatest struggle is with themselves and their morally flawed human natures—their natural inclinations toward laziness, insatiable appetites, self-centeredness, greed, and so on.

God and Religion Become Unnecessary

A third consequence of the belief that people are basically good is to render God and religion morally unnecessary. Why would basically good people need a God to hold themselves accountable to or a religion to provide them with moral standards?

Faith in Oneself and in Power

And fourth, those who believe that people are basically good will, obviously, believe that they themselves are good. This certitude about their own goodness leads to some very significant attitudes. One is that Leftists view those who differ with them not as merely wrong, but as bad. Another is faith in men (and women) holding power. Those who, like the American Founders, regard the human being as a fundamentally morally flawed creature do not trust the concentration of political power in anyone. The Left does.

No great body of wisdom, East or West, ever posited that people were basically good. This naive and dangerous notion originated in modern secular Western thought. It is another example of the absence of wisdom and the dangers ensuing from the death of God and religion in the West.

2. God-Based Morality
No God, No Good and Evil

To the Founders of the United States, from evangelical Christian to deist, it was axiomatic that God and God-based religion were indispensable to morality. That, of course, is the Judeo-Christian position and the only rational position. Only if there is a moral God do right and wrong really exist. If there is no God, "right" and "wrong" are opinions. In other words, if there is no God who says, "Do not murder" ("Do not kill" is a mistranslation of the Hebrew, which, like English, has two words for homicide), murder is not wrong. Many people may think it is wrong, and it may well comport with common sense, but it is still subjective opinion. There are no moral "facts" if there is no God; there are only moral opinions.

Years ago, I debated this issue at Oxford University with Professor Jonathan Glover, one of the leading moralists of our time. Because he is a man of great intellectual honesty, he readily acknowledged, even though he is an atheist, that without God, morality is subjective.[43] Glover is not alone among atheist thinkers who acknowledge that good and evil do not objectively exist if there is no God. Most serious moral thinkers do. Another atheist professor with whom I dialogued was Steve Stewart-Williams, lecturer in evolutionary psychology at Swansea University in Wales.[44] He, too, acknowledged the subjectivity of morality without God. And one of the most revered liberal (and atheist) philosophers of the modern era, Richard Rorty, wrote that for secular liberals, "there is no answer to the question, 'Why not be cruel?'"[45] You cannot get more honest than that regarding the absence of objective morality if there is no God.

Most secular individuals, however, do not acknowledge this, the most important fact about morality. They deny it because they recognize that if good and evil do not objectively exist, good and evil are no more real than "yummy" and "yucky," and they are exquisitely uncomfortable with this fact. Secularists want to have their cake and eat it, too. They want to deny the only possible source of objective morality, God, and still believe that good and evil really exist. They want this because life is a moral absurdity if there is no good and evil, and few people can make psychological or emotional peace with an absurd world. It is too painful for most decent secular people to realize that their moral relativism, their godless morality, means that cruelty is not really wrong, and there is no objective answer to Rorty's question.

As for the argument that human beings have a conscience that tells them that murder is wrong, those of us who believe in God as the source of morality would agree. But given the inability to locate this conscience in any laboratory, belief in the existence of a conscience is tantamount to belief in God. Those who believe that only matter is real, and that therefore only science can tell us what is real, cannot at the same time argue that there is a non-material, non-scientifically provable conscience. And if there really is this non-material, non-scientifically provable conscience, it is the non-material, non-scientifically provable God who created it.

The denial of God and of Judeo-Christian religions has, therefore, led to moral relativism. With no objective good and evil, morality has devolved into "What I think is right is right for me, and what you think is right is right for you," or "One man's terrorist is another man's freedom fighter."

In the late 1970s, in a public interview in Los Angeles, I asked one of the leading liberal writers of the past generation, Pulitzer Prize–winning historian Arthur Schlesinger Jr., if he would say that the United States was a morally superior society to that of the Soviet Union. Even when I repeated the question, and clarified that I readily acknowledged the existence of good individuals in the Soviet Union and bad ones in America, he refused to do so.

The Left fears and rejects the language of good and evil because they realize that it smacks of religious values and because it violates its moral relativism. This is also one of the most important differences between America and Europe. A *New York Times* article on European-American differences forthrightly acknowledged this divide: "The secularization of Europe, according to some political analysts, is one of the forces pushing it apart from the United States, where religion plays a potent role in politics and society, shaping many Americans' views of the world. *Americans are widely regarded as more comfortable with notions of good and evil, right and wrong, than Europeans*, who often see such views as reckless." (emphasis added) [46]

A major reason for the Left's loathing of American president George W. Bush was his use of moral language such as in his widely condemned description of the regimes of Kim Jong Il's North Korea, Mahmoud Ahmadinejad's Iran, and Saddam Hussein's Iraq as an "axis of evil." But if those tyrannical regimes were not "evil," nothing is. Which is the point to the Left. It often seems that the only evil according to the moral relativists of the Left is the judging of evil (even though, in a remarkable failure of self-awareness, the Left does it all the time).

Is abortion morally wrong? In the secular Left world, the answer is "It's between a woman and her physician." Whatever one's view of abortion, there is no clearer expression of moral relativism than every woman determining whether abortion is moral. To the individual with Judeo-Christian values, or even just common sense, the morality of ending the life of a human fetus is not determined anew by each individual. If it is, then "moral" means nothing more than personal opinion, and the tens of millions of abortions of female fetuses (largely in China and parts of India) performed for no reason other than a desire for a boy are perfectly "moral."

Probably the best-known verse in the Bible is "Love your neighbor as yourself" (Leviticus 19:18). It is a reflection of the secular age in which we live that few people are aware that the verse concludes with the words "I am God." The point of this verse is that this great ethical principle comes from God; otherwise it is just another man-made suggestion, no more compelling than "Cross at the green, not in between."

Let it be clear that nothing said here suggests that an atheist cannot be a good person or that all believers in God are good people. When we say that if there is no God, there is no good and evil, we are not saying that an atheist cannot be a good person. We are saying that there is no objective good and evil.

What has supplanted belief in the existence of moral truths are feelings about what is moral. Many children have been raised to ask, "How do I feel about it?" rather than "Is it right or wrong?" An example of this was the "Values Clarification" programs many American public schools utilized in the United States in the 1970s. Its name says it all. The program merely clarified the values the students held; it did not tell them what values are better or worse. How could it? If moral values are not objective, no values can be taught as true, or as superior to any other.

This has been confirmed by an extensive study of Americans ages eighteen to twenty-three conducted by sociologist Christian Smith of Notre Dame University and discussed by *New York Times* columnist David Brooks:

> Smith and company asked about the young people's moral lives, and the results are depressing. . . .
>
> When asked to describe a moral dilemma they had faced, two-thirds of the young people either couldn't answer the question or described problems that are not moral at all. . . .
>
> Moral thinking didn't enter the picture, even when considering things like drunken driving, cheating in school or

cheating on a partner. "I don't really deal with right and wrong that often," is how one interviewee put it. . . .

The default position, which most of them came back to again and again, is that *moral choices are just a matter of individual taste.* . . .

As one put it, "I mean, I guess *what makes something right is how I feel about it.* But different people feel different ways, so I couldn't speak on behalf of anyone else as to what's right and wrong. . . ."

Morality was once revealed, inherited and shared, but now it's thought of as something that emerges in the privacy of your own heart. (emphasis added)[47]

The death of God leads to the death of right and wrong as real, and ultimately to the death of universal moral standards, as opposed to feelings-based individual opinions.*

If Not to God, to Whom Is One Accountable?

A second reason God is necessary to morality is that if there is no God, there is no moral accountability to anyone but the self and/or society. One has to have a very elevated belief in the innate good-

---

* One other aspect of objective morality, or moral truths, needs to be explained. Objective right and wrong does not mean than an act is always wrong. It means that in any given situation there is a right and wrong. Many people who believe in objective morality confuse "objective" with "always." Objective morality means that good and evil really exist and are not matters of individual taste or feeling or preference. Therefore objective morality means that an action is right or wrong *for all people but not necessarily in every situation.* Very few actions are always wrong. It is usually wrong to lie, for example, but lying to Nazis searching for Jews to murder was not morally wrong—it was the highest form of morality. Therefore, "situational ethics" is not the same thing as moral relativism. Moral relativism means that every individual (or society) decides what is right or wrong. It completely negates objective morality. Situational ethics means what is right or wrong depends on the situation. It in no way negates objective morality. For example, it is the situation that determines when killing is wrong. According to the Bible itself, the situation determines when killing is murder. That is why the Ten Commandments say, "Do not murder" not "Do not kill." Murder is immoral killing—and it is the situation that determines when killing is moral and when it is immoral and therefore deemed murder. Pacifism is an excellent example of the flawed belief that an action—in this case, killing—is *always* immoral. Pacifism argues that it is wrong to take a life in every situation. For this reason, it has no basis in Judeo-Christian values, which hold that there is moral killing (self-defense, defending other innocents, taking the life of a murderer) and immoral killing (intentional murder of an innocent individual, wars of aggression, terrorism, etc.).

ness of human beings to believe that accountability to oneself will work. And one has to have a very elevated belief in the goodness of society and of its leaders—and their ability to catch and punish those who do evil—to believe that accountability to society will work.

But even with an exalted view of the self and of society, there is still no real accountability without God. By accountability, we are talking about reward and punishment; without reward and punishment, accountability means nothing. That is the bigger reason accountability to oneself is meaningless. In addition to how easy it is for the individual to convince himself of the righteousness of whatever he does, one cannot reward or punish oneself like society or God does.

All of the American Founders, whatever their theology, believed that individuals and nations are accountable to a God who rewards and punishes—generally speaking, nations in this world and individuals in the next.

3. Reason Without God Is Ineffective

Those who do not believe that moral values must come from the Bible or from God argue that they have a better source for values: reason. That is why the era that began the assault on religion is known as the Age of Reason. It ushered in the modern secular era, a time when the men of the "Enlightenment" assumed that mankind would be liberated from the irrational shackles of religious faith, and rely solely on reason to make a good world.

As it happened, the era following the decline of religion in Europe led not to unprecedented moral greatness, but often to unprecedented levels of irrationality, cruelty, and mass murder.

The secular argument posits that those of us who rely on reason will all agree that stealing is wrong because reason tells us so: We don't want to be stolen from, the argument goes, and therefore all reasonable men will conclude that stealing is wrong.

But this reasoning is flawed. What if I am stronger than others and can get away with stealing? What if I don't care about the general human good, just my own? What if the rush I get from stealing is worth it? Why then is my decision to steal, especially if I am pretty certain I will get away with it, irrational?

The fact is that it is not an irrational decision.

It is wishful thinking that reason alone inevitably leads to the good. If anything, goodness in the world would probably diminish if reason alone dictated human behavior. The firefighter with a family to support who risks his life to save an elderly person from a burning building is not acting on reason. Nor are the Christian missionaries who leave lucrative careers in the West to work among impoverished people in the Third World. Nor does the individual who takes care of his or her spouse who has Alzheimer's.

To argue that such actions are derived from reason alone is to argue that every person whose actions are guided by reason will engage in similar acts of self-sacrifice, and that anyone who does not engage in self-sacrifice is acting irrationally. But that itself is an irrational argument. Did those non-Jews in Europe who risked their lives to save a Jew during the Holocaust act on the dictates of reason? In a lifetime of studying rescuers' motives, I have never come across an instance of an individual who risked his or her life to save Jews because of reason. There is a good explanation: It was quite irrational for non-Jews to risk their lives—and often the lives of their family members as well—to save Jews.

In sum, there are at least five problems with reason as a guide to morality when divorced from God.

First, with regard to many vexing moral questions, there is no such thing as a purely rational viewpoint. What is the purely rational view on the morality of abortion? On public nudity? On medical experimentation on animals? On capital punishment for murder? On any of these issues, reason alone can argue for opposite positions. What impels people to do the right thing in these instances is *a value that is higher than reason* (though one should be able to rationally explain that value).

Second, as noted, reason can often argue for evil as easily as it can for good. Reason is only a tool, and therefore it is amoral. If you want to achieve good, reason is immensely helpful, and if you want to commit evil, reason is immensely helpful. It is sometimes rational to do what is wrong, and sometimes irrational to do what is right.

Third, human beings are usually incapable of morally functioning on the basis of reason alone. Our passions, psychological makeup, values, beliefs, emotions, and experiences all influence the ways in which even the most rational person determines what is moral and especially whether to act on it. Anyone who thinks that he guides all his moral decisions by reason alone is thinking irrationally.

Fourth, the belief that reason alone is sufficient to produce a moral world is itself irrational and must be based on an irrational belief—that people are basically good. After all, if people are not basically good, they are hardly likely to use reason solely to do the right thing.

Fifth, even when reason does lead to moral conclusions, it does not compel one to act on those conclusions. Let's return to the example of the non-Jew in Nazi-occupied Europe. Imagine that a Jewish family knocks on a non-Jewish family's door, asking to be hidden. Imagine further that on rational grounds alone (though I cannot think of any), the non-Jew decides that the moral thing to do is hide the Jews. Will he act on this decision at the risk of his life? Not if reason alone guides him. People don't risk their lives for strangers on the basis of reason. They do so on the basis of faith in something that far transcends reason, or just because their nature is such that they cannot say no to people whose lives they can perhaps save.

None of this means that reason is useless. Good would be impossible if people ignored reason. A reason-free world would be a nightmare. Reason and rational thought are hallmarks of human greatness. Reason is as necessary to goodness as oxygen is to life. But, like oxygen, reason is necessary, but not sufficient. Alone, reason is largely worthless in the greatest quest of all—producing large numbers of decent human beings and decent societies. To accomplish that, a moral God, belief in a divinely revealed moral text—such as the Ten Commandments—and, yes, reason, are all necessary. And even then, as history has made abundantly clear, there are no guarantees.

But if you want a quick evaluation of where godless reason leads, look at the irrationality and moral confusion that permeate the embodiment of reason without God—the Western university.

The Judeo-Christian value system and the American value system are rooted in a good and moral God who demands that His human creations choose goodness and morality—and use reason to help determine how to apply the divine moral will in any given situation.

4. Human Life Is Sacred and Humans Are at the Center of the Universe

To return to the question I have posed for decades: If your dog (or other beloved pet) and a stranger (a person whose identity you did not know) were both drowning, which would you save?

The answer depends on whether one's moral guidance is rooted primarily in feelings or in values that may conflict with one's feelings.

One of the most obvious and significant differences between secular and Judeo-Christian values concerns human worth. One of the great ironies of secular humanism is that it leads to a devaluing of humans. In secular thought, human beings are frequently depicted as essentially just another animal, and as one moves leftward, humans are often depicted as banes on the environment.

The God-based Judeo-Christian value system renders man far more valuable and significant than any secular value system possibly can. Indeed, it places man at the center of creation.*

The reason is simple: Only if there is a God who created man and made him "in His image" is man worth more than any other

---

* An ancient Talmudic dictum put it, "Every person is obligated to say, 'For me the world was created'" (Sanhedrin 37a).

creation. If we are not created in the image of God, we are created in the image of carbon dioxide and primordial biological matter. We are no more than self-conscious matter. Which attitude renders the human being more valuable is obvious.

Contemporary secular society has rendered human beings less significant than at any time in Western history.

The secular denial that human beings are created in God's image has led to a concerted effort on the part of secular thinkers, especially those on the Left, to minimize the difference between humans and animals. As Dan Wharton of the Chicago Zoological Society, a population biologist and research scientist at Columbia University, has written, "I have come to the conclusion that the so-called divide between animals and humans is really a laugh. The only concrete difference that I can find is that a few humans are better readers than most animals."[48]

Wharton's view that the "so-called" divide between animals and humans "is really a laugh" is the normative secular Left-wing view of humanity.

One result is that many people estranged from Judeo-Christian values (including more than a few Jews and Christians) support public awareness campaigns such as the previously noted "Holocaust on Your Plate," the effort by PETA to convince us that there is no difference between barbecuing chickens and burning Jews in the Holocaust—since humans and chickens are of equal worth.

The human-animal equation is not theoretical. A Tucson, Arizona, woman screamed to firefighters that her "babies" were in her burning house. Thinking that the woman's children were trapped inside, the firemen risked their lives to save the woman's three cats.[49]

Those inclined to dismiss these examples as either theoretical (the dog-stranger question) or extreme (the Tucson "mother" of cats) need to confront the very real question of animal experimentation to save human lives. More and more people believe as PETA does that even if it led to a cure for cancer, it is wrong to experiment on animals. (The defense that research with computers can teach all that experiments on animals teach is not true.) In fact, many animal rights advocates oppose killing a pig to obtain a heart valve to save a human life.

Belief in human-animal equivalence follows the death of Judeo-Christian values, and it serves not so much to elevate animal worth as to reduce human worth. Those who believe it is immoral to kill animals for any reason, including eating and humane medical experimentation, should reflect on this: While there are strong links between cruelty to animals and cruelty to humans, there are no links between kindness to animals and kindness to humans. Cruelty to animals frequently indicates a tendency toward cruelty to fellow human beings. But kindness to animals does not indicate that a person will be kind to other people. The Nazis, noted for their cruelty to human beings, were also the most pro-animal-rights group prior to the contemporary period. They outlawed experimentation on animals—but performed widespread experiments on human beings. And Hitler was famously affectionate toward his German shepherd, Blondie, while consigning millions of people to hellish misery and agonizing death.

The breakdown of Judeo-Christian values greatly diminishes human worth. If man is not created by God, in the divine image, the human being is stellar dust, the product of random chance, no more designed—or significant—than a grain of sand.

5. Holiness: We Are Not Animals

If humans are only animals, another key Judeo-Christian concept, the value of holiness is rendered moot.

People who do not believe in God or religion can surely lead ethical lives. But they are very unlikely to lead holy lives. By definition, the ideal of the holy, as understood by Judaism and Christianity and that unique amalgam known as Judeo-Christian values, needs God and religion.

Perhaps the best way to explain holiness is this: There is a continuum from the profane to the holy that represents the dual bases of human nature—the animal and the divine. The human being can be said to be created in both the image of God and in the image of animals. We are biologically animals, but in spiritual and moral terms we transcend mere biology. God is the most holy, and animals, as helpful, loyal, and lovable as many are, are at the opposite end of the holiness continuum. This is in no way an insult to animals. Saying dogs and lions are not holy is no more degrading to them than saying men are not cars. It's simply reflective of the fact that they cannot elevate themselves above the animal level, while human beings can.

There is a secular way to understand this. If we see a person eating food with his face in a bowl, we think that he's eating "like a pig" or "like an animal." Now, that is considered an insult to a person—because humans are supposed to elevate their behavior above the animal (this is a goal of Judeo-Christian and every other major religious tradition). But it is no insult to an animal. When an animal eats face-first out of a bowl, we do not think ill of it; but when a person mimics animal behavior, we do have a lower view of that person. So, even nonreligious society has imbibed some of the religious view that acting like an animal is not how a human being should generally act.

To better understand this, one needs to appreciate that holiness is not necessarily a moral category. It is not immoral to eat with one's face inside a bowl, given the general understanding of morality as whether an action "hurts anybody." But it is animal-like, not elevated, and therefore unholy.

Elevating human behavior toward the divine is one of the greatest achievements of religion and civil society.

If, in the sexual arena, we did behave like animals, society would eventually devolve. An aspect of societies that are deemed primitive is their not placing a marital fence around sexual intercourse. This can also be seen in the Western world's underclass, where sex and having children outside of marriage is normative and marriage has been in precipitous decline (to the detriment of all people living in those communities, especially the children who are often subjected to chaotic home lives and grow up to repeat the cycle). The religious ideal of confining sexual intercourse to marriage has played a major role in the creation of advanced civilization.

Speech is another example. In our increasingly secular world, the concept of elevating one's speech is increasingly rare. The idea is so foreign that perhaps most young people, raised in a secular home and society, would not even understand the concept. If you see a vehicle with a bumper sticker that contains an expletive, you can be sure that the owner of that vehicle does not regularly attend religious services.

The consequences of the death of the holy are ubiquitous. Secular Europe is far readier to feature nudity on public television than is Judeo-Christian America, and it is far more accepting of people walking around nude in public at beaches. The Judeo-Christian problem with public nudity at a beach or even at a nudist colony is not about religiously licit or illicit sexual behavior; it is that clothing elevates human beings above the animals, whose genitals are always uncovered.

And that is what the Judeo-Christian value system ultimately yearns for—the elevation of human conduct, rather than allowing us to behave like animals. In the final analysis, if the holy breaks down, the ethical and moral will do so as well.

6. Hate Evil

The core moral value of the Bible is not just to love our neighbor but to hate evil. Indeed, it is the only thing the Bible instructs people to hate—so much so that love of God is equated with hatred of evil. "Those who love God must hate evil," the Psalms declare.[50]

The notion of hating evil was, and remains, foreign to many. Ancients did not have a religious obligation to hate evil. How could they? Their gods were often cruel. Nor did all higher religions place hating evil at the center of their worldviews. In Eastern philosophy and religion, the highest goal was the attainment of enlightenment (Nirvana) through effacing the ego, not through hating and fighting evil. Evil and unjust suffering were regarded as part of life, and it was best to escape life, not necessarily fight it.

In addition, in many cultures, "face," "shame," and "honor" define moral norms, not standards of good and evil. In parts of the Muslim world, as we have seen, "honor killings"—the murder of a daughter or sister who has brought "shame" to the family (usually by refusing to marry the father's choice of a husband or by committing an alleged sexual sin)—are widely viewed as heroic.

In the West, with notable exceptions, Christians historically did not tend to regard evil as the greatest sin but rather unbelief, blasphemy, and sexual sin. Over time, however, Christians came to lead the battle against evil—from slavery to Communism. And today it is not coincidental that America, the country that most thinks in terms of good and evil, is the most religious of the Western industrialized countries.

In the contemporary Western world, most people who identify with the Left hate corporations, pollution, Christian fundamentalists, economic inequality, tobacco, and executing murderers. But they rarely hate the greatest evils of their day.

Communism, a way of life built on murder, lies, and deprivation of the most fundamental human rights, attracted vast numbers of people on the Left, and from the 1960s, it was opposed by only a small fraction of the Left. Even most people calling themselves liberal, not Leftist, spoke out against anti-Communism much more than against Communism.

Ask Leftists what they believe humanity must fight against, and they will likely respond poverty, inequality, and whatever they perceive as threats to the natural environment. In fact, the Left throughout the world generally has contempt for people who speak of "evil." The Left labels such people "Manichaeans," moral simpletons who see the world "in terms of black and white."

The American labeling of evil as such—not to mention often fighting these evils—is a major divide between America and Europe. As an editor of the leading French newspaper, *Le Monde*, wrote about Europe: "The notion of the world divided between Good and Evil is perceived with dread."[51] Similarly, the leading German weekly magazine, *Der Spiegel*, commented during the Bush administration that "Mr. Bush's recent speeches have made no retreat from the good vs. evil view of the world that the Europeans hate."[52]

Typical of the Left's deconstruction of good and evil is this series of questions posed on the Left-wing website Counterpunch by Gary Leupp, a professor of history and comparative religion at Tufts University: "Questions for discussion. Was Attila good or evil to invade Gaul? Saddam good or evil to invade Kuwait? Hitler good or evil to invade Poland? Bush good or evil to invade Iraq? *Are 'good' and 'evil' really adequate categories to evaluate contemporary and historical events?*" (emphasis added)

Western Europeans on the Left, and their American counterparts, have disdain for the language of good and evil and correctly attribute it to America's religious—that is, Judeo-Christian—values. Among those values is fighting evil. And to do that, you have to hate it. Because if you don't hate evil, you won't fight it. And good will lose.

7. Murderers Must Die

One cannot identify all Jews or all Christians with Judeo-Christian values. Even many sincerely religious Jews and Christians take certain positions that are contrary to traditional Judeo-Christian, and certainly biblical, values.

A particularly contentious example is the death penalty for murderers. Many Jews and Christians take the Left-wing position on the death penalty for murder. They believe that all murderers should be kept alive—that it is not only wrong to take the life of a murderer, but actually un-Jewish or un-Christian.

Jews opposed to capital punishment cite the Talmud (the second most important religious text to Jews), which is largely opposed to capital punishment. The rabbis of the Talmud, living as they did in a time of monstrous state cruelty in the Roman Empire, came to loathe state execution even though the Torah adamantly demanded it. Meanwhile Christian opponents of the death penalty for murder often cite Jesus on loving one's enemies. And Catholic abolition-ists also cite the late Pope John Paul II and the many cardinals and bishops who, though not denying the Church's teachings on the permissibility of the state to take the life of a murderer, oppose capi-tal punishment.

Yet the notion that a murderer must give up his life is one of the central values in the Torah, the Five Books of Moses. In fact, taking the life of a murderer is the only law that is found in all five books of the Torah. That is remarkable in and of itself. It is even more remarkable considering how few laws there are in the first book, Genesis. Yet the law is in Genesis, and it is given after God wiped out nearly all of what had become a universally wicked humanity as a fundamental value in the maintenance of moral civilization: "Whoever sheds the blood of man, by man shall his blood be shed; for in the image of God He created him (Genesis 9:6)."

The Torah's reasoning is that societies that allow all murder-ers to keep their lives consider murder a less serious crime than it is and thereby cheapen the worth of human life. The punishment for a crime is the most convincing way in which a society teaches its members how serious that crime is. This is easily demonstrated. Imagine a society that meted out the same punishment to murder-ers as to those who had parked their car in a no-parking zone. That society would obviously be communicating that it regards murder as no more serious a crime than illegal parking. In the same way, a society that allows all murderers to live deems murder less awful than one that takes away the life of a murderer.

Opponents of the death penalty argue that they oppose the tak-ing of any murderer's life precisely because they value human life so highly. They argue that you cannot teach that killing is wrong by killing. But that is the same as arguing that you can't teach that stealing is wrong by stealing (that is, confiscating) a thief's money or that you can't teach that kidnapping is wrong by kidnapping (that is, imprisoning) kidnappers.

To the Torah, the first source of Judeo-Christian values, murder is the greatest sin; the immoral shedding of human blood (as opposed to the moral shedding of human blood in self-defense, in a just war, or in the execution of a murderer) pollutes the world. That is why the Torah legislated that even an animal that killed a human should be put to death. The purpose was not to punish the animal; animals do not have free choice and cannot be morally culpable. And it was hardly to teach other animals not to kill. It was because a human life is so valuable, it cannot be taken without the taker forfeiting its life.

But, some will object, the Torah decrees the death penalty for many infractions, yet we don't put to death people who practice witchcraft, or commit adultery or other capital infractions. Why those who murder?

There are two answers.

First, the only capital crime mentioned in the Bible before there were Jews or Israel is murder. Other death penalties applied specifically to the people of Israel when they entered the Land of Israel—a unique code of behavior for a unique time in a unique place. And virtually none of them were carried out. Other than for murder, the primary purpose of declaring a sin worthy of capital punishment was not to actually execute the sinner, but to declare how serious the infraction was—especially when a society was establishing itself as the first one based on ethical monotheism. Capital punishment for murder, on the other hand, was clearly intended for all time and for all people. It is independent of the existence of Jews, and independent of the Jews living in Israel. It is fundamental to the existence of a humane order.*

Second, all the other death penalties are laws. But the death penalty for murder is not only a law; it is a value. Laws may be time-bound or even place-bound. Values are eternal. Thus the Chris-

---

* Even the State of Israel, which abolished the death penalty at its founding in 1948, executed the Nazi architect of the Holocaust, Adolf Eichmann. By doing so, Israel acknowledged that a humane civilization cannot allow some people to live.

tians who believe in the divinity of the Torah are not bound to the Torah's dietary laws (such as not eating pork and shellfish), but they are bound to the value of taking the life of murderers.

Finally, the Old Testament is preoccupied with justice. And allowing one who has unjustly deprived another person of life to keep his own is the ultimate injustice. It is not coincidental that the United States, the one major industrialized democracy to retain the death penalty for murder, is also the one most prepared to fight evil around the world.

8. Distinctions and Order

It is difficult to overstate the depth of the differences between the Judeo-Christian view of the world and that of its opponents on the Left. In addition to such basic issues as objective versus relative morality, it involves the question of whether there is order to the world. Basic to the biblical worldview is the proposition that God made order out of chaos—order expressed largely through separation and distinction.

Order is dependent upon distinctions, and order reflects the divine. Attempts to abolish those differences represent a denial of that order, a denial that leads to chaos, moral and otherwise. Here are some of the distinctions that are central to the Judeo-Christian worldview. All are under attack.

Good and Evil

Central to the Judeo-Christian value system is that good and evil exist and are polar opposites: "Woe unto those who call evil good, and good evil" (Isaiah 5:20). As the breakdown of good and evil as objective moral realities has been discussed in a number of contexts, I will note one additional example here. It was expressed by one of England's leading crime novelists, Ruth Rendell, regarding about as clear an evil as exists—the 9/11 terrorist attacks and Osama bin Laden. Jeanette Winterson of the *Guardian* wrote:

"My friend Ruth Rendell was in conversation at the Cheltenham Literary Festival last weekend. Her sell-out audience was conservative and over-50. Someone asked a question about pure evil, citing the terrorist attacks on America as an example. With great presence, Rendell replied that we could not categorise such attacks as evil, since they were carried out from the highest motives and in the name of freedom. The audience hated this reply—there was a collective and audible shudder. Yet who reading Bin Laden's speeches can doubt it? There is no cynicism in the man—he has never heard of a spin doctor . . ."[53]

God and Man

God and man constitute a separation that many modern people reject. For Marx and Engels "man is God" and "God is man," and many people today would essentially agree. The idea of God as infinitely higher than man offends the egalitarian impulse. Moreover, when man becomes the source of moral values, he becomes, in effect, his own God.

Man and Woman

". . . male and female He created them" (Genesis 1:26).

"A woman must not wear men's clothing nor a man wear women's clothing" (Deuteronomy 22:5).

This is the area of the greatest current cultural battle over obliterating a distinction. The Judeo-Christian view is that man and woman are distinct beings, and that civilization rests in large measure on preserving the male-female distinction. That is why Genesis mentions the creation of male and female only with regard to human beings, not with regard to the creation of the animals, even though, obviously, God also created male and female animals.

The Left is working to abolish this distinction. That is in part what the battle for the "transgendered" in "GLBT" is about—"Gay, Lesbian, Bisexual, Transgendered." It is not only about sympathy for those individuals who feel alienated from the biological sex into which they were born. It is about getting rid of the male-female distinction.

Some schools and government agencies have begun to offer

three options under "Gender": "Male, Female, Other." And more and more American high schools elect males to be homecoming queens and females to be homecoming kings—they have been well taught that male and female mean little or nothing.[54] More than a few universities have eliminated men's and women's bathrooms— they regard forcing students to identify as male or female as unfair to those who do not identify as either male or female and they do not wish to impose this distinction on any student. There are parents in Sweden and America who are raising their children with no sexual identity (mixed clothing, a gender-neutral name, no consistent references to "him" or to "her") They do not want to "impose" but rather have the child choose later which, if either, sex to identify as.

The battle over same-sex marriage is ultimately over this issue. If the sex of spouses does not matter, if the sex of parents does not matter, then male and female do not matter. Standing in the way of this movement to remove the male-female distinction are Judeo-Christian values.

Preserving the male-female distinction is a value that may be essential to civilization. Society needs to figure out how to maintain the oldest human distinction and still be fair and decent to sexual minorities. In this instance, as in so many others, the goal should be to maintain both standards and compassion.

Holy and Profane

A major Judeo-Christian distinction is that of the holy and the profane. Applied to speech, for example, this would mean that cursing is regarded much less seriously by those parts of society estranged from Judeo-Christian values. I deal with the cursing issue at length elsewhere. Applied to sex, those who believe in the holy-profane distinction regard sexual intercourse as having a dimension of holiness unknown to the secular schools that have reduced intercourse to being exclusively a health issue.

Differing attitudes toward public displays of sexuality also emanate from the Judeo-Christian–secular divide. When the American popular singer Janet Jackson bared her breast—accidentally or intentionally—on national television during a performance at the most widely watched sporting event in America, the Super Bowl, most religious Americans were disturbed, while commentators on the Left were disturbed only by those who were disturbed. Public and media nudity are often regarded by the Left as signs of societal enlightenment and by those committed to Judeo-Christian values as signs of civilizational decline.*

Human and Animal

As explained above, Judeo-Christian values strongly distinguish between humans and animals. Human life has infinite worth and sanctity; animal life does not. This does not allow humans to cause animals gratuitous suffering, however.

That Torah law and three others began the long road to protecting animals from needless suffering and awakening human beings to the fact that they must treat animals properly. The Ten Commandments require that even animals must have a day of rest; and Deuteronomy prohibited muzzling an animal when it works in the field[55] and banned yoking two different species of animals to the same plow.[56]

Great and Poor Art

Just as the distinction between good and evil in the moral realm has been reduced to personal opinion, so, too, has the distinction between great art and junk. There is no longer great art, only art that one enjoys or personally thinks is great. The art world, since the Left's domination of it began around the turn of the twentieth century, has abandoned its heritage of striving for greatness, for truth, and for beauty. The West's most prestigious art museums and art galleries routinely feature, and award, works that demonstrate no artistic greatness, beauty, or profundity. What is frequently most

---

* Like all generalizations, this one has exceptions. Not all nudity in film is gratuitous. The religious conservative U.S. senator who objected to *Schindler's List* on the grounds that the women being herded into the gas chamber were shown naked (from afar) went too far in objecting to nudity. That is exactly how it happened, and there was not a scintilla of titillation in that scene.

honored is that which affronts tradition and especially middle-class bourgeois values.

9. Nature Must Not Be Worshipped

It is difficult to overstate how radically different Old Testament thought was from that of the rest of the world from which it emerged. Among the most radical of these differences was the declaration that God created nature and exists entirely outside of it.

In every society, people deified nature and worshipped nature gods. There were gods of thunder and gods of rain. Mountains were worshipped, as were rivers, animals, and every natural force known to man. In ancient Egypt, gods included the Nile River, the frog, the sun, the gazelle, the bull, the cow, the serpent, the moon, and the crocodile.

Then came Genesis, which announced that a supernatural God, that is, a God who existed above and outside of nature, created nature. Therefore, nothing about nature was divine.

Professor Nahum Sarna of Brandeis University, the author of one of the most important commentaries ever written on the Book of Genesis, put it this way: "The revolutionary Israelite concept of God entails His being wholly separate from the world of His creation and wholly other than what the human mind can conceive or the human imagination depict."[57]

Another superb commentary on Genesis was written in the 1940s by Umberto Cassuto, a professor of Bible at the Hebrew University of Jerusalem: "Relative to the ideas prevailing among the peoples of the ancient East, we are confronted here with a basically new conception and a spiritual revolution. . . . The basically new conception consists in the completely transcendental view of the Godhead . . . the God of Israel is outside and above nature, and the whole of nature, the sun, and the moon, and all the hosts of heaven, and the earth beneath, and the sea that is under the earth, and all that is in them— they are all His creatures which He created according to His will."[58]

This was extremely difficult for the men of the ancient world to accept. And as society drifts from Judeo-Christian values, it is again becoming difficult to accept. Major elements in secular Western society are returning to forms of nature worship: The natural environment is increasingly regarded as sacred. Extreme expressions of nature worship actually regard human beings as blights on nature.

It is understandable that people who rely on feelings more than reason would exalt nature. It is easier—indeed more natural—to worship nature in all its grandeur than it is to worship an invisible and morally demanding God. What is puzzling is that many people who claim to rely on reason would do so. Nature is unworthy of worship. It is amoral and frequently cruel. Nature, "red in tooth and claw," has no moral laws, only the amoral law of survival of the fittest.

Why would people who value justice or kindness to the stranger or caring for the weak venerate nature? These moral qualities are unique to humanity. In nature, the weak are to be killed or left to suffer and die. A hospital is a profoundly unnatural, indeed anti-natural, creation: To expend precious resources on keeping the most frail alive is a violation of the natural order. The individual means nothing to nature; the individual is precious to humans.

The romanticizing of nature, let alone the ascribing of divinity to it, involves ignoring what really happens in nature. It is most unlikely that those American schoolchildren who conducted a campaign on behalf of freeing a killer whale (the whale in the film *Free Willy*) ever saw films of actual killer whale behavior. They should have watched the National Geographic videos that show, among other things, killer whales tossing a terrified baby seal back and forth before finally killing it. If they had, the schoolchildren might then have petitioned killer whales to free baby seals.

Without Man, the Environment Is Insignificant

Nature has been created for man's use, and on its own, without man, it has no meaning. Dolphins are adorable because human beings find them adorable. Without people to appreciate them or the role they play in the earth's ecosystem to enable human life, they are no more adorable or meaningful than a rock on Neptune.

That is the point of the Creation story—everything was made in order to prepare the way for the creation of the human being. God declared each day's creation "good," but declared the day of man's creation "very good."

Critics find three biblical notions about nature unacceptable: that man shall lord over it; that it was created for man and has no intrinsic value; and that it is not sacred.

With regard to man "conquering and subduing nature," this was one of the revolutionary ideas of the Old Testament that made Western medical and other scientific progress possible. *In all other ancient civilizations, nature (or the capricious and amoral gods of nature) ruled man.* Only by conquering and subduing nature does man develop cures for nature's diseases. Either we conquer cancer or cancer conquers us.

As for the objection that the Judeo-Christian notion of man as the pinnacle and purpose of nature is "arrogant" one can only say woe unto mankind if that objection prevails. When man is reduced to being only a part of the natural world, his status is reduced to that of a dispensable animal.

Let it be clear that the biblical view of man and nature does not in any way suggest that man has the right to poison the earth or to abuse animals. The former is unfair to future generations of human beings, and the latter is immoral.

But man is what matters. If DDT is necessary to keep millions of Africans from dying from malaria (as it had been to prevent Americans from dying of malaria), then DDT must be used to wipe out the anopheles mosquito. Western environmentalists have been responsible for the deaths of millions of Africans because of the ban on DDT. In 1970, the National Academy of Sciences estimated that "in little more than two decades, DDT has prevented 500 million deaths due to malaria that would otherwise be inevitable." [59]

But this has been of little consequence to the environmentalist movement, which has come to place the natural environment on a par with, and often higher than, human beings.

10. Material Well-Being Is One of Many Values

Judeo-Christian values place great importance on bettering man's material life. That is why the biblical prophets spoke so emphatically about clothing the naked and feeding the hungry. That is why many Christians left—and continue to leave—affluent countries to devote their lives to feed the hungry and to provide medical assistance in the most impoverished places on earth.

But beyond assuring that our fellow human beings have their basic material needs met, man's material condition is not as supreme a Judeo-Christian value as it is a Leftist one. It is certainly important, but man's moral and spiritual condition are at least as important. Moreover, there is the extremely important issue of the afterlife. Even the American Founders who are labeled "deists"—such as Franklin and Jefferson—strongly affirmed a belief in the afterlife. The Judeo-Christian traditions all affirmed an afterlife where the ultimate justice that will always elude mankind is finally achieved. Therefore there is no Judeo-Christian seeking of a material utopia on earth, as there is on the secular Left.*

A good example of the Judeo-Christian difference with the Left in this arena would be the lavish cathedrals the Catholic Church has built in many impoverished countries. To Leftists this is widely regarded as a great wrong. In their view, all that labor, not to mention the gold and treasure, should have been spent on the poor. To those who hold Judeo-Christian values, however, while feeding the hungry is a primary value, so is feeding the soul. A cathedral in a poor Latin American city is therefore vitally important. These beautiful churches and cathedrals have been among the few things, aside from family and friends, that afforded millions of poor people in Catholic countries a measure of comfort and joy.

To a materialist, the notion that poor people—or even people

---

* Many modern Jews believe that Judaism does not affirm an afterlife. They confuse modern Jews' beliefs with Judaism. In the *Encyclopedia Judaica*, the world's foremost secular work of scholarly Jewish reference, the article on "afterlife" begins: "Judaism has always affirmed a belief in the afterlife."

who are just not rich—would place non-material concerns over material ones is perverse. That is why Leftists do not understand why the non-rich, let alone the poor, would vote for any conservative party. An American bestseller in 2004, *What's the Matter with Kansas? How Conservatives Won the Heart of America*, by Left-wing author Thomas Frank, illustrated this point. The theme of his book was that Americans of a lower economic status who vote Republican do so against their own best interests. When I dialogued with Frank on the radio, he seemed incapable of understanding that many millions of Americans consider the Left's views on social issues—abortion, same-sex marriage, sex education in elementary schools, among others—more important than the alleged economic advantages of voting Democrat.

Biblical values deeply emphasized material progress. The Bible gave the very idea of moral and material progress to the world. Every other society in the world had a cyclical view of life—life just kept repeating itself throughout the generations. It was the Jewish prophets of the Old Testament who enunciated the divine obligation to care for the poor and the helpless. But such concerns were never the only Judeo-Christian values, and the poor in biblical nomenclature were truly destitute, not at all analogous to those classified as poor in America, for example. In 2005, those designated as "poor" in America lived in a home with two or more rooms per person and air-conditioning, and they owned a car, refrigerator, stove, clothes washer and dryer, and microwave. They also had two color televisions, cable or satellite TV reception, a VCR or DVD player and a stereo, and obtained medical care (even without health insurance). Nearly half owned their own homes.[60]

A final irony here is that preoccupation with material concerns does not lead to more personally altruistic behavior vis-à-vis the poor. Religious Americans give more charity to, and volunteer more time to help, the poor.[61]

11. Life Has Ultimate Meaning

If the God introduced by the Hebrew scriptures exists, life has ultimate meaning. If there is no such God, it does not. If we humans are made solely out of matter and exist solely because of random impersonal forces, our lives have no more meaning than inanimate objects.

This does not mean that people who do not believe in such a God cannot feel that they have a purpose and meaning for their own lives. Indeed, most people do. They have to because the need for meaning is the greatest of all human needs. It is even stronger than the need for sex. There are people who lead chaste lives who achieve happiness, but no one who lacks a sense of purpose or meaning can achieve happiness.

Nevertheless, the fact that people feel that their lives are meaningful—as a parent, a caregiver, an artist, a professional, or any of myriad ways in which we feel we are doing something meaningful—has no bearing on the question of whether life itself is ultimately meaningful. The two issues are entirely separate. A physician understandably views his healing of people as meaningful. But if there is no God, he will have to confront the fact that as meaningful as healing the day's patients has felt, that was just a feeling. Ultimately everything is meaningless because life itself is. In this sense, it is better for an individual's peace of mind to be a poor person who believes in God than a successful neurosurgeon who does not.

Therefore, while secular government is a good thing, secularism has been devastating for individuals and for societies. On the individual level, among these consequences have been increased unhappiness (all surveys report that religious Americans are happier than secular ones); increased reliance on drugs, sex, alcohol, and mind-numbing entertainment to get through life; moral confusion; a paucity of wisdom (for example, belief in male-female sameness); and a search for substitute religions such as Marxism, socialism, fascism, Communism, environmentalism, and pacifism.

Secularism is even leading to the disappearance of Western nations. In order to maintain the population of a group, its women must give birth to at least 2.1 children. But in thoroughly secularized Germany, for example, the birthrate in 2010 was 1.38.[62] Most other Western European nations also have a birthrate below replacement level. And while secularism gives people little reason to have children, Leftism has given people reasons not to have children: the preservation of the natural environment through zero population growth, and discouraging women from making motherhood their primary occupation.

Given the indispensability of God to meaning in life, to liberty, to human worth, and to the other values enumerated here, it is no wonder that "In God We Trust" is one of the three elements of the American Trinity. Perhaps more Americans would be aware of this if they were not taught in schools that push secularism to the point of virtually banning mention of God.

A godless America would no longer be America. It would be Europe between Mexico and Canada.

E Pluribus Unum—From Many One

The other day, I was in a small company—and there were Asians, Koreans, Middle Easterners, some other people. And they had been in America for, like, two, three, four years. And they talk American. They look American. Body language is American. I'm sure they already think American. Go to Korea and become Korean in one or two years' time. Good luck with that.

That's so special about this country.

—Mikheil Saakashvili, president of Georgia, February 2, 2012, FoxNews

THE MOTTO OF AMERICA, E Pluribus Unum, is rare, if not unique as a governing principle or motto of a country. For good reason: No other nation is made out of as "many" as America is. In virtually every society in history, the national or group identity was correlated with its ethnic or racial identity. No other nation calls itself a "nation of immigrants," as Americans—of all political persuasions—routinely call America.

At first the *pluribus* in E Pluribus Unum referred to the thirteen original colonies—and the motto was adopted in order to help forge these many colonies into *unum*, one nation. But from the beginning, the phrase came to refer to the many peoples who made up America. That is why the motto was retained after America united as one country.

If you are Japanese, you are Japanese because you were born to Japanese parents. There is no other way to be considered Japanese (even if a non-Japanese could in some rare instance become a citizen of Japan). The same has held true for virtually all other groups, from tribes to countries, throughout history.* America went against the human norm in adopting E Pluribus Unum. This motto ended any significance people attached to race, ethnicity, or blood, each of which has been among the most important values in all societies.

As a result, the American ability to assimilate people from every ethnic, national, and racial background has been unique. Non-Americans who are aware of it find it almost incredible. It runs entirely against the universal human predilection toward defining members of other races, ethnicities, and nationalities as the "other," an "other" who, moreover, cannot become "one of us."

This is even true for other Western democracies. European countries, in the second half of the twentieth century, began accepting large numbers of immigrants. However, it is very difficult, and often impossible, for immigrants of other races or ethnicities to be considered truly a member of a host European country. A third-generation Turk in Germany, born in Germany, fluent and accentless in German, is rarely considered a German by other Germans. In America, however, a first-generation Turk who is not fluent in

---

* Interestingly in light of the Judeo-Christian aspect of America's founding, one exception was the Jews. A person of any ethnic group could always join the Jewish people (the Jews have always been a people—or "nation," as the Hebrew Bible described them)—by affirming the Jews' religious beliefs.

English and speaks with a distinct accent is considered an American by other Americans. And the odds are that his children will not marry another Turkish-American but an American of some other background, quite possibly one of white Anglo-Saxon racial stock.

Anyone from anywhere and of any race or ethnicity can become an American in every sense of the word. This is one reason many of America's Founders asserted that a new type of person was being made in America. No longer would a man or woman be identified primarily by their ethnic, national, religious, or racial origins, but by their individual achievements and their willingness to identify as Americans.

Aside from its uniqueness, E Pluribus Unum is one of the reasons America developed so rapidly and achieved a level of prosperity that surpassed every other country. Lawrence Harrison, director of the Cultural Change Institute at Tufts University, makes this point in his book *Who Prospers: How Cultural Values Shape Economic and Political Success*. Harrison, who spent much of his life in Latin America as director of the U.S. Agency for International Development, pondered the question of why the United States developed economically and politically so much more so than Latin American countries, many of which were also blessed with huge areas of rich undeveloped land and immense natural resources.

One of his explanations is that, unlike the United States, Latin America engaged in what Harrison calls "familism," discrimination on the basis of blood relationships. People did not trust non-blood relations and therefore gave jobs and opportunities to family members—who, of course, were also members of the same ethnicity and race.

Outside of the United States, "familism" has been the human norm. From the beginning of societies, people divided the world by blood and marriage ties—that is, families and tribes. Much later, in some parts of the world, the nation-state developed and indigenous members of that nationality would owe allegiance to the nation-state. But overwhelmingly human beings trusted only members of one's family or tribe. America became the first society to reject family and national origin, and, eventually, ethnicity and race, too, as defining factors of one's identity.

Unlike other national identities, there is no racial or ethnic component to being American. We know what Norwegians, Japanese, Chinese, Ethiopians, and others are supposed to look like because there is a racial or ethnic component to being a member of these groups. But we have no idea what an American looks like because an American can look Norwegian, Japanese, Chinese, African, Arab, Latin, or like any combination of them. It is true that there was always a white Anglo-Saxon Protestant (WASP) look to the majority, but when non-WASPs began immigrating into America, they became as American as any WASP. That is why "God Bless America"—probably the American people's favorite national song and its unofficial anthem—could be written by a Russian Jewish immigrant named Israel Isidore Baline, aka Irving Berlin. He felt as American as someone whose ancestors came to America on the *Mayflower*.

Finally, E Pluribus Unum, with its rejection of tribal, familial, ethnic, and blood origins, made possible the essential American value—the individual. The individual matters most, not any group and not any family to which the individual belongs. The only group that matters is the American. This celebration of the individual has never been promulgated anywhere else in the world as it has in America. In earlier times, and in some areas until relatively recently, there was a racist element that deemed non-whites, especially blacks, as less than fully human, not to mention less than fully American. That element has largely disappeared. Today it is the Left that seeks to supplant E Pluribus Unum with multiculturalism, which is preoccupied with race, ethnicity, and national origins and opposes the notion of one American identity.

Hence the Left's preoccupation with "diversity," by which it means ethnic and racial diversity. "Diversity is our strength" is a Left-wing credo. It sounds true and admirable, but it is really an attempt to undo E Pluribus Unum by celebrating Pluribus, not Unum. Much of America's strength does indeed lie in its diverse *origins*, but

America's strength is diminished by diverse primary identities. It is not diversity, but the *ability to unify the diverse*, that is America's strength and greatness; and that can only be done by celebrating the individual and the nation those individuals form, America.

The consequence of E Pluribus Unum and the celebration of the individual over race and ethnicity has been the creation of the least racist society in the world. While the Left regularly calls America racist, non-white immigrants to America know how untrue that is. Apparently many millions of Africans did not believe the charge of America's racism. They went there for liberty and opportunity and got them.

NATIONALISM

Another value contained within the Unum in E Pluribus Unum is nationalism. American values celebrate one national identity, that of America—and, since the American value system is exportable, the citizens of every country can and should celebrate their national identity. Once again we have a major difference between Leftism and Americanism. Leftism seeks to do away with national identities and supplant them with one international identity (it uses multiculturalism to achieve the same end—the subversion of nationalism, especially American nationalism).

American nationalism is one of the most important sources of Left-wing hostility to America. America celebrates its national identity more than any Western European country, and almost more than any country in the world.

In the summer of 2008, Israel's ambassador to the United Nations, Dan Gillerman, and I were lecturers at a Jewish leadership retreat in Phoenix, Arizona. I asked what most impressed him about America. His immediate answer was "Its patriotism." He was deeply impressed, for example, that Americans sang or played the National Anthem before all major sporting events.

On the Left, Americans' celebration of American nationalism is widely dismissed as "flag waving" or even as dangerous "jingoism." "When fascism comes to America, it will come wrapped in the American flag" is a widely expressed sentiment of the Left. The original source of the statement is unknown but, not surprisingly, it was a professor who probably first said something like it. In 1938, Professor Halford Luccock of Yale Divinity School delivered a lecture in which he said: "When and if fascism comes to America it will not be labeled 'made in Germany'; it will not even be called fascism; it will be called, of course, 'Americanism.' "[63]

Yet there is something particularly morally—not to mention emotionally—healthy about having a national identity. It means that one feels moral and emotional attachments to others. The person who has ties to his country, his religion, his family, his friends, his volunteer group, his local community, his college, his coworkers, and so on is a far better person than one who only has ties to humanity. One does not—because one cannot—have ties to "humanity" that are as strong as the ties one has to a specific group. No normal person reacts to a plane crash that kills passengers from a distant country with the same emotional intensity that one feels toward a plane crash that kills fellow nationals. Likewise, one reacts even more intensely if all the passengers killed in a plane crash lived in one's hometown—even if one didn't personally know them. There is nothing morally wrong with such reactions.

We learn to care for others by first caring for family and friends, then for one's immediate community, and then for one's nation. Then we can—and should—feel for humans everywhere. People have done immense harm in the name of their nation, and people have done immense harm in the name of "humanity." The suppression of the natural human instinct to care about the particular has led to great evil.

The famous Soviet Jewish dissident Natan Sharansky wrote a book, *Defending Identity: Its Indispensable Role in Protecting Democracy*, on this very theme. In it he wrote, "Identity without democracy is totalitarian; democracy without identity is weak and self-betraying."

How weak is proved by what has happened in Western Europe. For one thing, these democracies with weakened national identities lose the will to fight for democracy. It is America that has been defending democracies, including those of Western Europe—often against the wishes of the Western Europeans themselves, as when, during the Cold War, the United States placed Pershing missiles in Europe despite massive protests.

The loss of identity in Europe has led not only to a lack of will to defend democracy; it has led to a lack of will to reproduce. With no religious identity and no national identity, even the desire to have children is affected. Why reproduce a group you don't care much about?

The affirmation of national identity is a major reason the American value system is applicable to all peoples. The American ideal is that Thais feel a strong Thai identity, that Uruguayans identify strongly with Uruguay, etc.

In addition to the intrinsic moral and national benefits of countries having strong national identities, the more countries that have a strong national identity, the greater the barrier to international institutions controlling the lives of nations and individuals. Any individual living in a free country has much more control over his life when his government has more power than international institutions do. In a free country one can vote whom one wants into power and out of power. The individual has no such control over who directs international institutions.

That is one reason Americans who affirm American values strongly oppose handing over power to international bodies such as the United Nations and the International Court of Justice. If a big government in one's own country diminishes the control the individual citizen has over his life, how much more so do large international institutions?

American Exceptionalism

This negative view of powerful international institutions is a defining aspect of what is known as American exceptionalism. It is the belief that America has better values than international institutions do and because of those values, not because of any inherent superiority, it should guide its own destiny. The cultural war in which America is engaged is in large measure about American exceptionalism. Conservative America generally believes in the concept; liberal America does not. Americans who believe in American exceptionalism do not have a high moral regard for the United Nations, do not trust the World Court more than American institutions, regard Amnesty International as a morally confused Left-wing organization, recognize the biases of the world's news media, do not share Hollywood's values, and regard "world opinion" as morally useless.

Liberal America regards American exceptionalism as chauvinistic and therefore dangerous. Even worse, American exceptionalism is the major obstacle to a central goal of Leftism—supplanting nationalism with internationalism. The belief that America usually knows better than the "world" what is right and wrong therefore infuriates the American and international Left, which places far more trust in world bodies and world opinion.

A related issue is international law. For the Left, law defines the good more so than it does for the Right. For the Right, especially the Judeo-Christian Right, morality is higher than law. Take the two sides' views of the American war in Iraq, for example. A primary reason the Left gave for opposing the war was that, in its view, it violated international law. Had it been authorized by the United Nations Security Council, as was the first war against Saddam Hussein's Iraq, it would have been considered legal and presumably not have elicited nearly as much opposition as it did (though the Left in America largely opposed the First Gulf War as well). But because the UN Security Council did not authorize the war, it was deemed illegal and therefore wrong.

On the other side are those who believe that morality trumps international legality as determined by the United Nations—which means nothing more than China, Russia, and France voting to authorize a war, thereby making it legal. Overthrowing the mass murderer-rapist-torturer Saddam Hussein was a moral good (irrespective of the presence or absence of WMD). If it violated UN-based international law, that reflected on the moral inadequacy of international law and how it is determined, not on the rightness or wrongness of Americans giving up life and wealth to depose Saddam Hussein.

The American exceptionalism view that morality is higher than legality is the Judeo-Christian view. Indeed, it is the view of all religions, and of common sense. How can it be otherwise? In Nazi Germany killing the mentally retarded was legal; while in Jim Crow America, it was illegal for a black to sit at a lunch counter with whites. Should moral people have followed those laws?

Yet for much of the secular world, especially the Left, law has come to constitute the highest definition of good—because if you do not believe in objective morality, you will posit objective law in its stead. For the Judeo-Christian world, law is very important. But laws are made by men, whereas the rule of morality comes from a higher source. Of course, such a belief has dangers. But the greater danger is thinking that law embodies morality. Virtually every individual who is widely regarded as having been a great moral figure—from Moses (who violated Egyptian law) to Dietrich Bonhoeffer (who violated German law) to Rosa Parks (who violated American Jim Crow laws)—achieved greatness because he or she knew when to violate the law. Too bad more Europeans did not place morality above law. There would not have been a Holocaust.

America Is Good

PRESIDENT GEORGE W. BUSH often spoke about the "goodness" of America (and about the "evil" of three world tyrannies). Was this language meaningful—or was it, as many critics at home and abroad contended, sanctimonious rhetoric?

As odd as it may sound, that an American president would refer to America as a good country and speak about good and evil are compelling arguments for America's goodness. The rhetoric that leaders use tells a great deal about them and about their nations.

Americans are so used to hearing such descriptions of their country that many of them would probably be surprised to learn that such rhetoric is largely confined to American leaders. It does not surprise most foreigners, however. They recognize it as quintessentially American; and they either find it impressive (if they agree with it) or highly objectionable (if they do not).

How, then, do other leaders describe their countries? The answer depends, of course, on which leaders and nations we are talking about. But whichever they are, their national self-description rarely includes the word "good." This is true regarding both tyrants and elected leaders. Adolf Hitler never spoke about the German people's goodness—goodness meant nothing to him or to Nazism—but about the inherent (racial) superiority of the *Deutsche Volk*. Nor do leaders of decent countries speak of their country's goodness. What leaders frequently invoke, especially in times of crisis, is their countries' *greatness*. The postwar French leader Charles de Gaulle famously said about his country, "France cannot be France without greatness." During World War II, Joseph Stalin often referred to Russia's greatness. China, Japan, Korea, and other nations with long histories refer to present or past national greatness. And many European national leaders speak with pride of their countries' social systems, of their commitment to international law and to European unity.

But American leaders speak of their country's *goodness*. That has always been America's self-image: as a nation with a moral mission—a nation that is, in Abraham Lincoln's words, "the last best hope of earth." Therefore, Americans have a national obligation to be good.

In contrast, the Left identifies a country having a sense of national mission with fanaticism and chauvinism. Like the European Left, the American Left does not use goodness rhetoric—it prefers the language of "fairness," "rights," and "equality" to the language of morality. Moreover, the Left does not see America as good, but as profoundly flawed from its inception, with its racism and slavery, to the present time.*

Is America good?

If "good" means more or less perfect or flawless, the answer is, of course, no. But America is good in the three ways the word matters: in comparison with other countries, especially historically powerful ones; in all the good it has done for the great majority of those who were born in or came to America; and with regard to all the good it has done, at tremendous cost, for vast numbers of people in other countries. No country has given nearly as many individuals the liberty, the life filled with opportunity, and the material well-being that America has given the great majority of its citizens. And no country has done as much or sacrificed as much for other people and other countries as has America. America has been the beacon of hope for mankind since its creation in 1776.

America's moral record is stained most especially by slavery, the anti-black racism that persisted among many Americans for a hundred years after the Civil War, and by its treatment of American Indians. There are no excuses for these evils. There is, however, moral perspective.

First, slavery was universal. For nearly all of history it was accepted as a normal part of life. Therefore what needs to be evaluated is not so much why there was slavery in America as why slavery was ended in America. The very basis of America, its commitment to liberty, made the existence of slavery in America a moral problem from the country's founding. And within twenty-eight years of the founding of the United States, in the year 1808, the United States and Great Britain outlawed the international slave trade.

Second, between 618,000 and 700,000 Americans died in a civil

---

* According to a 2008 Rasmussen poll, 78 percent of Republicans, but only 49 percent of Democrats, viewed America as "fair and decent." If Rasmussen also polled only those who identified as "Left," the number would have been much lower than 49 percent. The poll is cited in Michael Barone, "Is America a Good Country or Not?" *U.S. News & World Report*, April 10, 2008.

war fought over slavery. The most popular song of the Civil War era, and one of the most popular American songs ever written, was Julia Ward Howe's "Battle Hymn of the Republic," written just six months into the Civil War. As Americans know, it contained the words, "Let us die to make men free."

Third, it was the Founders' commitment to liberty that ultimately led to the end of slavery. No society or individual lives up to their highest ideals. But America's ideals were taken extremely seriously by America. It is no wonder that the United States became the only non-majority-black country in the world to elect a black leader. Indeed, America has so exorcised racism that—for nearly all Americans—electing the country's first black president was a triumph, but having a black president was no big deal.

Fourth, weighed against its moral flaws—which were shared by just about all other countries—one must weigh all the good America has done. No country has shed as much blood for others' liberty, or preserved liberty in so many countries, or became leader of what became known as the free world, or provided so much opportunity for immigrants from every place on earth. When there are natural disasters anywhere in the world, the world looks first to America. When there is great evil, victims of that evil look first to America. And when America liberates a people, whether their government had been a friend or foe, they know that America will not stay as conqueror or as occupier, that it will probably leave and that if it remains it will be solely to ensure that country's freedom and security. American troops have remained in Germany since World War II and in South Korea since the Korean War. Both nations are very fortunate for that fact—as they have both become free and economic giants. Of what other country's troops can that be said?

Fifth, imagine what the world would be if there were no America or if America ceased to be strong. As previously noted, if America ceased to be strong, let alone ceased to exist, liberty on earth would gradually be extinguished:

1. Islamists would take over many Muslim-majority countries (they may, in any event). Terrorists would have no foe capable of subduing them.

2. Free Taiwan would be overrun by the Communist regime in China.

3. Iran, other Islamic states, and Islamist groups would seek to annihilate free Israel—resulting in a Mideast war, perhaps nuclear, the probable deaths of millions, and possibly the destruction of Israel.

4. Tyrants throughout Africa would be emboldened.

5. The United Nations would become, even more so than today, a tool of anti-democratic regimes.

6. The non-democratic regime ruling Russia would increasingly suppress liberty in Russia and use force to re-create the former Russian/Soviet empire.

7. Latin American countries struggling to create democratic institutions would be subverted by anti-democratic regimes.

The world would become a far crueler place. It would descend to the law of the jungle where the mighty devour the weak. No good country would replace America as the world's superpower. Instead a variety of powerful countries—none of which had a comparable desire to be good—would replace America and either vie with one another for superpower status or divide the world into spheres of interest. Terror, torture, and tyranny would increase and become commonplace.

RUSSIA

Russia is one such alternative world power—at least militarily. Yet Russia is a country essentially devoid of a moral value system. Whatever moral role the Russian Orthodox Church once played was extinguished during the seven decades of Communist suppression of religion. Pockets of religious and secular morality notwithstanding, Russia is basically a nihilistic state. Under the leadership of Vladimir Putin, a former KGB director, Russia resumed playing a destructive role in world affairs. It supports and sells arms to some of the worst regimes in the world, forces its will on Ukraine and other neighboring states, and violently suppresses domestic critics who shed light on the autocratic government that rules the geographically largest nation in the world. Without America, Russia would be far more aggressive and seek to reestablish the Soviet Union. Who would stop it?

TURKEY

World media opinion has portrayed the Islamist regime in Turkey as the *New York Times* did in 2011, "a template that effectively integrates Islam, democracy and vibrant economics," and Recep Tayyip Erdogan as "its mildly Islamist prime minister."[64] However, the "mildly Islamist" prime minister has arrested secular and other opposition journalists.[65]

Erdogan's party has undone the secular Ataturk revolution. Turkey, long regarded as the bridge between the West and Islam, has rapidly moved away from the West and embraced an increasingly anti-Western Islamism. It seeks to regain the power and prestige of the Ottoman Empire. Armenians are not the only ones who fear such a prospect.

IRAN

The Islamic Republic of Iran is ruled by moral heirs of the Nazis. The totalitarian theocrats who rule Iran boast of their desire to initiate a second Holocaust against the Jews, all the while denying that the first Holocaust took place. And the country's treatment of Iranians who seek elementary human freedoms and of Iranian women is among the world's worst. It is the United States that prevents Iran from attaining the greater world influence it seeks.

NORTH KOREA

Without fear of American retribution, North Korea would likely attack South Korea, and threaten Japan. American troops in South Korea and American power are the greatest impediments to the psychopathological regime in North Korea engaging in international aggression.

EUROPE

Europe long ago gave up fighting for or believing in much other than living a life with as much economic security, as many days off, and as early a retirement age as possible. World War I killed European idealism. And whatever remained was destroyed by World War II. What I have written here about the Germans is true for nearly all of Europe: Instead of learning to fight evil, Europe has learned that fighting is evil. If there were no America, much of Western Europe would have come under Soviet control, and Russia—and in the future, perhaps Islamism—would be the most powerful forces in Europe.

ISLAMISM

As the *New York Times*, originally rather optimistic about the so-called Arab Spring, reported, the battle in the Arab world is not between Islamists and Western-type secular democrats but between Islamists. Without America, many Arab regimes would, with the support of other Muslim regimes, seek to destroy Israel and to spread Islamist doctrines among Muslims throughout the world, including Europe. At least one hundred million Muslims support violent jihad—meaning, among other things, the death of the West and its liberal values—and without America, who would stop them?

CHINA

As in Russia, traditional Chinese virtues were largely destroyed by Communism, and China, too, is essentially a nihilistic state whose government spends vast sums of foreign currency buying influence in some of the cruelest places on earth—such as Robert Mugabe's Zimbabwe and Mahmoud Ahmadinejad's Iran. Without America, China would seek to dominate Japan, become the major Asian power, and then the world's superpower.

UNITED NATIONS

The good performed by some of United Nations institutions, such as the World Health Organization and UNICEF, has been outweighed by the amount of bad the UN has either abetted or allowed. It has enabled genocide in Rwanda, done little or nothing to stop genocide in the Congo and Sudan, given a respectable forum to tyrannies, convened conferences (the Durban Conferences on racism) that simply became forums for anti-Semitism, and been preoccupied with vilifying one of its relatively few humane states, Israel.[66] Its moral failings were further exemplified by its placing Qaddafi's Libya on its Human Rights Commission, Iran on its Commission on the Status of Women, and North Korea on the Nuclear Disarmament Commission. It is not that the people who run the United Nations are bad people; it is that the United Nations is run by a majority of the world's governments, and they are run by bad people. Without America in the Security Council, the bad would nearly always prevail.

The World Should Adopt American Values

AMERICAN VALUES MADE AMERICA a unique force for good in the world, as well as a uniquely free and prosperous nation. There is no reason these values cannot do the same for any other country in the world.

No country has to become America, let alone Christian, in order to do so. On the contrary, according to the American value system, a country must keep its special identity. Let us imagine Honduras, a poor country in Central America. There is nothing basic to Honduran society that would prevent it from adopting the three American values. Indeed, with a commitment to Liberty, that is, a free economy and all the other freedoms enumerated here, there is every reason to believe that Honduras would begin to prosper. Of course, with that freedom, Hondurans—just like Americans—would also have to embrace In God We Trust, meaning that God, not government, is the source of liberty, and that each individual is morally accountable to God. And Hondurans would have to commit to E Pluribus Unum, meaning that blood- and family-based cronyism would be abandoned, that all citizens would take on one primary identity—Honduran—and that each individual's ability, not family ties, would determine Hondurans' ability to succeed or fail.

With the adoption of American values, nothing specifically Honduran would have to be given up—not its culture, its music, its religion, its language, its flag. On the contrary, given the nationalist aspect of American values, the more Honduran that Hondurans felt, the better their chances for success—providing, of course, the other values were also affirmed.

Now, Honduras provides a particularly easy example because it is already a Western country, and its religious base is Christian.

But what about a non-Western, non-Christian country? Could American values work there?

Absolutely.

No Muslim country would have to give up Islam. They would have to give up Islamism, the desire for a Sharia-based government, but not Islam. The individual Muslim would be free in such a state to lead as Sharia-observant a life as he wished. Would freedom mean that some Muslims would opt out of a religious life? Probably so—just as millions of Jews and Christians have chosen to do. But that is usually the fault of the respective religions. If a religion needs a ghetto or state coercion in order to keep its followers, it is not a respect-worthy religion. Religions need to sell themselves in free societies, not rely on an absence of freedom.

Nor would any Asian society have to give up its national, religious, or cultural traditions. Look at South Korea, which has only begun to adopt American values (without calling them by that name).

The tragedy is that the greatest value system ever devised cannot be exported if the would-be exporters no longer manufacture it. If Americans stop believing in the American Trinity, the future of humanity is dim indeed. No other system exists to promote liberty, let alone all the other values discussed here.

One might say that the United States of America has a cure for moral cancer. This book has been about that cure. A pain-filled world awaits.

ACKNOWLEDGMENTS

No book is written only by the author. That is certainly true of this book. While, of course, I bear sole responsibility for its contents, it can be said that many thousands of people have contributed significantly to this book.

In formulating my ideas, I have been blessed with something almost unique. I have been able to bounce my thoughts off millions of people, on almost every conceivable topic, and on a daily basis.

In addition to teaching, lecturing, and writing, I have been a radio talk show host for thirty years. As such I have been afforded two very rare intellectual gifts.

The first is the accumulated wisdom of a large national audience. There are few topics about which some listener does not know more than I do. And no matter what subject I raise, some listeners have actually experienced it. No topic has remained abstract. If my subject is immigration, immigrants and children of immigrants call in. If I am discussing male-female relations, men and women call in and open up as if they were in a room alone with their best friend or therapist. More to the point of this book, when the topic has been Islam, I have had any number of opportunities to speak with religious Muslims, secular Muslims, Christians and Jews who have lived in Muslim countries, professors who teach Islamic studies, and authors of books defending and books critical of Islam.

All teachers know how much they have learned from their students. Therapists readily acknowledge how much they have learned from patients. Imagine, then, how much wisdom one can accumulate from millions of "students" and "patients."

So, I first want to acknowledge my listeners and readers. Whether they call or write, whether they agree or disagree, they have taught me an immeasurable amount, not least how to communicate with people I differ with—a trait I hope is reflected in this book.

The other rare gift my profession has afforded me has been the ability to talk to virtually every great thinker, writer, and politician—including many whose views I strongly opposed—of the past generation.

There is an ancient Hebrew saying, "Acquire a friend, make for yourself a teacher." My friends have all been my teachers. From high school when I met my devoted friend and lifelong teacher, Joseph Telushkin, to today, my friends have given me, intellectually as well as emotionally, more than they can ever know.

For almost twenty-five years, I have spent almost every Saturday afternoon, after synagogue, with two couples, Drs. Stephen and Ruth Marmer and Allen and Susie Estrin. There is no idea, let alone personal issue, that we have not discussed in depth. Others who have shaped my life and thinking include (in alphabetical order) Joel Alperson, whose talents are only exceeded by working on behalf of our shared ideals, and who has devoted much of his life to preparing the publication of my forthcoming commentary on the Torah; Gary and Georgette Awad, a second generation Syrian-Lebanese couple, whom I always introduce as people who make the commandment, "Love your neighbor as yourself" effortless to obey; Shmuley Boteach, whom I enjoy debating almost as much I enjoy our friendship; Alan Briese, who in so many ways has made my life better and my work possible; Lynn and Sylvie Bradley, a Mormon couple who leave everyone they come into contact with better people, including me; Shlomo Cohen, friend for forty years, former head of the Israel Bar Association, and my favorite Lefty; Father Gregory Coiro, a Capuchin Franciscan friar who brings glory to his Church and joy to his friends; Paul Croshaw, who devoted years to making a moving and fun full-length film—*Baseball, Dennis, and the French*—on the role my radio show played in changing his life; Izzy and Rita Eichenstein, my friends since I moved to California in the late 1970s, whose lives have traveled down an emotionally wrenching religious path that I have been a part of and learned so much from; Leonid Feldman, my longtime friend whose path from atheist and Soviet dissident to prominent American rabbi is worthy of its own book; Robert Florczak, my friend, my favorite agnostic atheist, and a great artist and thinker; Michael and Jill Gotlieb, for thirty years of friendship and for Rabbi Michael's overseeing Sue's studying of Judaism; Larry Greenfield, who offered insightful advice on the manuscript and carries on the fight for American values in his own inimitable way; Lee Habeeb, whose insights into radio and into America have been invaluable; Michael and Barbara Ledeen, who have made enormous contributions to the fight against tyranny worldwide and who, along with Thurber, have warmly welcomed me into their Washington, D.C., home for decades; Mike Noble, whose name personifies the man and who has devoted his talent and time to help me get my ideas out to the world; Michael Nocita, a former Catholic priest whose friendship has been a thirty-year gift; Bahram and Doris Nour-Omid, two Persian Jews who play an important role in my life, and who exemplify what Iran has lost and America has gained in the Persian-Jewish exodus following the Khomeini revolution; Eyal Rav-Noy, a friend and one of the most brilliant young Jewish minds in America; Roger and Christine Silk, whose friendship has been one of the best things to happen to me professionally and personally in recent years; Ron Temkin, one of the few people I asked to read and critique the book in manuscript. Barry Wolfe, for his friendship, generosity, and wisdom; and David and Beverly Woznica, close friends for thirty years—watching Rabbi Woznica evolve into one of America's leading rabbis gives one hope for American Judaism.

My cup truly runneth over with such people in my life. And there are others whom I just do not get to see as often, too numerous to individually cite. Finally, I happily include my Salem

Radio Network colleagues from whom I have learned so much and who form an all-star team that I am honored to be a member of: Bill Bennett, Mike Gallagher, Hugh Hewitt, and Michael Medved. And while on the subject of my radio show, I thank the Salem Radio Network—in particular Ed Atsinger, Greg Anderson, and Tom Tradup—for giving me the national forum I have. They have devoted their lives to making a better America and a better world. And they have succeeded magnificently. They are a credit to their deep and animating Christian faith.

I am grateful to Jason Bunn, Roy Hadavi, Alexandra Kerr, Sean McConnell (whose daily contribution to my radio show has been instrumental), Jared Sichel, Christian Welborn, and Julia Whittle for their transcriptions of important materials and for myriad other ways they have helped me. And, of course, to my editor, Adam Bellow, and all others at HarperCollins, whose advice, encouragement, and patience have been deeply appreciated.

I particularly want to thank Allen Estrin and my wife, Susan Prager, who read, and reread, every one of 130,000 words. That I incorporated nearly every one of their edits, additions, and deletions is testimony to the excellence of their work.

Regarding Sue, words fail this professional communicator in describing the immensity of the role she plays in my intellectual life, not to mention the rest of my life. She is a sort of secret weapon during every one of my radio shows, as we instant-message (IM) one another while I broadcast. Ronald Reagan was quoted as having said that all it took for him to feel lonely was for Nancy to leave the room. I know what he meant.

To Allen, additional deeply felt thanks for the extraordinary job he does every day in producing my radio show and for founding and guiding a project that will preoccupy me for many years to come, the internet-based Prager University (www.PragerUniversity.com). It is an attempt, among its other goals, to undo the moral and intellectual damage too many universities have done in their politicization of the humanities. It offers, in five-minute courses, some of the finest minds in the world presenting honest and entertaining food for the mind on virtually every subject. I hope that readers of this book will join the millions of people around the world who have already visited this website.

Finally, I thank America. Indeed this book may be considered one American's thank-you to his country. I have no illusions about America's flaws, and I am well aware that there are other free countries in the world. But no place would have given this grandchild of poor Jewish immigrants to America the opportunities that America has given me. Moreover, in most other countries I would be "Dennis the Jew." In America, I am "Dennis."

My mother, Hilda Prager, died during the writing of this book and I think of her every day. I lost my biggest fan; and my father, Max Prager, lost his best friend of seventy-three years. The book is written in her memory and dedicated to my two beloved sons, David and Aaron, who, thank God, as different as they may be from one another, love each other and love America.

Dennis Prager
La Cañada Flintridge, California
February 2012

ADDENDUM

Leftism-Americanism Differences

This chart is a list of Leftist beliefs and positions contrasted with American and conservative beliefs and positions. It is presented with the understanding that not every individual who considers himself Leftist or liberal holds every one of these positions. This is a listing of Leftist positions, not of Leftists. To cite but one example, there are many individuals on the Left who are in favor of capital punishment, but opposition to capital punishment is a Leftist position.

In keeping with the subject of this book, nearly all of the conservative positions may also be called "American" positions since they emanate, as explained in the chapters on American values, from the American Trinity of Liberty, In God We Trust, E Pluribus Unum.

	American/ Conservative Values	Liberal/Left Values
Primary Concern	Liberty	Material equality
One's Primary Identity	National	World citizen
How to Make a Good Society	Develop each citizen's character.	Abolish inequality.

	American/ Conservative Values	*Liberal/Left Values*
The State	Small	Large
Source of Moral Standards	American and Judeo-Christian values	Individual conscience, the heart, science
Attitude toward Wealth	Create more.	Redistribute.
Morality	Universal	Relative (to individual and/or society)
Primary Sources of Evil	The individual and the state	Socioeconomic forces
Humanity's Primary Division	Good/evil	Rich/poor; strong/weak
Trinities	1. Liberty, God, E Pluribus Unum 2. Life, Liberty, Pursuit of Happiness	1. Liberty, Equality, Fraternity 2. Race, Gender, Class
Family Ideal	Family headed by married father and mother	There is no ideal, only love.
Corporal Punishment of Children	Properly administered, it can be an important tool in raising a good person.	Always wrong. Abusive. Should be illegal.
Morality of Abortion	Determined by society. Wrong unless life of mother is threatened.	Determined only by mother. Society has no say.
Death Penalty for Murder	Sometimes morally necessary.	Always morally wrong.

	American/ Conservative Values	Liberal/Left Values
Individual's Income	Belongs to the individual except for what is absolutely necessary for maintaining limited government.	The state determines what it wants and leaves remainder to individual.
School Vouchers	For: Public schools' monopoly has a negative impact on education.	Against: Vouchers will weaken public schools.
Place of Religion in America	Religious society with secular government	Secular society and secular government
American Interventions Abroad	With few exceptions, they have been noble efforts to spread liberty.	With few exceptions, they have been engaged in for economic and/or imperialist reasons.
View of American Exceptionalism	Positive: an affirmation of America's historic role to be a bright shining light on a hill	Negative: an essentially chauvinistic doctrine
Nuclear weapons	The greater America's superiority, the more secure America and the world will be.	Ideally, neither America nor any country will own any.
Greatest Threat to the World	Evil: at this time Islamist violence	Environmental catastrophe: at this time, global warming
Teenage Sex	Family and society have great influence on teenage behavior. Therefore teen sex is to be discouraged by family and society.	Society has little influence. Teens will engage in sex no matter what. Therefore society must emphasize— and teach—safe sex.

	American/ Conservative Values	Liberal/Left Values
Multiculturalism and Diversity	1. America has always been multiethnic, not multicultural.	1. America's strength comes from its cultural and other forms of diversity.
	2. Some cultures are superior to others.	2. Neither American nor European nor any other culture is superior to any other.
	3. E Pluribus Unum: Promote American identity among all Americans.	3. Promoting "American identity" is jingoistic.
Racism	America is the least racist society.	Racism remains endemic to America and its institutions.
Black Americans	Should be treated no differently from any other Americans. Lowering standards to accommodate blacks demeans blacks and their achievements and undermines American values.	As victims of white America both historically and today, blacks deserve and justice demands race-based affirmative action.
Litigation	Frivolous lawsuits are undermining the quality of American life.	Few lawsuits are truly frivolous and those that are are the price of preventing the stronger and richer from abusing the poorer and weaker.
Violent Crime in America	In most cases, caused by individuals with defective consciences and value systems	In most cases, caused by poverty and/or racism
The Best Hope for Mankind	The United States of America	The United Nations

	American/ Conservative Values	**Liberal/Left Values**
War	Often the only answer to great evil. Death camps were liberated by soldiers, not peace activists.	"War is not the answer."

Notes

Introduction: Humanity at the Crossroads: The Future Will Be Leftist, Islamist, or American

1. "Iran Plans for a World Without America," *Investor's Business Daily*, August 4, 2011.

2. There are moments, however, in the life of other countries when such values are espoused. Margaret Thatcher's Great Britain was perhaps the most prominent example.

3. Thomas Friedman, *New York Times*, January 30, 2010.

Chapter 1: What Is Leftism?

1. Reuters, cited in *Los Angeles Times*, May 4, 2000. Here is how the *New York Times* reported it: "Despite spending more than $2 billion over two decades to improve education and attract more white students, the Kansas City School District has essentially been judged a failure by a state education review board, which has denied it accreditation."

2. David Brooks, "Tools for Thinking," *New York Times*, March 27, 2011.

3. "How Rich People Spend Their Time," *Washington Post*, June 23, 2008.

4. *Today*, NBC, March 3, 2009, www.youtube.com/watch?v=oE0gHtQXWhI.

5. *Wall Street Journal*, February 17, 2009.

6. Psychiatrist-author Theodore Dalrymple has written perhaps the best single work on the role of the welfare state in creating the underclass: *Life at the Bottom: The Worldview That Makes the Underclass* (Chicago: Ivan R. Dee, 2001).

7. Speech to the Economic Club of New York, December 14, 1962.

8. Karl Marx, *Critique of Hegel's Philosophy of Right*, 1843.

9. See, for example, Arthur C. Brooks, "A Nation of Givers" *American*, March/April 2008: http://www.american.com/archive/2008/march-april-magazine-contents/a-nation-of-givers.

10. "Iowa Town Renames Good Friday to 'Spring Holiday,'" ABC News, March 29, 2010.

11. "Hawking expresses a radically skeptical view of reality in general," in Steven Weinberg, "The Universes We Still Don't Know," *New York Review of Books*, February 10, 2011. Weinberg, a Nobel laureate in physics, disagrees with Hawking: "Like most people, I think that there is something real out there. . . . I can't help believing in an objective reality."

12. Darrow's speech is in William Safire, *Lend Me Your Ears: Great Speeches in History* (New York: Norton, 1997). For a discussion of the religious view of free will and human nature, see Joseph Telushkin, *A Code of Jewish Ethics,* vol. 1, *You Shall Be Holy* (New York: Bell Tower, 2006), chapter 2.

13. *BBC Sport*, November 16, 2000.

14. "Seles's Assailant Gets Suspended Sentence," *New York Times*, April 4, 1995.

15. The audio and the transcript of the entire dialogue are available at my website, www.dennisprager.com.

16. It is not widely known, or it has simply been forgotten, that America won the Vietnam War in 1973 when North Vietnam signed the Paris Peace Accords conceding "the South Vietnamese People's right to self-determination." North Vietnam agreed to cease its aggression against South Vietnam, and the United States agreed to supply the South Vietnamese government with arms to defend itself if the North reneged on the agreement and attacked again. The North did renege, resuming its attacks almost immediately. At the time, even the Nobel Committee believed peace had been achieved and both Vietnams would endure. It awarded the Nobel Peace Prize to American secretary of state Henry Kissinger and North Vietnam's Le Duc Tho. Tellingly, Le Duc Tho declined to accept the award. See Bruce Herschensohn, *An American Amnesia: How the U.S. Congress Forced the Surrenders of South Vietnam and Cambodia* (New York: Beaufort Books, 2010). Also see the Bruce Herschensohn video on this subject at Prager University, www.prageru.com.

17. Music critic James H. North, *Fanfare*, September–October 2010, p. 304.

18. Anthony Tommasini, "Top 10 Composers: The Vienna Four," *New York Times*, January 10, 2011.

19. "EU Declares Vacation Travel a Human Right," *Economic Policy Journal*, April 20, 2010.

The European Union has declared travelling a human right, and is launching a program to subsidize vacations with taxpayers' dollars for those too poor to afford their own trips. Antonio Tajani, the European Union commissioner for enterprise and industry, proposed a strategy that could cost European taxpayers hundreds of millions of euros a year. "Travelling for tourism today is a right. The way we spend our holidays is a formidable indicator of our quality of life," Mr. Tajani told a group of ministers at the European Tourism Stakeholders Conference in Madrid on April 15.

A pilot vacation program is scheduled to be launched in 2013, when EU taxpayers will be footing 30% of vacation bills for seniors, youths between the ages of 18 and 25, disabled people, and families facing "difficult social, financial or personal" circumstances.

20. "Egyptians Turn Against Liberal Protesters," *Wall Street Journal*, August 2, 2011.

21. "How Did Rich People Vote and Why?" *New York Times*, November 11, 2008.

22. Dennis Prager, "Why the Democrats use 12-year-olds," August 3, 2004, http://townhall.com/columnists/dennisprager/2004/08/03/why_the_demo crats_use_12-year-olds.

23. Some of the examples I noted are worth citing:

"Has it come to this? The desperation of the GOP? Insulting a 12 yr old girl. You sure are a class act."

"You're an asshole for saying that Wexler girl has not earned the right to criticize Cheney. Fuck YOU dick head."

"I have found that my own kids, aged 5 and 6 now can make very profound statements and can be very wise."

"Ilana Wexler earned the right to criticize anyone she wants to on the day she was born an American, you idiot!"

"Picking on little girls—too pathetic for comment, really. I will pray for you. Geek."

"You are a very sad person if picking on the kid at the convention is your idea of clever writing."

"You have some nerve picking on a child. But I guess that is what we should all expect from Republicans now. Bible thumping and self righteousness all the while raping and molesting children when they think no one is looking. So, blow it out your ass."

"In re: your incredibly harsh words for Ilana Wexler . . . Go Fuck Yourself."

24. This is frequently asserted—as a negative, of course—by the Left. See, for example, the column by Charles M. Blow, "Religious Outlier," *New York Times*, September 3, 2010.

25. A superb book with which to begin a study of anti-Americanism is Paul Hollander, *Anti-Americanism: Critiques at Home and Abroad, 1965–1990* (New York: Oxford University Press, 1992). Hollander was a professor of sociology at the University of Massachusetts.

26. David Brooks, "All Hail Moore," *New York Times*, June 26, 2004.

27. Peter O'Neil, "Feminist's Anti-U.S. Speech Causes Uproar," *Vancouver Sun*, October 02, 2001.

28. Gore Vidal, the *New Statesman*, October 15, 2001.

Chapter 2: *Why the Left Believes What It Believes*

1. *Anderson Cooper 360*, CNN, October 31, 2011.

2. Dennis Prager, "Are People Basically Good?" *Jewish Journal of Los Angeles*, October 20, 2010.

3. Dennis Prager, "Human Nature, Judaism and Liberals: Response to My Critics," *Jewish Journal of Los Angeles*, November 3, 2010.

4. In fact, the historical consensus is that Hitler and the Nazis actually toned down their anti-Semitism in order to win more votes.

5. Thomas Sowell, "Next stop: Supreme Court?" Townhall.com, May 23, 2002.

Chapter 3: *Why the Left Succeeds*

1. http://www.dailykos.com/story/2008/12/26/677292/-Dennis-Prager -Endorses-Marital-Rape.

2. For an important discussion of this exhibition and what it says about the Left's assault on culture, see Heather MacDonald, "Radical Graffiti Chic," *City Journal*, Spring 2011.

3. In Vasconcellos's words:
"I grew up in the 1930s in a constrained, traditional, Catholic family. I was educated in both public schools and Catholic (Jesuit) schools, through college and law school. In school, I was a high-achiever, receiving awards and excellent grades. In adulthood, I became a prominent lawyer in a prestigious firm. My first campaign for a seat in the state legislature in 1966 was successful, and I have now been reelected eleven times. Yet, through it all, I had almost no sense of my self, no self-esteem. . . . I had been conditioned to know myself basically as a sinner, guilt-ridden and ashamed, constantly beating my breast and professing my unworthiness."
See http://www.lightparty.com/Visionary/ImportanceSelfEsteem.html.

4. Vasconcellos: "It has become essential to my political views and priorities. My legislative record has paralleled and in some ways become a reflection of my personal growth. In its essence, after all, politics properly understood is nothing more than the making of policy for all of us together, the sum of our individual beings."

5. See R. F. Baumeister, J. M. Boden, and L. Smart, "Relation of Threatened Egotism to Violence and Aggression: The Dark Side of High Self-Esteem," *Psychological Review* 103, no. 1 (1996), pp. 5–33.

6. Paul C. Vitz, "The Problem with Self-Esteem," http://www.catholiceducation .org/articles/education/ed0001.html.

7. Lori Gottlieb, "How to Land Your Kid in Therapy," *Atlantic*, July/August 2011.

8. For a devastating discussion of this subject, see *Intellectuals: From Marx and Tolstoy to Sartre and Chomsky* (New York: Harper Perennial, 1990), written by one of the preeminent historians of our time, Paul Johnson.

9. "New state law requires textbooks to include gays' achievements," *Los Angeles Times*, July 15, 2011.

10. "Scholars note that at the time Western European countries abolished capital punishment it had widespread public support (Zimring and Hawkins, 1986; Simon and Blaskovich, 2002; Hood and Hoyle, 2009). Steiker (2002: 108)." James Unnever, "Global support for the death penalty," *Punishment & Society* 2010 12:463. Unnever is a professor of criminology at the University of South Florida, Sarasota-Manatee.

11. "The Power of Christian Young Men," *Selected Addresses and Papers of Woodrow Wilson* (New York: Boni & Liveright, 1918), pp. 49–55. Reproduced at http://www.wallbuilders.com/LIBissuesArticles.asp?id=19484.

12. *Wall Street Journal,* November 4, 2001.

13. "Yale Press Bans Images of Muhammad in New Book," *New York Times*, August 12, 2009.

14. For a transcript of the relevant portions of the interview, see Dennis Prager, "College Taught Her Not to Be a Heterosexual," Townhall.com, April 19, 2005. http://www.dennisprager.com/columns.aspx?g=d9342985-b046-46ea-bc19 -ab36da1454f5&url=college_taught_her_not_to_be_a_heterosexual.

15. "Harvard President Sees Rise in Anti-Semitism on Campus," *New York Times*, September 21, 2002.

16. "Northwestern University to Investigate What Happened When Sex Toy Was Demonstrated in Optional Panel," *New York Daily News*, March 3, 2011. Also see Dennis Prager, "The $50,000 Orgasm," *National Review Online*, March 8, 2011.

17. http://www.holocaustresearchproject.org/einsatz/.

18. "The Einsatzgruppen Reports," Holocaust Library, 1989.

19. Jonah Goldberg, *National Review Online*, February 4, 2011.

20. "Israel Outraged as EU Poll Names It a Threat to Peace," *Guardian*, November 2, 2003.

21. *BBC News*, April 9, 2004.

22. "U.S. Image in Australia Isn't So Good, Poll Finds," *New York Times*, March 29, 2005.

23. *BBC News*, April 6, 2005.

24. "U.S. Needs to Go Goodwill Hunting," *Washington Post*, November 30, 2005.

25. *The Guardian*, November 3, 2006.

26. "Poll: Over 40% of Canadian Teens Think America Is 'Evil,'" *Canada Free Press*, June 30, 2004.

27. "British Believe Bush Is More Dangerous Than Kim Jong-Il," *Guardian*, November 3, 2006.

28. Reuters, May 24, 2002.

29. "An Operation Gone Wrong," *Washington Post*, October 7, 1997.

30. *Morning Edition*, NPR, November 6, 2009, http://www.npr.org/templates /story/story.php?storyId=120162816.

31. Edward S. Shapiro, *Crown Heights: Blacks, Jews, and the 1991 Brooklyn Riot* (Waltham, MA: Brandeis University Press, 2006), p. xi.

32. Ari L. Goldman, "Telling It Like It Wasn't," *New York Jewish Week*, August 9, 2011.

33. The audio is in my possession, and can be heard at www.dennisprager.com.

34. *Rolling Stone*, fortieth anniversary edition, 2007.

35. http://tpmdc.talkingpointsmemo.com/2009/10/grayson-explains-what -it-means-to-be-a-democrat-we-have-a-conscience.php.

36. "After 50 Years of Covering War, Looking for Peace and Honoring Law," *New York Times*, December 16, 2001.

37. ABC News, August 31, 2011.

38. *NBC Nightly News*, reported by CNN, September 15, 2009.

39. CNN Politics, September 16, 2008.

40. *Daily Beast*, August 22, 2008.

41. *New York Times*, December 5, 2009.

42. "Pelosi Hammers GOP for 'Anti-worker Agenda,'" *Hill*, August 15, 2011.

43. *Raleigh News & Observer*, April 30, 2011.

44. Rick Perlstein, "Christian Empire," *New York Times*, January 7, 2007. Needless to say, these people who speak about American Christian fascists would label anyone who used the term *Islamo-fascist* an "Islamophobic" bigot. Again, those who do not fight real evil fight make-believe evil.

45. Frank Rich, "The Rage Is Not About Health Care," *New York Times*, March 27, 2010.

46. Cited by Jonah Goldberg, *National Review Online*, January 5, 2001.

47. MSNBC, November 10, 2010.

48. Glenn Greenwald, "Who Has Moral Courage?" *New York Times*, August 17, 2010.

49. Charles Krauthammer, "Moral Myopia at Ground Zero," *Washington Post*, August 20, 2010.

50. For a list of leading Democrats who believed Saddam was hiding WMDs, see www.snopes.com/politics/war/wmdquotes.asp.

51. Fareed Zakaria, "Why Do They Hate Us?" *Newsweek*, October 15, 2001.

52. Deborah Solomon, "The Way We Live Now, 7/11/04: Questions for William F. Buckley; Conservatively Speaking," *New York Times*, July 11, 2004.

53. It also leads, all too frequently, to the emasculation of boys. Then many women looking to marry wonder where masculine men are.

54. "For Little Children, Grown-Up Labels as Sexual Harassers," *Washington Post*, April 3, 2008.

55. *Oregonian*, July 22, 2007.

56. http://www.nrc.gov/reading-rm/doc-collections/fact-sheets/3mile-isle .html.

57. http://www.unscear.org/unscear/en/chernobyl.html#Health.

58. *Guardian*, January 10, 2010.

59. Ibid.

60. http://www.iaea.org/newscenter/features/chernobyl–15/cherno-faq.shtml.

61. "Chernobyl Death Toll Grossly Underestimated," Greenpeace International, April 18, 2006.

62. Andrew Bolt, "Time to Stop Nuke Hysteria," *Herald Sun* (Australia), March 16, 2011.

63. James E. Enstrom and Geoffrey C. Kabat, "Environmental Tobacco Smoke and Tobacco Related Mortality in a Prospective Study of Californians, 1960–98," *British Medical Journal*, March 7, 2003.

64. Diane Macedo, "Scientist's Firing After 36 Years Fuels 'PC' Debate at UCLA," FoxNews, August 31, 2010.

65. Michael B. Siegel, "A Smoking Ban Too Far," *New York Times*, May 5, 2011.

66. *Face to Face with Connie Chung*, CBS, December 10, 1990.

67. "Hysteria Is Easier Than Science, and It Pays Better," *Baltimore Sun*, August 7, 1996.

68. http://www.nejm.org/doi/full/10.1056/NEJM199406163302401#t=article.

69. http://www.nejm.org/doi/full/10.1056/NEJM199506223322502#t= abstract.

70. Ed Uthman, M.D., "On Breast Implant Hysteria," http://web2.iadfw.net /uthman/rants/on_implant_hysteria.html, March 31, 1996.

71. *NBC Nightly News*, November 17, 2006.

72. Cited in Christopher Jencks, *The Homeless* (Cambridge, MA: Harvard University Press, 1995), p. 2.

73. Meredith Broussard, "Nuts to That: The People Profiting from Food Allergies," *Slate*, August 31, 2009.

74. "Global Warming: Truth or Dare?" *Activist Teacher*, February 27, 2007.

75. "Is 'Climate Change' Nudging Us Closer to a New Ice Age?" *Seminole County Environmental News Examiner*, January 13, 2010.

76. George Will, "The Law of Doomsaying," syndicated column, February 15, 2009.

77. http://activistteacher.blogspot.com/2007/02/global-warming-truth-or -dare.html.

78. Richard S. Lindzen, "The Climate Science Isn't Settled," *Wall Street Journal*, November 30, 2009.

79. http://www.petitionproject.org/seitz_letter.php.

80. "Open Kyoto to Debate: An Open Letter to Prime Minister Stephen Harper," *National Post*, April 11, 2006.

81. http://epw.senate.gov/public/index.cfm?FuseAction=Minority.Blogs& ContentRecord_id=de6a54bf-802a-23ad-45ed-60ae6f3febe2.

82. *Vanity Fair*, May 2006.

83. *Time*, April 21, 2008.

84. As Michael Moore said on CNN's *Larry King Live* in 2008, in refusing to condemn Rev. Jeremiah Wright's "God damn America" sermon: "I do not believe, as a white guy, that I am in any position to judge a black man who has had to live through [American racism]."

Chapter 4: The Left's Moral Record

1. Stéphane Courtois et al., *The Black Book of Communism* (Cambridge, MA: Harvard University Press, 1999), p. 4.

2. "The Germans murdered about as many non-Jews as Jews during the war, chiefly by starving Soviet prisoners of war (more than three million) and residents of besieged cities (more than a million) or by shooting civilians in 'reprisals'

(the better part of a million, chiefly Belarussians and Poles)." Timothy Snyder, *Bloodlands: Europe Between Hitler and Stalin* (New York: Basic Books, 2010), p. x.

3. The Canada–based Human Security Report Project says the number is about half the IRC number. In either case, the number is in the millions, genocide-like numbers of which almost no one in the world is aware. See "DR Congo war deaths 'exaggerated,'" *BBC News*, January 20. 2010.

4. Barry Gewen, *New York Times*, December 21, 2009.

5. Donald Rayfield, *Stalin and His Hangmen: The Tyrant and Those Who Killed for Him* (New York: Random House, 2005), p. xii.

6. "Muslims Must Embrace Our British Values, David Cameron Says," *Telegraph*, February 5, 2011.

7. "Cameron Criticizes 'Multiculturalism' in Britain," *New York Times*, February 5, 2011.

8. "Nicolas Sarkozy Declares That Multiculturalism Has Failed," *Telegraph*, February 11, 2011.

9. "Germany's Angela Merkel: Multiculturalism Has 'Utterly Failed,'" *Christian Science Monitor*, October 17, 2010.

10. George Will, "Britain Tackles the Welfare State," *Washington Post*, August 10, 2011.

11. "Antiwar Rallies Draw Millions Around the World," *Los Angeles Times*, February 16, 2003.

12. "American Fury as German Justice Minister Compares Bush to Hitler," *Telegraph*, September 20, 2002.

13. "No Parade for Hans," *New York Times*, November 14, 2009.

14. Quoted in *New York Times*, January 30, 2005.

15. Editorial, *Los Angeles Times*, January 27, 2006.

16. Michael Oren, *Washington Post*, September 23, 2011.

17. The interview was recorded and is available from www.dennisprager.com.

18. Paisley Dodds, "Amnesty Takes Aim at 'Gulag' in Guantanamo," Associated Press, May 25, 2005.

19. David Bosco, "Gulag v. Guantanamo," *New Republic*, June 3, 2005.

20. Democratic representatives Barbara Lee, Michael Honda, and Laura Richardson of California; Melvin Watt of North Carolina; Bobby Rush of Illinois; Marcia Fudge of Ohio; and Emanuel Cleaver II of Missouri.

21. The *Miami Herald* labeled the seven members of the CBC who went to Cuba, "The Clueless Seven." From the *Herald*'s editorial: "If only the group had met with even one prisoner of conscience or one of the wives, mothers, daughters

or sisters of the 75 independent journalists, librarians and human-rights advocates imprisoned in Cuba's 'Black Spring' of 2003. . . . Or the seven could have traveled three hours from Havana to see the hunger-striking dissidents led by Jorge Luis Garcia 'Antunez' Perez in Placetas. Or they could have asked to see Oscar Elias Biscet, a doctor serving 25 years in prison for following the peaceful resistance of Martin Luther King Jr. . . . Or what of the mothers of three young men who were tried in a day and killed the next by firing squad in 2003 for trying to hijack a ferry from Havana Harbor? No passenger was hurt, but that didn't stop the Cuban government from sending a swift and terrifying message to the country's Afro-Cuban masses."

22. A *Washington Post* editorial noted that Representative Barbara Lee said that "'Cubans do want dialogue. They do want talks.' Funny, then, that in five days on the island the Congress members found no time for dialogue with Afro-Cuban dissident Jorge Luis Garcia Perez. . . . Mr. Garcia, better known as 'Antunez,' is a renowned advocate of human rights who has often been singled out for harsh treatment because of his color. 'The authorities in my country,' he has said, 'have never tolerated that a black person (could dare to) oppose the regime.' His wife, Iris, is a founder of the Rosa Parks Women's Civil Rights Movement, named after an American hero whom Afro-Cubans try to emulate. The couple have been on a hunger strike since Feb. 17, to demand justice for an imprisoned family member."

23. *Wall Street Journal*, April 11, 2003.

24. Alan Cooperman, "Israel Divestiture Spurs Clash. Jewish Leaders Condemn Move by Presbyterian Church," *Washington Post,* September 29, 2004.

25. "Norway: Parliament Shuns Israeli Products," *Ynetnews.com*, December 22, 2005.

26. "CUPE in Ontario Votes to Boycott Israel," CBC News, May 27, 2006.

27. Ronen Bodoni, "South African Union Joins Boycott of Israel," *YnetNews.com*, June 8, 2006.

28. "The Anti-Israel Divestment Campaign: Churches," ADL website.

29. *New York Times*, April 17, 2007.

30. Ireland Palestine Solidarity Campaign, Press Release, May 29, 2008.

31. *Jerusalem Post*, September 17, 2009.

32. *Counterpunch*, December 13, 2001.

33. Ibid.

34. Quoted in *Commentary*, June 2002.

35. See Deborah E. Lipstadt, *Denying the Holocaust* (New York: Plume, 1994).

36. The distinction is one of actions versus feelings. The anti-Semite hates Jews. The individual who works against Jews does not necessarily hate Jews.

37. Joshua Muravchik, "A Portrait of a Self-Hostile Jew and Holocaust Survivor," *Wall Street Journal*, March 3, 2004.

38. *New York Times*, December 30, 2009.

39. Cited by Ruth Wisse, professor of Yiddish literature at Harvard University, in "Drowning in the Red Sea," *Jewish Review of Books*, Fall 2011.

40. "U.N. Official Answers Questions About Fierce Criticism of Israel," *Forward*, July 21, 2011.

41. "London Mayor Defends the Use of Palestinian Suicide Bombers," *Haaretz*, July 19, 2005.

42. Deborah Orin, "Howard's Hatefest," *New York Post*, December 16, 2003.

43. Quoted in *Chronicle of Higher Education*, November 29, 2009.

44. Agence France-Presse, January 13, 2011.

45. "MOCA Gala's Main Dish Is Performance Art," *Los Angeles Times*, November 12, 2011. One can see what it looks like at http://www.latimes.com/entertainment/news/arts/la-et-moca-gala-abramovic-20111112,0,1348643.story?track=rss.

46. *New York*, June 8, 1970.

47. The *New York* magazine article also reported on a prior party for the Black Panthers at the home of another major figure in the American entertainment world, Sidney Lumet:

"The emotional momentum was building rapidly when Ray 'Masai' Hewitt, the Panthers' Minister of Education and member of the Central Committee, rose to speak. . . . 'Some of you here,' he said, 'may have some feelings left for the establishment, but we don't. We want to see it die. We're Maoist revolutionaries, and we have no choice but to fight to the finish.'

"For about 30 minutes Masai Hewitt laid it on the line. He referred now and again to 'that M— F— Nixon' and to how the struggle would not be easy, and that if buildings were burned and other violence ensued, that was only part of the struggle that the power structure had forced the oppressed minorities into."

48. *Time*, January 25, 1982.

49. "Smoke's No Joke for Tom and Jerry," *BBC News*, August 21, 2006.

50. George Will, *Newsweek*, January 1, 2011.

51. *New York Law Journal*, March 25, 2002.

52. "Equal Cheers for Boys and Girls Draw Some Boos," *New York Times*, January 14, 2007.

53. Gerald Uelman (dean of Santa Clara University School of Law), "The Price of Free Speech: Campus Hate Speech Codes," http://www.scu.edu/ethics/publications/iie/v5n2/codes.html.

54. *Los Angeles Times*, April 22, 1997.

55. This and many of the following examples of free speech banned are to be found on the website of Professor Eugene Volokh of UCLA School of Law: http://www2.law.ucla.edu/volokh/harass/breadth.htm#39.

56. "CCLU Threatened School District with Injunction," *Windsor Locks (CT) Journal*, June 21, 2004.

57. Cited by John Leo, *U.S. News & World Report*, July 10, 2005.

58. http://blogcritics.org/politics/article/what-we-learned-from-the-alito/.

59. "Alito and the Ted Kennedy 'Study,'" *National Review Online*, January 9, 2006.

60. "Alito Accused of Racism," *Washington Times*, January 11, 2006.

61. *Washington Post*, April 3, 2010.

62. Edwy Plenel, editorial director, *Le Monde*, September 14, 1998.

63. Cited by Professor Amitai Etzioni of George Washington University, http://www.gwu.edu/~ccps/etzioni/B317.html.

64. Kate N. Grossman, "NU [Northwestern University] Sex: Academic Freedom in Action," *Chicago Sun-Times*, March 6, 2011.

65. http://www.youtube.com/watch?v=JJyWWM9OHKA.

66. For an extensive discussion of the roles of Democrats and Republicans in civil rights legislation, see Ann Coulter, *Demonic* (New York: Crown Forum, 2011), chapter 10. Like all other powerful and attractive conservative women, Coulter has been caricatured and demonized by the Left and the media. But this book is a painstakingly researched and carefully documented work that every open-minded liberal should read. Closed-minded liberals should also read it, but I suspect they are not reading this endnote.

67. The Left-wing rewriting of the Kennedy assassination has not stopped. See "Was Everyone Quite So Nuts? Frank Rich and Adam Moss on 1963 vs. 2011," *New York*, November 22, 2011.

68. "Why Nearly 60 Percent of Russians 'Deeply Regret' the USSR's Demise," *Christian Science Monitor*, December 23, 2009.

69. George Will, "Conservatives More Liberal Givers," *RealClearPolitics*, March 27, 2008.

Chapter 5: On Evaluating Religions

1. "U.N. Body Adopts Resolution on Religious Defamation," Reuters, March 26, 2009.

2. The Southeastern Center for Contemporary Art's "Awards in the Visual Arts" competition, 1988.

3. G. E. Von Grunebaum, *Islam: Essays in the Nature and Growth of a Cultural Tradition* (Whitefish, MT: Kessinger, 2007), p. 114.

4. See, for example, King's famous letter from a Birmingham, Alabama, jail for its constant allusions to God and Christianity.

Chapter 6: The Moral Record of Islam

1. Here are the freedom rankings of the forty-seven Muslim-majority countries according to the Freedom House "Freedom in the World" 2010 survey:

Country	Ranking	Country	Ranking
Afghanistan	Not Free	Malaysia	Partly Free
Albania	Partly Free	Maldives	Partly Free
Algeria	Not Free	Mali	Free
Azerbaijan	Not Free	Mauritania	Not Free
Bahrain	Not Free	Morocco	Partly Free
Bangladesh	Partly Free	Niger	Partly Free
Brunei	Not Free	Nigeria	Partly Free
Burkina Faso	Partly Free	Oman	Not Free
Chad	Not Free	Pakistan	Partly Free
Comoros	Partly Free	Qatar	Not Free
Djibouti	Partly Free	Senegal	Partly Free
Egypt	Not Free	Sierra Leone	Partly Free
Gambia	Partly Free	Somalia	Not Free
Guinea	Not Free	Saudi Arabia	Not Free
Indonesia	Free	Sudan	Not Free
Iran	Not Free	Syria	Not Free
Iraq	Not Free	Tajikistan	Not Free
Jordan	Not Free	Tunisia	Not Free
Kazakhstan	Not Free	Turkey	Partly Free
Kosovo	Partly Free	Turkmenistan	Not Free
Kuwait	Partly Free	United Arab Emirates	Not Free
Kyrgyzstan	Not Free	Uzbekistan	Not Free
Lebanon	Partly Free	Yemen	Not Free
Libya	Not Free		

2. A talk by Brian Whitaker, Middle East editor for the *Guardian*, at the School of Oriental and African Studies in London, January 26, 2010. It can be found at an Arab website: http://www.al-bab.com/arab/articles/text/soas100126.htm.

3. Cited by Brian Whitaker in his book, *What's Really Wrong with the Middle East* (London: Saqi Books, 2009), and at an Arab website: http://www.al-bab .com/arab/background/social_reform.htm.

4. *Arab Human Development Report 2003: Building a Knowledge Society*, United Nations Development Programme, Regional Bureau for Arab States, 2003, p. 82.

5. *Economist*, July 17, 2010.

6. *Islamica*, no. 17.

7. Professor Efraim Karsh, head of the Mediterranean Studies program at King's College London, University of London, *Islamic Imperialism: A History*, (New Haven, CT: Yale University Press), 2007, p.4.

8. *Newsweek*, October 15, 2001.

9. Bernard Lewis, *The Political Language of Islam* (Chicago: University of Chicago Press, 1988), p. 72.

10. Ibn Khaldun, *The Muqaddimah*, translated by Franz Rosenthal, Bollingen Series, (Princeton, NJ: Princeton University Press, 1967), p. 183.

11. Denis MacShane, Labor Party MP, *Guardian*, November 11, 2007.

12. Charles Krauthammer, "Moral Myopia at Ground Zero," *Washington Post*, August 20, 2010.

13. "Terrorism's Christian Godfather," *Time*, January 28, 2008.

14. M. Boudjemaa, "Terrorism in Algeria: Ten Years of Day-to-Day Genocide," in *Africa and Terrorism, Joining the Global Campaign*, edited by Jakkie Cilliers and Kathryn Sturman (Pretoria, South Africa: Institute for Security Studies, 2002).

15. "Jordanians Turn Against al-Qa'eda Leader over Bombings," *Telegraph*, November 12, 2005.

16. Will Durant, *The Story of Civilization*, vol. 1, *Our Oriental Heritage* (New York: Simon & Schuster, 1935), p. 459. (Prior to the latter half of the twentieth century, Westerners generally referred to Islam as "Mohammedanism.")

17. Donald Little, "Coptic Conversion to Islam Under the Mahri Mamluks, 692–755/1293–1354," *Bulletin of the School of Oriental and African Studies,* University of London, (1976) 39: p. 567.

18. Ibid., p. 568.

19. Dennis Prager and Joseph Telushkin, *Why the Jews: The Reason for Antisemitism* (New York: Simon & Schuster, 2003), p. 96.

20. Karen Armstrong, *Muhammad: A Biography of the Prophet* (New York: HarperOne, 1993), p. 179.

21. S. D. Goitein, *Jews and Arabs: Their Contacts Through the Ages* (New York: Schocken Books, 1964), p. 64.

22. See Joel Kraemer, "War, Conquest and the Treatment of Minorities in Medieval Islam," in *Violence and Defense in the Jewish Experience*, edited by Salo Baron and George Wise (Philadelphia: Jewish Publication Society of America, 1977), p. 150.

23. For the complete listing of provisions in the Pact of Umar, see Fordham University's *Medieval Sourcebook*, http://www.fordham.edu/halsall/source/pact -umar.html.

24. Salo Baron, *A Social and Religious History of the Jews*, 2nd ed., vol. 3 (New York: Columbia University Press, 1957), p. 141.

25. Raul Hilberg, *The Destruction of the European Jews* (Chicago: Quadrangle, 1961), p. 5; Bernard Lewis, *The Jews of Islam* (Princeton, NJ: Princeton University Press, 1987), pp. 25–26.

26. Baron, *A Social and Religious History of the Jews*, p. 141.

27. Edward Stourton, "Iraqi Christians Under Fire," *Telegraph*, July 21, 2011.

28. Baron, *A Social and Religious History of the Jews*, p. 140.

29. Ibid., p. 124.

30. Goitein, *Jews and Arabs*, p. 80.

31. Ibid., pp. 74–78.

32. E. W. Lane, *An Account of the Manners and Customs of the Modern Egyptians*, 1837, republished as *Manners and Customs of the Modern Egyptians* (New York: Cosimo Classics, 2005), p. 537.

33. H. H. Ben-Sasson, ed., *A History of the Jewish People* (Cambridge, MA: Harvard University Press, 1976), pp. 847–48.

34. See Shimon Shamir, "Muslim-Arab Attitudes Towards Jews in the Ottoman and Modern Periods," in Baron and Wise, eds., *Violence and Defense in the Jewish Experience*, p. 195.

35. See "Palestine Before the Zionists," by Harvard professor David Landes, *Commentary*, February 1976.

36. Albert Memmi, *Jews and Arabs*, translated by Eleanor Levieux (Chicago: J. P. O'Hara, 1975), pp. 32–33.

37. Ibid., p. 33.

38. Speech to UN seminar on religious tolerance and freedom, delivered December 5, 1984, quoted in Anti-Defamation League's *News*, February 7, 1985.

39. Cited by Middle East Media Research Institute and quoted by Jonah Goldberg in "Pigs, Jews and War," *National Review Online*, November 1, 2002.

40. Cited in "Saudi Arabia's Curriculum of Intolerance," Center for Religious Freedom of Freedom House, 2006, http://www.freedomhouse.org/uploads/special_report/48.pdf.

41. Reported by the European Commissioner for Justice, Freedom, and Security Franco Frattini, who is responsible in the EU for combating racism and anti-Semitism in Europe. *Jerusalem Post*, August 26, 2011.

42. PA TV (Fatah), January 29, 2010. Translated by Palestinian Media Watch, February 4, 2010.

43. Edward Stourton, "Iraqi Christians Under Fire," *Telegraph*, July 21, 2011.

44. *BBC News*, October 29, 2005.

45. "Beheaded Girls Were Ramadan 'Trophies,'" *Australian*, November 9, 2006.

46. *Time*, February 21, 2011.

47. On the court's website: www.federalshariatcourt.gov.pk.

48. "Q&A: Pakistan's Controversial Blasphemy Laws," *BBC News*, March 22, 2011.

49. *The Vanguard*, Lagos, allafrica.com/stories/2002/1240005.html.

50. *Five Years On: No Justice for Sexual Violence in Darfur*, Human Rights Watch, April 6, 2008.

51. "Islamists Rally for Pakistan's Blasphemy Laws," *Wall Street Journal*, January 10, 2011.

52. See the article by Taseer's son, Aatish Taseer, in *Telegraph*, January 8, 2011.

53. *Telegraph*, Calcutta, January 23, 2011.

54. *Chicago Tribune*, May 3, 1998.

55. Sheila Musaji, "The Death of Aqsa Parvez Should Be an Interfaith Call to Action," *American Muslim*, December 14, 2007. http://www.theamericanmuslim.org/tam.php/features/articles/the_death_of_aqsa_parvez_should_be_an_interfaith_call_to_action/.

56. Quoted in Robert R. Reilly, *The Closing of the Muslim Mind* (Wilmington, DE: Intercollegiate Studies Institute, 2010), p. 12.

57. Ibid., p. 6.

58. http://pewresearch.org/pubs/1814/muslim-public-opinion-hamas-hezbollah-al-qaeda-islam-role-in-politics-democracy?src=prc-latest&proj=peoplepress.

59. http://pewglobal.org/2010/12/02/muslims-around-the-world-divided-on -hamas-and-hezbollah/#prc-jump.

60. Timur Kuran, *The Long Divergence: How Islamic Law Held Back the Middle East* (Princeton, NJ: Princeton University Press, 2011), p. 305.

Chapter 7: Islam, America, and the West

1. *www.Ijtihad.com*, October 2001.

2. Peter Brownfeld, "Muslims Who Love America," *www.Ijtihad.com*, February 14, 2005.

3. "Swedes Begin to Question Liberal Migration Tenets," *New York Times*, February 26, 2011.

4. Valerie Strauss and Emily Wax, "Where Two Worlds Collide: Muslim Schools Face Tension of Islamic, U.S. Views," *Washington Post*, February 25, 2002.

Chapter 8: Responses to Arguments on Behalf of Islam

1. Sura 2:256.

2. Dalia Mogahed, executive director for Gallup's Center for Muslim Studies, "The Battle for Hearts and Minds: Moderate vs. Extremist Views in the Muslim World," Gallup, 2006.

3. Fareed Zakaria, "Why Do They Hate Us?" *Newsweek*, October 15, 2001.

4. Ibid.

5. *Commentary*, July–August 2010.

6. Ayaan Hirsi Ali, *Wall Street Journal*, August 18, 2010.

7. *Islamica*, no. 20.

8. http://www.beliefnet.com/Faiths/Islam/2001/09/Fractured-Fundamen talisms.aspx?p=1.

9. *Islamica*, no. 20.

10. PBS, May 25, 2010.

11. *Reliable Sources*, with Howard Kurtz, CNN, August 22, 2010.

12. Nathan Burchfel, "Chris Cuomo: Christians Shouldn't Condemn Jihad Because of Crusades," *NewsBusters.org*, August 26, 2010.

13. Bernard Lewis, "Learning the Lingo: Jihad vs. Crusade," *Wall Street Journal*, September 27, 2001.

14. "Muslim Bus Drivers Refuse to Let Guide Dogs on Board," *Daily Mail*, July 19, 2010.

15. "Muslim Cab Drivers Refuse to Transport Alcohol, and Dogs," ABC News, January 26, 2007.

16. Cited in Brownfeld, "Muslims Who Love America."

17. Muqtedar Khan, "A Memo to American Muslims," http://www.ijtihad .org/memo.htm.

18. Cited in Brownfeld, "Muslims Who Love America."

Chapter 9: The American Trinity

1. *New York Times*, February 21, 2005.

2. Steven Waldman, *Founding Faith: How Our Founding Fathers Forged a Radical New Approach to Religious Liberty* (New York: Random House, 2009), p. xi.

3. "Did the Founders Want Government Small?" *Too Much*, the online newsletter on excess and inequality published by Institute for Policy Studies, Washington, DC, February 20, 2010.

4. Thomas Kidd, *God of Liberty: A Religious History of the American Revolution* (New York: Basic Books, 2010), p. 7.

5. I elaborate on this in my book *Happiness Is a Serious Problem* (New York: HarperCollins, 1999).

6. Claire Berlinski, in her important book on Margaret Thatcher, summarized the former British prime minster's views of the literally demoralizing impact of socialism (Western democratic socialism, that is, Leftism):
"In all its incarnations, wherever and however it was applied—[socialism] was morally corrupting. [It] turned good citizens into bad ones; it turned strong nations into weak ones; it promoted vice and discouraged virtue; and . . . it transformed formerly hardworking and self-reliant men and women into whining, weak and flabby loafers. Socialism was not a fine idea that had been misapplied; in was an inherently *wicked* idea. This was Thatcher's single contribution to the debate. It was a point she emphasized again and again: 'In the end, the real case against socialism is not its economic inefficiency, though on all sides there is evidence of that. Much more fundamental is its basic immorality.'
"To a Western world preoccupied with guilt, decline and decay, Thatcher's message has a particularly significant resonance. It is hardly a secret that many of us are still wondering whether capitalism is the right path. It is the *only* right path, says Thatcher, and the only one men and women of virtue—not greed, but *virtue*—should take."
Claire Berlinski, *"There Is No Alternative": Why Margaret Thatcher Matters* (New York: Basic Books, 2008), pp. 7–8, 13.

7. Kidd, *God of Liberty: A Religious History of the American Revolution*, pp. 245–46.

8. *The Works of John Adams* (Boston, 1854), vol. 9, pp. 228–9. http://books .google.com/books?id=PZYKAQAAIAAJ&pg=PA228#v=onepage&q&f=false.

9. Waldman, *Founding Faith*, p. 37.

10. Ibid., p. 23. Waldman is not a conservative and his book was widely praised among secular reviewers.

11. Recorded by James Madison, *Records of the Federal Convention*, 1787. http://www.americanrhetoric.com/speeches/benfranklin.htm.

12. Alexis de Tocqueville, *Democracy in America*, translated by George Lawrence, edited by J. P. Mayer (Garden City, NY: Anchor, 1969), pp. 294–95.

13. Waldman, *Founding Faith*, p. xv.

14. Franklin to unknown recipient, December 13, 1757. *The Papers of Benjamin Franklin*, vol. 7, cited in Waldman, *Founding Faith*, p. 22.

15. Waldman, *Founding Faith*, p. xv.

16. Ibid., pp. 36–37.

17. Adams, letter to Thomas Jefferson, April 19, 1817, quoted in Cappon, *Adams-Jefferson Letters*, p. 509, cited in Waldman, *Founding Faith*, p. 36.

18. John Adams letter to Benjamin Rush, January 21, 1810, quoted in Norman Cousins, *In God We Trust* (New York: Harper, 1958), p. 101.

19. Kidd, *God of Liberty*, p. 8.

20. Ibid., p. 2.

21. Waldman, *Founding Faith*, pp. 95, 96.

22. Kidd, *God of Liberty*, p. 117.

23. *The Age of Reason,* part 1, *Recapitulation.*

24. This was reconfirmed for me in an interview with one of the leading American historians, Pulitzer Prize–winning Brown University professor Gordon S. Wood. It was broadcast on my radio show on September 1, 2011.

25. Kidd, *God of Liberty*, p. 87.

26. Waldman, *Founding Faith*, p. 23.

27. Ibid., p. 60.

28. Leviticus 25:10.

29. Kidd, *God of Liberty*, pp. 169, 213.

30. Micah 6:8.

31. David Gelernter, *Americanism: The Fourth Great Western Religion* (New York: Doubleday, 2007), pp. 1, 2.

32. Paul Johnson, "The Almost-Chosen People," *First Things*, June/July 2006.

33. Kidd, *God of Liberty*, p. 113.

34. Thomas Jefferson, first inaugural address. In the address, Jefferson answered his own question, an answer that runs completely counter to Leftist ideology: "Still one thing more, fellow citizens, a wise and frugal government, which shall restrain men from injuring one another, shall leave them otherwise free to regulate their own pursuits of industry and improvement, and shall not take from the mouth of labor the bread it has earned. This is the sum of good government . . ."

35. Steven C. Bullock, *Revolutionary Brotherhood: Freemasonry and the Transformation of the American Social Order, 1730–1840* (Chapel Hill: University of North Carolina Press, 1966), p. 16.

36. Philip Kossoff, *Valiant Heart: A Biography of Heinrich Heine* (New York: Cornwall Books, 1983), pp. 125–26.

37. Kidd, *God of Liberty*, p. 100.

38. John Adams, letter to Benjamin Rush, August 1, 1812, in *Old Family Letters* (Philadelphia: Lippincott, 1892), cited in Waldman, *Founding Faith*, p. 37.

39. James Madison, *Federalist* No. 51.

40. From Witherspoon's sermon "The Dominion of Providence Over the Passions of Men," delivered in May 1776. Cited in Waldman, *Founding Faith*, p. 96.

41. "Terror Inquiry Looks at Suspect's Time in Britain," *New York Times*, December 29, 2009.

42. Tim Rutten, "Keeping L.A. Safe," *Los Angeles Times*, December 29, 2010.

43. Glover later became professor of ethics at King's College, University of London. The debate was published in *Ultimate Issues* 9, no. 1 and is available from http://stores.dennisprager.com/06A/DPUI9_1.html.

44. He was a guest on my radio show after Cambridge University Press published his book *Darwin, God and the Meaning of Life: How Evolutionary Theory Undermines Everything You Thought You Knew* (2011).

45. Richard Rorty, *Contingency, Irony, and Solidarity* (New York: Cambridge University Press, 1989), p. xv.

46. "Faith Fades Where It Once Burned Strong," *New York Times*, October 13, 2003.

47. David Brooks, "If It Feels Right . . . ," *New York Times*, September 12, 2011.

48. *Huffington Post*, February 12, 2011.

49. *Arizona Daily Star*, December 8, 2004.

50. Psalm 97:10. See also Psalm 45:7: "Love righteousness and hate evil."

51. Cited by Patrice de Beer, *Yale Global Online*, November 8, 2004.

52. *Spiegel Online International*, February 21, 2005.

53. Jeanette Winterson, *Guardian*, October 16, 2001.

54. Two examples: "Lesbian Couple Elected High School Homecoming King and Queen; Parents React," *Yahoo News*, October 31, 2011; and "Male Student Elected Homecoming Queen," http://www.bgay.com/bnews/news71001_male _student_elected_homecoming_queen.htm.

55. Deuteronomy 25:4.

56. Deuteronomy 22:10.

57. Nahum Sarna, *The JPS Torah Commentary: Genesis* (Philadelphia: Jewish Publication Society of America, 1989).

58. U. Cassuto, *A Commentary on the Book of Genesis, Part One: From Adam to Noah*, translated by Israel Abrahams (Jerusalem: Magnes Press, 1961).

59. "The Life Sciences: Recent Progress and Application to Human Affairs the World of Biological Research Requirements for the Future," National Academy of Science, the National Academies Press, 1970, p.432. http://www.nap.edu /openbook.php?record_id=9575&page=432.

60. These statistics are from U.S. census reports and government agencies. See the entire report, as compiled by Robert Rector of the Heritage Foundation: http://www.heritage.org/research/reports/2007/08/how-poor-are-americas -poor-examining-the-plague-of-poverty-in-america.

61. See, for example, Arthur Brooks: http://www.american.com/archive/2008 /march-april-magazine-contents/a-nation-of-givers.

62. "Baby Gap: Germany's Birth Rate Hits Historic Low," *Time World*, May 23, 2010. As a liberal journal, *Time* ascribed the low German birthrate to economic factors: economic recession and a lack of government-sponsored day care.

63. *New York Times*, September 12, 1938. The *Times* erroneously spelled his first name "Hanford." One can see the original article photocopied at http:// technoccult.net/archives/2010/03/03/who-really-said-when-fascism-comes -to-america-it-will-come-wrapped-in-the-flag-and-waving-a-cross/.

64. "In Turkey's Example, Some See Map for Egypt," *New York Times*, February 5, 2011.

65. "Charges Against Journalists Dim the Democratic Glow in Turkey," *New York Times*, January 4, 2012.

66. On Durban and anti-Semitism, see, for example, "Germany Pulls Out of Durban III Anti-racism Conference," *Jerusalem Post*, September 2, 2011.

INDEX

Index

ABOUT THE AUTHOR

Dᴇɴɴɪꜱ Pʀᴀɢᴇʀ ᴡʀɪᴛᴇꜱ ᴀ syndicated column, hosts a radio show carried by 120 stations, and appears regularly on major Fox venues. He is the author of *Happiness Is a Serious Problem* and *Think a Second Time*.